Early Quaker Records of Philadelphia

Pennsylvania

Volume 1
1682–1750

Anna Miller Watring

HERITAGE BOOKS
2019

HERITAGE BOOKS

AN IMPRINT OF HERITAGE BOOKS, INC.

Books, CDs, and more—Worldwide

For our listing of thousands of titles see our website
at
www.HeritageBooks.com

Published 2019 by
HERITAGE BOOKS, INC.
Publishing Division
5810 Ruatan Street
Berwyn Heights, Md. 20740

International Standard Book Number
Paperbound: 978-1-68034-895-8

CONTENTS

INTRODUCTION

According to Horace Mather Lippincott in *Early Philadelphia Its People and Progress* (1917), stated that:

> "The first Friends' Meeting was held at Shackamaxon, in the now Kensington district of Philadelphia, at the house of Thomas Fairman, opposite the Treaty Elm, in 1681. The settlement of the city rendered this place inconvenient and Richard Townsend, who came with Penn in the Welcome, says in his "Testimony" that one boarded meeting house was set up where the city was to be, so that this structure must have been the first concern of the settlers, even before their dwellings, and while the caves were yet in use.
>
> On the 9th of January, 1693, a meeting of Friends was held in Philadelphia and Thomas Holme, John Songhurst, Thomas Wynne and Griffith Owen were selected to make the choice of a site for a meeting house and build it. In August of the next year the Quarterly Meeting directed the building of a house in the Centre Square where now the City Hall stands, to be fifty by forty-six and of brick. At the same time another meeting house was projected for the Evening up on the river bank [called the Bank meeting house] on Front above Sassafras Street [later called Race Street]. This house was fifty by thirty-eight feet, and was but a temporary affair of frame, being replaced by another of brick in 1703 which stood on the west side of Front above Race."

In 1772 the Philadelphia Monthly Meeting for the Northern District and Philadelphia Monthly Meeting for the Southern District were established. The first Monthly Meeting for the Northern District was held at the Bank meeting house on 3rd month, 24th day, 1772. They later built a meeting house in Key's Alley and moved the monthly meeting there in 1789. The Monthly Meeting for the Southern District met first at a building on Fourth Street near Chestnut but soon shifted to a building on the south side of Pine Street, below Second. The remaining portion of the original meeting was sometimes called the Middle District Monthly Meeting.

In the section titled "Miscellaneous Marriages, 1672-1750" on page 116, where two dates are given, the first date is the date the couple were left at liberty to marry; the second date is the date on which it was reported that the marriage had been accomplished. A single date indicates that one or the other event had occurred.

F. Edward Wright
Westminster, MD
1997

BIRTHS AND DEATHS
1688-1750

Children of Robert and Ann Adams: Margaret Adams b. 2/15/1749; Ann Adams b. 3/31/1753; Christian Adams b. 4/14/1754.

Children of Nehemiah and Rebecca Allen: Nathaniel Allen b. 5/16/1744; Nehemiah Allen b. 10/1/1747; Elizabeth Allen b. 11/18/1749-50; Thomas Allen b. 8/19/1751; Rebecca Allen b. 11/23/1753; Mary Allen b. 11/19/1757.

Children of William and Elizabeth Alloway: William Alloway b. 6/9/1695; Sarah Alloway b. 1/14/1696.

Mary Ambler, daughter of Joseph and Sarah Ambler, b. 8/5/1689.

Children of Richard and Sophia Armitt: John Armitt b. 10/8/1702; Stephen Armitt b. 4/17/1705.

Children of Stephen and Sarah Armitt: Sarah Armitt b. 9/15/1733; Ann Armitt b. 4/29/1735; John Armitt b. 9/21/1737; Richard Armitt b. 12/13/1739; Samuel Armitt b. 8/12/1742; Mary Armitt b. 6/6/1748.

Children of William and Mary Attmore: Thomas Attmore b. 4/20/1747; William Attmore b. 7/28/1750.

Thomas Balston, son of Thomas and Ann Balston, b. 11/23/1701.

Children of Davis and Mary Bassett: Abigal Bassett b. 8/22/1749; Josiah Bassett b. 10/14/1751; Beulah Bassett b. 1/18/1755; Paul Bassett b. 10/30/1757; Reuben Bassett b. 11/15/1759; Josiah Bassett b. 10/4/1764.

Mary Bell, daughter of Samuel and Mary Bell, b. 1/15/1738-9.

Children of Benjamin and Mary Betterton: William Betterton b. 6/17/1731; Mary Betterton b. 2/22/1733; Sarah Betterton b. 10/24/1735; Benjamin Betterton b. 10/2/1737; Ann Betterton b. 12/24/1739; Chalkley Betterton b. 1/7/1741; Sarah Betterton b. 2/15/1744; Martha Betterton b. 12/5/1745; Hannah Betterton b. 11/15/1747.

Children of John and Abigail Bettle: William Bettle b. 7/11/1699; Hannah Bettle b. 4/4/1701-2; Samuel Bettle b. 5/20/1704.

Elizabeth Bickley, daughter of Thomas Gardiner of Burlington, N. J., d. 3/15/1714.

Children of Abraham and Elizabeth Bickley: Susanna Bickley b. 3/11/1702; Samuel Bickley b. 4/2/1703; Hannah Bickley b. 9/9/1704; Susanna Bickley b. 1/19/1705-6; Abraham Bickley b. 2/24/1707; Mary Bickley b. 1/21/1708-9; Mary Bickley b. 8/5/1710; Isaac Bickley b. 6/6/1712; Benjamin Bickley b. 3/9/1714.

Rebeckah Blackburn, daughter of Christopher and Abigail Blackburn, b. 1/16/1700.

Children of Christopher and Rachel Blackburn: Christopher Blackburn b. 5/12/1703; Ann Blackburn b. 3/22/1704; Christopher Blackburn b. 4/8/1705.

Children of William and Elizabeth Boulding: Ann Boulding b. 7/31/1693; Elizabeth Boulding b. 6/17/1795; William Boulding b. 8/28/1698.

Rachell Bradford, daughter of Thomas and Alice Bradford, b. 4/11/1705.

Children of Joseph and Esther Brientnall: Jane Brientnall b. 7/28/1740; Esther Brientnall b. 6/10/1726.

Children of John and Rosina Bringhurst of Amsterdam, Holland: Rosina Elizabeth Bringhurst b. 6/24/1688; John Bringhurst b. 12/25/1691; Ann Barbera Bringhurst b. 1/29/1693; John George Bringhurst b. 3/15/1697.

Children of John and Mary Bringhurst: Mary Bringhurst b. 11/18/1720; John Bringhurst b. 9/9/1722; Elizabeth Bringhurst b. 12/4/1723-4; James Bringhurst b. 10/7/1730; Joseph Bringhurst b. 1/20/1732-3; Deborah Bringhurst b. 7/15/1636.

Children of Thomas and Mary Brown: Alexander Brown b. 11/11/1702-3; Elizabeth Brown b. 4/13/1705.

Child born to Jonathan and Rebecca Carmalt, 5/13/1728.

Children of Jonathan Carmalt and Hannah, his second wife: James Carmalt b. 8/6/1735; Caleb Carmalt b. 7/2/1737; Rebecca Carmalt b. 6/7/1739; John Carmalt b. 7/27/1742; William Carmalt b. 9/11/1746; Mary Carmalt b. 5/30/1752; William Carmalt b. 2/3/1755.

Samuel Carpenter and Hannah, his wife, formerly Hannah Hardiman from South Wales, mar. in 1684, removed to Gloucester, N. J. where he died in 1747.

Children of Samuel and Hannah Carpenter: Hannah Carpenter b. 1/3/1685-6; Samuel Carpenter 12/9/1687-8; Joshua Carpenter b. 1/28/1689; John Carpenter b. 3/5/1690; Rebecca Carpenter b. 2/24/1692.

Hannah Carpenter, daughter of John and Ann (Hoskins) Carpenter, b. 9/23/1711.

Johannes Cassell came from Krisheim in the Palatinate in High Germany, a weaver, in the unity of friends. Arrived 12/20/1686 with five children; Arnold, Peter, Elizabeth, Mary and Sarah. He died 2/17/1691 and was buried at Germantown.

Children of Arnold and Susanna Cassell: Johannes Cassell b. 7/10/1694; Daniel Cassell b. 7/27/1696; Veronica Cassell b. 11/10/1697; Arnold Cassell b. 1/3/1700; Nicholas Cassell b. 11/11/1702; Daniel Cassell b. 2/7/1705; Susanna Cassell b. 9/8/1706; Elizabeth Cassell b. 7/2/1710.

Children of Edward and Rachel Cathrall: Isaac Cathrall b. 8/20/1733 (m. Ann Kay); Hannah Cathrall b. 4/22/1736; Benjamin Cathrall b. 12/9/1737; Sarah Cathrall b. 2/30/1740; Mary Cathrall b. 10/5/1744; Edward Cathrall b. 10/12/1747.

Children of George (Thomas?) and Martha Chalkley: George Chalkley b. 4/11/1701; Rebecca Chalkley b. 2/1/1703; Child b. 9/?/1704 and lived abt. two hours; Robert Chalkley b. 9/6/1705.

Children of William and Beulah Clark: William Clark b. 10/14/1746; Beulah Clark b. 4/1/1748; William Clark b. 7/18/1749; Joseph Clark b. 1/7/1751; Elizabeth Clark b. 1/20/1753; Sarah Clark b. 11/22/1754; Samuel Clark b. 3/5/1757.

Children of Geo. and Deborah Claypoole: Deborah Claypoole b. 8/1/1716 and d. 12/12/1730; Mary Claypoole b. 12/21/1717-18 and d. 12/18/1730; Hannah Claypoole b. 10/3/1719 and d. 5/2/1721; Samuel Claypoole b. 2/6/1721 and d. 9/1/1728; Hannah Claypoole b. 2/24/1722 and d. 12/12/1730; Abraham Claypoole b. 1/20/1722-23; John Claypoole b. 7/5/1724 and d. 3/18/1725.

Children of Thomas and Ann Clifford: Sarah Clifford b. 1/10/1745-6; Elizabeth Clifford b. 3/25/1747; Thomas Clifford b. 10/10/1748; John Clifford b. 1/8/1750; George Clifford b. 6/6/1753; Ann Clifford b.

1/16/1755; Edward Clifford b. 6/28/1756; Deborah Clifford b. 3/29/1759; Thomazine Clifford b. 10/7/1760.

Samuel Coates, son of Thomas and Beulah Coates, b. 6/7/1710/11.
Mary Coates, wife of Thomas Coates and daughter of Josiah and Mary Langdale, b. 3/26/1713.
Samuel Coates and Mary Langdale mar. 4/13/1734.

Children of Samuel and Mary Coates: Samuel Coates b. 3/17/1735; Margaret Coates b. 5/11/1736; Mary Coates b. 1/26/1738; Beulah Coates b. 11/28/1739-40; Samuel Coates b. 11/14/1741-2; Sarah Coates b. 7/1/1743; Alice Coates b. 7/11/1744; Langdale Coates b. 8/4/1745; Thomas Coates b. 8/27/1746; Josiah Coates b. 9/10/1747; Samuel Coates b. 8/24/1748.

Hannah Cockfield, daughter of Joshua Cockfield, b. 12/14/1716.

Children of James and Mary Cresson: Mary Cresson b. 12/9/1693; Elizabeth Cresson b. 12/17/1695; James Cresson b. 12/26/1696; Liddie Cresson b. 12/10/1699.

Children of Solomon and Anna Cresson: Mary Cresson b. 9/23/1703; Anna Cresson b. 5/20/1705; Rachel Cresson b. 5/17/1707; James Cresson b. 8/2/1709; Solomon Cresson b. 8/4/1711; Rebecca Cresson b. 6/27/1713; John Cresson b. 6/28/1715.

Children of James and Sarah Cresson: Caleb Cresson b. 8/29/1742; Joshua Cresson b. 2/30/1744.

Children of James and Rachel Davis: Sarah Davis b. 6/13/1741; Samuel Davis b. 3/17/1743; Martha Davis b. 4/22/1745; James Davis b. 1/17/1747; Rachel Davis b. 2/17/1749.

Mary Dawson, daughter of Isaac and Jane Dawson, b. ?/17/1742-3.

Sarah Day, daughter of John and Hannah Day, b. 1/16/1691-2.

Children of Jonathan and Mary Dickinson: Jonathan Dickinson b. 1/12/1695-6 in Elizabeth Parish, near Black River, Jamiaca; Joseph Dickinson b. 2/4/1698 in Phila; John Dickinson b. 1/27/1701 in Phila.

Children of Jacob and Jane Dubree: James Dubree b. 4/22/1698; Jacob Dubree b. 1/12/1701-2; Joseph Dubree b. 3/20/1705 and d. 5/18/1707; Joseph Dubree b. 10/7/1707; John Dubree b. 10/31/1710.

Children of Manuell and Elizabeth Dungworth: John Dungworth b. 3/26/1715; Hester Dungworth b. 9/6/1716; Elizabeth Dungworth b. 6/25/1718; Elizabeth Dungworth b. 1/2/1720-1; Emmanuel Dungworth b. 8/14/1722; Richard Dungworth b. 4/16/1727.

Children of Hugh and Elizabeth Durberow: John Durberow b. 10/24/1686; Hugh Durberow b. 11/11/1688-9; Daniel Durberow b. 3/4/1691; Isaac Durberow b. 11/8/1693-4; Hannah Durberow b. 11/20/1695-6; Joseph Durberow b. 2/20/1699; Elizabeth Durberow b. 8/21/1700; Mary Durberow b. 11/1/1702-3; Jacob Durberow b. 12/3/1704-5.

Sarah Durberow, daughter of John and Sarah Durberow, b. 9/19/1715.

Children of Daniel and Sarah Durberow: Hannah Durberow b. 9/27/1718; Stephen Durberow b. 2/6/1722; Elizabeth Durberow b. 6/18/1723; Daniel Durberow b. 11/6/1724-5.

Children of Nathaniel and Ann Edgecombe: Joseph Edgecombe b. 11/7/1701-2; Nathaniel Edgecombe b. 9/22/1703.

Children of Thomas and Mary Eldridge: James Eldridge b. 12/20/1704-5; Mary Eldridge b. 3/11/1710.

Children of Caleb and Mary Elfreth: Martha Elfreth b. 5/8/1726; Gove Elfreth b. 10/13/1728; Sarah Elfreth b. 8/26/1730.

Margaret Elgar, daughter of Joseph and Margaret Elgar, b. 9/21/1720.

Children of John and Annabella Elliott: John Elliott b. 7/20/1739; Annabella Elliott b. 8/3/1743; Mary Elliott b. 4/3/1746; Samuel Elliott b. 8/26/1748; Hannah Elliott b. 10/3/1750; Jane Elliott b. 9/7/1753,

Children of David and Mary Elwell: Rebecca Elwell b. 4/10/1744; David Elwell b. 10/11/1746.

Children of George and Hannah Emlen: George Emlen b. 5/7/1695; Samuel Emlen b. 2/15/1697; Caleb Emlen b. 4/9/1699; Joshua Emlen b. 2/14/1701; Hannah Emlen b. 12/3/1703-4; Ann Emlen b. 3/19/1705; Mary Emlen b. 11/1/1707-8; Sarah Emlen b. 1/19/1709-10.

Children of Thomas and Hannah England: Sarah England b. 2/14/1701; Hannah England b. 3/17/1703; Abraham England b. 1/20/1705-6.

Children of Jonathan and Hannah Evans: Elizabeth Evans b. 1/3/1740-1; Samuel Evans b. 8/6/1742; Joel Evans b. 12/24/1743-4; Mary Evans b. 10/7/1746; William Evans b. 3/4/1749; Benjamin Evans b. 9/16/1751; John Evans b. 5/30/1753; [Jonathan Evans b. 1/25/1759].

Children of Nathan and Jane Fawcett: John Fawcett b. 12/17/1705-6; Nathan Fawcett [son of Nathan, dec'd] b. 7/5/1707.

Children of William and Hannah Fishbourn: Abraham Fishbourn b. 8/18/1702; Samuel Fishbourn b. 9/8/1703.

Joshua Fisher and Sarah Rowland mar. 7/27/1733 at a meeting in Pilot Town, Sussex Co.

Children of Joshua and Sarah Fisher: Esther Fisher b. 5/28/1734; Lydia Fisher b. 3/4/1736; Thomas Fisher b. 3/6/1741; Samuel Fisher b. 9/6/1745; Miers Fisher b. 4/10/1748; Jabez Maud Fisher b. 7/10/1750; [Sarah Fisher b. 6/1/1759.]

Children of Henry and Ann Flower: Samuel Flower b. 12/17/1708-9; Benjamin Flower b. 11/30/1710-11; Benjamin Flower b. 4/3/1715.

Children of Daniel and Sarah Flower: Sarah Flower b. 1/22/1709-10; Joseph Flower b. 4/1/1700.

Mary Foulke, daughter of Cadwallader and Mary Foulke, b. 5/6/1731.

Francis Fox, son of James and Elizabeth Fox, b. 3/22/1691.
George Fox, son of George and Susanna Fox, b. 2/21/1697.

Children of John and Rebecca Garrigues: Jacob Garrigues b. 11/17/1750-1; Rachel Garrigues b. 11/9/1755; Mary Garrigues b. 8/20/1756.

Children of Samuel and Mary Garrigues: Isaac Garrigues b. 7/13/1741; John Garrigues b. 1/22/1742-3; Rebecca Garrigues b. 8/29/1744; William Garrigues b. 7/23/1746; Samuel Garrigues b. 1/22/1747-8; James Ralph Garrigues b. 8/25/1749; Ann Garrigues b. 2/9/1751; Mary Garrigues b. 11/14/1752; Edward Garrigues b. 1/30/1756; Susanna Garrigues b. 10/16/1759; Benjamin Garrigues b. 9/10/1761.

Benjamin Gibbs, son of Benjamin and Ann Gibbs, b. 7/1/1750.

Children of John and Ann Gillingham: Sarah Gillingham b. 7/4/1736; Mary Gillingham b. 12/4/1738-9; Ann Gillingham b. 5/13/1741; Susanna Gillingham b. 3/7/1743; Elizabeth Gillingham b. 11/19/1745-6.

Children of Richard and Bridgett Gove (of Plymouth, England): Sarah Gove b. 1/8/1677; Mary Gove b. 10/31/1679; Martha Gove b. 5/4/1683; Elizabeth Gove b. 10/16/1686 and d. 9/17/1687.

Bridgett Gove, wife of Richard Gove, d. 9/13/1687.

Children of George and Mary Gray: George Gray b. 6/13/1693; Joseph Gray b. 4/20/1696.

Isaac Greenleaf, son of Isaac and Elizabeth Greenleaf, b. 12/1/1750-1.

Children of Thomas and Mary Griffitts: Isaac Griffitts b. 2/17/1719; Mary Griffitts b. 1/20/1720-1.

Rebecca Griscom, daughter of Tobias and Grace Griscom, b. 10/29/1745. Children of John and Mary Guest: Richard Guest b. 3/26/1702; Mary Guest b. 7/10/1703; Hannah Guest b. 12/6/1705-6.

Children of John Hallowell: Phebe Hallowell b. 5/15/1738; Elizabeth Hallowell b. 10/18/1739; Catherine Hallowell b. 11/10/1741; Israel Hallowell b. 5/27/1743; Hannah Hallowell b. 12/24/1745-6; John Hallowell b. 2/24/1748.

Jervis Hanney (Hennis), son of John and Elizabeth Hanney (Hennis), b. 11/24/1717.

Children of John and Jane Harper: Mary Harper b. 11/22/1713-14; Joseph Harper b. 12/28/1718-19.

Children of Richard and Hannah Hill: Richard Hill b. 6/28/1701; Hannah Hill b. 3/9/1703; Elizabeth Hill b. 12/8/1704-5.

Children of John and Joanna Hill: Howard Hill b. 8/10/1750; John Hill b. 10/4/1751; Joseph Hill b. 7/25/1753; Ann Hill b. 10/29/1754; Joanna Hill b. 2/6/1756; Thomas Hill b. 6/17/1757.

Children of John and Rachel Hillborn: Elizabeth Hillborn b. 3/4/1731; Joseph Hillborn b. 5/31/1732; Frances Hillborn b. 2/8/1734; John Hillborn b. 7/26/1736; Myles Hillborn b. 9/6/1738; Amos Hillborn b. 3/26/1741; Thomas Hillborn b. 12/3/1744-5.

Children of Thomas and Mary Hodges: Mary Hodges b. 11/22/1704; Margaret Hodges b. 8/15/1706; Jane Hodges b. 8/10/1708.

Children of Thomas and Elizabeth Hooten: Thomas Hooten b. 7/6/1687; Elizabeth Hooton b. 9/4/1689.

Children of Benjamin and Hannah Hooton: John Hooton b. 9/18/1743; Mary Hooton b. 3/31/1745; Rebecca Hooton b. 5/20/1746; Sarah Hooton b. 10/7/1747; Thomas Hooton b. 11/5/1749-50; Joseph Hooton b. 4/25/1751 and d. 1/10/1768; Hannah Hooton b. 8/21/1753; Esther Hooton b. 8/26/1754; Susanna Hooton, b. 12/8/1755; Benjamin Hooton b. 6/18/1757; Elizabeth Hooton b. 9/13/1759.

John Howell, son of Thomas and Elizabeth Howell, b. 3/9/1702.

Children of Joseph and Hannah Howell: Elizabeth Howell b. 2/19/1742-3; Jacob Howell b. 3/11/1744; Sarah Howell b. 6/23/1745; Samuel Howell b. 10/6/1746; Arthur Howell b. 8/20/1748 and mar. Mary Mott 12/10/1778; Joseph Howell b. 6/31/1750; William Howell b. 9/7/1751; Rachel Howell b. 7/7/1753; Israel Howell b. 10/6/1754.

Children of William and Mary Hudson: Samuel Hudson b. 7/27/1690; Mary Hudson b. 12/3/1691-2; Elizabeth Hudson b. 4/19/1693 (Samuel and Elizabeth were born at their grandfather Samuel Richardson's plantation near Germantown, the rest in Philadelphia); Sarah Hudson b. 10/28/1694; William Hudson b. 1/31/1696; John Hudson b. 10/10/1697; Susanna Hudson b. 12/17/1698-9; Elinor Hudson b. 6/8/1700; John Hudson b. 12/25/1701-2; Hannah Hudson b. 1/28/1704 (mar. Jacob Metcalf); Rebecca Hudson b. 3/30/1705; Timothy Hudson b. 5/8/1706; Rachel Hudson b. 9/11/1707; Timothy Hudson b. 12/13/1708-9.

Children of Samuel and Mary Hudson: William Hudson b. 7/6/1722; Hannah Hudson b. 8/28/1723; Mary Hudson b. 9/16/1724; Elizabeth Hudson b. 6/24/1721.

Children of John and Hannah Hudson: Rebecca Hudson b. 6/27/1726; William Hudson b. 5/26/1728; John Hudson b. 5/26/1728 and d. 6/5/1728; Deborah Hudson b. 1/5/1729-30 at Jos. Coopers, in Jersey.

Philip James, son of Philip and Esther James, b. 10/15/1702.

William Janney, son of Randall and Frances Janney, b. 1/27/1704.

John Jennings, a doctor, bur 11/13/1688-9.

Mary Jerman, daughter of Edward and Elizabeth Jerman, b. 7/3/1702.

Children of Martin and Mary Jervis: Elizabeth Jervis b. 2/16/1699; John Jervis b. 9/11/1704; Sarah Jervis b. 10/26/1708.

Children of John and Rebecca Jervis: Charles Jervis b. 2/7/1731; Elizabeth Jervis b. 2/7/1733; Mary Jervis b. 11/10/1735; John Jervis b. 6/3/1742.

Elizabeth Jones, daughter of Joseph and Margaret Jones, b. 12/23/1705-6.
Mary Jones, daughter of Samuel and Hannah Jones, b. 3/25/1712.

Children of John (Bolter) and Elizabeth Jones: James b. 1/18/1705-6; Francis Jones b. 12/13/1707-8; Elizabeth Jones b. 10/5/1709; Ann Jones b. 8/15/1711; Francis Jones b. 7/14/1716; James Jones b. 12/14/1717; Charles Jones b. 1/18/1718-9; Samuel Jones b. 2/19/1721; John Jones b. 6/7/1723.

Children of Isaac and Mary Jones: Abraham Jones b. 7/22/1738; Martha Jones b. 1/1/1741-2; Isaac Jones b. 1/22/1743-4; Joseph Jones b. 2/18/1746; Benjamin Jones b. 6/9/1750; Mary Jones b. 2/8/1747-8.

Owen Jones, 2nd son of Jonathan and Gainer Jones of Merion, b. 9/18/1711.

Susanna Jones, daughter of Hugh and Lowry Evans and wife of Owen, b. 11/25/1719-20.
Owen and Susanna Jones mar. 3/30/1740.

Children of Owen and Susanna Jones: Jane Jones b. 1/5/1740-1; Lowry Jones b. 10/30/1742; Owen Jones b. 1/15/1744-5; Susanna Jones b. 7/4/1747; Hannah Jones b. 10/28/1749; Ann Jones b. 3/13/1752 n.s; Martha Jones b. 3/10/1754; Rebecca Jones b. 7/3/1757; Sarah Jones b. 5/13/1760; Jonathan Jones b. 7/15/1762.

Children of Jonathan Jones: Jonathan Jones b. 3/19/1748 o.s; Samuel Jones b. 7/23/1751 o.s; Elizabeth Jones b. 12/15/1753 n.s; Charles Jones b. 12/31/1755 n.s.

Children of Robert and Mary Jordan: Robert Jordan b. 8/6/1732; Richard Jordan b. 1/14/1734-5; Joseph Jordan b. 11/25/1735-6; Stanbury Jordan b. 12/11/1737-8; Mary Jordan b. 9/26/1739.

Children of William and Marianna Kelley: Mary Kelley b. 12/25/1698; William Kelley b. 1/3/1699-1700.

Robert Kent bur 1/8/1688.

Sarah Knowles, daughter of Francis and Sarah, b. 10/22/1723.

Children of John and Sarah Lancaster: Jonathan Lancaster b. 8/11/1715 and d. 2/?/1716; David Lancaster b. 8/11/1715 and d. 2/?/1716; Jane Lancaster b. 1/4/1716-7; Thomas Lancaster b. 5/12/1719; John Lancaster b. 12/6/1721-2; Joseph Lancaster b. 1/9/1724-5.

John Lewis b. 3/23/1696.
Hannah Lewis, daughter of Adam and Hannah Lewis: b. 1/13/1708-9.

Children of William and Mary Lingard (Lingardman): William Lingard (Lingardman) b. 8/8/1710; Mary Lingard (Lingardman) b. 8/26/1712.

Children of John and Joan Linton: Mary Linton b. 8/10/1723; Mary Linton b. 11/7/1724-5; John Linton b. 11/16/1726; Mary Linton b. 2/3/1729.

John Lock, son of John and Mary Lock, b. 3/31/1717.

Children of Ralph Loftus: Elizabeth Loftus b. 7/23/1740; Samuel Loftus b. 7/15/1745.

Thomas Lloyd, son of David and Grace Lloyd, b. 11/27/1697-8.

Children of Wm. and Mary Maltby: John Maltby b. 3/4/1690, parish of Eastwood, Nottingham; Mary Maltby b. 1/7/1692, parish of Eastwood, Nottingham; Elizabeth Maltby b. 10/25/1694, parish of Eastwood, Nottingham; William Maltby b. 10/18/1695, at sea on the Bristol Merchant; David Maltby b. 1/20/1699-1700, at Philada.

Benjamin Marshall, son of Christopher and Sarah Marshall, b. 8/14/1737.

Children of Joseph and Rachel Marshall, Joseph Marshall b. 5/12/1739; Ralph Marshall b. 11/29/1740; Hannah Marshall b. 10/16/1742; George Marshall b. 5/30/1744; John Marshall b. 10/20/1748; Jacob Marshall b. 10/23/1750.

Naomy Maule, daughter of John and Charity Maule, b. 7/8/1710.
Sarah Maule, daughter of Thomas and Susanna Maule b. 3/5/1750.

(No parents given): Matthew Metcalf b. 2/12/1724; Hannah Metcauˆ b. 5/17/1726; Mary Metcalf b. 12/21/1727; Rachel Metcalf b. 9/27/1729;

BIRTHS

Sarah Metcalf b. 2/27/1731; William Metcalf b. 6/12/1732; Jacob Metcalf b. 6/12/1732; Susanna Metcalf b. 6/4/1734; Hannah Metcalf b. 9/4/1735.

(No parents given): Sarah Michener b. 2/24/1687; Rebecca Michener b. 10/1/1692; Hannah Michener b. 10/1/1692; William Michener b. 10/14/1696; John Michener b. 9/29/1701; Elizabeth Michener b. 9/29/1701.

John Mifflin the younger, from Wiltshire, and Elizabeth Hardy from Derbyshire, mar. 12/6/1683-4 at the house of Henry Lewis, near Schuylkill.

The children of John and Elizabeth Mifflin who left issue and married among Friends: Edward; George; John; Jonathan, b. 4/12/1704; Jane.

Jonathan Mifflin and Sarah Robinson mar. in Philadelphia 3/30/1723.

Children of Jonathan and Sarah Mifflin: Samuel Mifflin b. 12/13/1724-5; Elizabeth Mifflin b. 3/19/1727; Sarah Mifflin b. 8/16/1729; Patience Mifflin b. 11/3/1735-6.

Children of William and Ann Miller: John Miller b. 1/24/1732-3; Hannah Miller b. 10/191734; Mary Miller b. 7/19/1741.

Children of James and Elizabeth Milner: Rebecca Milner b. 7/19/1747; Sarah Milner b. 12/11/1749; Isaac Milner b. 1/30/1753; Hannah Milner b. 1/30/1756.

Children of John Milner: Thomas Milner b. 11/31/1748; John Milner b. 10/27/1755; Mary Milner b. 11/2/1760; Martha Milner b. 11/17/1763; Sarah Milner b. 10/9/1765.

Children of Anthony and Elizabeth Morris: James Morris b. 5/8/1688; William Morris b. 5/23/1695; Elizabeth Morris b. 4/28/1697; Isaac Morris b. 10/24/1701; Sarah Morris b. 11/16/1703-4; Israel Morris b. 10/25/1705; Luke Morris b. 8/25/1707.

Children of Anthony (brewer) and Phebe Morris: Anthony Morris b. 11/14/1705; James Morris b. 7/8/1707; John Morris b. 4/23/1709; Samuel Morris b. 5/20/1710; Samuel Morris b. 9/21/1711; Mary Morris b. 8/17/1713; Joseph Morris b. 1/10/1714-5; Elizabeth Morris b. 8/21/1716; Benjamin Morris b. 10/30/1717.

Hannah Morris, daughter of Anthony and Elizabeth Morris, b. 5/4/1717.

Children of Morris Jr. and Susanna Morris: Jonathan Morris b. 11/7/1744-5; Sarah Morris b. 4/5/1747; Susanna Morris b. 4/2/1749; Rebecca Morris b. 7/13/1754.

Children of Joseph and Mary Noble: Samuel Noble b. 5/25/1721; Mary Noble b. 5/31/1722; Martha Noble b. 2/15/1731-2.

Children of Isaac and Mary Norris: Mary Norris b. 10/5/1694; Hannah Norris b. 4/1/1696; Sarah Norris b. 8/2/1697; Joseph Norris b. 11/29/1698-9; Rachel Norris b. 12/28/1699; Isaac Norris b. 8/23/1701; Elizabeth Norris b. 11/7/1703-4; Deborah Norris b. 8/18/1705; Thomas Norris b.(at Joseph Pikes in Cork)11/29/1706-7; John Norris b.4/28/1709; Prudence Norris b. 4/22/1710; Charles Norris b. 3/9/1712; Margaret Norris b. 6/16/1713; Samuel Norris b. 7/12/1714.

Children of Evan and Mary Owen: Robert Owen b. 10/12/1712; Martha Owen b. 4/12/1714; Esther Owen b. 9/18/1716; Aurelius Owen b. 1/1/1718-19.

Children of Robert and Susanna Owen: Mary Owen b. 3/3/1719; Hannah Owen b. (illegible); Rachel Owen b. 6/19/1724.

George Palmer, son of Thomas and Sarah Palmer, b. 11/26/1705-6.

Children of John and Mary Parker: Jane Parker b. 1/24/1701-2; Abraham Parker b. 10/9/1705; John Parker b. 12/28/1709-10.

Children of Anthony and Rachel Peel: John Peel b. 11/27/1723-4; Ann Peel b. 1/26/1733.

Children of Israel and Rachel Pemberton: Israel Pemberton b. 3/19/1715; James Pemberton b. 6/26/1723; John Pemberton b. 9/25/1727; Charles Pemberton b. 5/4/1729.

John Penn, son of Gov. William and Hannah Penn, b. 11/28/1699-70.

Isaac Pennington, son of Edward and Sarah Pennington, b. 9/22/1700.

Children of Samuel and Elizabeth Pennock: Joseph Pennock b. 7/18/1737-8; John Pennock b. 4/11/1740; Samuel Pennock b. 8/20/1748.

Joseph Peters, son of Reece and Ann Peters, b. 9/26/1712.

Sarah Pleadwell, daughter of Edward and Grace Pleadwell, b. 2/23/1720.

Children of Samuel and Abigail Powell: Ann Powell b. 2/10/1702; Samuel Powell b. 12/26/1704-5.

Children of Samuel Powell: Abigail Powell b. 5/21/1735; Samuel Powell b. 8/28/1738; Sarah Powell b. 7/22/1747.

Children of William and Jane Rakestraw: Martha Rakestraw b. 10/15/1748; Bevan Rakestraw b. 11/10/1753.

Mary Reeve, daughter of John and Sarah Reeve, b. 6/28/1720.

Children of Joseph and Mary Reynear: Isaac Reynear b. 7/3/1721; Stephen Reynear b. 11/15/1723-4; Hannah Reynear b. 8/10/1727; Rachel Reynear b. 10/18/1730.

Mary Reynear, widow of Joseph, mar. Samuel Bell (see Bell).

Children of Samuel and Elizabeth Rhoads: Mary Rhoads b. 6/1/1738; Samuel Rhoads b. 7/6/1740; Hannah Rhoads b. 12/4/1743-4.

Children of William and Mary Riall: John Riall b. 4/7/1696; Susan Riall b. 5/13/1698; William Riall b. 1/9/1701; Joseph Riall b. 4/5/1703.

Margaret Richards, daughter of David and Sarah Richards, b. 8/5/1761.

Elizabeth Richardson, daughter of Joseph and Hannah Richardson, b. 3/21/1743.

Children of Joseph Richardson and Mary, his 2nd wife: Hannah Richardson b. 10/6/1748; Mary Richardson b. 9/30/1750; Joseph Richardson b. 12/4/1752; Nathaniel Richardson b. 2/2/2754; Rebecca Richardson b. 4/5/1758.

Children of Francis and Mary Richardson: Mary Richardson b. 4/15/1743; Grace Richardson b. 2/6/1745; Francis Richardson b. 3/15/1746; George Richardson b. 2/27/1747; Hannah Richardson b. 2/4/1748; Elizabeth Richardson b. 3/29/1749; Thomas Richardson b. 10/16/1750; John Richardson b. 1/6/1752 n.s; Deborah Richardson b. 8/28/1753.

John Ricketts, son of Isaac and Elizabeth Ricketts, b. 11/13/1689.

Children of John and Mary Roberts: Margaret Roberts b. 6/10/1703; Elizabeth Roberts b. 10/28/1705.

Children of Thomas and Martha Roberts: Mary Roberts b. 2/9/1707; Martha Roberts b. 12/1/1708; Sarah Roberts b. 12/13/1710-11.

Children of Matthew and Sarah Robinson: David Robinson b. 5/17/1701; Margaret Robinson b. 10/30/1703; Lydia Robinson b. 7/27/1705.

William Sanders, son of Charles and Sarah Sanders, b. 12/17/1698.

Children of William and Hester Sanders: Elizabeth Sanders b. 9/19/1723; John Sanders b. 5/14/1725; Hannah Sanders b. 9/18/1726.

Children of William and Sarah Sandwith: Mary Sandwith b. 4/2/1732; Elizabeth Sandwith b. 12/16/1734-5; William Sandwith b. 8/12/1746.

Children of Samuel Sansom: Mary Sansom b. 1/20/1737-8; Samuel Sansom b. 1/15/1738-9 (mar. Hannah Calender 5/25/1762); John Sansom b. 12/5/1741-2; Elizabeth Sansom b. 12/5/1741-2; Sarah Sansom b. 3/30/1744; Joseph Sansom b. 2/30/1747; Hannah Sansom b. 6/14/1749.

Benjamin Sharpless, son of Benjamin and Edith Sharpless, b. 1/6/1741. Hannah Sharpless, wife of Benjamin and daughter of Edmund Hollinshead, b. 7/25/1738.
Benjamin and Hannah Sharpless mar. 8/25/1763.

Doctor John Shelson (Shillson), of Plymouth, d. 10/27/1688.

Children of Jacob and Elizabeth Shoemaker: Thomas Shoemaker b. 5/27/1725; David Shoemaker b. 12/22/1726-7; Jonathan Shoemaker b. 12/22/1726-7.

William Sitgreaves, son of William Sitgreaves b. 12/14/1729-30.

Children of William and Mary Sitgreaves: Thomas Sitgreaves b. 9/25/1731; Sarah Ann Sitgreaves b. 4/4/1733.

Children of James and Susanna Skerrett: John Skerrett b. 11/20/1748-9; Emme Skerrett b. 6/15/1750; Joseph Skerrett b. 9/18/1752; Esther Skerrett b. 2/12/1755; James Skerrett b. 2/27/1760; Susanna Skerrett b. 8/25/1762; James Skerrett b. 1/27/1766.

Children of Daniel and Sarah Stanton: Abigail Stanton b. 11/24/1736; Sarah Stanton b. 7/5/1741.

Children of Stephen and Mary Stapler: John Stapler b. 1/7/1748; Margaret Stapler b. 10/6/1750; Thomas Stapler b. 7/29/1751; Mary Stapler b. 3/1/1758.

Children of James and Martha Steel: Sarah Steel b. 12/4/1699-1700, Chichester, Eng; Martha Steel b. 6/20/1701; Mary Steel b. 12/1/1702-3, Philad.

Children of Peter and Margery Stretch: Sarah Stretch b. 6/28/1705; Joseph Stretch b. 12/20/1709-10.

Children of Joseph and Lydia Stretch: Sarah Stretch b. 7/13/1733; John Stretch b. 1/14/1734-5; Lydia Stretch b. 12/23/1737-8; Thomas Stretch b. 2/30/1739.

Children of John and Mary Test: Henry Test b. 1/18/1749-50; Ann Test b. 5/29/1755; Sarah Test b. 7/30/1757.

Children of Christopher and Mary Thomson: Sarah Thomson b. 6/17/1711; Hannah Thomson b. 6/11/1715.

Elizabeth Tilbury, daughter of Thomas and Ann Tilbury, b. 12/17/1742-3.

Children of Charles and Abigail Townsend: Sarah Townsend b. 2/24/1732; Isaac Townsend b. 10/21/1733; Susanna Townsend b. 12/14/1737-8; Hannah Townsend b. 9/21/1742; Lydia Townsend b. 10/28/1745; John Townsend b. 11/6/1747; Mary Townsend b. 11/6/1747.

Children of William and Elizabeth Walker: Susanna Walker b. 6/29/1690; Susanna Walker b. 10/13/1691; Elizabeth Walker b. 7/11/1693.

Chidden of Nicholas and Jane Waln: Elizabeth Waln b. 1/27/1697; Nicholas Waln b. 1/24/1699; William Waln b. 1/15/1700-1.

Children of Richard and Ann Waln: Nicholas Waln b. 6/23(5)/1707 and was bur 7/3/1707; Nicholas Waln b. 1/19/1709.

Children of Richard and Ann Waln: Jane Waln b. 6/6/1711 and was bur 6/17/1711; Jane Waln b. 12/20/1712 and was bur 8/4/1714; Ann Waln b. 12/16/1714-5; Richard Waln b. 4/5/1717; Susanna Waln b. 4/9/1719; Robert Waln b. 1/21/1721; Joseph Waln b. 10/18/1722; Mary Waln b. 6/15/1724.

Jeremiah Warder and Mary Head mar. in Philad. 2/13/1735.

Children of Jeremiah and Mary Warder: John Warder b. 11/6/1736-7; Lydia Warder b. 11/13/1737-8; John Warder b. 5/19/1739; Sarah Warder b. 9/1/1740; Joseph Warder b. 3/25/1742; Rebecca Warder b. 2/11/1743; Jeremiah Warder b. 5/31/1744; Sarah Warder b. 6/5/1745; Mary Warder b. 11/23/1746-7; Susanna Warder b. 5/17/1749; John Warder b. 2/24/1751; Sarah Warder b. 1/28/1753.

Children of Isaac and Veronica Warner: John Warner b. 8/13/1717; Arnold Warner b. 4/8/1719; Susanna Warner b. 9/23/1721; Ann Warner b. 10/2/1723; Jane Warner b. 8/7/1726; Elizabeth Warner b. 11/23/1730; Lydia Warner b. 1/15/1732; Isaac Warner b. 6/4/1735; Hannah Warner b. 12/26/1738; Margaret Warner b. 3/14/1743.

Children of Samuel and Mary Wetherill: Thomas Wetherill b. 4/5/1744; Mary Wetherill b. 1/17/1745-6; Joseph Wetherill b. 12/16/1747-8; Elizabeth Wetherill b. 3/23/1750; Samuel Wetherill b. 6/10/1752 n.s; Ann Wetherill b. 8/13/1755.

Joseph Wharton, son of Thomas and Rachel Wharton, b. 9/25/1689.
Joseph Wharton, son of Thomas and Rachel Wharton, b. 6/4/1707.

Children of Joseph and Hannah Wharton: Samuel Wharton b. 3/3/1732; Thomas Wharton b. 11/15/1730; Joseph Wharton b. 1/21/1733-4; John Wharton b. 11/17/1737-8; William Wharton b. 1/12/1739-40; George Wharton b. 1/14/1741-2; Charles Wharton b. 11/11/1743; Isaac Wharton b. 7/15/1745; Carpenter Wharton b. 6/30/1747; Benjamin Wharton b. 12/12/1749-50.

Children of William and Sarah White: Liddia White b. 2/24/1703; Elizabeth White b. 6/29/1705; Mary White b. 8/3/1704;

Children of Zachariah and Sarah Whitpain: Mary Whitpain b. 6/28/1689; John Whitpain b. 10/25/1691.

Children of George and Mary Wilson: Mary Wilson b. 6/31/1732; Ann Wilson b. 3/8/1734; William Wilson b. 7/13/1739; Joseph Wilson b. 8/13/1741; Hannah Wilson b. 7/21/1743; George Wilson b. 11/10/1745; Elizabeth Wilson b. 7/5/1749.

Richard Wistar, son of Caspar and Catherine Wistar, b. 5/6/1727.
Sarah Wistar, wife of Richard and daughter of Bartholomew and Sarah Wyatt, b. 6/6/1733 in Mannington, Salem Co.
Richard Wistar and Sarah Wyatt mar. 9/27/1751 at Salem.

Children of Anthony and Jane Woodcock: Jane Woodcock b. 7/26/1747; Catherine Woodcock b. 9/26/1749.

Children of Robert and Elizabeth Worrell: Hannah Worrell b. 4/10/1742; Jonathan Worrell b. 9/3/1743; Rachel Worrell b. 8/26/1748; Rebecca Worrell b. 9/14/1753.

Joseph Worthington, son of Daniel and Sarah Worthington, b. 5/29/1715.

Barbara Wright, daughter of Benjamin Wright, b. 8/4/1703.

Children of Mordecai and Catherine Yarnall: Sarah Yarnall b. 8/27/1734; Ellen Yarnall b. 8/7/1736; Hannah Yarnall b. 6/6/1738; Catherine Yarnall b. 11/1/1740-1.

Children of Mordecai Yarnall and Mary, his 2nd wife: Mary Yarnall b. 3/13/1746; Mordecai Yarnall b. 8/9/1747; Edward Yarnall b. 10/14/1748; Lydia Yarnall b. 3/6/1750; Ann Yarnall b. 9/9/1751; Elizabeth Yarnall b. 10/26/1752; Peter Yarnall b. 2/17/1754; Deborah Yarnall b. 6/15/1756; Jane Yarnall b. 12/9/1757 and d, age 11 mo.

Mary Young (Yong), daughter of Morgan and Mary Young (Yong), b. 12/26/1690.

Children of Jonathan and Mary Zane: Nathaniel Zane b. 5/17/1729; Mary Zane b. 6/1/1731; Hannah Zane b. 12/25/1732; Mary Zane b. 1/19/1734; Nathan Zane b. 2/22/1737; Rebecca Zane b. 3/7/1739; Jonathan Zane b. 1/23/1741; Mary Zane b. 10/11/1743; Deborah Zane b. 7/13/1745; Joel Zane b. 7/6/1746; Jesse Zane b. 9/23/1748; Liddia Zane b. 7/29/1750; William Zane b. 3/7/1754.

Children of Isaac and Sarah Zane: Hannah Zane b. 10/23/1734; Phebe Zane b. 2/16/1737; Isaac Zane b. 10/23/1738-9; John Zane b. 12/9/1740-1; Isaac Zane b. 4/24/1743; Daniel Zane b. 4/4/1746; Phebe Zane b. 12/28/1748-9; Daniel Zane b. 12/6/1750-1; Sarah Zane b. 5/7/1752; Sarah Zane b. 6/10/1753; Sarah Zane b. 9/29/1754.

DEATHS AND BURIALS
1687-1750

Elizabeth Gove, dau of Richard and Bridgett, d. 9/17/1687.
Bridgett Gove, wife of Richard, d. 9/13/1687.
Nathaniel Watson d. 9/4/1688.
Henry Jones d. 4/2/1688.
Doctor John Chelsey (Shillson in will) d. 10/27/1687.
Widdow Hammond d. 6/7/1688.
Doctor John Jennings bur 11/13/1688.
John Longhurst bur 11/25/1688.
Anthony Moar bur 11/?/1688 (last day of month).
John Saxbie bur 12/26/1688.
Mary Jones bur 12/5/1688.
Thomas Whooten, Senr, bur 12/11/1688.
Ann Snowden bur 1/4/1688.
Robert Kent bur 1/8/1688.
Edward Evirard bur 1/14/1688.
Benjamin King bur 1/?/1689, on last day of month.
Daniel Prit bur 2/5/1689.
Richard Wall bur 2/6/1689.
Joshua Carpenter, son of Samuel and Hannah, bur 1/18/1689.
William Stanley bur 2/21/1689.
Elizabeth Carpenter, dau of Joshua and Elizabeth, bur 3/2/1689.
Hannah Chambers, dau of Benj. and Hannah, bur 3/2/1689.
Mary Tailor bur 3/24/1689.
Randoll Smallwood bur 3/26/1689.
John Kinsey, brother of Thomas Fairman's wife, bur 6/28/1689.
Robert Fairman, son of Thomas and Elizabeth, bur 7/2/1689.
Richard Fox bur 7/16/1689.
Thomas Carter bur 7/17/1689.
John Patrick, uncle of Zachariah and John Whitpayne, bur 7/21/1689.
Zepheniah Phipps, son of Joseph and Sarah, bur 7/24/1689.
Samuel Morris, son of Anthony and Mary, bur 9/4/1689.
Elizabeth Test, wife of John, bur 12/1/1689.
Nathaniel Ible bur 12/12/1689-90.
John Eckley bur 12/14/1689-90.
Henry Robins bur 1/3/1689-90.
John Hutchins bur 1/3/1690.
Mary Emblin, wife of George, bur 1/22/1690.
Sarah Lee, William Southby's dau-in-law, bur 2/15/1690.
John Deplone, son of John, bur 3/4/1690.
Daniel Furnis, son of Henry, bur 3/(last day)/1690.
Mary Delavall, dau of John and Hannah, bur 4/3/1690.

Mary Ambler, dau of Joseph and Sarah, bur 4/9/1690.
Elizabeth Ible, dau of Nathaniel and Elizabeth, bur 4/11/1690.
John Morris, son of Anthony, bur 4/14/1690.
Simon Jones, son of Daniel and Mary, bur 4/25/1690.
Elizabeth Alling, dau of Nemiah and Mary, bur 4/25/1690.
____ Hodgsons, wife of Doctor Hodgsons, bur 4/26/1690.
Anthony Deplone, son of John and Waneky, bur 4/27/1690.
Joseph Wharton, son of Thomas and Rachel, bur 5/4/1690.
William Gibbs bur 5/5/1690.
Sarah Lee, dau of William and Joan, bur 5/16/1690.
Hannah Lee, dau of William and Joan, bur 5/18/1690.
Mary Jones, dau of John and Mary, bur 5/24/1690.
Elizabeth Hooton, dau of Thomas and Elizabeth, bur 6/6/1690.
Thomas Bristoll, "color macker", bur 6/12/1690.
Daniel Pearce, son of Nicholas and Mary, bur 7/6/1690.
James Barker bur 6/7/1690.
Barnabas Wilcox bur 7/14/1690.
Daniel Oliver, son of Evan and Jane, bur 7/15/1690.
Mary Warner, wife of George, bur 7/24/1690.
Israel Roberts, son of Thomas and Catherine, bur 7/25/1690.
Morris Morgan, son of Morris and Catherine, bur 8/1/1690.
Elizabeth Wallice, dau of Robert and Easter, bur 8/1/1690.
Mary Forrist, dau of William and Joan, bur 8/6/1690.
Robert Wallice, son of Robert and Esther, bur 8/11/1690.
Caleb Fincher, son of Francis and Mary, bur 8/11/1690.
John Taylor, son of Anthony and Jane, bur 8/16/1690.
George Harmer, son of George and Mary, bur 8/16/1690.
Samuel Longshaw, son of Thomas and Christian, bur 9/5/1690.
Mary Jones, dau of Daniel and Mary, bur 9/7/1690.
Thomas Williard, son of Thomas and Judith, bur 9/7/1690.
Mary Pritchet, dau of Thomas and Barbara, bur 9/8/1690.
John Pearce, son of Richard and Ann, bur 9/10/1690.
Mary Wade, dau of John and Marling, bur 9/10/1690.
William Harwood, son of William and Susanna, bur 9/16/1690.
Thomas Howard, son of Benjamin and Mary, bur 9/21/1690.
Mordecai Morgan, son of William and Elizabeth, bur 10/3/1690.
Thomas Smith bur 10/25/1690.
Sarah Chambers, dau of Benj. and Sarah (Hannah?), bur 12/13/1690.
Daniel Thomas, son of Michael and Winnifred, bur 12/19/1690.
Susana Walker, dau of William and Elizabeth, bur 1/16/1690-1.
Rebeckah Banton, wife of Peter, bur 6/28/1691.
Pieter Banton, son of Pieter and Rebecka, bur 6/30/1691.
Sarah Kelly bur 7/13/1691.
Edward Ible bur 7/23/1691.
William Jenings, son of Samuel and Ann, bur 9/22/1691.

Jeremiah Gabitas, son of William and Abigail, bur 10/9/1691.
Abigail Gabitas, wife of William, bur 10/12/1690.
Ann Boulding, wife of William, bur 10/19/1691.
William Hearne, son of William and Sarah, bur 11/18/1691.
Christopher Row, son of Robert and Mary, bur 11/28/1691.
John Thomas bur 12/20/1691.
Susannah Walker, dau of William and Elizabeth, bur 1/13/1690-1.
Thomas Winn bur 1/17/1691-2.
Kinsey Firman, son of Thomas, bur 1/3/1692.
Symon Edgcomb, son of Nathaniel and Sarah, bur 2/14/1692.
Mary Brant, dau of Albertus and Susan, bur 2/18/1692.
Katherine Beetle, dau of John and Elizabeth, bur 3/1/1692.
John Williams (cooper), Sophia Armitts father, bur 3/12/1692.
Isac Ricketts bur 4/26/1692.
Francis Fincher, son of Francis and Mary, bur 5/27/1692.
Agnes Morris, wife of Anthony, bur 5/28/1692.
Sarah Eckley, widow of John, bur 6/24/1692.
Nathaniel Allen bur 6/24/1692.
Sarah Hardin bur 6/31/1692.
Hanna Masters, wife of Thomas, bur 7/2/1692.
Dorothy Fox, dau of James and Elizabeth, bur 8/28/1692.
Sarah Wilcox, widow of Barnabas, bur 9/21/1692.
John Goodson, son of John and Sarah, bur 9/28/1692.
Robert Turner, son of Robert and Susanna, bur 10/18/1692.
Alce Hudson, dau of William and Ann, bur 10/22/1692.
Philip Richards, son of Philip and Mary, bur 12/4/1692.
Zachariah Whitpain bur 1/20/1693.
Hanna Chambers, wife of Benjamin, bur 1/27/1693.
Dennis Rotchford bur 2/7/1693.
Ruth Stockdaile, dau of William and Ruth, bur 2/9/1693.
Doctor Robinson, of East Jersey, d. 3/19/1693.
Rebecka Carpenter, dau of Samuel and Hannah, bur 4/1/1693.
John Sutton bur 5/4/1693.
Richard Dean bur 5/12/1693.
John Delavall bur 10/6/1693.
Mary Preston, dau of Samuel and Rachel, bur 7/7/1693.
Margrett Lloyd, dau of Thomas, bur 7/13/1693.
Joseph Umphrey d. 7/14/1693.
William Stocdaile bur 7/23/1693.
Susanna Walker, dau of William and Elizabeth, bur 8/5/1693.
William Newton, son of Basill and Barbadoes, d. 7/15/1693.
John Delavall, son of John, dec'd, and Hannah, d. 8/15/1693.
Ann Murrey, wife of Humphrey, d. 8/15/1693.
John Cox d. 11/4/1693-4.
Elizabeth Luff d. 12/2/1693-4.

Sarah Edgecomb, dau of Nathaniel and Sarah, bur 1/18/1693-4.
Elizabeth Jacques, dau of Thomas, bur 4/22/1694.
John Frederick Didon bur 6/13/1694.
William Brilewin, bricklayer, bur 6/22/1694.
William Hudson bur 6/30/1694.
Edmund Warner, son of Edmund and Rachel, bur 6/29/1694.
Sarah Cerres bur 7/4/1694.
Elizabeth Houton bur 7/8/1694.
William Coddington, son of Thomas and Mary, bur 7/8/1694.
Thomas Lloyd bur 7/12/1694.
David Griffith bur 7/24/1694.
Robert Hoskins, son of Richard and Hester of Barbadoes, bur 7/26/1694.
Christopher West, son of James and Prudence, bur 8/17/1694.
Dyana Hardyman, wife of Abraham, bur 8/27/1694.
William Hunt bur 9/6/1694.
Elizabeth Kelly, wife of William, bur 9/7/1694.
William Smith bur 9/11/1694.
Katherine Dean, widow of Richard, bur 9/14/1694.
Joyse Jenings, dau of Samuel and Ann, bur 9/14/1694.
William Saleway bur 9/15/1694.
Christopher West, son of James and Prudence, bur 9/17/1694.
Young Morgan bur 9/24/1694.
Katherine More, dau of Anthony and Jane, bur 9/25/1694.
Elizabeth White, wife of Joseph, bur 10/2/1694.
Margrett Powell, wife of David, bur 10/7/1694.
Mary Rotchford, widow of Dennis, 10/25/1694.
Elizabeth Miller, wife of Thomas, bur 11/3/1694.
Jonathon Duckitt bur 11/5/1694.
Elizabeth Ewer, wife of Robert, bur 11/9/1694.
Thomas Woodroof, son of Thomas (of Salem), bur 11/9/1694.
Grace Rakestraw, wife of William, bur 11/11/1694.
Thomas Hollyman bur 11/12/1694.
Hannah Owen, dau of Griffith and Sarah, bur 11/22/1694.
Rebecka Jones, wife of John, bur 12/1/1694.
Evan Oliver bur 12/2/1694.
Joseph Carpenter, son of Samuel and Hannah, bur 2/26/1695.
Lloyd Preston, son of Samuel and Rachel, bur 3/22/1695.
Nathaniel Edgcomb, son of Nathaniel and Sarah, bur 5/26/1695.
Jane Rawle, wife of Francis, Sr, bur 12/9/1695.
Elizabeth Moore, wife of John, bur 1/1/1696.
Elizabeth Beedle, wife of John, bur 1/3/1696.
Jane Oliver, widow of Evan, bur 1/5/1696.
Elinor Allen, widow of Nathaniel, bur 1/14/1696.
Jacob Hout, son of Caspar and Elizabeth, bur 1/20/1696.
Thomas Densy, son of John and Sarah, bur 1/21/1696.

Elizabeth Boulding, dau of William and Elizabeth, bur 2/12/1696.
James Kinsey, son of John and Sarah, bur 2/29/1696.
William Chanders, son of Thomas and Frances, bur 6/6/1696.
Ruth Piller, dau of James and Gainer, bur 6/7/1696.
Elizabeth Clements, dau of Matthew and Elizabeth, bur 6/14/1696.
Mary Mitchner, dau of John and Sarah, bur 6/24/1696.
Sarah Luff, dau of Hue and Sarah, bur 7/10/1696.
Elizabeth Beaks, dau of William and Elizabeth, bur 7/11/1696.
Elizabeth Brintnall, dau of Jane and David, bur 7/12/1696.
Edward Doughty bur 10/7/1696.
John Whittraine bur 12/3/1696-7.
Francis Rawly, Senr, bur 12/25/1696-7.
Nathaniel Duckitt bur 2/1/1697.
Robert Barrow, of Westmoreland, bur 2/6/1697 (shipwrecked on the
    coast of Florida in company with Jonathan Dickinson and others).
Elizabeth Coates, dau of James and Mary, bur 4/5/1697.
Elizabeth Walker, widow of William, bur 5/26/1697.
Elizabeth Boulding, dau of William and Elizabeth, bur 5/22/1697.
Joseph Chanders, son of Thomas, dec'd, and Frances, bur 5/30/1697.
George Holten, son of Author and Elizabeth, bur 6/19/1697.
Elizabeth Coats, dau of James and Mary, bur 5/4/1697.
Hennery Hern, son of William and Sarah, bur 7/27/1697.
Judith Griffith, wife of Thomas, bur 8/9/1697.
E. Howell, wife of Philip, d. 8/16/1697.
Samuel Harwood, son of William and Susanna, d. 9/5/1697.
Thomas Masters, son of Thomas and Isabella, d. 9/19/1697.
Margrett Lynum, wife of John, d. 12/13/1697-8.
John Bowen d. 11/6/1697-8.
Samuel Harding, son of Thomas and Esther, d. 11/19/1697-8.
Esther Coleman, dau of Stephen and Sarah, d. 11/6/1697-8.
Mary Kelly, dau of William and Mirianna, d. 1/8/1698.
Hannah Day, dau of John and Hannah, d. 1/27/1698.
____ Say, dau of William and Mary, d. 1/27/1698.
Jane Dawson, wife of Manuell, d. 1/30/1698.
Mary Say, wife of William, d. 2/1/1698.
Thomas Prichard d. 2/2/1698.
Thomas Andrews d. 2/14/1698.
John Hudson, son of William and Mary. d. 3/7/1698.
Edy Sanders, wife of Paul, d. 2/3/1698.
Thomas Hart, son of John and Mary, d. 2/7/1698.
Alce Beakes, dau of William and Elizabeth, d. 2/8/1698.
Millicent Hoskins d. 2/9/1698.
John Decon d. 3/15/1698.
Elizabeth Richards, dau of Philip and Mary, d. 3/16/1698.
Phebe Pemberton, dau of Phineas, d. 3/30/1698.

George Fox, son of George and Susanna, d.4.13.1698.
Nathan Peg, son of Daniel and Rebeckah, d. 4/25/1698.
Ruth Badcock, dau of Henry and Mary, d. 5/6/1698.
John Sanders, son of John and Elizabeth, d. 6/29/1698.
Jenkin Lewiss d. 7/29/1698.
Phillip Richards d. 8/19/1698.
John Litchfield d. 8 19 1698.
Mary Woodmansey, late Wardell, wife of Thomas, d. 2/2/1699.
Thomas Bulkley, son of Samuel and Anne, d. 2/18/1699.
Mary Kelley, dau of William and Marianna, d. 1/8/1699.
Rachel Jones, widow of Henry, d. 2/24/1699.
Sarah Harwood, wife of John, d. 5/3/1699.
William Masters, son of Thomas and Isabella, d. 5/11/1699.
Joanna Pryor d. 5/25/1699.
Mary Havard, dau of John and Sarah, d. 5/13/1699.
Mary Johnson, dau of Tertullian and Johanna, d. 6/9/1699.
Sarah Edgecombe, dau of Nathaniel and Sarah, d. 6/11/1699.
Daniel Smith d. 6/12/1699.
Isaac Ashton d. 6/15/1699.
Stephen Coleman d. 6/16/1699.
Margrett Radley, dau of Daniel and Mary, d. 6/17/1699.
Ann Lee, wife of Lawrence, d. 6/24/1699.
Phillis Hooper, wife of Abraham, d. 6/21/1699.
Thomas Morriss d. 6/28/1699.
William Johnson d. 6/30/1699.
Deborah Dean, dau of Richard and Katherine, d. 7/1/1699.
Jane Morriss, dau of Thomas, d. 7/1/1699.
Sarah Smith, wife of Thomas, d. 7/1/1699.
Abraham Hardiman d. 7/1/1699.
Samuel Lambert d. 7/1/1699.
Nathaniel Dean, son of Richard and Katherine, d. 7/2/1699.
Thomas Smith, son in law to Thomas Sisum, d. 7/2/1699.
Hester Hoskins, wife of Richard, d. 7/2/1699.
Katherine Hardin d. 7/3/1699.
Mary Spikeman, wife of Randolph, d. 7/3/1699.
George Fox, son of James and Elizabeth, d. 7/4/1699.
John Stepthen, servant to Rv? Haydock of Liverpool, d/ 7/4/1699.
William Alloway d. 7/5/1699.
Thomas Smith d. 7/5/1699.
Joseph Durborow, son of Hugh and Elizabeth, d. 7/5/1699.
Abigail Harwood, dau of William and Susanna, d. 7/7/1699.
Thomas Smith, son of Thomas, dec'd, d. 7/10/1699.
William Trotter d. 7/11/1699.
John Jennett d. 7/12/1699.
Samuel Skott d. 7/12/1699.

Tho: Rich d. 7/12/1699.
Paul Newman d. 7/12/1699.
Lawrence Lee d. 7/13/1699.
Elizabeth Martin d. 7/13/1699.
Grace Pearson, widow of Thomas, d. 7/14/1699.
Thomas Duckett d. 7/14/1699.
Mary Gracy, wife of George, d. 7/14/1699.
William Harwood d. 7/15/1699.
Thomas Willson d. 7/15/1699.
Katherine Reyneer Johnson, wife of Reyneer, d. 7/16/1699.
John Reyneer Johnson, son of Reyneer and Katherine, d. 7/16/1699.
Guinn Laycock, wife of William, d. 7/16/1699.
Deborah Morgan, dau of Edward, dec'd, d. 7/18/1699.
John Straton, servant to James Fox, d. 7/18/1699.
James Fox d. 7/19/1699.
Charles Sanders d. 7/21/1699.
Margrett Beardsley, widow of Alexander, d. 7/22/1699.
Elizabeth Giles, servant to Daniel Radley, d. 7/22/1699.
Sarah Cox, widow, d, 7/23/1699.
Rebecka Ward, widow Hardings servant, d. 7/23/1699.
Patience Gove, wife of Richard, d. 7/24/1699.
Sarah Norris, dau of Isaac and Mary, d. 7/26/1699.
Mary Morris, wife of Anthony, d. 7/27/1699.
Thomas Loansdale d. 7/28/1699.
Mary Sibthorp, wife of Christopher, d. 7/28/1699.
Elizabeth Lounsdale, dau of Thomas and Margrett, d. 7/29/1699.
Rebecka Morris, dau of Thomas, dec'd, and Margrett, d. 7/29/1699.
John Sanders d. 7/29/1699.
Mary Richards, widow of Phillip, d. 7/29/1699.
William Atkinson, son of Christo., dec., and Margret, drowned 7/30/1699.
Thomas Proctor, servant of Margrett Atkinson, drowned 7/30/1699.
Elizabeth Hoskins, dau of Richard and Esther, dec'd, d. 8/1/1699.
George Goldsmith d. 8/1/1699.
Arthur Cook d. 8/2/1699.
Roger Gill d. 8/3/1699 of malignant yellow fever which prevailed greatly this year.
Barberah Prichard, widow of Thomas, d. 8/3/1699.
Mary Busby, wife of John, d. 8/3/1699.
Jane More, dau of Jane, widow, d. 8/3/1699.
Mary Addams, wife of S. Addams, d. 8/5/1699.
Thomas Fitchwater d. 8/6/1699.
John Busby d. 8/6/1699.
Edward Richardson d. 8/7/1699.
Thomas Langston d. 8/7/1699.
Evan Owen d. 8/7/1699.

John Pain d. 8/7/1699.
John Southby, son of William, d. 8/9/1699.
Peter Castle d. 8/10/1699.
Johanna Johnson, wife of Tertullian, d. 8/10/1699.
Ester Hardin, wife of Thomas, d. 8/11/1699.
Elizabeth Alloway, widow of William, d. 8/11/1699.
Rachell Reneer Johnson, dau of Reneer Johnson, d. 8/12/1699.
Mary Allen, wife of Nehemiah, d. 8/12/1699.
Margrett Lansdale, widow of Thomas, d. 8/13/1699.
William Maltby d. 8/14/1699.
Elizabeth Hoot, wife of Casper, d. 8/14/1699.
Catherine Hoot, dau of Casper and Elizabeth, d. 8/15/1699.
Elizabeth Calcup d. 9/6/1699.
Margrett Miller, servant to Richd. Woodworth, d. 10/31/1699.
William Thomson, son of Robert and Sarah, d. 11/5/1699.
John Walker, son of Manuell and Margrett, d. 11/8/1699.
Hannah Blake, widow of Edward, late of New Castle, d. 12/7/1699.
Rich. Boyce, servant of Abraham Hooper, d. 12/7/1699.
Sarah Edgecombe, wife of Nathaniel, d. 12/24/1699.
Mary Masters, dau of Thomas and Sabilla, d. 12/27/1699.
Hannah Masters, dau of Thomas and former wife Hannah, d. 1/4/1699-
1700.
Miriam Harriott, wife of Samuel, d. 1/24/1699-1700.
Jonathan Mifflin, son of H.John and Elizabeth, d. 3/15/1700.
Caleb Flower, son of Daniel and Sarah, d. 5/8/1700.
Ann Howood, dau of John and Sarah, dec'd, d. 5/3/1700.
Rebecka Pillar, dau of James and Tamar, d. 6/14/1700.
John Merriwether, son of Richd., dec'd, and Mary, d. 6/14/1700.
Elinor Hudson, dau of William and Mary, d. 6/27/1700.
John Jessup d. 7/7/1700.
Joseph Clifton, son of Henry, d. 7/8/1700.
John Moore, son of Anthony and Jane, d. 7/29/1700.
Joseph Rakestraw, son of William and Grace, dec'd, d. 8/1/1700.
Elizabeth Rakestraw, wife of William, d. 8/8/1700.
Sarah Aston, dau of Joseph and Sarah, d. 9/18/1700.
Robert Stacy d. 10/5/1700.
John Willson, son of Thomas, dec'd, d. 10/5/1700.
John Watson d. 10/16/1700.
William Dixson, son of William of Maryland, d. 10/28/1700.
Edith Cruch, Sarah Colemans cousin, d. 10/24/1700.
William Fletcher, son of ___, dec'd, d. 11/24/1700.
James Fox, son of James. dec'd, and Elizabeth, d. 11/30/1700.
Abraham Decow, son of Jacob, dec'd, and Hannah, d. 1/8/1700-01.
Mary Parrot, dau of James and Martha, d. 3/29/1701.
Thomas Lloyd, son of David and Grace, d. 4/3/1701.

Abigail Blackburn, wife of Christopher, d. 4/6/1701.
Jonathan Denniss, a Barbadoes Friend, d. 4/12/1701.
Hester Bonny, wife of Robert, d. 5/18/1701.
Sarah Hotton, dau of Arthur and Elizabeth, d. 5/18/1701.
George Chalkley, son of Thomas and Martha, d. 6/12/1701.
James West d. 6/26/1701.
David Vaughan d. 7/26/1701.
Morjana Bringhurst, dau of John, dec'd, and Rosina, d. 7/11/1701.
Isaac Jones, son in law of Ellis Jones, d. 8/11/1701.
Samuel Siddall d. 8/14/1710.
Ann Fox, widow of James, Jr., d. 8/27/1701.
Edward Pennington d. 11/11/1701.
Thomas Bonny, son of Robert and Hester, d. 11/27/1701.
John Gilbert, son of John, d. 1/7/1701-2.
Zechariah Whittrain, son of Zechariah, dec'd, and Sarah, d. 1/20/1701-2.
Abraham Carpenter, son of Samuel and Hannah, d. 2/9/1702.
Richard Blany d. 2/16/1702.
Mary Claypoole, wife of George, d. 2/28/1702.
Martha Parrott, wife of James, d. 2/27/1702.
Elizabeth Fox, wife of James, Senr, dec'd, d. 2/27/1702.
Margrett Estacke d. 2/18/1702.
Francis Fox, son of James and Elizabeth, dec'd, d. 3/12/1702.
Frances Hendricks, wife of John, d. 3/17/1702.
Mary Lean, dau of Robert and Elizabeth, both dec'd, d. 3/21/1702.
Mary Wright, dau of Benjamin and Barbara, d. 3/21/1702.
Rebecka Coleman, dau of William and Rebecka, d. 3/25/1702,
Charles Jackson, son of Ralph and Elizabeth, d. 3/27/1702.
Elizabeth Say, d. 3/28/1702.
Samuel Powell, son of William and Elizabeth, d. 4/8/1702.
George Walker, son of Emanuell and Margrett, d. 4/14/1702.
Sarah Dilwin, dau of William and Sarah, d. 4/20/1702.
Richard Guest, son of John and Mary, d. 4/18/1702.
Elizabeth Durbree, dau of Hugh and Elizabeth, d. 4/29/1702.
Mary Peg, dau of Daniel and Barbara, d. 5/7/1702.
Catherine Owen, dau of Griffith and Sarah, d. 5/19/1702.
John Kight, son of James, d. 5/25/1702.
Orelius Hoskins, child of Richd. and Hester, d. 5/27/1702.
Rebecka Clifton, wife of Henry, d. 5/2/1702.
Sissily Bradford, wife of Thomas, d. 5/11/1702.
Prudence West, widow of James, d. 6/10/1702.
Mary Fox, child of James, Jr., and Ann, dec'd, d. 5/16/1702.
Sarah Kinsey, wife of John, d. 7/12/1702.
Susanna Bickley, dau of Abraham and Elizabeth, 7/15/1702.
Isaac Shout, son of Thomas and Elizabeth, d. 7/16/1702.
Ann Richards, wife of John, d. 6/24/1702.

John Roberts of Hartford, smith, d. 8/1/1702.
Thomas Roberts d. 8/2/1702.
Elizabeth Every, wife of John, d. 8/3/1702.
Margrett Walker, wife of Joseph, dec'd, d. 8/11/1702.
Dorothy Woodmansey, wife of William, d. 8/14/1702.
Joell Blackburn son of Christopher, d. 8/14/1702.
George Walker d. 9/1/1702.
John Martin d. 9/11/1702.
Grace Beak, wife of John of Barbadoes, d. 10/4/1702.
Sarah Owen, wife of Griffith, d. 10/22/1702.
Mary Gove, dau of Richard, d. 10/26/1702.
Daniel Pegg d. 12/23/1702-3.
Joseph Buckley, son of Samuel and Ann, d. 1/5/1702-3.
Sarah Caine, wife of John, d. 1/29/1702-3.
James Radley, son of Daniell and Mary, d. 1/31/1702-3.
Mary Rochford, dau of Denniss and Mary, d. 3/9/1702-3.
Elinor Richardson, wife of Samuel, d. 4/29/1703.
Thomas Pryor, son of Thomas and Lydia, d. 5/8/1703.
William Fairman, son of Thomas and Elizabeth, d. 5/10/1703.
Benjamin Ireson, son of John, d. 5/12/1703.
Abraham Fishburn, son of William and Hannah, d. 5/28/1703.
Christopher Blackburne, son of Christo. and Rachel, d. 6/3/1703.
Margrett Leeds, widow, d. 6/30/1703.
Sarah Jones, dau of John and Ann, b. 7/13/1703.
Daniell Zachary, son of Daniel and Elizabeth, d. 7/19/1703.
Samuel Bulkley d. 7/22/1703.
Mary Evans, dau of Edward and Lucia, d. 8/3/1703.
Mary Noble, wife of Abel, d. 11/16/1703.
James Wood, son of James and Jane, d. 12/17/1703.
Cornelius Sturges d. 2/15/1704.
Richard Love d. 3/25/1704.
William Janney, son of Randol and Frances, d. 3/25/1704.
Mary Fincher, dau of Joshua and Elizabeth, d. 4/4/1704.
Sarah Knowles. dau of John and Elizabeth (now Griffith), d. 5/2/1704.
Ann Blackburn, dau of Christopher and Rachel, d. 5/15/1704.
Elizabeth Jackson, wife of Ralph, d. 5/26/1704.
Nathan Stanbury, son of Nathan and Mary, d. 6/10/1704.
John Haywood, son of John and Mary, d. 6/22/1704.
Joseph Kirll d. 7/24/1704.
Bancroft Heald, son of Samuel, d. 7/24/1704.
Mary Kirll, wife of Joseph, d. 9/28/1704.
Robert Hutchinson d. 11/16/1704.
Hannah Carline, wife of ____ Carline, d. 11/22/1704.
Jonathan West, son of James and Prudence, d. 12/21/1704.
John Mills d. 1/17/1704-5.

Ann Warner of Moreland d. 2/12/1705.
Ann Densey, dau of John and Sarah, d. 2/15/1705.
Rebeckah Shippen, wife of Edward, d. 2/26/1705.
Christopher Pound, son of Robert and Mary, d. 3/6/1704-5.
William Plumstead, son of Clement and Sarah, d. 3/14/1704-5.
Henry Jenings d. 4/3/1705.
Lusce Brown, wife of Joseph, d. 4/14/1705.
John White, son of Thomas and Rebekah, d. 5/1/1705.
Ellis Coleman d. 5/2/1705.
Caleb Lawrence, son of William and Ann, d. 5/5/1705.
John Parsons bur 6/19/1705.
Rebecka Chalkley, dau of Thomas and Martha, d. 6/26/1705.
Fincher Flower, son of Daniel and Sarah, d. 6/13/1705.
Christopher Blackburn, son of Christo. and Rachell, d. 6/16/1705.
Sarah Plumstead, wife of Clement, d. 6/17/1705.
Catherine Herberdink, wife of Levien, d. 6/31/1705.
Alce Guest, widow of George, d. 7/3/1705.
Joshua Jonson, son of Joshua, d. 7/3/1705.
Rebekah Hudson, dau of William,. and Mary, d. 7/10/1705.
Robert Wood, son of James and Jane, d. 7/14/1705.
George Peet d. 7/15/1705.
John Martin the elder d. 7/16/1705.
Anne Reed, widow of Charles, d. 9/4/1705.
Richard Hill, son of Rich. and Hannah, bur 9/12/1705.
Mary Hunt, wife of John, d. 11/28/1705-6.
Reneer Johnson d. 1/6/1705-6.
Abigaill Watson, dau of John and Abigaill, d. 12/26/1705-6.
Mathew Robinson, son of Mathew and Sarah, d. 1/1/1705-6.
William Claypoole, son of George and Mary, d. 2/25/1706.
Elizabeth Sanders, widow of John, d. 3/4/1706.
Love Fisher, dau of John and Sarah, d. 3/4/1706.
Mary Parrott, dau of James and Sarah, d. 3/6/1706.
Thomas Ryall, son of William and Mary, d. 3/10/1706.
Richard Snead, son of William and Mary, d. 4/27/1706.
Jane Corne_?, wife of John, d. 4/30/1706.
Benjamin Carle, son of Samuel and Sarah, d. 5/2/1706.
Elizabeth Flower, wife of Henry, d. 5/19/1706.
Nathaniel Ruggle d. 6/25/1706.
John Holton, son of Arthur and Elizabeth, d. 6/27/1706.
Joan Jones, wife of Griffith, d. 6/29/1706.
Benjamin Flower, son of Henry and Elizabeth, d. 7/8/1706.
John Blackburne, son of Christo. and Rachell, d. 8/4/1706.
Mary Powell, dau of William and Elizabeth, d. 8/7/1706.
Mary Flower, dau of Daniel and Sarah, d. 8/14/1706.
Robert Chalkley, son of Thomas and Martha, d. 8/19/1706.

Mary Harwood, dau of William, dec'd, and Susanna, d. 8/22/1706.
Mary Lukens d. 9/17/1706.
Elizabeth Powell, wife of William, Jr., d. 8/30/1706.
Josiah Durberow, son of Hugh and Elizabeth, d. 9/19/1706.
Ester Couper, wife of James, d. 10/15/1706.
Mary Webb, mother of John Webb, d. 10/26/1706.
Ruth Wood, dau of James and Jane, d. 10/29/1706.
Richard Sutton, son of Richard and Mary, d. 1706.
Mary Sutton, dau of Richard and Mary, d. 1706.
Elizabeth Wood, dau of James and Jane, d. 11/6/1706-7.
Rebeckah Williams d. 11/5/1706-7.
Clause Burnes, child of Dyer, d. 12/6/1706-7.
Rachell Palmer, wife of John, d. 12/7/1706-7.
Abraham Jones, son of John and Margrett, d. 12/22/1706-7.
Rachell Sobb, dau of Christopher and Rebecka, d. 1/2/1706-7.
John Green d. 2/7/1707.
Elizabeth Guest, dau of John and Elizabeth, d. 2/22/1707.
Abraham Hooper d. 2/28/1707.
_____ Rakestraw, child of William and Elizabeth, d. 9/4/1707.
Elizabeth Dilwin, dau of William and Sarah, d. 9/4/1707.
Ruth Duckett, widow of Thomas, d. 5/10/1707.
Joseph Dubree, son of Jacob and Jane, d. 5/18/1707.
Arthur Holton, son of Arthur and Elizabeth, d. 5/23/1707.
Thomas White, son of Thomas and Rebecca, d. 5/27/1707.
Abraham England, son of Thomas and Hannah, d. 6/2/1707.
William Woodmansey d. 6/6/1707.
Thomas Usher, son of Jacob and Ruth, d. 6/27/1707.
John Palmer, son of John (and Rachel, dec'd), d. 6/28/1707.
Mary Griffith, dau of Joseph and Sarah, d. 7/11/1707.
Joseph Ashton d. 7/19/1707.
Ann Preston, dau of Henry and Susanna, d. 8/16/1707.
William Martindale, son of John, d. 8/19/1707.
Hannah Gaunt, wife of Daniel, d. 9/4/1707.
Ann Powell, dau of Samuel and Abigail, d. 10/12/1707.
John Shippen, son of son of Edward, Senr., and Hester, d. 10/24/1707.
John Ashton, ship carpenter, d. 10/29/1707.
Ellin Waln, dau of Nicholas and Jane, d. 11/14/1707.
Ruth Harwood, dau of Samuel, d. 11/22/1707.
Jane Lewiss, wife of John, sawyer, d. 12/10/1707.
John Hart, son of John and Mary, bricklayer, d. 12/20/1707.
Joan Southbe, wife of William, d. 1/2/1707.
Elizabeth Sanders, dau of John and Sarah, bricklayer, dec'd, d. 1/3/1707.
Elizabeth Bennett, widow of Edmond, 1/8/1707.
William Powell, son of John and Ann, d. 1/10/1707.
Francis Jones, son of John and Elizabeth, bolter, d. 1/15/1707.

Rebecka Belloes, dau of Mathias and Maudlin, d. 1/16/1708.
Thomas Hodges d. 1/29/1708.
Ester Hobbs, wife of Thomas, d. 2/1/1708.
Nathan Faucitt d. 2/2/1708.
Mary Rakestraw, dau of John and Ruth, d. 2/4/1708.
Ann Hutchinson, widow of Robert, d. 2/8/1708.
Timothy Hudson, son of William and Mary, d. 2/11/1708.
Mary Spencer, dau of Samuel and Hester, d. 2/18/1708.
Benjamin Jones, son of John and Ann, cordwainer, d. 2/24/1708.
John Davis d. 2/28/1708.
Francis Hamms, son of Henry, dec'd, and Rebecka, d. 2/29/1708.
John Jones, merchant, d. 3/4/1708.
Elizabeth England, wife of Philip, d. 3/17/1708.
Richard Sutton d. 3/30/1708.
John Densey, carpenter, d. 4/3/1708.
John Flower, son of Daniel and Sarah, d. 4/11/1708.
Owen Morris, sawyer, drowned 4/19/1708.
James Wood, dau of James and Jane, cooper, d. 5/4/1708.
John Densey, son of John, dec'd, and Sarah, d. 5/15/1708.
Mary Jones, son of John and Margrett, joyner, d. 5/16/1708.
John Richardson, son of Francis and Elizabeth, d. 5/16/1708.
Margrett Guy, dau of John and Jemimah, d. 6/16/1708.
Millicent Fisher, dau of William and Bridget, joyner, d. 6/22/1708.
Margrett Shout, dau of William, dec'd, d. 6/27/1708.
Mary Eldridge, dau of Thomas and Mary, cordwainer, d. 7/3/1708.
Nicholas Walne, son of Richard and Ann, d. 7/9/1708.
Thomas Sytford d. 7/14/1708.
Jane Teague, wife of Penticost. d. 9/21/1708.
John Soper, son of John, d. 10/7/1708.
Hannah Stretch, dau of Peter and Mary, d. 10/8/1708.
Mary Dean d. 10/21/1708.
Susanna Rakestraw, dau of William and ____, dec'd, d. 10/22/1708.
Thomas Stacy, son of John and Alce, d. 11/11/1708.
Nathan Faucitt, son of Nathan, dec'd, and Jane, d. 11/30/1708.
Mary Hudson, wife of William, d. 12/17/1708.
Joshua Jacob d. 12/22/1708.
Martha Grant d. 12/27/1709.
Timothy Hudson, son of William and Mary, d. 1/1/1709.
Naomy Grey, wife of George, d. 1/4/1709.
Hannah Lewiss, wife of Adam, d. 1/24/1709.
Henry Carter, brickmaker, d. 3/21/1709.
Barbarah Wright, dau of Benjamin and Barbarah, d. 4/7/1709.
Mary Bickley, dau of Abraham and Elizabeth, d. 4/8/1709.
Ann Pound, dau of Robert and Mary, d. 4/14/1709.
Samuel Nichols, sawyer, d. 4/19/1709.

Ann Knowles, dau of John and Ann, d. 5/25/1709.
Richard Spencer, son of Samuel and Hester, d. 5/26/1709.
Thomas Scott, son of Abraham and Hannah, d. 6/1/1709.
Elizabeth Tiby, wife of John, d. 6/2/1709.
Roger Townsend d. 6/11/1709.
Joshua Tittery, potter, d. 7/13/1709.
Elizabeth Warder, dau of Richard and Ann, d. 7/17/1709.
Sarah Thomson, dau of Christopher and Mary, d. 7/19/1709.
John Belloes, son of Mathias and Maudling, d. 7/20/1709.
Mary Smith, sister of John Bud, the Brewers wife, d. 8/4/1709.
Elizabeth Maccomb, dau of John and Elizabeth, d. 8/9/1709.
Rebecka Coleman, dau of Stephen, dec'd, and Sarah, d. 8/29/1709.
John Otter d. 9/2/1709.
Elizabeth Wright, dau of Benj. and Barbarah, d. 9/29/1709.
Joseph Griffith, smith, d. 10/14/1709.
William Waite d. 10/21/1709.
Margrett Jenings, widow of Henry, d. 10/26/1709.
Sarah Goodson, wife of John, d. 11/3/1709-10.
Evan Prothero d. 11/20/1709-10.
Benjamin Cotty, son of Abell, d. 12/12/1709-10.
Ruth Usher, dau of Jacob and Ruth, d. 12/22/1709-10.
Mary Dubree, dau of Jacob and Jane, d. 1/14/1709/10.
Ester Wilson d. 2/20/1710.
John Palmer d. 2/22/1710.
Ester Humphrey, wife of Joshua of Ancocas, d. 3/15/1710.
John Coats, son of William and Mary, d. 3/28/1710.
Elizabeth Prothero, widow of Evan, d. 11/24/1710.
Robert Pound, butcher, d. 4/2/1710.
Mary Dixson, dau of Elizabeth of Cohansey, d. 4/11/1710.
Thomas Carter, brickmaker, d. 5/3/1710.
William Powell. son of William and Sarah, d. 5/19/1710.
Ann Painter, dau of Geo. and Lydia, d. 5/23/1710.
Joseph Rudman. son of Thomas and Sarah, d. 5/27/1710.
Susanna Worrils, widow of Thomas, d. 5/29/1710.
Samuel Coats, son of Thomas and Beulah, d. 6/7/1710.
Mary Radley, dau of Daniell and Mary, d. 6/13/1710.
Ann Story, wife of Thomas, d. 6/19/1710.
Elinor Mole, wife of Roger of Cohansey, d. 6/22/1710.
John Poole, son of Nathaniel and Elizabeth, d. 6/23/1710.
Daniel Tittery d. 7/8/1710.
Richard Snead, son of William, dec'd, and Mary, d. 7/14/1710.
Ellis Morris, son of Owen, dec'd, and Mary, d. 7/14/1710.
Ann Wills, dau of William and ____, dec'd, d. 7/17/1710.
John Estaw, son of James and Mary, d. 7/19/1710.
Thomas Plumstead, son of Clement and Elizabeth, d. 7/19/1710.

Thomas Colvert, son of Thomas and Mary, d. 7/21/1710.
William Stacey, son of William and Alce, dec'd, d. 7/30/1710.
Sarah Newbold, late Ashton, wife of Godfrey, d. 7/30/1710.
Mary Herberdinck, wife of Levin, d. 7/30/1710.
_____ Cresson, widow, mother of Solomon, d. 8/1/1710.
John Jackson, son of Stephen and Elizabeth, d. 8/3/1710.
Samuel Morris, son of Anthony and Phebe, Jr., d. 8/8/1710.
Nathan Shenton, late from England, d. 8/11/1710.
Thomas Owen, son of Edward, dec'd, from Maryland, d. 8/29/1710.
James Bonney, son of Robert and Frances, d. 8/29/1710.
Edward Jerman, son of Edward and Elizabeth, d. 9/8/1710.
John Barney, Senr., d. 9/28/1710.
Elizabeth Boulding, wife of William, d. 10/20/1710.
George Embly d. 10/24/1710.
Richard Redman, son of Richard and Provided. d. 10/26/1710.
Margrett Robinson, dau of Mathew and Sarah, d. 11/1/1711.
Mary Usher, wife of Joseph, d. 11/6/1711.
Hannah Hart, wife of John, merchant, and dau of John Maccomb, d.
    2/19/1711.
Benjamin Wright d. 3/26/1711
William Rakestraw, son of John and Ruth, d. 3/27/1711.
Benjamin Masters, son of Thomas and Sabella, d. 4/30/1711.
James Morris, son of James and Margaret, d. 5/3/1711.
Thomas Ryall, son of William and Mary, d. 5/14/1711.
Ann Evans, dau of Edward and Luce, d. 5/28/1711.
Prudence Norris, dau of Isaac and Mary, d. 5/31/1711.
Hannah Pleedwell, dau of Edward and Grace, d. 5/31/1711.
Elizabeth Hart, dau of John, mercht, and Hannah, dec'd. d. 6/1/1711.
Elizabeth Maccomb, wife of John, d. 6/4/1711.
Sarah Flower, dau of Daniell and Sarah, d. 6/8/1711.
Richard Parker d. 6/12/1711.
William Dilwin d. 6/14/1711.
Mary Coats, dau of William and Mary, d. 6/17/1711.
Elizabeth Cheatam, dau of John and Ann, d. 6/22/1711.
William Till, joyner, d. 6/23/1711.
James Atkinson d. 6/24/1711.
Hannah Poole, dau of Nathaniel and Elizabeth, d. 6/24/1711.
William Clark, son of William and Rebecka, d. 6/27/1711.
Elizabeth Jerman, dau of Edward and Elizabeth, d. 6/25/1711.
Ann Warder, wife of Richard, d. 6/28/1711.
Alce Bradford, wife of Thomas, d. 6/28/1711.
Elizabeth Stapler, wife of Stephen, d. 6/29/1711.
Mary William, Thomas Wharton's kinswoman, d. 6/29/1711.
Joseph Smith d. 6/30/1711.
Mary Parker, dau of George and Ester, d. 6/30/1711.

Rebecka Comb, wife of Samuel, couper, d. 6/31/1711.
An_? Bettson, wife of Thomas, d. 7/7/1711.
Thomas Wells d. 7/10/1711.
Sarah Harris, dau of William and Alice, d. 7/13/1711.
Martha Ross Huggins, wife of Nicholas Ross Huggins, d. 7/16/1711.
Thomas Coats, son of Thomas and Bula, d. 7/19/1711.
Joshua Gilbert, blacksmith, d. 7/19/1711.
Hannah Hammon, James Steel's mother-in-law, d. 7/26/1711.
Abell Cottey, watchmaker, d. 7/30/1711.
Martha Wolliston, widow of Thomas, d. 8/4/1711.
Hannah Embley, dau of George and Hannah, d. 8/6/1711.
Richard Heath, son of Robert and Susannah, d. 8/8/1711.
George Harwood, son of Samuel, d. 8/8/1711.
George Walker, son of Manuell and Margrett, d. 8/9/1711.
Bridgett Jennett, widow of John, d. 8/11/1711.
John Gilbert d. 8/13/1711.
Thomas Garner, son of Thomas of Burlington, d. 8/13/1711.
John Warder, son of Richard, pipemaker, d. 8/14/1711.
Ann Paul, dau of John and Mary, d. 9/4/1711.
Rachel Norris, dau of Isaac and Mary, d. 9/15/1711.
Mathias Belloes d. 10/4/1711.
John Webb, taylor, d. 10/13/1711.
Rosannah Bringhurst d. 11/4/1711-12.
Jane Moore, widow, d. 12/24/1711-12.
William Smith, son of William and Mary, d. 1/2/1711-12.
Barbara Pratchin, widow, d. 1/9/1711-12.
William Masterman d. 1/16/1711-12.
Martha Chalkley, wife of Thomas, d. 1/30/1712.
Thomas Miller, carpenter, d. 2/12/1712.
Mary Tucker, wife of James, d. 2/29/1712.
John Rakestraw, son of John and Ruth, d. 4/15/1712.
Mary Howard, dau of John and Mary, d. 5/19/1712.
Elizabeth Jackson, dau of Stephen and Elizabeth, d. 5/22/1712.
Elizabeth Torr, wife of Richard, d. 6/3/1712.
Edward Hill d. 6/4/1712.
Mary Radley, dau of Daniel and Mary d. 6/4/1712.
Elizabeth Poole, wife of Nathaniell, d. 6/7/1712.
Nathan Stanbury, son of Nathan and Mary, d. 6/8/1712.
Benjamin Flower, son of Henry and Ann, d. 6/11/1712.
Patience Marcy, dau of Samuel and Sarah, d. 6/18/1712.
Elizabeth Hill, dau of Edward, dec'd, and Mary, d. 6/23/1712.
Sarah Pemberton, dau of Israel and Rachel, d. 6/24/1712.
Ann Parsons, widow of John, d. 6/25/1712.
Elizabeth Taylor, wife of Samuel, d. 6/29/1712.
Peeter Ozburn, whitesmith, d. 7/2/1712.

Elizabeth Robinson, dau of Mathew and Sarah, d. 7/2/1712.
Thomas Plumstead, son of Clement and Elizabeth, d. 7/5/1712.
Ester Betle, dau of John and Abigail, d. 7/9/1712.
Sarah Smith, dau of William and Sarah, d. 7/15/1712.
Mary Bonny, dau of Robert and Frances, d. 7/18/1712.
John Vaughn bur 7/27/1712.
Edward Shippen bur 8/3/1712.
Martha Roberts, dau of Thomas and Martha, bur 8/23/1712.
Ester Brown, dau of John, bur 8/23/1712.
Elizabeth Cannons, dau of Thomas and Mary, bur 8/24/1712.
Hannah Stapler, dau of Stephen and Elizabeth, dec'd, bur 10/2/1712.
Ester Cuff, dau of Absalom and Martha, bur 10/2/1712.
John Ricketts, son of Isaac, dec'd, bur 10/3/1712.
Robert Owen, son of Evan and Mary, bur 10/9/1712.
Margarett Cook, widow of Arthur, bur 10/18/1712.
Margrett Jones, widow, at ye center, bur 11/21/1712.
Elizabeth Elphrey, dau of Henry and Sarah, bur 11/24/1712.
John Richardson of Duck Creek, bur 2/3/1713.
William Ward, master of a sloop, bur 2/22/1713.
Peter Roberts, son of Thomas and Martha, bur 2/22/1713.
Abigail Hoffman, wife of Marmaduke, bur 2/26/1713.
James Matreviss, a chandler, bur 2/26/1713.
Thomas Knight, son of John and Sarah, bur 4/14/1713.
Ann Hind, dau of Robert and Mary, bur 5/6/1713.
Samuel Cook, son of ___, who died at sea, and Elinor, bur 5/26/1713.
Abigail Beedle bur 5/31/1713.
Benjamin Denniss, son of Thomas and Mary, bur 6/13/1713.
Oliver Thomas, joyner, a newcomer, bur 6/17/1713.
Barbara Beedle, dau of John and Abigail, dec'd, bur 6/23/1713.
Benjamin Gummery, son of John and Deborah, bur 6/24/1713.
Deborah Gummery, dau of John and Deborah, bur 6/27/1713.
Richard Cocks, son of Thomas and Mary, bur 7/3/1713.
___ Jones, wife of Joseph, bur 7/4/1713.
Abigail Powell, wife of Samuel, bur 7/6/713.
Elizabeth Taylor, dau of Samuel, bur 7/10/1713.
Hannah Ranstead, dau of Caleb and Mary, bur 8/2/1713.
Grace Rakestraw, dau of William and Ann, bur 8/28/1713.
Mary Jones, dau of John and Ann, cordwainer, bur 9/3/1713.
Margrett Norriss, dau of Isaac and Mary, bur 9/4/1713.
James Kight bur 9/6/1713.
Martha Eldridge, wife of Jonathan of Jersey, bur 9/24/1713.
Hannah Atkinson, widow of James, bur 10/15/1713.
Elizabeth Furniss, wife of Thomas, bur 10/18/1713.
Rebecka Richardson, dau of Francis and Elizabeth, bur 10/27/1713.
John Lingard, son of William and Mary, bur 12/9/1713.

Katherine Owen bur 12/18/1713-14.
Henry Badcocke, son of Henry and Mary, bur 1/8/1713-14.
Katherine Starr, wife of Arthur, bur 1/20/1713-14.
John Lowden of New Garden, in Chester County, bur 1/21/1713-4.
Lucie Evans, wife of Edward, joyner, bur 1/289/1713-4.
Ann Cross, dau of Joseph and Ann, bur 2/1/1713.
Samuel Carpenter, merchant, bur 2/13/1714.
Thomas Hust, son of Thomas and Elinor, bur 2/23/1714.
John Durborow, son of John and Sarah, bur 3/5/1714.
Elizabeth Bickley, wife of Abraham, bur 3/16/1714.
Elizabeth Richardson, wife of Francis, bur 3/20/1714.
Elizabeth Fisher, dau of William and Tabitha, bur 3/21/1714.
Thomas Lewiss, son of Richard and Mary, bur 3/22/1714.
Sarah Lewiss, dau of Jenkin, dec'd, bur 3/22/1714.
Isaac Dickinson, son of Jonathan and Mary, bur 3/25/1714.
Phineas Pemberton, son of Israel and Rachel, bur 3/25/1714.
James Jones, son of John and Elizabeth, bur 3/26/1714.
Katherine Vaughan, apprentice to John Jones, bolter, bur 3/28/1714.
Priscilla Guest, dau of John and Mary, bur 3/28/1714.
Mary Hind, dau of Robert and Mary, bur 3/29/1714.
Thomas Powell, son of William and Sarah, bur 4/1/1714.
Ester Spencer, dau of Samuel and Ester, bur 4/1/1714.
Elizabeth Coats, dau of James, dec'd, and Mary, bur 4/1/1714.
Ann Coats, dau of James, dec'd, and Mary, bur 4/2/1714.
John Mifflin bur 4/4/1714.
Sarah Rakestraw, wife of Thomas. bur 4/4/1714.
Sarah Warder, dau of John, dec'd, and Agnes, bur 4/6/1714.
Francis Janney, wife of Randall, bur 4/7/1714.
John Parsons, son of John, ship carpenter, bur 4/8/1714.
Lidia Painter, wife of George, bur 4/10/1714.
Cornelius Parker, son of John and Mary, bur 4/11/1714.
William Coats, son of William and Mary, brickmaker, bur 4/14/1714.
Mary Yieldhall, dau of Robert and Joan, bur 4/15/1714.
Mary Moore, dau of Anthony, bur 4/15/1714.
Thomas Coats, son of Thomas and Beulah, bur 4/19/1714.
William Harriss, son of William and Alce, bur 4/21/1714.
Mary Lingard, dau of William and Mary, bur 4/25/1714.
Mary Webb, dau of Robert, dec'd, and Elizabeth, now wife of Samuel
    Richardson, bur 4/29/1714.
Hannah Hind, dau of Robert and Mary, bur 4/29/1714.
Mary Price, dau of Thomas and Elizabeth, bur 4/30/1714.
Tamor Piller, wife of James, bur 5/1/1714.
Mary Orum, dau of Benjamin and Elizabeth, bur 5/1/1714.
Sarah Webb, dau of Joseph, dec'd, and Hannah, now wife of John Lea,
    bur 5/2/1714.

William Williams, son of Edward and Margaret, bur 5/3/1714.
Sarah Robinson, dau of Matthew and Sarah, bur 5/8/1714.
Eliza: West, dau of John and Joan, died at William Manningtons and was
      bur 5/13/1714.
Sarah Mitchell, dau of Thomas and Sarah, bur 5/15/1714.
Samuel Evans, son of David and Elizabeth, bur 5/16/1714.
Hannah Fisher, dau of John and Sarah, bur 5/16/1714.
Jaspar Robins, son of William and Rebecka, bur 5/18/1714.
Elizabeth Lyle, dau of Morris and Mary, bur 5/27/1714.
Benjamin Bickley, son of Abraham and Elizabeth, dec'd, bur 5/29/1714.
Mary Peeters, dau of Benjamin and Ann, bur 5/31/1714.
Martha Claypoole, dau of George, bur 6/1/1714.
Hannah Evans, dau of Edward and Lucie, dec'd, bur 6/2/1714.
Hannah Hill, dau of Richard and Hannah, bur 6/4/1714.
Benjamin Richardson, son of Francis and Elizabeth, dec'd, bur 6/5/1714.
John Hastings, son of Samuel, bur 6/9/1714.
Ann Martindale, dau of John and Mary, bur 6/10/1714.
Martha Zealy, dau of John and Margaret, bur 6/16/1714.
John Dyer, son of John and Elizabeth, bur 6/17/1714.
Martha Potts, dau of Thomas and Martha, bur 6/18/1714.
John Cadwallett, son of Edward, dec'd, and Rebecka, bur 6/19/1714.
Rachell Moore, dau of Richard and Margrett, bur 7/9/1714.
Edward Jerman bur 7/10/1714.
Mary Cockfield, dau of Joshua and Elizabeth, bur 7/11/1714.
William Gumley, apprentice to Solomon Cresson, bur 7/17/1714.
John Zealy bur 7/21/1714.
Martha Large, dau of Ebenezer and Margrett, bur 7/28/1714.
William Harriott, son of Samuel, bur 7/28/1714.
Samuel Flower, son of Daniel and Sarah, bur 8/4/1714.
Mary Till, dau of William, dec'd, and Ann, bur 9/11/1714.
William Jones, Griffith Jones brother, bur 9/16/1714.
William Forrist bur 10/12/1714.
Joseph Ransted bur 10/14/1714.
Joseph Cart, son of Samuel, dec'd, and Sarah, bur 10/28/1714.
John Harwood, shoemaker, d. 11/3/1714.
Jeremiah Gray, baker, d. 11/11/1714.
James Oldman, son of Thomas and Elizabeth, d. 11/13/1714.
Miriam Kelly, wife of William, d. 11/18/1714.
Thomas Oldman d. 11/21/1714.
Chalkley Grainger, son of Joshua and Elizabeth, d. 11/28/1714.
Ruth Usher, wife of Jacob, d. 12/12/1714.
John Gumley, Solomon Cressons apprentice, d. 12/20/1714.
Sarah Hudson, dau of William and Mary, d. 1/1/1714.
Edmund Vernum d. 1/14/1714.
John James, son of Thomas and Sarah, d. 1/31/1715.

C____ Cadwallader, child of John and Mary, d. 2/?/1715.
John Biddle d. 2/23/1714.
Mary Stanberry, wife of Nathan, d. 2/25/1715.
Arthur Holton, baker, d.3.5.1715.
Ann James, widow of Edward, d. 3/15/1715.
George Hopper, son of George and Joyce, d. 5/2/1715.
David Pew d. 5/8/1715.
Elizabeth Peters dau of Thomas, d. 5/19/1715.
Ann Warner, wife of John, d. 5/19/1715.
Mary Peters, dau of Benjamin and Ann, d. 5/24/1715.
Cornelius Lingard, son of William and Mary, d. 5/28/1715.
Martha Potts, dau of Thomas and Martha, d. 5/29/1715.
Samuel Carpenter, son of Samuel and Hannah, mercht, d. 6/4/1715.
Ann Loyd, dau of John and Sarah, smith, d. 6/29/1715.
Mary Loyd, dau of John and Sarah, smith, d. 7/2/1715.
Reece Evans, son of David and Elizabeth, d. 7/5/1715.
____ Thomas, son of Evan, joyner, d. 7/12/1715.
Jonathan Lancaster, son of John and Sarah, d. 9/3/1715.
James Loyd, son of John and Sarah, smith, d. 9/11/1715.
Sarah Buckley, wife of Phineas, d. 9/19/1715.
James Piller, carpenter, d. 9/21/1715.
Sarah Durberow, wife of John, d. 9/24/1715.
Benjamin Chambers d. 9/27/1715.
Clement Plumstead, son of Clement and Elizabeth, d. 9/27/1715.
____ Knowles, dau of John and Ann, d. 9/29/1715.
William Ryall d. 10/5/1715.
Randall Janney d. 10/7/1715.
Jane Hillary, wife of Samuel, d. 10/10/1715.
Hannah Warner, dau of Isaac and Mary, d. 10/26/1715.
Joshua Nichols d. 10/29/1715.
Henry? Hodge, wife of Henry, d. 11/11/1715.
____ Potts, son of John and Rebecka, d. 11/25/1715.
Samuell Carpenter, son of Samuell and Hannah, d. 11/29/1715.
Robert Yieldhall d. 11/29/1715-16.
Jemimah Guy, wife of John, d. 12/21/1715-16.
Samuell Durberow, son of Hugh and Elizabeth, d. 1/13/1715-16.
Eveny Watson d. 2/8/1715-16.
Humphrey Murray d. 2/28/1716.
John Cheatum d. 5/6/1716.
Jane Billin, wife of John, d. 5/9/1716.
Hannah Kight, wife of James, Jr., d. 5/17/1716.
John Stacy, son of John, d. 6/1/1716.
Naomy Ellison, servant to Samuel Stretch d. 6/8/1716.
Hannah Coates, dau of Geo. and Grace, d. 6/13/1716.
David Lancaster, son of John and Sarah, d. 9/11/1716.

Joshua Ranstead d. 6/14/1716.
Rachell Preston, wife of Samuell, d. 6/15/1716.
Mary Hawood, wife of Samuell, d. 6/15/1716.
Abigail Chalkley, dau of Thomas and Martha, d. 6/19/1716.
_____ Plumstead, dau of Clement and Elizabeth, d. 6/20/1716.
Robert Stacy, son of John, d. 6/23/1716.
Sarah Knight, wife of John, d. 6/26/1716.
Robert Wilkins, son of William, d. 7/1/1716.
Charles Ripton, son of Josias of Great Broughton in Cumberland,
    England, d. 7/2/1716.
John Haistins, son of Samuell, d. 7/9/1716.
John Mannington, son of William, d. 7/10/1716.
John Mifflin, senior of ye three of ye name, d. 7/4/1716.
Isaiah Warner, son of Swan and Ester, d. 7/15/1716.
Benjamin Cart, son of Samuel and Sarah, d. 7/22/1716.
William Butler, son of John, d. 7/22/1716.
William Price, son of Thomas and Elizabeth, d. 7/23/1716.
Martha Rakestraw, dau of Thomas, d. 7/24/1716.
_____ Bonny, dau of Robert and Frances, d. 7/24/1716.
Charles Couper, son of John and Rachel, d. 7/26/1716.
James Tomlinson, son of John and Luce, d. 7/28/1716.
Mary Torr, dau of Richard, d. 7/29/1716.
_____ Everton, wife of Nath., d. 7/29/1716.
_____ Rednap, son of Joseph and Elizabeth, d. 8/6/1716.
Elizabeth Rednap, wife of Joseph, d. 8/9/1716.
Mary West, wife of Charles, d. 8/9/1716.
Hannah Large, dau of Ebenezer, d. 8/9/1716.
Henry Hillary, son of Samuell and Jane, d. 8/11/1716.
George Daviss, son of John and Mary, d. 8/16/1716.
Elizabeth England, dau of Joseph, d. 8/19/1716.
John Faucitt, son of John, dec'd, and Jane, d. 8/20/1716.
Paul Sanders d. 8/26/1716.
Thomas Renshaw, son of John and Elizabeth, d. 9/7/1716.
Samuel Bilton d. 9/16/1716.
Grace Spikeman, wife of Randolph, d. 10/13/1716.
Mary Hind, dau of Robert and Mary, d. 10/19/1716.
Merriam Boyden, widow of James, d. 10/23/1716.
John Harriott, son of Samuel, d. 12/8/1716-17.
An_ Cheatom, widow of John, d. 12/23/1716-17.
Benjamin Blackbu n, son of Christopher and Rachel, d. 1/2/1716-17
Paul Sanders, Jr, d. 1/27/1717
John Warner, Sr, d. 2/12/1717.
William Oxley d. 2/15/1717.
John Parker d. 3/7/1717.
Irons Pearses, late from Duck Creek, d. 4/13/1717.

Barberah Wright, widow of Benjamin, d. 4/20/1717.
Sarah Lingard, dau of William and Mary, d. 4/20/171.
David Price, son of Thomas and Elizabeth, d. 4/25/1717.
Joshua Cockfield d. 4/26/1717.
James Scull, son of Edward and Sarah, d. 4/29/1717.
Thomas Coats, son of Thomas and Bulah, d. 4/30/1717.
James Logan, son of James and Sarah, d. 5/2/1717.
John Wale, son of Joseph and Martha, d. 5/6/1717.
John Shoemaker, son of George and Rebecka, d. 5/21/1717.
Mary Thomas, wife of David, d. 5/22/1717.
Charles Brogdon, son of Charles and Susanna, d. 5/3/1717.
Ann Hudson, dau of John and Abigail, d. 5/23/1717.
Sarah Thomas, wife of William, d. 6/9/1717.
Thomas Moore, son of William and Martha, d. 6/9/1717.
Frances Griffith, dau of Nathaniel and Elizabeth, d. 6/12/1717.
Mary Armstrong, dau of Christian Broadgate, d. 6/13/1717.
Griffith Owen d. 6/19/1717.
John Ireson, son of William and Dorcas, d. 6/26/1717.
Ann Scofield, wife of Henry, d. 6/31/1717.
Caleb Ranstead, son of Caleb and Mary, d. 7/8/1717.
William Cliffton d. 7/19/1717.
Samuell Cresson, son of Solomon and Hannah, d. 7/19/1717.
Susannah Colly, wife of John, d. 8/1/1717.
Sarah Scull, wife of Nicholas, d. 8/11/1717.
Elizabeth Ring, dau of Samuel and Hannah, d. 8/12/1717.
Mathew Andrews d. 8/17/1717.
William Boulding d. 8/19/1717.
Thomas England d. 8/22/1717.
John Cannon, son of Thomas and Mary, d. 8/24/1717.
Thomas Chalkley, son of Thomas and Martha, d. 9/10/1717.
Patience Mifflin, dau of John and Elizabeth, d. 9/23/1717.
James Baley, Senr. d. 10/29/1717.
David Thomas d. 10/31/1717.
Susanna Redman, widow of John, d. 11/24/1717-18.
Jeremiah Armitt, son of Thomas and Elizabeth, d. 12/16/1717-18.
Hannah Carpenter, dau of Samuel and Hannah, d. 1/14/1718.
Mary Powly, wife of George, d. 2/7/1718.
Ann Preston, dau of Paul and Elizabeth, d. 3/2/1718.
Thomas Cannon, son of Thomas and Mary, d. 3/4/1718.
James Estaw, son of James and Hannah, d. 3/7/1718.
Sarah Preston, dau of Paul and Elizabeth, d. 3/8/1718.
Thomas Cannon, son of Thomas and Mary, d. 3/4/1718.
James Estaw, son of James and Hannah, d. 3/7/1718.
Sarah Preston, dau of Paul and Elizabeth, d. 3/8/1718.
Elizabeth Clare, dau of William and Ester, d. 3/9/1718.

Rebecka Coleman, dau of William and Rebecka, d. 3/11/1718.
Samuell Carpenter, son of John and Ann, d. 3/18/1718.
Sarah Fishburn, dau of William and Hannah, d. 4/9/1718.
Samuel Hood, grandson of John of Darby, d. 4/17/1718.
Elizabeth Haney, dau of Martin Jerviss, d. 4/18/1718.
Martha Knowles, dau of John and Ann, d. 4/18/1718.
Thomas Wharton d. 5/31/1718.
William Cresson, son of Solomon and Hannah, d. 6/19/1718.
George Fishwater, son of George and Mary, d. 7/1/1718.
John Besell. son of William and Hannah, d. 7/5/1718.
Mary Knowles, dau of John and Ann, d. 7/11/1718.
James Jones, son of John and Elizabeth, d. 7/18/1718.
John Whitpaine d. 7/23/1718.
Deborah Potts, dau of Jonas and Mary, d. 7/24/1718.
Mary Carpenter, wife of Samuel, son of Joshua, d. 8/1/1718.
Mary Walton, dau of Michael and Elizabeth, d. 8/12/1718.
Elizabeth Andrews d. 6/16/1718.
Elinor Shires, dau of George and Deborah, d. 9/3/1718.
Henry Griffitts, son of Nathaniel and Elizabeth, d. 9/10/1718.
Ann Jones, wife of John, d. 9/18/1718.
Hannah Estaw, dau of James and Hannah, d. 9/24/1718.
Samuel Hastins, son of Samuel and Mary, d. 9/24/1718.
Rachel Caster, dau of John and Elizabeth, d. 9/27/1718.
Abraham Shute, son of Thomas and Elizabeth, d. 10/7/1718.
Letitia Cadwalader, dau of John and Martha, d. 10/14/1718.
Deborah Shires, wife of George, d. 10/19/1718.
William Rakestraw d. 11/5/1718.
Hannah Miller, wife of Thomas, d. 11/28/1718.
Jane Upfould d. 12/5/1718.
Francis Jones, son of John and Elizabeth, boulter, d. 12/24/1718.
Jane Waln, wife of John, d. 12/26/1718.
Benjamin Peters, son of Thomas and Mary, d. 1/7/1718.
Joseph Blackburn, son of Christopher and Rachel, d. 1/8/1718.
An_ Carpenter, wife of John, d. 1/20/1718.
Charles Pemberton, son of Israel and Rachel, d. 1/24/1718.
Rebecka Potts, dau of John and Rebecka, d. 1/26/1719.
Rachel Large, dau of Ebenezer and Rachel, d. 2/2/1719.
Isaac Bickley, son of Abraham and Elizabeth, d. 2/3/1719.
Rebecka York d. 2/7/1719.
Ann Cox, dau of Thomas, d. 3/5/1719.
Elizabeth Clare, dau of William and Hester, d. 3/9/1719.
Mary Mifflin, dau of George and Hester, d. 3/17/1719.
John Knowles, son of Francis and Sarah, d. 3/18/1719.
Thomas Moore, son of Richard and Margrett, d. 4/7/1719..
Samuel Richardson d. 4/10/1719.

John Watson, son of John and Abigail, d. 4/17/1719.
Thomas Paschall, son of William and Sarah, d. 4/29/1719.
Deborah Mitchell, dau of Thomas and Sarah, d. 5/7/1719.
Charles Plumstead, son of Clement and Elizabeth, d. 5/16/1719.
John Parker, son of John, dec'd, and Mary, d. 6/9/1719.
George Coats, son of George and Grace, d. 6/10/1719.
Thomas Broadgate, son of Thomas and Christian, d. 6/11/1718.
Mary Dillworth, dau of John and Mary, d. 6/16/1719.
Elizabeth Dungworth, dau of Emanuell and Elizabeth, d. 6/21/1719.
Hannah Roberts, dau of Thomas and Martha, d. 6/26/1719.
Mary Orum, dau of Benj. and Elizabeth, d. 6/26/1719.
Elizabeth Hodge, dau of Henry and Frances, dec'd, d. 6/28/1719.
Hannah Edghill, dau of Simon and Rebecka, d. 6/29/1719.
Richard Harrison, son of Richard and Hannah, d. 6/29/1719.
Benjamin Peters, son of Benj. and Ann, d. 7/1/1719.
Josiah Elfrey, son of Jeremiah and Sarah, d. 7/1/1719.
Ann Mumford, dau of Thomas and Mary, d. 7/1/1719.
Elizabeth Parrott, dau of James and Sarah, d. 7/4/1719.
Benjamin Morriss, son of Anthony and Phebe, d. 7/7/1719.
Henry Elfrey d. 7/10/1719.
Thomas Coleman, son of Thomas and Elizabeth, d. 7/17/1719.
Mary Bissell, dau of William and Mary, d. 7/181719.
Samuel Mickoll, son of Samuell and Thomasin, d. 7/26/1719.
William Keely d. 8/1/1719.
James Sanders, son of Richard and Sarah, d. 8/3/1719.
John Sopors d. 8/9/1719.
William Taylor d. 8/12/1719.
Sarah Flower, dau of Daniel and Sarah, d. 8/16/1719.
Deborah Burrows d. 8/25/1719.
John James, son of Thomas and Sarah, d. 8/25/1719.
Judith Head, dau of John and Rebecka, d. 8/25/1719.
Elizabeth Parrock, dau of Ja: and Sarah (2nd of ye name), d. 9/9/1719.
Elizabeth Fisher, dau of William, Jr, and Tabitha, d. 9/10/1719.
Sarah Parrock, wife of James, d. 9/18/1719.
Liddia Parrock, dau of James and Sarah, d. 9/19/1719.
Mary Dickinson, wife of Jonathan, d. 10/3/1719.
Elizabeth Koile, wife of Michael, d. 10/25/1719.
Thomas Hardin, son of Thomas and Carolina, d. 10/27/1719.
Hannah Lambert, dau of John, dec'd, d. 11/3/1719.
Rebecka Williams d. 11/4/1719.
Joseph Everett, malster, d. 11/8/1719.
Ann Lloyd, wife of James, d. 11/25/1719.
Mary Baley, dau of James and Sarah, d. 11/25/1719.
John Williamson, son of John and Mary, d. 12/14/1719.
Susanna Brintnall, wife of John, d. 12/17/1719.

Elizabeth Smart, wife of John, d. 12/20/1719.
James Loyd d. 1/7/1719.
Michell Kile, son of Michell, d. 1/13/1719.
Ann Roberts, dau of Edward and Marcy, d. 1/15/1719.
Joseph Taylor d. 1/21/1719.
Hugh Parsons, taylor, d. 2/1/1720.
Jane Roberts d. 2/5/1720.
Elizabeth Dickson, dau of Andrew and Margrett, d. 2/23/1720.
Mary Clare, dau of William and Hester, d. 2/26/1720.
Elizabeth Pride, wife of Abraham, d. 3/20/1720.
Sarah Mitchell, dau of Thomas and Sarah, d. 3/22/1720.
Joseph Wale, son of Joseph and Martha, d. 4/27/1720.
Rebecka Key, dau of John and Sarah, d. 5/9/1720.
Ebenezer Robinson, son of Ebenezer and Mary, d. 5/29/1720.
Sabilla Masters, wife of Thomas, d. 6/23/1720.
Henry Knight, son of John and Hannah, d. 6/25/1720.
Joseph Wale d. 6/26/1720.
Hannah Peel, dau of Anthony and Rachel, d. 6/26/1720.
Hannah Hart, dau of John and Mary, d. 6/28/1720.
Nathaniel Querdon d. 6/29/1720.
James Bud, son of John and Rebecka, d. 7/1/1720.
Joseph Cooper, son of James and Hester, dec'd, d. 7/4/1720.
Mary Cresson, dau of Solomon and Anna, d. 7/4/1720.
Hannah Burden, dau of Thomas, dec'd, and Katherine, d. 7/4/1720.
Sarah Bissell, dau of William, d. 7/8/1720.
Martha Roberts, dau of Thomas and Martha, d. 7/15/1720.
Elizabeth Rochford, dau of Denniss and Elizabeth, d. 7/16/1720.
John Brown d. 7/20/1720.
Elizabeth Fitchwater d. 7/30/1720.
Mary England, dau of Daniel and Elizabeth, d. 9/4/1720.
Elizabeth Hughs, dau of David and Doroth_, d. 9/11/1720.
Elizabeth Fairman, widow of Thomas, d. 9/18/1720.
Jeremy Ryall d. 9/20/1720.
Margrett Edgar, wife of Joseph, d. 9/24/1720.
Rebecka Roberts, dau of Thomas and Martha, d. 9/25/1720.
Mary Ranstead, wife of Caleb, d. 10/4/1720.
Priscilla Bradford, wife of Thomas, d. 10/24/1720.
Elizabeth Plumstead, wife of Clement, d. 10/30/1720.
Martha Chalkley, dau of Thomas and Martha, d. 11/3/1720.
Richard Warder d. 11/15/1720.
John Widdowfield d. 11/23/1720.
Robert Finlow d. 12/3/1720.
Martha Wale, widow of Joseph, d. 12/3/1720.
Margrett Robinson, dau of Mathew and Sarah, d. 1/12/1720.
Joseph Dixson d. 1/19/1720.

John Howell d. 1/26/1720.
John Lloyd, smith, d. 1/26/1720.
Nathan Stanbury d. 2/2/1720.
Sarah Smith, wife of Richard, d. 2/2/1721.
William Powell, Sr., d. 2/30/1721.
Martha Bellow, dau of Mathew, dec'd, d. 3/25/1721.
John Walker d. 4/18/1721.
Mathew Birchfield, son of Mathew and Alice, d. 4/22/1721.
Samuel Fishburn, son of William and Hannah, d. 4/24/1721.
Arelius Owen, child of Evan and Mary, d. 5/2/1721.
Hannah Claypoole, dau of George and Deborah, d. 5/2/1721.
Thomas Mumford, son of Thomas and Mary, d. 5/29/1721
Thomas Knight, son of John and Hannah, d. 6/12/1721.
Tho: Holmes d. 6/28/1721.
Aron Goforth, son of Aron and Mary, d. 7/3/1721.
Grace Pleadwell, wife of Edward, d. 8/10/1721.
Anthony Morriss d. 8/24/1721.
Robert Pound, son of Robert, dec'd, and Mary, d. 9/26/1721.
Sarah Knowles, dau of Francis and Sarah, d. 9/28/1721.
James Baley, dau of James and Sarah, d. 10/8/1721.
Rebecka Corker, wife of William, d. 10/8/1721.
Rachell Pemberton, dau of Israell and Rachell, 10/12/1721.
Thomas Mornington, son of William and Susannah, d. 10/15/1721.
Levine Herbendick d. 10/26/1721.
David Powell, son of John and Ann, dec'd, d. 11/5/1721.
John Kirll, son of Joseph, d. 11/19/1721.
Mary Bryan, dau of Thomas and Susannah, d. 11/21/1721.
Elizabeth Bryan, dau of Thomas and Susannah, d. 11/21/1721.
Thomas Bryan, son of Thomas and Susannah, d. 11/28/1721.
Nicholas Waln bur 12/4/1721.
Nicholas Waln, son of the aforesaid Nicholas, d. 12/11/1721.
Richard Wharton, son of Thomas, dec'd, and Rachel, d. 1/5/1721.
Mary Radley, wife of Daniel, d. 1/6/1721.
Robert Fraim d. 1/17/1721.
John Daviss d. 1/30/1721.
Samuel Powell, Sr, d. 2/3/1722.
Ann Garratt, wife of William, d. 2/7/1721.
Susannah Mannington, wife of William, d. 2/22/1721.
Phebe Morris, dau of Anthony and Phebe, d. 3/7/1722.
Samuel Michol, son of Samuel and Thomason, d. 3/23/1722.
Mary Belloes, dau of Mathew, dec'd, and Maudling, d. 3/27/1722.
James Radley, son of Daniel and Mary, d. 3/28/1722.
Elizabeth Jacob, wife of Caleb, d. 3/29/1722.
Elizabeth Durberow, wife of Hugh, d. 4/1/1722.
Isaac Lenior, son of Isaac and Mary, d. 4/2/1722.

Joseph Usher d. 4/12/1722.
Jonathan Dickinson d. 4/18/1722.
Mary Lock, wife of John, d. 4/21/1722.
William Broadgate, son of Thomas and Christian, d. 5/8/1722.
Margrett Roland d. 5/14/1722.
Ishmael Roland d. 5/22/1722.
Tabitha Goforth, wife of Aron, Senr, d. 5/29/1722.
Marmaduke Burden, son of Thomas, dec'd, and Katherine, d. 6/6/1722.
Elizabeth Griffitts, dau of Nathaniel and Elizabeth, d. 6/21/1722.
Sarah Robinson, dau of Ebenezer and Mary, d. 6/23/1722.
William Southbe d. 7/7/1722.
Thomas Powell d. 7/9/1722.
Christopher Blackburn d. 7/16/1722.
Elizabeth Hill, dau of Richd. and Hannah, d. 7/27/1722.
Elizabeth Hastins, dau of Samuell and Mary, d. 8/12/1722.
William Hodson, son of Samuel and Mary, d. 8/26/1722.
Miriam Grainger, dau of Joshua and Elizabeth, d. 9/12/1722.
Sarah Webb, dau of Joseph and Mary, d. 9/24/1722.
Tabitha Birchfield, dau of Mathew and Alce, d. 10/6/1722.
Sarah Hardin dau of Francis and Elizabeth, d. 10/7/1722.
George Painter d. 10/30/1722.
Jacob Shoemaker d. 11/10/1722.
John Durberow, son of John and Rebecka, d. 11/11/1722.
William Makins, son of Thomas and Sarah, d. 11/12/1722.
Thomas Bradford d. 11/26/1722.
William Peters, son of Reece and Ann, d. 12/1/1722.
Ann Oxley, widow of William, d. 2/3/1723.
Joseph Paschall, son of Joseph and Elizabeth, d. 4/16/1723.
Thomas Chalkley, son of Thomas and Martha, d. 5/2/1723.
Rachel Logan, dau of James and Sarah, d. 5/28/1723.
Margrett Hugg, wife of Elias, d. 6/4/1723.
Mary Mifflin, dau of George and Hester, d. 6/8/1723.
Samuell Harwood, son of Samuel, d. 6/24/1723.
Aquilla Roas d. 6/25/1723.
Elizabeth Ranstead d. 6/31/1723.
Aron Birchfield, son of Mathew and Alce, d. 6/31/1723.
Isaac Lenoyer d. 8/4/1723.
James Warner, son of William and Ann, d. 9/29/1723.
Mary Linton, dau of John and Joan, d. 9/29/1723.
Isaac Merrit, carpenter, d. 10/4/1723.
Thomas Paschall, son of William and Sarah, d. 10/7/1723.
Imanuel Walker d. 10/12/1723.
Susanna Rakestraw, dau of Thomas and Mary, d. 10/20/1723.
Thomas Masters d. 11/11/1723.
Sarah Emson, dau of Cornelius, Jr, and Hannah, d. 11/22/1723.

Abraham Fitchwater, son of George and Mary, d. 1/12/1723.
Caleb Jacobs d. 1/16/1723.
Elizabeth Hastins, wife of Joshua, d. 1/19/1723.
Richard Lewiss, taylor, d. 2/1/1724.
Sarah Reeves, dau of John and Sarah, d. 2/10/1724.
Joshua Hastins d. 3/7/1724.
Patience Loyd, widow of Thomas, d. 4/26/1724.
Joseph Fisher, son of Samuel and Sarah, d. 5/12/1724.
Henry Knight, son of John and Hannah, d. 5/12/1724.
John Anniss, commander of the ship London, d. 5/15/1724.
Philip James d. 5/22/1724.
Mary Fisher, dau of John and Sarah, d. 5/25/1724.
Rebecka Bud, wife of John, d. 5/29/1724.
Joan Humphrey d. 6/3/1724.
Hester Shippen, widow of Edward, d. 6/7/1724.
_____ Morriss, dau of Anthony and Phebe, d. 6/14/1724.
Ruth Lansdall d. 6/17/1724.
Ann Waln, wife of Richard, bur 6/25/1724.
John Thomson, son of Gilbert, d. 6/22/1724.
Elizabeth Oldman, widow of Thomas, d. 6/23/1724.
James Bud, son of John and Rebecka, dec'd, d. 6/28/1724.
George Mifflin, son of George and Ester, d. 7/5/1724.
Mary Lawrence, dau of Joshua and Amy, d. 7/7/1724.
John Huddy, baker, d. 7/10/1724.
Jacob Harmar, dau of George and Honor, d. 7/16/1724.
Samuel Cart, son of Samuel and Sarah, d. 7/24/1724.
Edmond Stevens d. 7/30/1724.
Samuel Mifflin, son of John, dec'd, and Elizabeth, d. 8/1/1724.
John Edghill, son of Simon and Rebeckah, d. 9/24/1724.
Alce West, dau of Charles, d. 10/8/1724.
Thomas Redman 10/14/1724.
Phineas Pemberton, son of Israel and Rachel, d. 11/4/1724.
Mary Large, wife of Ebenezer, d. 11/14/1724.
Thomas Peters d. 11/26/1724.
Lettins Robbins, dau of William and Rebecka, d. 12/2/1724.
Ann Spikeman, wife of Randolph, d. 12/25/1724.
Mary Roberts, dau of Edward and Mary, d. 12/25/1724.
John Burge, son of William and Elizabeth, d. 1/24/1724.
William Dunn, a blind man, d. 1/25/1724.
Hannah Paschall, dau of William and Sarah, d. 2/14/1725.
_____ Bailor, a ship carpenter, d. 3/4/1725.
John Claypoole, son of George and Deborah, d. 3/18/1725.
John Watson d. 3/25/1725.
Rachel Norris, dau of Humphrey and Rachel, d. 4/4/1725.
Joseph Wood d. 4/12/1725.

Benjamin Cassell, son of Arnold and Susanna, d. 4/19/1725.
John Fisher, smith, d. 4/23/1725.
Randolph Spikeman d. 5/11/1725.
George Colvert d. 5/12/1725.
Joshua Hastings, son of Samuel, d. 5/12/1725.
Dorothy Tatnall, dau of Thomas and Ann, d. 5/14/1725.
Thomas Tatnell, son of Thomas and Ann, d. 5/16/1725.
Mary Barnes, widow of John, d. 5/16/1725.
Mary Hastings, dau of Samuel, d. 5/18/1725.
John Sanders, son of William and Hester, d. 5/28/1725.
Jane Brintnall, wife of David, d. 6/26/1725.
Benjamin Horn, son of Edward and Elizabeth, d. 7/13/1725.
Bridgett Fisher, wife of William, d. 7/27/1725.
Joseph Harris of Maryland, d. 7/28/1725, at William Fishburns.
Ann Parr, daughter of Samuel and Ann, d. 8/10/1725.
Maudlin Nixson, wife of Thomas, d. 8/11/1725.
Peter Brown, a shallop man, d. 8/28/1725.
Susanna Warner, dau of William and Ann, d. 8/30/1725.
Mary Fisher, dau of Jonathan and Mary, d. 8/31/1725.
John Ogdon, son of John and Hannah, d. 9/3/1725.
George Shires d. 9/5/1725.
Hannah Coffin, wife of Jacob, d. 9/21/1725.
Anna Cresson, dau of Solomon and Anna, d. 10/3/1725.
Agnes Stretch, wife of Samuel, d. 10/12/1725.
Owen Roberts d. 10/16/1725.
Thomas Fitchwater, son of George and Mary, d. 10/22/1725.
Ralph Jackson d. 10/27/1725.
Jude Watsom, son of John, d. 11/2/1725.
Sarah Smith, dau of John and Margrett, chocolatt grinder, d. 11/11/1725.
David Evans, son of David and Elizabeth, d. 11/18/1725.
Lidia Tomson d. 2/16/1726.
William Kelly, son of William, dec'd, d. 3/9/1726.
William Corker d. 4/14/1726.
Mary Wood, dau of James, d. 6/21/1726.
Hannah Preston, dau of Paul and Elizabeth, d. 7/1/1726.
Margaret Careton, dau of William, d. 7/7/1726.
Sarah Powell, a noted midwife, wife of William, d. 7/13/1726.
Hannah Knowles, dau of Francis and Sarah, d. 7/18/1726.
William Mason d. 8/2/1726.
Sarah Buckley, wife of Joseph, d. 8/7/1726.
Sarah Kelly, dau of William, dec'd, and Elizabeth, d. 9/7/1726.
Sarah Williams, Sarah Redmans aunt, d. 9/11/1726.
Joseph Rakestraw, son of Thomas, d. 9/29/1726.
Ester Tomlinson d. 10/4/1726.
Mary Griffitts, dau of Nathaniel and Elizabeth, d. 10/7/1726.

Elizabeth Lindley, dau of Thomas, d. 10/8/1726.
Ann Hood, dau of Thomas, d. 10/13/1726.
Mary Lewiss, widow of Richd. of Germantown, d. 10/14/1726.
Liddia Parr, dau of Samuel and Ann, d. 10/19/1726.
Millicent Fisher, dau of William and Tabitha, d. 10/19/1726.
Daniel Parker, son of George, butcher, d. 10/20/1726.
Charles Logan son of James and Sarah, d. 10/26/1726.
Thomas Framton d. 10/27/1726.
Sarah Roberts, wife of John, d. 11/1/1726.
Elizabeth Richardson, widow of Samuel, d. 11/8/1726.
Thomas Renshaw, son of John, d. 11/12/1726.
Ann Richardson, lived at Ed. Horns, d. 11/15/1726.
William Webb, son of Joseph and Mary, d. 11/17/1726.
William Laycock, son of Joseph, d. 11/23/1726.
Mary Pain d. 11/31/1726.
Deborah Siddal, dau of Ezekall and Sarah, d. 12/11/1726.
Sophia Shores, wife of Cornelius, d. 12/12/1726.
Mary Kalve, wife of John, d. 12/16/1726.
An Peters, wife of Reece, Jr., d. 12/17/1726.
John Wilson, merchant. d. 12/20/1726.
Elizabeth Griffith, wife of Thomas, d. 12/23/1726.
John Hinton, son of William and Jane, d. 12/22/1726.
Mary Emly, late Mary Hudson, wife of Joshua, d. 12/23/1726.
Hannah Hill, wife of Richard, d. 12/28/1726.
Thomas Griffith d. 1/5/1726.
Francis Rawle d. 1/7/1726.
Robert Pennill, son of Joseph of Chester Co., d. 1/9/1726.
Miriam Radley, dau of Daniel, d. 1/20/1726
Thomas Norriss, son of Isaac and Mary, d. 1/22/1726.
James Satterwith of Burlington, d. 1/29/1727.
David Powell, son of David, d. 1/30/1727.
Isaac Warner d. 2/10/1727.
Joseph Maltby, son of John, d. 2/10/1727.
John Phillips d. 2/16/1727.
Joseph Wattson d. 2/20/1727.
Mary Williams, dau of Isaac and Mary, d. 3/19/1727.
Ester Benson, dau of John, d. 5/10/1727.
Sarah Ogdon, dau of John and Hannah, d. 5/13/1727.
Mary Cook d. 6/3/1727.
Rachell Guest, dau of George and Elizabeth, d. 6/3/1727.
Joseph Goforth, son of Aron, Jr, and Mary, d. 6/3/1727.
Joseph Buckley d. 6/4/1727.
_____ Adams, dau of Thomas and Ruth, d. 6/6/1727.
Joseph Lancaster, son of John and Sarah, d. 6/11/1727.
John Townsend d. 6/17/1727.

Samuel Addams, son of Thomas and Ruth, d. 6/23/1727.
Elizabeth Sanders, dau of Richard, d. 6/25/1727.
Isaac Boulton, son of Samuel, d.6/26/1726.
William Coats, son of Enoch and Rose, d. 7/2/1727.
William Brooks, son of Edward and Elizabeth, d. 7/13/1727.
Ellis Jones d. 7/16/1727.
William Paschall, son of William and Sarah, d. 8/4/1727.
Thomas Wolliston, son of Thomas, d. 8/9/1727.
Ann Peters, dau of Reece, d. 8/11/1727.
_____ Stapler, dau of William, d. 8/14/1727.
Nathaniel Edgcomb d. 8/19/1727.
Mathew Birchfield d. 9/5/1727.
John Stacy d. 9/7/1727.
Sarah Hearn, wife of William, d. 9/14/1727.
Susanna Cassle, widow of Arnold, d. 9/14/1727.
John Goodson d. 10/28/1727.
_____ Dickinson, dau of Francis and Thomas Masters kinswoman, d.
   11/7/1727.
John Kaloe d. 11/11/1727.
Joanna Flower, dau of Henry, d. 11/14/1727.
Josiah Betell, son of John and Abigail, d. 2/27/1728.
Elizabeth League d. 3/10/1728.
Thomas Rakestraw d. 3/17/1727.
John Hood, son of John, d. 4/5/1728.
Thomas Denham d. 5/4/1728.
Mathew Wilton, son of John, d. 5/21/1728.
Hannah Carpenter, widow of Samuell, d. 5/25/1728.
Hannah Fishburn, wife of William and dau of Hannah Carpenter, d.
   5/26/1728.
Jane Dubree, wife of Jacob, d. 6/2/1728.
George Shoemaker, son of George, d. 6/4/1728.
Samuel Hudson, son of John and Hannah, d. 6/12/1728.
William Fisher d. 6/14/1728.
Samuel Nichos, son of John, d. 6/16/1728.
William Webb, son of Joseph, d. 6/19/1728.
Samuel Cox, son of Thomas, d. 6/21/1728.
John Key, son of John, d. 6/29/1728.
Rachell Worthinton, dau of Robert, d. 6/30/1728.
John Spence, son of John and Rachel, d. 7/3/1728.
Joshua Vernen, son of Jacob, d. 7/5/1728.
Mary Linton, dau of John and Joan, d. 7/7/1728.
Ezekell Siddall d. 7/7/1728.
Joshua Fincher d. 7/13/1728.
Benjamin Preston, son of Paul, d. 7/20/1728.
Thomas Hopkins, son of Robert, d. 7/22/1728.

Thomas Oliver d. 8/4/1728.
Joshua Fisher, son of Jonathan, d. 8/9/1728.
Samuel Claypoole, son of George and Deborah, d. 9/1/1728.
Sarah Hodgson, wife of Daniell, d. 9/4/1728.
Deborah Durberow, dau of Daniell and Sarah, d. 9/13/1728.
Joshuah Richardson d. 9/17/1728.
Sarah Durberor, wife of Daniell, d. 9/21/1728.
Sarah Durberow, dau of Daniell, d. 9/21/1728.
Elizabeth Noble, dau of Joseph and Mary, d. 9/22/1728.
Sarah Elfre, wife Henry, d. 9/23/1728.
Sarah Redman, widow of Thomas, d. 9/23/1728.
Thomas Cox, son of Thomas and Martha, d. 10/2/1728.
Mary Rakestraw, widow of Thomas, d. 10/4/1728.
_____ Rakestraw, son of Thomas and Mary, d. 10/4/1728.
William Cox, son of Thomas and Martha, d. 10/6/1728.
Sarah Coats, dau of William, d. 10/8/1728.
Thomas Siddon d. 10/8/1728.
Mary Worley, wife of Francis, d. 10/12/1728.
Mary Paschall, dau of Joseph and Elizabeth, d. 10/18/1728.
Eleanor Vernon. dau of Jacob, d. 10/19/1728.
Thomas Coats, son of Enoch and Rose, d. 10/21/1728.
Isaac Shoemaker, son of Benj. and Sarah, d. 10/29/1728.
Elizabeth England, wife of Joseph, d. 11/1/1728.
William Hudson, son of John and Hannah, d. 11/14/1728.
Sarah Ranstead, wife of Caleb, d. 11/16/1728.
Mary Moreton, wife of John, d. 11/19/1728.
Joseph Trotter, son of Joseph and Dinah, d. 12/21/1728.
Stephen Stapler, son of Stephen, dec'd, d. 12/26/1728.
Thomas Addams d. 12/27/1728.
Rebecka Owen, dau of Edward and Susanna, d. 1/1/1728.
Thomas Pryor d. 1/6/1729.
Ester Benson, dau of John and Mary, d. 3/19/1729.
William Dowell d. 3/23/1729.
John May of Cape May d. 3/29/1729.
Sarah Robinson, wife of Richard, d. 4/10/1729.
William Ireson, son of William and Dorcas, d. 5/8/1729.
Richard Warder, son of Richard and Rebecka, d. 5/14/1729.
Hannah Tomson, dau of Christopher and Mary, d. 6/5/1729.
Rebecka Watson, dau of John, d. 6/5/1729.
Jane Yieldhall, widow of Robert, d. 6/7/1729.
Edward Muggleston d. 6/11/1729.
Francis Richardson d. 6/18/1729.
Elizabeth Wilton, wife of John, d. 6/20/1729.
Thomas Tomson, son of Christopher, d. 6/21/1729.
Elizabeth Couper, dau of Joseph and Mary, d. 6/27/1729.

William Alloway, son of William, d. 6/23/1729.
Susanna Stapler, dau of William, d. 6/25/1729.
William Carter, son of William and Mary, d. 6/27/1729.
Richard Hill d. 7/5/1729.
Sarah Gibbons d. 7/12/1729.
Elizabeth Ranstead, dau of Caleb, d. 7/18/1729.
Mary Master, dau of Thomas and Hannah, d. 8/2/1829.
William Hern d. 8/3/1729.
Richard Preston d. 8/13/1729.
James Coleman, son of Thomas, d. 8/13/1729.
Joshua Burch of Barbadoes, d. 9/16/1729.
Mary Ryall d. 9/28/1729.
John Knight d. 10/13/1729.
Margrett Williams, wife of Edward, d. 10/19/1729.
Katherine Miller, wife of James, d. 10/19/1729.
Mary Pearce, wife of Thomas, d. 11/11/1729.
Josiah Elliss d. 12/1/1729.
Sarah Dilwin, widow of William, d. 12/16/1729.
John Dickinson, son of Jonathan, dec'd, d. 1/3/1729.
Deborah Emly, wife of Joshua, d. 1/16/1729.
Benjamin Jackson, son of Stephen and Elizabeth, d. 1/3/1730.
John Furness d. 2/21/1730.
Cornelius Empson, son of Cornelius and Hannah, d. 4/6/1730.
Mary Wilson, wife of George, d. 6/7/1730.
Mary Bissell, dau of William and Hannah, d. 6/10/1730.
Margrett Rawle, wife of William, d. 6/12/1730.
Rebecka Couper, dau of Samuel, d. 6/21/1730.
John Morton d. 6/29/130.
Joshua Parr, son of Samuel and Ann, d. 6/29/1730.
Rachell Lowdon, dau of Widow Lowdon, d. 7/1/1730.
James Brooks, son of Edward and Elizabeth, d. 7/2/1730.
Sarah Clifton, dau of Henry and Letitia, d. 7/17/1730.
Elizabeth Oldman, dau of Thomas and Mary, d. 7/24/1730.
Robert Lowdon, son of Widow of Lowdon, d. 8/5/1730.
Isaac Hues, son of Moses and Sarah, d. 8/12/1730.
_____ Ireson, wife of John, d. 8/19/1730.
_____ Carey, wife of Sampson, d. 8/23/1730.
William Thomson, dau of Robert and Sarah, d. 8/25/1730.
Joseph Burger d. 8/26/1730.
Mary Badcock, wife of Henry, d. 9/8/1730.
John Hudson d. 9/12/1730.
George Claypoole d. 10/23/1730.
John Ireson d. 10/31/1730.
Merabe Preston, wife of Abell, d. 11/16/1730.
Elizabeth Lewiss, dau of James and Sarah, d. 11/22/1730.

John Bissell, son of William and Hannah, d. 11/25/1730.
Mary Adams, dau of Thomas and Ruth, d. 12/1/1730.
William Shippen, son of Edward, dec'd, d. 12/3/1730.
Jane Robinson, dau of Edward, a lame man, d. 12/6/1730.
Joseph Bissell, son of William and Hannah, d. 12/7/1730.
Hannah Roberts, dau of Edward and Marcy, d. 12/11/1730.
Deborah Claypoole, dau of George and Deborah, d. 12/12/1730.
Hannah Claypoole, dau of George and Deborah, d. 12/12/1730.
Elizabeth Rochford, dau of Dennis, d. 12/12/1730.
Benjamin Harner, son of George and Honour, d. 12/14/1730.
Hannah Burden, dau of Thomas and Mary, d. 12/15/1730.
Joannah Present d. 12/16/1730.
Edward Roberts, son of Edward and Marcy, d. 12/17/1730.
Mary Claypoole, dau of George and Deborah, d. 12/18/1730.
Thomas Mekins, Jr., d. 12/18/1730.
Thomas Lindsey, son of Thomas and Hannah, d. 12/18/1730.
Elizabeth Warder, dau of Richd. and Rebecka, d. 12/21/1730.
Abraham Spencer, son of John and Rachell, d. 12/21/1730.
Edward Boon d. 12/21/1730.
Isaac Claypoole, son of George and Deborah, d. 12/22/1730.
Elizabeth Claypoole, dau of George and Deborah, d. 12/22/1730.
Mary Hitchcock, dau of Nicholas and Elizabeth, d. 12/26/1730.
Susannah Hudson, dau of William, Jr., and Jane, d.12/26/1730.
Susannah Shoemaker, dau of George, d. 12/26/1730.
Mary Pemberton, dau of Israell and Rachel, d. 1/1/1730,
Marcy Roberts, wife of Edward, d. 1/2/1730.
William Hudson, son of William, Jr., and Jane, d. 1/2/1730.
Susannah Peters, dau of Thomas and Mary, d. 1/3/1730.
Mary Griffits, dau of Natha. and Elizabeth, d. 1/4/1730.
Joseph Ireson, son of William and Dorcas, d. 5/5/1730.
Mary Harriss, dau of ____ and Alce, d. 1/6/1730.
Francis Prescott d. 1/7/1730.
Priscilla Wolliston, dau of Thomas and Ellinor, d. 1/7/1730.
Samuel Parr, son of Samuel and Ann, d. 1/8/1730.
John Richardson, son of Francis and Letitia, d. 1/8/1730.
Joseph Fisher, son of Jonathan and Mary, d. 1/8/1730.
John Fisher, son of Jonathan and Mary, d. 1/8/1730.
John Thomas, son of Richard and Elizabeth, d. 1/10/1730.
John Champion d. 1/11/1730.
William Ingledue, son of Blanton, bur 1/14/1731.
Elizabeth Anniss, dau of William and Patience, bur 1/15/1731.
April Key, dau of John, bur 1/17/1731.
Caleb Vernon, son of Jacob and Elinor, bur 1/20/1731.
Aquilla Roberts, son of John and Mary, bur 1/21/1731.
Arnold Cassle bur 1/22/1731.

Ester Hutt, dau of Daniel and Ester, bur 1/23/1731.
John Linton, son of John and Joan, bur 1/24/1731.
Rachell Head, dau of John, bur 1/24/1731.
John Burden, son of Thomas and Mary, bur 1/26/1731.
Sarah Hutt, dau of Daniel and Hester, bur 1/28/1731.
Mary Ashmalham, dau of Thomas, bur 1/28/1731.
Rachel Ingram, dau of John and Ann, bur 1/31/1731.
William Burr, son of William Burr, bur 2/1/1731.
Richard Noble, son of Joseph and Mary, bur 2/1/1731.
Abell Fordum bur 2/2/1731.
George Biles, son of Jonathan and Ann, bur 2/2/1731.
John Kinsey, son of John and Mary, bur 2/4/1731.
Abraham Fishburn, son of William and Hannah, bur 2/6/1731.
Abraham Moore, son of Widow Moore, bur 2/12/1731.
William Paschall, son of William and Sarah, bur 2/15/1731.
Rachell Rogers, dau of Nicholas, bur 2/18/1731.
William Fincher, son of Joshua, dec'd, bur 2/19/1731.
Isaac Johnson, son of Joshua, hatter, bur 2/20/1731.
George Fincher, son of John and Katherine, bur 2/24/1731.
Mary Allawase, wife of William, bur 3/3/1731.
William Allen, son of Nathaniell and Hannah, bur 3/16/1731.
Daniell Hodgson bur 5/17/1731.
Mary Folk, dau of Cadwallader and Mary, bur 5/17/1731.
Mary Lawrence, dau of Joshua and Anne, bur 6/12/1731.
John Norris, son of Isaac and Mary, bur 6/15/1731.
John Carver bur 6/17/1731.
Henry Tomson bur 6/24/1731.
Ruben Foster, son of Reuben, bur 6/30/1731.
Elizabeth Hardin, wife of Francis, bur 6/31/1731.
Mary Tomlinson, dau of Benjamin, bur 7/5/1731.
Nathaniel Queans, son of Jonathan and Mary, bur 8/1/1731.
Richard Scofield d. 8/28/1731.
John Powell, son of Samuel, couper, bur 8/30/1731.
James Parrock, Jr, bur 9/9/1731.
Sarah Hatton, dau of Thomas, bur 9/11/1731.
Mary Cannon, wife of Thomas, bur 9/18/1731.
Mary Fitchwater, wife of George, bur 9/19/1731.
Joseph Webb bur 9/19/1731.
Rebecka Trotter bur 9/20/1731.
William Paschall, son of Joseph, bur 10/22/1731.
Martha Cadwallader, dau of ____ and Rebecka, bur 11/12/1731.
William Harmer bur 11/26/1731.
William Powell, son of William, couper, bur 12/21/1731.
Ann Lawrence, wife of William, bur 1/4/1732.
Dr. Griffith Owen, son of Dr. Griffith Owen, bur 1/4/1732.

Henry Hodge bur 1/7/1732.
Mary Ogdon bur 1/12/1732.
Mary Queans, dau of Jonathan and Mary, bur 1/19/1732.
Thomas Hobbs bur 1/22.1732.
Richard Townsend bur 1/30/1732.
Samuel Stretch bur 1/31/1732.
Mary Bolding, wife of William, bur 2/27/1732.
Edward Williams bur 3/12/1732.
Samuel Robbins, son of Thomas, bur 3/14/1732.
Hannah Hastings, wife of John, bur 4/8/1732.
Joan Forrest, widow of William, bur 5/1/1732.
Sarah Couper, wife of Samuel, bur 5/5/1732.
Henry Tew, son of Samuel and Mary, bur 5/8/1732.
Michall Point, son of Isaac, bur 5/9/1732.
Reuben Forster, son of Ruben, bur 5/16/1732.
Margrett Holway, dau of Thos and Jane, bur 5/28/1732.
Samuell Alton, son of Samuell and Mary, bur 5/30/1732.
Rachell Spence, wife of Samuel, bur 6/1/1732.
Susanna Harwood bur 6/3/1732.
David Powell bur 6/6/1732.
Mary Hastings, wife of Samuel, bur 6/16/1732.
Phebe Eldridge, wife of Obediah, bur 6/17/1732.
Thomas Foulk, son of Cadwalader and Mary, bur 6/22/1732.
William Truman, son of Richard, bur 7/4/1732,
Thomas Cannan bur 7/7/1732.
James Estaw, son of Elizabeth, 7/29/1732.
John Sharcross bur 8/11/1732.
Moses Riley bur 8/11/1732.
Sarah Brooks, dau of Edward, bur 9/5/1732.
Richard Redman bur 9/6/1732.
Paul Preston bur 9/7/1732.
George Harmor bur 9/19/1732.
Joseph Cross bur 9/24/1732.
Joseph England bur 9/26/1732.
David Brentnall bur 9/28/1732.
William Corker bur 10/4/1732.
Thomas Roberts, taylor, bur 10/5/1732.
James Couper bur 10/6/1732.
_____ Couper, wife of James, bur 10/6/1732.
Ann Preston, widow of William, bur 10/6/1732.
John Loyd, smith, bur 10/7/1732.
David Shewring bur 10/8/1732.
William Lawrence bur 10/12/1732.
Marcy Dillwin, wife of John, bur 10/19/1732.
Jean Jones, widow of Ellis, bur 10/21/1732.

William Moore, son of William, bur 10/23/1732.
Ann Warner bur 10/27/1732.
Katherine Burden bur 10/4/1732.
Thomas Bedson bur 11/17/1723.
William Powell, couper, bur 11/17/1732.
Robert Hind, son of Robert and Mary, bur 11/20/1732.
Anthony Morriss, son of Anthony, Jr, bur 11/31/1732.
Caspar Hoods bur 12/11/1732.
Mary Stacy, dau of John, bur 1/4/1732.
Liddya Mifflin, dau of Jonathan and Sarah, bur 1/5/1732.
Mary Davis, widow of John, taylor, bur 1/14/1732.
Ann Townsend, widow of Richard, bur 1/15/1732.
Thomas Flarney bur 1/15/1732.
_____ Carter, wife of James, bur 2/3/1733.
Joshua Elfrey bur 2/4/1733.
John Green bur 2/7/1733.
John Harris bur 2/8/1733.
Sarah Randall, wife of Warwick, bur 2/15/1733.
Aron Goforth, Jr, bur 4/6/1733.
Martha Roberts, widow of Thomas, bur 4/6/1733.
John Hartley bur 4/22/1733.
Henry Vanbibber bur 5/31/1733.
Sarah Owen, widow of Griffith, bur 6/4/1733.
Ann Emmerson, wife of Lambert, bur 6/9/1733.
Thomas Coleman, son of William and Rebecka, bur 6/10/1733.
Daniel Boyden bur 6/15/1733.
Elizabeth Hitchcock, wife of Nicholas, bur 6/26/1733.
Robert Jordan, son of Robert and Mary, bur 6/28/1733.
Bartholomew Candry bur 7/17/1733.
Samuel Harrott bur 7/22/1733.
John Wood bur 8/1/1733.
_____ Callender, son of William and Katherine, bur 8/5/1733.
Mary Noble, wife of Joseph, bur 8/6/1733.
Joseph Norriss, son of Isaac and Mary, bur 8/7/1733.
John Roads of Manalony bur 8/9/1733.
George Chalkley, son of Thomas and Martha, bur 8/14/1733.
Mary Goforth, widow of Aron, Jr, bur 8/15/1733.
Letitia Elfrey, wife of Jeremy, bur 9/16/1733.
Joseph Elfrey, son of Caleb, bur 9/25/1733.
Thomas Makin bur 9/27/1733.
Mary Loyd, wife of Peter, bur 9/30/1733.
Jones Bune bur 10/1/1733.
Michall Walton bur 10/20/1733.
Jane Lancaster, dau of John and Sarah, bur 10/25/1733.
Thomas Boyles, taylor, bur 10/29/1733.

Sarah Parker, dau of George, bur 11/14/1733.
Henry Saddin but 11/23/1733.
William Lingard bur 11/27/1733.
Samuel Couper, butcher, bur 12/8/1733.
Thomas Oldman bur 1/3/1734.
John Spence bur 1/7/1734.
Ann Wilcox, widow of Joseph, bur 1/17/1734.
Hannah Masters, wife of Thomas, bur 1/14/1734.
Martha Cockshaw, wife of Jonathan, bur 2/4/1734.
William Sanders bur 2/10/1734.
Mathew Phillips bur 1/19/1734.
Elizabeth Whartenaby bur 2/23/1734.
Grace Coates, wife of George, bur 2/24/1734.
Mary Dubree, dau of Joseph. bur 2/29/1734.
Mary Tew (or Chew), wife of Dr Samuel, bur 3/27/1734.
Margrett Evans, dau of David and Elizabeth, bur 4/12/1734.
William Wood, son of Joseph, bur 4/17/1734.
Margrett Hudson, dau of William and Jane, bur 5/8/1734.
Sarah Goforth, dau of Aron, bur 5/10/1734.
Sarah Bettson, dau of Thomas, Jr, bur 5/21/1734.
Joshua Wister, son of Caspar, bur 5/23/1734.
Rachel Townsend, dau of Ja:, bur 5/23/1734.
John Cadwalader bur 5/24/1734.
Andrew Williams, son of Thomas, bur 6/4/1734.
Susanna West, dau of Edward, bur 6/6/1734.
Margrett Fisher, dau of John, bur 6/8/1734.
William Fisher bur 6/9/1734.
Susanna Peters, dau of Thomas, bur 6/15/1734.
Jane Austin, widow of John, bur 7/14/1734.
Mary Little, alias Davis, bur 7/16/1734.
Samuel Nichols, bricklayer, bur 8/25/1734.
John Lock, son of John, bur 9/17/1734.
Margrett Peters, dau of Thomas, Sr, bur 9/19/1734.
Sarah Sanders, wife of Richard, bur 9/21/1734.
Sarah Hopewell, wife of Joseph, bur 9/25/1734.
Phebe Flascott, wife of John, bur 9/28/1734.
Jacob Turner bur 10/10/1734.
Abraham Cox bur 11/2/1734.
Cadwalader Foulk, son of Cadwallader, bur 5/28/1734.
Thomas Williams bur 10/10/1734.
Sarah Lewis, wife of James, bur 11/16/1734.
Mary Howell, wife of George, bur 11/19/1734.
Phillip Romman bur 12/25/1734.
Mary Williams, wife of Oliver, bur 1/8/1734.
Christian Morriss bur 1/18/1734.

Ann Whittrain, widow of John, bur 2/1/1735.
Ann Poole, wife of Nathaniel, bur 2/6/1735.
Sarah Carpenter, wife of Abraham, bur 3/28/1735.
Isaac Norriss bur 4/5/1735.
Olive Longhurst, wife of John, bur 4/6/1735.
Mary Wood, dau of Joseph, bur 4/10/1735.
Mary Enock, dau of David, bur 4/27/1735.
Jane Richardson bur 5/4/1735.
Rachel Trotter, dau of Joseph and Dinah, bur 5/7/1735.
John Lancaster bur 5/23/1735.
Sarah Goodwin, Jr, dau of John and Sarah, bur 6/3/1735.
Margrett Hudson, dau of William and Jane, bur 6/4/1735.
Rachel Wharton, dau of Thos, dec'd, and Rachel, bur 6/7/1735.
Mary Burdon, dau of Thomas and Mary, bur 6/12/1735.
Daniel Roberts, son of John and Mary, bur 6/13/1735.
Mary Furness, wife of Joseph, bur 6/14/1735.
Mary Ashburnham, dau of Thomas and Hannah, bur 6/14/1735.
An Shout, dau of Thomas, chandler, bur 6/21/1735.
Mary Claypoole, wife of James, bur 6/22/1735.
Samuel Powell, son of Sam'l, Jr, and Mary, bur 6/24/1735.
Sarah Truman, dau of Thomas, bur 6/26/1735.
Hannah Jones, dau of John and Barbarah, bur 7/1/1735.
Thomas Wilson, son of George, bur 7/3/1735.
Henry Badcock bur 7/11/1735.
Edward Horn bur 7/14/1735.
John Williams, son of John, bur 8/5/1735.
Elizabeth Engledue, wife of Blaxton, bur 8/10/1735.
Elizabeth Elfrey, wife of Jeremiah, bur 8/23/1735.
Benjamin Hartley bur 8/31/1735.
William Egrell bur 10/20/1735.
Sarah Jackson, widow of Ralph, bur 10/23/1735.
John Songhurst bur 9/3/1735.
Rebecka Nichols, wife of Antony, bur 11/8/1735.
Charles Messer bur 11/10/1735.
Thomas Betson, son of Thomas, bur 1/21/1735.
Sarah Knowles bur 8/12/1735.
Hannah Hodge, widow of Henry, bur 1/26/1736.
Thomas Shoemaker, bur 3/23/1736.
Mary Roman, widow of Philip. bur 3/23/1736.
Sarah Hopewell, dau of Joseph, bur 3/29/1736.
Elizabeth Townsend, widow of James, bur 3/30/1736.
Sarah Spurrier, widow of Theophilus, bur 4/11/1736.
Michall Point bur 4/13/1736.
Theophilus Spurrier bur 5/3/1736.
Mary Hitchcock, dau of Joseph, bur 5/7/1736.

Sarah Willerson, widow of William, bur 5/8/1836.
Cadwalader Foulk, son of Cadwallader and Mary, bur 5/18/1736.
Nathaniel Allen bur 5/21/1736.
Jane Hart bur 5/24/1736.
Elizabeth Shoemaker, dau of Jacob, bur 6/4/1736.
Samuel Cox, son of Abraham and Martha, bur 6/5/1736.
Samuel Cockrom, son of Samuel, bur 6/7/1736.
James Townsend, son of James, bur 6/12/1736.
John Freman bur 6/13/1736.
James Garratt bur 6/14/1736.
Sarah Wister, dau of John, bur 6/14/1736.
John Jenkins bur 6/15/1736.
Jane Marl, wife of Thomas, bur 6/15/1736.
Martha Sinn, wife of Joseph, bur 6/17/1736.
Mary Jenkins, widow of John, bur 6/18/1736.
Sarah Reeves, wife of John, bur 6/18/1736.
Dove Hill bur 6/20/1736.
Elizabeth Mifflin, widow of John, bur 6/21/1736.
Jacob Jones, son of Jacob, bur 6/21/1736.
John Dilwin, son of John, bur 6/21/1736.
Thomas Marl, son of John, bur 6/24/1736.
Samuel Roberts, son of John, bur 6/25/1736.
Samuel Coats, son of Samuel, bur 6/26/1736.
John Ogden, son of John, bur 6/26/1736.
Jacob Coffin bur 6/26/1736.
George Hous, son of George, bur 7/2/1736.
Elizabeth Dean bur 7/4/1736.
Charles Townsend, son of Charles, bur 7/4/1736.
William Rakestraw bur 7/8/1736.
Hannah Durberow, wife of Hugh, bur 7/15/1736.
Rebecka Mitchell, dau of Abram, bur 7/24/1736.
John Hastings bur 7/27/1736.
Hannah Muckans bur 8/2/1736.
Mary Lacy, wife of Thomas, bur 8/3/1736.
Rachel Preston, dau of Richard, bur 8/7/1736.
Mary Lewiss, dau of Adam, bur 8/9/1736.
Sarah Gates, wife of Josiah, bur 8/10/1736.
Benjamin Main bur 8/15/1736.
Hannah Preston, wife of Abell, bur 8/25/1736.
Elizabeth Shout, dau of Jacob, bur 8/26/1736.
Mary Bittle, dau of John, bur 9/5/1736.
Thomas Miller bur 9/6/1736.
Thomas King, son of Joseph, bur 9/15/1736.
John Marshall bur 9/22/1736.
George Widdowfield, son of John, bur 9/22/1736.

Mary Taylor, wife of John, bur 9/23/1736.
Elizabeth Marton bur 10/6/1736.
John Jones, son of Jacob, bur 10/6/1736.
Joshua Point, son of Michall, bur 10/7/1736.
Patience Amiss, wife of William, bur 10/15/1736.
Jacob Jones, son of Jacob, bur 10/24/1736.
Frances Strickland, dau of Thomas, bur 10/25/1736.
George Hart, son of John, Jr, bur 10/27/1736.
Elizabeth Shout, dau of Thomas, bur 10/28/1736.
Thomas Firman, son of Benjamin, bur 10/31/1736.
Benjamin Firman, son of Benjamin, bur 10/31/1736.
_____ Whitehead, dau of James, bur 11/2/1736.
Samuel Brook, son of Ralph, bur 11/5/1736.
Ann Vernon, dau of Jacob, bur 11/5/1736.
Amos Strickland, son of Thomas, bur 11/6/1736.
Walmanus Aldridge bur 11/6/1763.
Rachel Wharton, dau of Joseph, bur 11/6/1736.
John Bittle bur 11/11/1736.
Mary Hays bur 11/14/1736.
Elizabeth Paschall, dau of Joseph, bur 11/14/1736.
Elizabeth Wright, wife of Jonathan, bur 11/16/1736.
Robert Reed bur 11/18/1736.
Abigail Hood, dau of Abram, bur 11/19/1736.
Mary Warner, dau of William, bur 11/19/1736.
Margrett Collins bur 11/20/736.
Sarah Betterson, dau of Benjamin, bur 11/20/1736.
Joseph Jones bur 11/22/1736.
Elinor Hill bur 11/27/1736.
Anthony Allen bur 11/29/1736.
Mary Jerviss, dau of Francis, Jr, bur 11/29/1736.
Thomas Brison bur 11/30/1736.
Margrett Shoomaker, widow of Jacob, Sr, bur 11/30/1736.
Ester Lewiss, dau of John, bur 11/31/1736.
Mary Zeans, dau of Jonath, bur 12/3/1736.
Mary Embly, dau of Samuel, bur 12/3/1736.
Elizabeth Marton bur 12/7/1736.
Joshua Fern bur 12/7/1736.
Thomas Masters, son of Thomas, bur 12/11/1736.
Joshua French bur 12/12/1736.
George Biles, son of Jonathan, bur 12/17/1736.
Anthony Morriss, son of James and Elizabeth, bur 12/25/1736.
Sarah Sugars bur 12/27/1736.
Richard Jordan, son of Robert, bur 1/27/1736.
Mary Gray, widow of George, bur 1/29/1736.
Joseph Huston bur 1/29/1737.

Nicholas Cassell bur 2/10/1737.
Abell Preston bur 2/20/1737.
Anthony Ludlow bur 3/6/1737.
Josiah Gates bur 3/16/1737.
Susanna Bond, wife of Thomas, bur 3/16/1737.
John Brinhart bur 2/17/1737.
Susanna Crokum bur 3/20/1737.
Sarah Key, wife of John, bur 3/24/1737.
Richard Townsend bur 3/30/1737.
Hannah Ogdon, wife of John, bur 5/22/1737.
Mary Mitchell, dau of Abraham, bur 5/28/1737.
Mary Emly, another dau of Samuel, bur 5/30/1737.
Mary Renshaw bur 6/2/1737.
John Harper bur 6/9/1737.
Mary Kirk, dau of James, bur 6/9/1737.
Sarah Williston, dau of Thomas, bur 6/24/177.
Susanna Dillwin, dau of John, bur 7/9/1737.
James Eriom bur 7/13/1737.
Benjamin Shoemaker, son of Benjamin, bur 7/16/1737.
Thomas Marl bur 7/17/1737.
John Trapnell bur 7/18/1737.
David Brooks bur 7/23/1737.
Sarah Williston, wife of Thomas, bur 7/25/1737.
Elizabeth Shout, dau of Thomas, bur 7/28/1737.
Sarah Hart, dau of John, bur 8/11/1737.
Hannah Brintnall, dau of John, bur 8/12/1737.
Liddia Ranstead, dau of Caleb, bur 8/20/1736.
Sarah Widdowfield, dau of John, dec'd, bur 8/20/1737.
Mary Redman, dau of Thomas, bur 9/8/1737.
Benjamin Sherman bur 9/18/1737.
Rachell Peel, wife of Anthony, bur 10/1/1737.
John Birmingham, son of Thomas, bur 10/4/1737.
Mary Dubree, dau of Jacob, Jr, bur 10/9/1737.
Samuel Bowles bur 10/12/1737.
Owen Evan, shoemaker, bur 12/26/1737-8.
Mary Johnson, dau of William, bur 1/7/1737-8.
Martha Guest, dau of John, bur 1/9/1737-8.
Mary Jervis, wife of Richard, bur 1/12/1737-8.
Cornelius Shours bur 1/13/1737-8.
Elizabeth Bittle bur 1/14/1737-8.
William Coates, son of Thomas, bur 1/26/1738.
John Bainbridge, son of James and Rachel, bur 2/2/1738.
Sarah Shoemaker, wife of Benjamin, bur 4/10/1738.
Mary Sansom, dau of Samuel, bur 4/11/1738.
Lydia Stretch, dau of Joseph and Lydia, bur 5/5/1738.

Mary Benezett, dau of Anthony and Joyce, bur 5/12/1738.
Anthony Morris, son of Samuel and Hannah, bur 5/15/1738.
Samuel Jobson, son of Samuel, bur 6/6/1738.
Mary Jackson, a young woman grown, dau of Stephen, bur 6/23/1738.
Hannah Tidmarsh, wife of William, d. 6/26/1738.
John Hains d. 6/26/1738.
John Stanton, son of Daniel, d. 7/5/1738.
Jane Halloway, wife of Thomas, d. 7/12/1738.
Elizabeth Flower, dau of Enoch, d. 7/25/1738.
Samuel Powell, shoemaker, d. 8/3/1738.
James Morris, son of James, d. 8/12/1738.
Clement Plumsted, son of William, d. 8/10/1738.
Sarah Price d. 8/12/1738.
Joseph Paschall d. 8/24/1738.
Giles Brimble d. 8/26/1738.
Mary Reynolds, dau of John and Mary, d. 8/31/1738.
Thomas Shute, Jr, d. 9/1/1738.
Jonathan Mifflin, son of Jonathan, d. 9/1/1738.
Mary Owen, widow of Evan, d. 9/13/1738.
Sarah Brown, dau of Peter, d. 9/15/1738.
Sarah Mekins, widow of Thomas, d. 9/18/1738.
Hannah Ogden, dau of John, d. 9/19/1738.
Hannah Robinson d. 9/20/1738.
Lydia Gray, wife of Samuel, d. 10/6/1738.
Mary Carlilse, dau of Abraham, d. 10/7/1738.
John Williams d. 10/8/1738.
Jacob Usher d. 10/10/1738.
John Prichard d. 10/10/1738.
Amy Widdowfield, dau of John, d. 11/2/1738.
William Thomas d. 10/14/1738.
William Clymer, son of Christopher, d. 10/15/1738.
William Griscom, son of Tobias, d. 11/13/1738.
Mary Fern d. 11/13/1738.
Mary Elfryth, wife of Jeremiah, d. 12/9/1738.
Robert Gerrard d. 12/18/1738.
Rachel Elfryth, dau of Jeremiah, d. 12/20/1738.
William Carter d. 12/21/1738.
Hannah Hastings, dau of Samuel, d. 12/24/1738.
Daniel Dawson, son of Daniel, d. 1/6/1738.
Elizabeth Howell d. 1/8/1738.
Daniel Willcox d. 1/9/1738.
John Prisgar, son of John, d. 1/11/1738.
Daniel Tucker, killed by a negro, 1/27/1739.
Catherine Chandler d. 1/31/1739.
William Johnson d. 2/1/1739.

Joan Kelly d. 2/12/1739.
John Paynter, son of Richard, d. 2/24/1739.
Susannah Lowns, dau of James, d. 3/12/1739.
Mary Williams d. 3/21/1739.
Thomas Wooleston, he used stools to walk with, d. 3/23/1739.
Mary Carlile, dau of Abraham, d. 5/2/1739.
Mary Allin, wife of Richard, d. 5/7/1739.
Hannah Kelton d. 5/23/1739.
Rachel Bainbridge, wife of James, d. 6/1/1739.
Ann Hitchcock, wife of Joseph, d. 6/15/1739.
Anna Cresson, dau of John, d. 6/7/1739.
Edward Fishbourne, son of William, d. 6/21/1739.
Elizabeth Syng, dau of Daniel, d. 6/24/1739.
Sarah Clifton, wife of John, d. 7/10/1739.
Charles Loftis, son of Ralph, d. 7/12/1739.
Mary Dubree, dau of Jacob, d. 7/17/1739.
Elizabeth Plumsted, dau of William and Rebecca, d. 7/21/1739.
Thomas Stretch, son of Joseph and Lydia, d. 7/21/1739.
Sarah Truman, son of Thomas, d. 7/22/1739.
Ann Cadwallader, dau of Thomas, d. 7/30/1739.
Daniell Standish d. 8/10/1739.
Mary Nichols, wife of Edward, d. 8/10/1739.
Nicholas Rogers d.. 8/12/1739.
Rachell Lowns, dau of James, d. 8/13/1739.
Richard Allen d. 8/14/1739.
Elizabeth Hall d. 8/26/1739.
Mary Taylor d. 8/29/1739.
John Roberts d. 9/5/1739.
Samuel Powell, son of Samuel, d. 9/6/1739.
Samuel Jobson d. 9/8/1739.
Clement Plumsted, son of William and Rebecca, d. 9/13/1739.
Elizabeth Joiners, wife of John, d. 9/25/1739.
Elizabeth Abbott d. 9/25/1739.
Mary Hopkins d. 10/1/1739.
Rebecca Tolier d. 10/3/1739.
Mary Peirce d. 10/5/1739.
William Robins d. 10/8/1739.
Joan Linton, wife of John, d. 10/13/1739.
Samuel Ashton, son of Samuel, d. 10/16/1739.
Francis Knowles d. 10/20/1739.
Joseph Parker, son of William, d. 10/25/1739.
Caleb Elfreth d. 10/31/1739.
Benjamin Fairman d. 11/1/1739.
Samuel Wells, son of Edward, d. 11/1/1739.
Patience Ratchford, dau of Solomon, d. 11/19/1739.

Dennis Ratchford d. 11/10/1739.
Susannah Morris d. 11/21/1739.
Elizabeth Ratchford, widow of Dennis, d. 11/28/1739.
Rachell Peasly, wife of Jonathan, d. 1/16/1739.
Elizabeth Clymer, dau of Christopher, d. 1/20/1739.
John Wister, son of John, d. 1/24/1739.
Sophia Armitt, wife of Richard, d. 1/25/1740.
John Abbott, son of Robert, d. 1/29/1740.
Phebe Zane, dau of Isaac, d. 2/2/1740.
Esther Warner, wife of Swan, d. 2/10/1740.
Susanna Lloyd, wife of Thomas, d. 2/10/1740.
Rebeccah Brockden, dau of Charles, d. 3/1/1740.
Deborah Clymer, dau of Christopher, d. 3/6/1740.
Isaac Zanes, son of Isaac, d. 3/7/1740.
Hugh Durborah d. 3/20/1740.
Nathaniell Griffitts d. 4/3/1740.
John Flower, son of Enoch, d. 4/3/1740.
Margrett Comer d. 4/8/1740.
Rebeccah Zanes, dau of Jona., d. 4/11/1740.
Solomon Fussell, son of Solomon, d. 4/12/1740.
John Powell, son of Samuel, dec'd, d. 4/22/1740.
Thomas Reece d. 4/27/1740.
Francis Wells d. 4/29/2740.
John Meredith, son of Reece, d. 4/30/1740.
William Haselton d. 5/4/1740.
Daniell Stanton, son of Daniell, d. 5/5/1740.
Hannah Jervis, son of John, d. 5/7/1740.
Joseph Hood, son of Daniel, d. 5/15/1740.
Isaac Warner, son of Edward, d. 5/15/1740.
John Warder, son of Jeremiah, d. 5/15/1740.
William Evans, son of Edward, d. 5/21/1740.
Joseph Dubree, son of Jacob, Jr, d. 5/24/1740.
Elizabeth Guess, son of John, d. 5/25/1740.
Margrett Robinson, dau of Thomas, d. 5/27/1740.
Elizabeth Peters, dau of Thomas, d. 5/28/1740.
Miriam Miller, widow, d. 6/18/1740.
Rebeccah Brockden, dau of Charles, d. 6/19/1740.
Elizabeth Robinson, dau of Thomas, d. 6/22/1740.
Mary Dawson, dau of Daniel, d. 6/25/1740.
Sarah Loyd d. 6/28/1740.
Elizabeth Scull, dau of James, d. 6/28/1740.
Mary Ashton, wife of Thomas, d. 7/18/1740.
Hannah Allen, wife of Nathaniell, d. 7/20/1740.
Elinor Hurst, dau of Thomas, d. 7/26/1740.
Elinor Acklin d. 8/14/1740.

John Holton, son of John, d. 8/18/1740.
Thomas Flower d. 8/19/1740.
Sarah Harry d. 9/13/1740.
John Clark, son of John, d. 9/14/1740.
Elizabeth Joyners, dau of John, d. 9/25/1740.
Elizabeth Abbott, widow, d. 9/25/1740.
William Davis d. 9/26/1740.
Agnes Akin d. 10/2/1740.
Elizabeth Goforth d. 10/8/1740.
Thomas Masters d. 10/18/1740.
Christian Garrigue, wife of Isaac, d. 10/29/1740.
Jacob Dubree d. 11/2/1740.
Rebeccah Plumsted, wife of William, d. 11/20/1740.
Mary Robins d. 11/29/1740.
Margrett Nichols, dau of Anthony, d. 1/18/1740.
Ann Griffitts, dau of Nathaniell, dec'd, d. 1/30/1741.
Edward Roberts d. 2/3/1741.
James Scull d. 2/3/1741.
James Vippin d. 3/15/1741.
Mary Carver, dau of Richard, d. 3/15/1741.
Deborah Cordry, wife of Hugh, d. 4/3/1741.
Susannah Guess, wife of John, d. 4/23/1741.
Beulah Coates d. 4/29/1741.
John Pennock, son of Samuel, d. 5/2/1741.
Mary Shoemaker d. 5/27/1741.
Oswell Peel d. 5/28/1741.
John Wood d. 6/2/1741.
John Jervis, son of John, d. 6/2/1741.
Owen Owen d. 6/6/1741.
Hannah Parker, dau of Alexander. d. 6/7/1741.
John Broadgate d. 6/12/1741 (a malignant yellow fever now
    spreads much).
Mary Nash, wife of Joseph, d. 6/16/1741.
Jacob Varnum d. 6/17/1741.
William Cadwill d. 6/18/1741.
Gabriell Winters d. 6/19/1741.
Peter Wishart d. 6.19.1741.
Benjamin Eastburn d. 6/20/1741.
John Evans, son of John, d. 6/24/1741.
Hannah Morris d. 6/25/1741.
James Steele, Jr, d. 6/28/1741.
Peter Brown, son of Peter, d. 6/29/1741.
Elizabeth Hatton, dau of Thomas, d. 6/30/1741.
Sarah Thomas, widow, d. 7/1/1741.
David Davis d. 7/3/1741.

John Ambler d. 7/5/1741.
Elizabeth Primmer, dau of Richard, d. 7/5/1741.
John Heaton d. 7/6/1741.
Samuel Shute d. 7/6/1741.
Mary Harley d. 7/7/1741.
Richard Orms d. 7/9/1741.
Griffith Owen d. 7/9/1741.
Deborah Powell, dau of Samuel, Jr, d. 7/11/1741.
Thomas Hatton d. 7/13/1741.
Samuel Fisher d. 7/15/1741.
Thomas Hogg, son of Thomas Hogg, d. 7/16/1741.
Sarah Woods, widow, d. 7/17/1741.
John Haselton, son of William, d. 7/25/1741.
Margrett Rhodes, dau of Jacob, d. 7/25/1741.
Martha Cooms, dau of John, d. 7/29/1741.
Elizabeth Hill, wife of Hugh, d. 8/6/1741.
Sarah Curey, dau of William and Sarah, d. 8/14/1741.

"Our dear and worthy friends being on a religious visit at the Island of
    Tortola there died and were buried by the side of each other to the
    best of my information, as follows: Thomas Chalkley the 3rd day of
    the 9th month, 1741; John Cadwallader about the 26th day of the 9th
    month, 1741; John Estaugh the 6th day of the 10th month, 1741".

Captain John Richmond d. 8/15/1741.
Abraham Carlisle d. 8/19/1741.
Mary Carlisle, wife of Abraham, Jr, d. 8/19/1741.
Samuel Jones, son of John, bolter, d. 8/29/1741.
Charles Townsend, son of Charles, d. 8/31/1741.
Caleb Burchell d. 9/8/1741.
John Cannon, son of William, d. 9/8/1741.
Jane Clark, wife of John, d. 9/16/1741.
William Walton d. 9/16/1741.
Hannah Eldridge, dau of Obediah and Mary, d. 9/20/1741.
Joseph Costord, son of John, d. 9/21/1741.
William Langdall, son of John, d. 9/21/1741.
Miriam Sharp. son of James, d. 9/23/1741.
Esther Parker, wife of George, d. 9/24/1741.
Abraham Leddon d. 9/30/1741.
William Clare d. 10/5/1741.
Ann Holland, wife of William, d. 10/7/1741.
Grace Price, wife of David, d. 10/8/1741.
Stephen Stapler d. 10/10/1741.
Mary Warren, dau of Isaac, d. 10/12/1741.
Martha Powell, dau of Samuel, d. 10/14/1741.

William Rawle d. 10/16/1741.
Joseph Paschall d. 10/26/1741.
Isaac Norris, son of Isaac and Sarah, d. 11/1/1741.
Martha Walker d. 11/4/1741.
Peter Marriott d. 11/7/1741.
Jonathan Jones, son of Jacob, d. 11/7/1741.
Ann Rakestraw d. 11/10/1741.
Samuell Griscom, son of Tobias, d. 12/7/1741.
Alexander Bullard d. 12/8/1741.
Deborah Cassell, wife of Nicholas, d. 12/20/1741.
Mary Mode, dau of William, d. 12/28/1741.
James Steele d. 1/5/1741.
Margret Simms, wife of John, d. 1/5/1741.
Martin Jervis d. 2/23/1742.
Elizabeth Chandler, widow, d. 2/25/1742.
Simon Edgell d. 2/26/1742.
Sarah Knowles, dau of Francis, dec'd, d. 3/16/1742.
William Fishbourne d. 3/29/1742.
Elizabeth Morris, wife of James, d. 4/3/1742.
Mary Mifflin, dau of John, d. 4/3/1742.
John Dilwyn, son of John, d. 4/11/1742.
Mary Armitt, dau of Joseph, d. 4/12/1742.
Elizabeth Shute, wife of Joseph, d. 5/3/1742.
Honnor Harmer, formerly Honnor Oxley, d. 5/4/1742.
Joseph Taylor d. 5/6/1742.
Mary Davis, dau of Joseph, d. 5/7/1742.
Hannah Mode, wife of William, d. 5/9/1742.
Amy Dowty d. 5/10/1742.
Thomas Bissell, son of William, d. 5/11/1742.
John Sansom, son of Samuel, d. 5/11/1742.
Mary Rhodes, dau of Adam, d. 5/14/1742.
Sarah Siddon, dau of Samuel, d. 5/14/1742.
Martha Biddle, dau of John, d. 5/14/1742.
Norton Prior, son of Norton, d. 5/15/1742.
Elizabeth Miflin, dau of John, d. 5/18/1742.
James Chetham, son of Joseph, d. 5/18/1742.
Elizabeth Jones, dau of Charles, d. 5/19/1742.
Beulah Reynolds, dau of John, d. 5/20/1742.
Elizabeth Kinsey, dau of John, d. 5/20/1742.
Jonathan Varnum, son of Jonathan, d. 5/21/1742.
Deborah Loyd d. 5/21/1742.
Hannah Jordan, dau of Robert, d. 5/21/1742.
John Jones d. 5/29/1742.
Ann Dudley d. 5/29/1742.
Ann Bittle, dau of John, d. 5/29/1742.

Isaac Warner, son of John, d. 6/1/1742.
William Dawson, son of Isaac, d. 6/4/1742.
Job Goodson d. 6/6/1742.
William Wister, son of John, d. 6/7/1742.
James Claypoole, son of James, d. 6/12/1742.
George Cassell, son of Nicholas, d. 6/14/1742.
Anthony Morris, son of Samuel and Hannah, d. 6/15/1742.
Joseph Drinker, d. 6/17/1742.
James Barker d. 6/20/1742.
Deborah Dawson, dau of Daniel, d. 6/22/1742.
Margarett Preston, wife of Samuel, d. 6/23/1742.
Sarah Mitchell d. 6/24/1742.
Mary Dubree, dau of Joseph, d. 6/24/1742.
Rebeccah Renshaw, dau of Richard, d. 6/24/1742.
Samuel Jordan, son of Robert and Mary, d. 7/2/1742.
James Morris, son of James, d. 7/3/1742.
Samuell Siddon d. 7/11/1742.
Sarah Kelly d. 7/11/1742.
Elizabeth Edgell, dau of Mary, d. 7/23/1742.
Esther Clare d. 8/3/1742.
Robert Jordan d. 8/7/1742.
Joseph Lynn d. 8/13/1742.
Samuel Ashton d. 8/29/1742.
William Shelly, son of Abraham, d. 8/30/1742.
Elizabeth Jones, widow of John, d. 9/21/1742.
James Robinson d. 9/23/1742.
Mary Snead d. 9/26/1742.
Isaac Nicholson, son of Joshua, d. 9/28/1742.
Sarah Flower d. 10/3/1742.
Nathaniell Griffits, son of Elizabeth, d. 10/8/1742.
William Hudson d. 10/17/1742.
Sarah Stretch d. 11/6/1742.
Mary Cathrill, dau of Edward, d. 11/6/1742.
Ann Biles, dau of Jonathan, d. 11/18/1742.
Ann Sciamn, dau of John, d. 11/22/1742.
John Dawson d. 11/27/1742.
John Ogden d. 12/6/1742.
William Woodley d. 12/16/1742.
Elizabeth Singleton, dau of John, d. 12/23/1742.
Charles Roberts d. 1/4/1742.
George Wharton, son of Joseph, d. 1/7/1742.
Hannah Sciamn, dau of John, d. 1/8/1742.
Joanna Morgan, wife of Evan, d. 1/9/1742.
Ann Owen, widow of Owen, d. 2/4/1743.
Reese Loyd d. 2/5/1743.

John Perry d. 2/8/1743.
Mathew Robinson d. 2/14/1743.
Lydia Condell d. 3/2/1743.
Isabel Marshall, dau of Christopher, d. 3/4/1743.
Margrett Nichols d. 3/11/1743.
John Loyd, son of Mordecai, d. 3/18/1743.
John Oxley d. 2/23/1743.
Samuell Redman, son of Thomas, d. 4/3/1743.
Joice Brown, dau of Thomas, d. 4/9/1743.
William Clare, son of John, d. 4/14/1743.
Dinah Glover d. 4/19/1743.
John Reed d. 4/21/1743.
Elizabeth Shute, dau of William, d. 4/22/1743.
Anthony Benezett, son of Anthony, d. 4/23/1743.
Nathaniel Ritter d. 4/24/1743.
John Stevenson, son of James, d. 5/1/1743.
Ann Loftis, dau of Ralph, d. 5/3/1743.
Phineas Pemberton, son of Israel and Sarah, d. 5/9/1743.
John Key d. 5/10/1743.
Joseph Brown, son of Isaac, d. 5/10/1743.
Robert Owen d. 5/14/1743.
Isaac Norris, son of Isaac and Sarah, d. 5/14/1743.
Joshua Lawrence d. 5/15/1743.
Tilton Brown, son of Isaac, d. 5/21/1743.
John Jenkins, son of Stephen and Hannah, d. 5/22/1743.
Richard Prior, son of Norton, d. 5/23/1743.
Hannah Warner, dau of Edward and Ann, d. 5/24/1743.
Abigail Clark, dau of Benjamin, d. 5/26/1743.
Mary Jervis d. 5/27/1743.
John Hart d. 5/29/1743.
Joell Neave d. 6/8/1643.
Spicer Brown, son of Isaac, d. 6/3/1743.
Jonathan Slatter d. 6/8/1743.
Sarah Thompson, wife of Robert, d. 6/11/1743.
Cherrish Gates d. 6/11/1743.
Sarah Massey. dau of Wight, d. 6/11/1743.
Sarah Mitchell, wife of Thomas, d. 6/18/1743.
Samuel Coates, son of Samuel, d. 6/22/1743.
Abraham Bickley d. 6/23/1743.
Elizabeth Durberah, wife of Joseph, d. 6/27/1743.
John Jones, son of Charles, d. 6/27/1743.
Mary Cathrill, dau of Edward and Rachell, d. 7/6/1743.
Samuel Preston d. 7/12/1743.
Elizabeth Townsend d. 7/16/1743.
Cadwallader Foulke d. 7/17/1743.

Elizabeth Boulds d. 7/21/1743.
Esther Sewers, wife of Francis, d. 7/23/1743.
Sarah Shute d. 7/28/1743.
Ann Sugar, wife of Thomas, d. 8/2/1743.
Hannah Roberts, dau of Hugh, d. 8/7/1743.
John Chamberlain d. 8/17/1743.
Rebeccah Cresson, dau of John, d. 8/19/1743.
Margrett Walker d. 9/1/1743.
Mary Wood, wife of Joseph, d. 10/14/1743.
Sarah Whitelock, dau of Isaac, d. 10/23/1743.
Ann Pound d. 10/29/1743.
Mary Needham d. 11/7/1743.
Mary Paschall, dau of Benjamin, d. 11/8/1743.
Nathan Trotter, son of Nathan, d. 11/31/1743.
James Trotter, son of Joseph, d. 11/19/1743.
Benjamin Clark d. 11/29/1743.
Martha Bennett, dau of William, d. 12/3/1743.
Elizabeth Condell, wife of William, d. 12/9/1743.
James Lowns, Jr, d. 12/16/1743.
John Jones, late of Merioneth, d. 12/26/1743.
Mary Denton d. 1/22/1743.
Sarah Massey d. 1/23/1743.
Amy Lawrence, dau of Amy. d. 2/8/1744.
William Hurst, son of William, d. 2/24/1744.
Antho: Sturgis d. 3/7/1744.
Amos Lewis d. 3/16/1744.
Coleman Fisher, son of William, d. 3/23/1744.
Benjamin Tomlinson d. 4/5/1744.
Robert Bittle, son of John, d. 4/6/1744.
Thomas Loftis, son of Ralph, d. 4/6/1744.
Timothy Saunders, son of Joseph, d. 4/9/1744.
Alice Campbell, wife of Thomas, d. 4/13/1744.
Joseph Eldridge, son of Obadiah, d. 4/13/1744.
Abraham Mitchell. son of Abraham, d. 4/15/1744.
Thomas Singleton, son of John, d. 4/20/1744.
Mary Stretch, dau of Thomas, d. 4/27/1744.
Thomas Jones d. 4/28/1744.
Mary Green, dau of John, d. 4/30/1744.
Robert Jones, son of Robert, d. 5/1/1744.
Grace Richardson, dau of Joseph, d. 5/5/1744.
Mary Kinsey, dau of John, d. 5/7/1744.
James Parker, son of William, d. 5/12/1744.
Elizabeth Williamson, dau of Mathew, d. 5/17/1744.
Richard Saunders d. 5/22/1744.
George Willson, son of George, d. 5/26/1744.

Mary Cruck d. 5/30/1744.
Tabitha Fisher d. 6/5/1744.
Stephen Simmons d. 6/5/1744.
Mary Atkinson, dau of William, d. 6/10/1744.
John Stanton, son of Daniel, d. 6/17/1744.
Margrett Morgner d. 6/18/1744.
Lydia Stretch, dau of Joseph, d. 6/18/1744.
Elizabeth Brimble d. 6/19/1744.
John Body d. 6/23/1744.
John Moor d. 6/24/1744.
Thomas James, son of Edward, d. 6/24/1744.
Elizabeth Shelly, dau of Abraham, d. 6/27/1744.
Deborah Cooper, dau of Jacob, d. 6/28/1744.
Ann Ingram, wife of John, d. 7/2/1744.
Samuel Evans, son of Jonathan, d. 7/4/1744.
Hannah Carver d. 7/18/1744.
Enoch Coates d. 7/20/1744.
Rebeccah Hog d. 7/22/1744.
Sarah Logan, dau of William, d. 7/23/1744.
Thomas Somner d. 8/3/1744.
Mary Reynolds, dau of John, d. 8/8/1744.
Jonathan Peasley d. 8/12/1744.
Isaiah Warner d. 8/13/1744.
Sarah Norris, wife of Isaac, d. 6/15/1744.
Thomas Roberts, son of Mary, d. 8/19/1744.
John Baker d. 8/20/1744.
Martha James, wife of Joseph. d. 8/21/1744.
Zachariah Williams d. 8/22/1744.
Abraham Whitehall d. 8/23/1744.
Thomas Powell, son of Samuel, d. 8/23/1744.
Alice Rochford, wife of Solomon, d. 9/6/1744.
Thomas Annis d. 9/7/1744.
Elizabeth Redman, dau of Thomas, d. 9/11/1744.
Eliza Hard, aged 90 and past, d. 9/18/1744.
Tace Price, dau of Isachar, d. 9/24/1744.
Hannah Cresson, wife of Solomon, d. 10/1/1744.
Peter Brown, son of Peter, d. 10/1/1744.
Thomas Gardner, son of Joseph, d. 10/2/1744.
Mary Warder, dau of Jeremiah, d. 10/5/1744.
Everard Bolton d. 10/9/1744.
Lydia Williams d. 10/11/1744.
Sarah Coates, dau of Samuel, d. 10/13/1744.
Richard Warder d. 10/14/1744.
Septimus Austin, son of Samuel, d. 10/16/1744.
Joseph Clerk, son of David, d. 10/18/1744.

Jonathan Peters, son of Hannah, d. 11/9/1744.
Penelope Whitehead d. 11/18/1744.
Deborah Clifton, dau of John, d. 11/18/1744.
Mary Thompson, wife of Christopher, d. 11/20/1744.
John Tompkins d. 12/10/1744.
Benjamin Paschall d. 12/14/1744.
Peter Loyd d. 12/17/1744.
Sarah Wagstaff, wife of James, d. 12/25/1744.
Mary Biddle d. 1/4/1744.
Sarah Marshall, dau of Thomas, d. 1/7/1744.
Katherine Fisher, wife of John, d. 1/9/1744.
Mary Siddon, wife of Antho:, d. 1/18/1744.
Stephen Armitt, son of Stephen and Sarah, d. 2/7/1745.
Sarah Hayward d. 2/10/1745.
John Bittle, son of John, d. 2/24/1745.
Mary Mason d. 2/26/1745.
Priscilla Brown, wife of Peter, d. 2/27/1745.
Thomas Hornby d. 3/15/1745.
Joseph Tempas, son of Joseph, d. 3/22/1745.
Clement Plumsted d. 3/26/1745.
Hannah James, dau of Thomas, d. 4/4/1745,
Daniel England d. 4/5/1745.
Ann Shute, wife of Atwood, d. 4/11/1745,
Thomas Hill, son of Hugh, d. 4/12/1745.
Sarah Winter d. 4/19/1745.
Sarah Howell, dau of John, d. 4/24/1745.
John Furnis, son of Thomas, d. 4/26/1745.
Thomas Saunders, son of Peter, d. 4/29/1745.
John Young d. 5/1/1745.
William Fisher, son of Thomas, d. 5/5/1745.
Sarah Parrock d. 5/6/1745.
Francis Trimble, son of Francis, d. 5/7/1745.
Jonathan Paschall, son of Stephen, d. 5/7/1745.
Thomas Jones, son of Lewis, d. 5/8/1745.
Samuel Davis, son of James, d. 5/8/1745.
Richard Robinson d. 5/9/1745.
Deborah Foulke, dau of Judah, d. 5/9/1745.
Isaac Shute, son of Isaac, d. 5/10/1745.
William Burge d. 5/10/1745.
Robert Bewen, son of Thomas, d. 5/14/1745.
John Nailer d. 5/22/1745.
John Shelley, son of Abraham, d. 5/23/1745.
Daniell Radley d. 5/24/1745.
Elizabeth Pole, dau of John, d. 5/25/1745.
Charles Wardell, son of William, d. 5/26/1745.

David Kinsey, son of John, d. 5/26/1745.
Sarah Mifflin, wife of Jonathan, d. 5/29/1745.
John Clare, son of John, d. 6/4/1745.
Joseph Nailer, son of Elizabeth, d.6/7/1745.
George Parker d. 6/8/1745.
Mary Zanes, dau of Jonathan, d. 6/8/1745.
Mary Jackson d. 6/14/1745.
Jonathan Mifflin, son of Jonathan, d. 6/16/1745.
Elizabeth Elfreth, dau of Mary, d. 6/19/1745.
John Dilwyn, son of John, d. 6/21/1745.
Isaac Hill, son of James, d. 6/26/1745.
Jane Evans, dau of Edward, d. 7/6/1745.
Mary Hicks, dau of Augustine, d. 7/8/1745.
Martha Rawles d. 7/18/1745.
Rachell Cruckshanks, wife of Alexander, d. 7/20/1745.
Thomas Strickland d. 7/26/1745.
Samuel Redman d. 8/2/1745.
Martha Bankson, dau of Peter, d. 8/3/1745.
Thomas Tolbert d. 8/8/1745.
Hannah Cresson, dau of John, d. 8/16/1745.
Joseph James d. 8/30/1745.
Benjamin Trotter, son of Nathan, d. 9/3/1745.
Elizabeth Henderson d. 9/4/1745.
Hannah Pierson d. 9/8/1745.
Rebeccah Kearney d. 9/13/1745.
Adam Lewis d. 9/15/1745.
Lydia Peel d. 9/23/1745.
David Evans d. 9/26/1745.
Mary Prisgar, dau of Mary, d. 10/8/1745.
Jane Lightfoot, wife of William, d. 10/11/1745.
Elizabeth Tomkins, dau of Elizabeth, d. 10/15/1745.
Rebeccah Evans, dau of Edward, d. 10/22/1745.
Mary Lewis, dau of Hannah, d. 10/26/1745.
John Massey, son of Wight, d. 10/29/1745.
Samuel Norris d. 11/5/1745.
Elizabeth Burge d. 11/19/1745.
Richard Saunders d. 11/21/1745.
Samuel Reynolds, son of John, d. 11/30/1745.
Sarah Cart d. 12/7/1745.
John Cresson, son of John, d. 12/11/1745.
Elizabeth Sansom, dau of Samuel, d. 12/14/1745.
Jeremiah Marle, son of John, d. 12/20/1745.
Daniel Dawson d. 1/1/1746.
George Chandler d. 2/9/1746.
John Koster d. 2/20/2746.

Priscilla Thomas d. 3/4/1746.
Isaac Woodward d. 3/5/1746.
Martha Roberts d. 3/8/1746.
James Cresson d. 3/25/1746.
Charles Kinesly d. 3/28/1746.
Deborah Fisher, dau of Thomas, d. 3/29/1746.
John Maccoombs d. 4/1/1746.
Martha Eldridge, dau of Obediah, d. 4/1/1746.
John Cruckshank, son of Alexander, d. 4/1/1746.
Sarah Jervis, dau of John, d. 4/3/1746.
Frances McCormish, dau of Patrick, d. 4/7/1846.
Hannah McCormish, dau of Patrick, d. 4/12/1746.
Benjamin Wood, d. 4/14/1746.
John Maule, son of Thomas, d. 4/15/1746.
James Haines, son of John, d. 4/15/1746.
Martha Roberts, dau of Rachel, d. 4/15/1746.
Robert Thompson d. 4/19/1746.
Thomas Husherson d. 4/19/1746.
Henry Clifton d. 4/20/1846.
Christian Brown d. 4/26/1746.
Hugh Hill d. 4/28/1746.
Evan Evans, son of Evan, d. 4/28/1746.
Ann Mccornish, dau of Patrick, d. 4/30/1746.
Mary Jackman, wife of Thomas, d. 7/9/1745.
Jane Taylor, dau of John, d. 7/17/1745.
Henry Drinker d. 5/1/1746.
Samuel Stanton, son of Daniel, d. 5/2/1746.
Grace Pole, dau of John, d. 5/3/1746.
James Moon d. 5/4/2746.
Elizabeth Jackson d. 5/6/1746.
Anthony Noble d. 5/8/1746.
Benjamin Blacklidge d. 5/10/1746.
Martha Hurst d. 5/11/1746.
Enis Sidon, son of Job, d. 5/12/1746.
Margrett Sharp d. 5/13/1746.
Mary Saul, dau of Joseph, d. 5/13/1746.
Andrew Robertson, son of Thomas, d. 5/14/1746.
John Dennis, son of Henry, d. 5/15/1746.
Barbara Jones d. 5/17/1746.
Hannah Dubree, dau of Joseph, d. 5/17/1746.
Mary Davis, dau of William, d. 5/17/1746.
Sarah Page, dau of John, d. 5/21/1746.
Elizabeth Pole, dau of John, d. 5/24/1746.
Hannah Lownes, dau of Joseph, d. 5/25/1746.
Ambrose Doile d. 5/26/1746.

Margery Stretch, wife of Peter, d. 5/27/1746.
Daniel Parker, son of William, d. 5/30/1746.
Mary Warder, dau of Jeremiah, d. 5/30/1746.
Sarah Pemberton, wife of Israel, Jr, d. 6/1/1746.
John Guest, son of John, d. 6/1/1746.
William Davis, son of William, d. 6/2/1746.
Martha Davis, dau of James, d. 6/3/1746.
Evan Rhodes, son of Adam. d. 6/4/1746.
George Peters, son of Benjamin, d. 6/6/1746.
Phebe Parry d. 6/7/1746.
Thomas Shaw, son of John, d. 6/8/1746.
Elizabeth Massey, wife of Wight, d. 6/9/1746.
Thomas Hawkins d. 6/9/1746.
John Morriss, son of John, d. 6/9/1746.
John Brientnall, son of John, d. 6/9/1746.
Thomas Hilbourn, son of John, d. 6/10/1746.
Hannah Mifflin, dau of Benjamin, d. 6/10/1746.
Priscilla Roberts, dau of Isaac, d. 6/11/1746.
Mary Pennock, dau of Samuel, d. 6/12/1746.
Hannah Wolley, dau of Thomas, d. 6/12/1746.
Sarah Nailer, dau of Elizabeth, d. 6/13/1746.
Jane Hinton, wife of William, d. 6/14/1746.
Sarah Peters, dau of Benjamin, d. 6/14/ 1746.
Priscilla Each, dau of Gideon, d. 6/14/1746.
Jordan Brow, son of Thomas, d. 6/16/1746.
Sarah Hoskins d. 6/17/1746.
Sarah Richardson, wife of Joseph, d. 6/17/1746.
Sarah Clifford, dau of Thomas, d. 6/17/1746.
Mary Brown, wife of Preserve, d. 6/18/1746.
Robert Dawson d. 6/20/1746.
Rachell Peters, wife of Benjamin, d. 6/20/1746.
Mary Phillips, dau of Mary, d. 6/20/1746.
Elizabeth Evans, dau of Jonathan, d. 6/26/1746.
Elizabeth Zanes, dau of Ebenezer, d. 6/28/1746.
Benjamin Redman, son of Thomas, 6/29/1746.
Henry Paul, son of Joseph, d. 6/27/1746.
George James d. 6/31/1746.
Ann Griscom, dau of Tobias, d. 7/1/1746.
Thomas Davis, son of Christian, d. 7/4/1747.
Simon Edgell d. 7/7/1746.
Christian Davis, dau of Christian, d. 7/10/1746.
Grace Bayes, dau of Mary, d. 7/11/1746.
Silus Priers, son of Silus, f. 7/13/1746.
Mary Priers, dau of Silus, d. 7/13/1746.
Jonathan Vorell, son of Robert, d. 7/23/1746.

Jane Jelson d. 7/25/1746.
William Wardell d. 7/26/2746.
Rachell Price, dau of Isachar, d. 7/26/1746.
Elizabeth Hughs, wife of William, d. 8/3/1746.
William Brooks, son of Edward, d. 8/8/1746.
Mary Hooten, dau of John, d. 8/13/1746.
Nehemiah Allen d. 8/14/1746.
Elizabeth Tomlinson, dau of Ebenezer, d. 8/15/1746.
Andrew Creamer d. 8/22/1746.
Christopher Dingey d. 8/22/1746.
Solomon Cresson d. 9/10/1746.
Peter Stretch d. 9/11/1746.
Mary Walker, dau of Thomas, d. 9/11/1746.
Mary Christopher d. 9/14/1746.
Samuel Lobdale, son of Isaac, d. 9/20/1746.
Thomas Mitchell, son of John, d. 9/25/1746.
Sarah Righton d. 9/29/1746.
Ellis Pew d. 10/3/1746.
Elizabeth Brown, dau of Peter, d. 10/3/1746.
Jane Landale, dau of John, d. 10/3/1746.
Margrett Hill, wife of James, d. 10/5/1746.
Thomas Griffitts d. 10/10/1746.
David Elwell d. 10/15/1746. about 30 years.
John Renshaw, son of Richard, d. 10/19/1746.
William Lingard d. 10/27/1746.
Israell Jones d. 10/28/1746.
Margrett Simms, dau of John, d. 10/31/1746.
Sarah Robinson d. 11/9/1746.
Robert Hind d. 11/15/1746.
Mary Marriott, wife of Thomas, d. 11/17/1746.
Jane Vanaker, wife of Henry, d. 11/25/1746.
Ann Hill, dau of James, d. 11/27/1746.
Hannah Richardson, wife of Joseph, d. 12/4/1746.
Ann Guess. dau of Jonathan, d. 1/7/1747.
Isabel Carver, wife of John, d. 1/16/1747.
John Durborah d. 1/22/1747.
Sarah Griscom, dau of Samuel, d. 1/25/1747.
Hannah Knight, dau of John, d. 2/2/1747.
Rebeccah Redman d. 2/14/1747.
Martha Cadwallader d. 2/16/1747.
Elizabeth Jones, dau of Jacob, d. 2/17/1747.
Susanna Roberts, dau of Hugh, d. 2/18/1747.
Robert Strettle, Jr, d. 2/28/1747.
Sarah Shoemaker, dau of Thomas, d. 3/1/1747.
Tabitha Campbell, wife of Thomas, d. 3/16/1747.

Thomas Cross d. 3/17/1747.
Joshua Johnson d. 3/22/1747.
Rachell Wharton d. 4/10/1747.
Thomas Croasdell d. 4/13/1747.
John Brientnall d. 4/22/1747.
Elizabeth Shelly, dau of Abraham, d. 4/27/1747.
Ann Guess, dau of John, d. 5/5/1747.
William Clark, son of William, d. 5/8/1847.
David Ewell, son of Mary, d. 5/15/1747.
Joseph Saunders, son of Joseph, d. 5/16/1747.
Rebeccah Paschall, dau of Stephen, d. 5/17/1747.
Ann Pledwell, wife of Edward, d. 5/18/1747.
Jane Waln d. 5/18/1747.
Hannah Pennock, dau of Samuel, d. 5/18/1747.
Margrett Langdall, dau of John, d. 5/18/1747.
Joseph Armitt d. 5/19/1747.
William Carmalt, son of Jonathan, d. 5/19/1747.
Sarah Jones, dau of Joseph, d. 5/25/1747.
Samuel Head, son of John Jr, d. 5/25/1747.
William Sandwith, son of Samuel, d. 5/30/1747.
Margrett Hooton, son of Benjamin, d. 5/31/1747.
William Whitepain, son of Zachariah, d. 6/2/1747.
Shimah Brockden, dau of Elizabeth, d. 6/2/1747.
John Ingram d. 6/3/1747.
Joseph Morris, son of Joseph, d. 6/3/1747.
William Curry, son of William, d. 6/3/1747.
John Bittle, son of John, d. 6/3/1747.
Elizabeth Hart, son of Thomas, d. 6/3/1747.
John Class, son of Humphrey, d. 6/3/1747.
Israell Ryall d. 6/4/1747.
Jane Paschall, dau of William, d. 6/4/1747.
Christian Broadgate, wife of Thomas, d. 6/6/1747.
Mary Mitchell, dau of Thomas, d. 6/7/1747.
Jacob Durborow, son of Jacob, d. 6/7/1747.
Samuel Paschall, son of Stephen, d. 6/9/1747.
James Morris, son of Joseph, d. 6/10/1747.
Lydia Mitchell, dau of Abraham, d. 6/10/1747.
Hannah Burchall, dau of Rebecca, d. 6/11/1747.
Abigail Jenkins, dau of Charles, d. 6/11/1747.
Sarah Flower, dau of Enoch, d. 6/11/1747.
Stephen Armitt, son of Stephen, d. 6/14/1747.
Thomas Snow, son of Peter, d. 6/16/1747.
Mary Marshall, dau of Joseph, d. 6/19/1747.
William Clare, son of John, d. 6/20/1747.
Peter Snow, son of Peter, d. 6/23/1747.

John Hilbourn d. 6/24/1747.
Charles Brockden, Jr, d. 6/24/1747.
Mary Carmack d. 6/24/1747.
Jane Pemberton, dau of Israel, Jr, d. 6/24/1747.
David Davis, son of Lydia, d. 6/25/1747.
Ann Atwood, wife of William, d. 6/26/1747.
Lydia Stretch, dau of Joseph, d. 6/26/1747.
Samuel Jones, son of Charles, d. 6/27/1747.
Langdale Coates, son of Samuel, d. 6/29/1747.
Daniel Zanes, son of Israel, d. 6/30/1747.
Joseph Palmer, son of Blandina, d. 6/30/1747.
Jane Worrell, dau of Robert, d. 7/3/1747.
Rebeccah Hogg d. 7/4/1747.
Hannah Robinson, dau of Thomas, d. 7/4/1747.
Samuel Morris, son of Daniel, d. 7/7/1747.
Elizabeth Stretch, dau of Thomas, d. 7/8/1747.
John Palmer, son of Blandina, d. 7/8/1747.
Joseph Wells, son of Edward, d. 7/9/1747.
Ann Rakestraw, dau of William, d. 7/9/1747.
Elizabeth Gray, dau of Samuel, Jr, d. 7/12/1747.
John Fletcher d. 7/13/1747.
Joseph Marshall, son of Thomas, d. 7/13/1747.
Joseph Atkinson, son of William, d. 7/13/1747.
Elizabeth Wells, dau of Edward, d. 7/15/1747.
Ann Smith, dau of Christian, d. 7/17/1747.
Thomas Redman d. 7/17/1747.
John Boice d. 7/17/1747.
Sarah Hood, wife of Thomas, d. 7/17/1747.
William Garrigue, son of Isaac, d. 7/18/1747.
Gideon Each, son of Gideon, d. 719/1747.
Isaac Garrigue, son of Isaac, d. 7/22/1747.
Samuel Powell, Jr, 7/23/1747.
Mary Erwin d. 7/24/1747.
Jesse Bourne d. 7/25/1747.
Jane Roberts, dau of Hugh, d. 7/25/1747.
Mary Garwood, dau of Martha, d. 7/28/1747.
Richard Hazelton, son of Miriam, d. 8/1/1747.
Sarah Williams d. 8/2/1747.
Martha Lincorn, dau of Mary, d. 8/2/1747.
Elizabeth Marles, dau of Jesse, d. 8/2/1747.
Mary Stephens, dau of Jane, d. 8/6/1747.
John Marshall, son of Joseph, d. 8/7/1747.
Jacob Howell, son of Joseph, d. 8/11/1747.
John Jackson, son of Samuel, d. 8/13/1747.
Ann Pierce d. 8/18/1747.

Joseph Thomas, son of Moses, d. 8/25/1747.
John Flower, son of Enoch, d. 8/27/1747.
Lewyn Taylor, son of Isaac, d. 8/31/1747.
Blandina Palmer d. 9/4/1747.
Thomas Mitchell d. 9/6/1747.
Mary Taylor, dau of Isaac, d. 9/13/1747.
Samuel Rhodes, son of Adam, d. 9/13/1747.
Sarah Ingram d. 9/18/1747.
Elizabeth Robinson, dau of Thomas, d. 9/18/1747.
Sarah England, daughter of Thomas, d. 9/19/1747.
Joseph Richards d. 10/4/1747.
James Sharp d. 10/4/1747.
Sarah Walker d. 10/9/1747.
Mary Lyons, dau of Mary, d. 10/14/1747.
Abraham Carlisle 10/16/1747.
Benjamin Peters d. 10/16/1747.
Sarah Clifton d. 10/19/1747.
Mary Hooten, dau of Benjamin, d. 10/20/1747.
James Cresson, son of Sarah, d. 10/23/1747.
Joseph Clifton, son of John, d. 10/29/1747.
Thomas Redman, son of Penelope, d. 10/29/1747.
Jonathan Varnon d. 10/31/1747.
Gideon Each d. 11/3/1747.
Benjamin Mifflin, son of John, d. 11/14/1747.
Elizabeth Lightfoot, dau of Thomas, d. 11/18/1747.
Joseph Paul, son of Joseph, d. 11/20/1747.
Hannah Duncan, wife of Robert, d. 11/25/1747.
Jean Guess, dau of Jonathan, d. 11/25/1747.
Edward Wells d. 11/29/1747.
Thomas Cannon, son of Sarah, d. 11/29/1747.
Elizabeth Durborah, dau of Joseph, d. 12/4/1747.
John Loftus, son of Ralph, d. 12/8/1747.
Hannah Cox d. 12/17/1747.
Joseph Haines, son of John, d. 12/21/1747.
George House, son of Joseph, d. 12/27/1747.
David Davis d. 1/4/1747.
Tomasin Mickle, wife of Samuel, d. 1/9/1747.
Joseph Butler, son of Deborah, d. 1/12/1747.
Nathaniel Pool d. 1/13/1747.
Joseph Hallowell, son of Joseph, d. 1/21/1747.
Elizabeth Scull, dau of Jasper, d. 1/21/1747.
Joseph Gardner d. 1/23/1747.
Elizabeth Hallowell, dau of Joseph, d. 1/24/1747.
Jane Bolton d. 1/25/1747.
Sarah Stanton, dau of Daniel, d. 2/3/1748.

Elizabeth Coates, dau of Thomas, d. 2/4/1748.
Hannah Shelton d. 2/7/1748.
Josiah Stanton, son of Daniel, d. 2/9/1748.
Elizabeth Parker, wife of William, d. 2/17/1748.
Mary Carlilse d. 2/21/1748.
Hannah Empson d. 3/1/1748.
Mary Norris d. 3/3/1748.
Sarah Annis, dau of William, d. 3/3/1748.
Hannah King, dau of Joseph, d. 3/9/1748.
William Tidmarsh d. 3/12/1748.
Mary Hind d. 3/12/1748.
John Williams d. 3/15/1748.
Charles Pemberton d. 3/23/1748.
Mary Austen, dau of Samuel, d. 3/26/1748.
Ann Chads d. 3/27/1748.
William Fisher, son of Thomas, d. 3/30/1748.
Ann Abbott, dau of Samuel, d. 4/4/1748.
Hezediah Shaw d. 4/5/1748.
William Trotter, son of William, d. 4/6/1748.
Mary McNabb, dau of John, d. 4/9/1748.
Elizabeth England, dau of Thomas, d. 4/4/1748.
Mary Maull, dau of Thomas, d. 4/14/1748.
Hugh Fitzrandolph d. 4/23/1748.
Sarah Scull, dau of Jasper, d. 5/1/1748.
William Annis d. 5/7/1748.
Violl Chubb d. 5/8/1748.
Sarah Richardson, dau of Francis, d. 5/10/1748.
Mary Jones d. 5/14/1748.
Sarah Savery, dau of William, d. 5/21/1748.
Martha Gardner d. 5/27/1748.
Sarah Ireson, dau of William, d. 5/27/1748.
Charity Harmon, dau of Tuball, d. 6/1/1748.
Deborah Huntsman d. 6/2/1748.
Joseph Govett d. 6/3/1748.
Jane Sharrot d. 6/4/1748.
Richard Armitt d. 6/7/1748.
Rebeccah Evans, dau of Rebeccah d. 6/8/1748.
Mary Wilson, dau of George, d. 6/12/1748.
Peter Robinson, son of Peter, d. 6/14/1748.
John NcNabb, son of John, d. 6/17/1748.
Thomas Biddle, son of John, d. 6/21/1748.
Sarah Jones, dau of Mary, d. 6/24/1748.
Sarah Fisher d. 7/1/1748.
Sarah Sansom, dau of Samuel, d. 7/1/1748.
Sarah Webb d. 7/2/1748.

Mary Boyce d. 7/6/1748.
William Bissell d. 7/7/1748.
Joseph Paul, son of Joseph, d. 7/8/1748.
John Dillwyn d. 7/10/1748.
William Stretch d. 7/17/1748.
Amy Page, dau of John, d. 7/17/1748.
Thomas Butler, son of Deborah, d. 7/19/1748.
Dorothy Aspden, wife of Mathias, d. 7/21/1748.
Joanna Smith. d. 7/21/1748.
Mary Williams, wife of Isaac, d. 7/29/1748.
Mathew Garrigue d. 8/6/1748.
Samuel Shoemaker, son of Samuel, d. 8/9/1748.
Richard Hayes d. 8/4/1748.
Ann Tilbury, wife of Thomas, d. 8/19/1748.
Isaac Warner d. 8/25/1748.
Ann Parr, wife of Samuel, d. 8/27/1748.
Joice Cory, dau of Samuel, d. 8/29/1748.
Elizabeth Harmer d. 8/31/1748.
John Warner d. 9/2/1748.
Thomas Hill, son of Mary, d. 9/3/1748.
William Goodwin, son of John, d. 9/4/1748.
Elizabeth Warner d. 9/4/1748.
John Kinsey, son of John, d. 9/9/1748.
Isaac Dawson d. 9/12/1748.
Samuel Carpenter d. 9/14/1748.
Joseph Dubree d. 9/18/1748.
Thomas Burden d. 9/23/1748.
Ann Pound d. 9/26/1748.
Thomas Shute d. 10/3/1748.
Esther Saunders d. 10/5/1748.
Sarah Wagstaff d. 10/7/1748.
Nathan Norbury d. 10/8/1748.
Ann Lambert d. 10/10/1748.
Hannah Falconer d. 10/12/1748.
Caleb Emlen d. 10/13/1748.
Samuel Coates d/ 10/5/1748.
Sarah Branson, wife of William, d. 10/6/1748.
Lydia Davis d. 10/29/1748.
Silvanus Jones d. 10/30/1748.
Mary Carter d. 11/2/1748.
Joseph Stretch, son of Joseph, d. 11/3/1748.
Tace Lewis, dau of Jacob, d. 11/4/1748.
Thomas Broadgate d. 11/13/1748.
George Wilson d. 11/13/1748.
William Atmore, son of William, d. 11/19/1748.

George Gray d. 11/22/1748.
William Bennett d. 12/1/1748.
Sarah Lee d. 12/8/1748.
Abraham Moss d. 12/9/1748.
Cadwallader Foulke, son of Judah, d. 12/9/1748.
Samuel Paschall, son of Thomas, d. 12/18/1748.
Martha Vanhusten d. 12/21/1748.
Ruth Harmer d. 12/25/1748.
Isaac Brown d. 12/26/1748.
Sarah James d. 12/26/1748.
William Chapman d. 1/1/1749.
Mary Watson d. 1/5/1749.
Elizabeth House, dau of Joseph, d. 1/7/1749.
Robert Waln, son of Robert, d. 1/7/1749.
John Cox d. 1/12/1749.
James Davis d. 1/13/1749.
Elizabeth Chetham, wife of Joseph, d. 1/19/1749.
Sarah Densey d. 1/20/1749.
Dorcas Ireson, wife of William, d. 1/26/1749.
Joshua Fisher d. 1/29/1749.
Sarah Hughs d. 1/30/1749.
Jane Dawson, dau of Jane, d. 1/30/1749.
Mary Williams, dau of Daniel, d. 2/7/1749.
Thomas Thomas, son of Moses, d. 2/15/1749.
Peter Brown d. 2/20/1749.
Samuel Davis, son of Rachel, d. 2/21/1749.
Benjamin Dever d. 2/24/1749.
Ann Wood d. 2/26/1749.
Mary Linkhorn, dau if Isaac, d. 2/27/1749.
Jane Harper, widow of John, d. 2/28/1749.
Lydia Stretch, dau of Joseph, d. 3/1/1749.
Hannah Talbott, wife of John, d. 3/5/1749.
Susanna Bland d. 3/21/1749.
Thomas Robinson d. 3/27/1749.
John Morris, son of John, d. 3/27/1749.
John Knight, son of John, d. 3/28/1749.
Elizabeth Lobdell, dau of Isaac, d. 3/29/1749.
Rebeccah Mitchell, dau of Abraham, d. 4/3/1749.
Elizabeth Dawson, dau of Jane, d. 4/4/1749.
Edward Cathrell, son of Edward, d. 4/11/1749.
Mary Worley, dau of Nathan, d. 4/12/1749.
Benjamin Bagnell, son of Benjamin, d. 4/13/1749.
Joseph Noble, son of Samuel, d. 4/17/1749.
John Williamson d. 4/18/1749.
Mary Saul, wife of Joseph, d. 4/19/1749.

John James, son of Aaron, d. 4/21/1749.
Thomas Austen, son of Edward, d. 4/25/1749.
Sarah Wagstaff, dau of James, d. 4/26/1749.
Joseph Drinker d. 4/28/1749.
Robert Dawson, son of Mary, d. 5/7/1749.
Rachel Dennis, dau of Henry, d. 5/9/1749.
Daniell Hoods d. 5/10/1749.
Francis Farris d. 5/10/1749.
Ann Owen d. 5/11/1749.
Daniel Williams, son of Daniel, d. 5/13/1749.
Silas Prier, son of Silas, d. 5/13/1749.
Jane Williams, dau of Daniel, d. 5/14/1749.
Thomas Nixson d. 5/16/1749.
Joseph Garrigues, son of John, d. 5/22/1749.
James Haffe d. 6/2/1749.
Isaac Dawson, son of James, d. 6/2/1749.
Thomas Smith, son of Hugh, d. 6/2/1749.
William Parker, son of William, d. 6/5/1749.
Thomas Allen, son of Nehemiah, d. 6/7/1749.
Martha Chalkley d. 6/13/1749.
Josiah Harman, son of Tuball, d. 6/13/1749.
William Griscom, son of Samuel, d. 6/18/1749.
Mary Brown, son of Preserve, d. 6/19/1749.
Elizabeth Hargrave, wife of Charles, d. 6/23/1749.
Charles Gray, son of William, d. 6/29/1749.
Edward Pledwell d. 7/4/1749.
Thomas Hart d. 7/5/1749.
Edward Yarnall, son of Mordecai, d. 7/12/1749.
Mary Tarent d. 7/20/1749.
Esther Scull d. 7/26/1749.
Mary Foulke, dau of Judah, d. 8/10/1749.
Thomas Peters d. 8/12/1749.
Ann Brockden, wife of Richard, d. 8/13/1749.
Rebecca Evans, dau of Sarah, d. 8/13/1749.
Katherine Schreogle d. 8/16/1749.
Jane Each d. 8/18/1749.
Ann Griscum, dau of Tobias, d. 8/23/1749.
Abigail Scull, dau of Jasper, d. 9/1/1749.
Septimus Hough d. 9/3/1749.
Sarah Hart, wife of John, d. 9/7/1749.
Rebecca Hart, dau of said John, d. 9/7/1749.
Isaac Deshler, son of David, d. 9/18/1749.
Isaac Shute d. 10/7/1749.
Ann Prier, wife of Silas, d. 10/9/1749.
John Huntsman d. 10/10/1749.

Mary Warner d. 10/13/1749.
Margrett Gray, dau of William, d. 10/29/1749.
Marcy Lawrence, dau of William, d. 10/30/1749.
Deborah Johnson, wife of John, d. 11/26/1749.
Martha Jones, dau of Doughty, d. 11/29/1749.
Anthony Saull, son of Joseph, d. 11/30/1749.
William Dilworth, son of William, d. 12/6/1749.
Margaret Ogilby, dau of John, d. 12/11/1749.
Mary Griffit d. 12/15/1749.
John Carlisle, son of Abraham, d. 12/18/1749.
George Howell d. 12/23/1749.
Samuel Powell, cooper, d. 12/24/1749.
Everard Ogilby, son of John, d. 1/3/1749.
Peter Snow d. 1/17/1749.
Grace Dennis, wife of Henry, d. 1/27/1749.
Martha Ogilby, dau of Patrick, d. 2/2/1750.
Thomas Paschall, son of Thomas, d. 2/6/1750.
Lydia Govett, dau of Esther, d. 2/8/1750.
Thomas Buckley d. 2/9/1750.
Benjamin Hartley d. 2/10/1750.
Sarah Mifflin, dau of John, d. 2/19/1750.
Thomas Hooton, son of Benjamin, d. 2/20/1750.
George Hallowell, son of John, d. 3/5/1750.
Mordecai Loyd d. 3/6/1750.
John Lynn, son of Joseph, d. 3/3/1750.
John Kinsey d. 3/13/1750.
George Fitzwater d. 3/19/1750.
Rachel Gilpin, dau of Thomas, d. 3/23/1750.
Thomas Burges d. 3/25/1750.
Henry Lewis d. 3/27/1750.
Mary Tritter, wife of Benjamin, d. 3/28/1750.
Mary Test, wife of John, d. 3/28/1750.
Sarah Altrich d. 4/3/1750.
William Jervis, son of John, d. 4/6/1750.
Mary Ogilby, dau of John, d. 4/9/1750.
Sarah Moor, dau of John, d. 4/10/1750.
Samuel Baker, son of Joseph, d. 4/11/1750.
Charles Jones, son of Joseph, d. 4/12/1750.
Margrett Evans, dau of Evan, d. 4/14/1750.
Ann Stretch, dau of Thomas, d. 4/16/1750.
John Biddle d. 4/18/1750.
Thomas Taylor, son of Sarah, d. 4/22/1750.
John Gardner d. 4/30/1750.
Catherine Rhoades, dau of Samuel, d. 5/7/1750.
Kenderdine Davis, son of Richard, d. 5/10/1750.
Rachel Abbott, dau of Samuel, d. 5/11/1750.

James Paynter d. 5/13/1750.
Rebecca Edgell d. 5/13/1750.
Martha Gardner, dau of Sarah, d. 5/13/1750.
Samuel Shoemaker, son of Samuel, d. 5/15/1750.
Margrett Rown, dau of Margrett, d. 5/27/1850.
Hannah Steel, dau of Rebeccah, d. 5/30/1750.
Hannah Robinson, dau of Hannah, d. 6/5/1750.
Jacob Britton d. 6/5/1750.
Mary Harrison d. 6/7/1750.
Elizabeth Mifflin, dau of Benjamin, d. 6/8/1750.
James Bonnell, son of Samuel, d. 6/8/1750.
Rebecca Saul, dau of Joseph, d. 6/9/1750.
Hannah Sanson, dau of Samuel, d. 6/9/1750.
Ann Renshaw, dau of Richard, d. 6/12/1750.
Mary Paschall, dau of Stephen, d. 6/12/1750.
Thomas Butler, son of John, d. 6/13/1750.
Mary Lawton d. 6/14/1750.
Grace Griscom d. 6/14/1750.
Susannah Lawrence, wife of William, d. 6/16/1750.
Esther Spencer d. 6/17/1750.
Joseph Durberah d. 6/19/1750.
Joseph Wishart d. 6/27/1750.
Elizabeth Jones, dau of John, d. 6/29/1750.
John Hallowell d. 7/2/1750.
John Moor d. 7/5/1750.
John Elfryth d. 7/6/1750.
Elizabeth Goforth d. 7/7/1750.
Samuel House, son of Samuel, d. 7/11/1750.
Samuel Robins d. 7/12/1750.
John Hilborn d. 7/18/1750.
Mary Hill d. 7/23/1750.
Mary Nichols, wife of Anthony, d. 7/25/1750.
Susannah Galloway d. 7/26/1750.
Richard Thomas d. 7/29/1750.
Susannah Hayes, wife of William, d. 7/29/1750.
Susannah Fussell, wife of Solomon, d. 8/2/1750.
Deborah Mott d. 8/5/1750.
Elizabeth Peters, dau of William, d. 8/8/1750.
Thomas Wooley d. 8/11/1750.
Sarah Boor d. 8/14/1750.
William Boor, son of said Sarah, d. 8/21/1750.
John Britton d, 8/23/1750.
Abigail Morton d. 8/24/1750.
Sarah Williams d. 9/8/1750.
Elizabeth Hallowell d. 9/10/1750.
Hannah Hallowell, wife of John, d. 9/10/1750.

Ann Saunders d. 9/10/1750.
Edward Warner, son of Edward, d. 9/25/1750.
Mary Roberts, son of Hugh, d. 9/26/1750.
Elizabeth Green, dau of Sarah, d. 9/28/1750.
Samuel Coster d. 10/2/1750.
Elizabeth Mifflin, dau of John, d. 10/2/1750.
John Martindall d. 10/5/1750.
Elizabeth Worley, wife of Nathan, d. 10/7/1750.
Deborah Warner d. 10/11/1750.
Ann Renshaw, wife of Richard, d. 10/14/1750.
Margrett Davis, dau of Lydia, d. 10/16/1750.
James Tempest, son of Rachel, d. 10/17/1750.
William Clark, son of William, d. 10/20/1750.
Priscilla Edmunson d. 10/23/1750.
Violl Chubb, son of Sarah, d. 10/24/1750.
Isaac Lobdell, son of Isaac, d. 10/26/1750.
Samuel Parr d. 11/1/1750.
Asher Mott, son of Asher, d. 11/1/1750.
James Davis, son of Rachel, d. 11/4/1750.
Doughty Jones, son of Doughty, d. 11/9/1750.
Elinor Chambliss d. 11/10/1750.
Mary Burr, dau of Henry, d. 11/11/1750.
Thomas Gardner, son of John, d. 11/12/1750.
Joseph Emlen d. 11/17/1750.
Thomas Hollinshead d. 11/17/1750.
Charles Wright d. 11/18/1750.
Sarah Cooper, dau of Jacob, d. 11/20/1750.
Richard Worrell, son of Robert, d. 11/24/1750.
James Morris d. 1129/1750.
Sarah Webb, dau of Joseph, d. 12/5/1750.
Mary Ranbury, dau of William, d. 12/5/1750.
Abraham Claypoole d. 12/10/1750.
Lydia Yarnall, dau of Mordecai, d. 12/13/1750.
Joseph Warner, son of Joseph, d. 12/26/1750.
Mary Lawrence, dau of William, d. 12/27/1750.
Deborah Winn, dau of Thomas, d. 12/28/1750.
Elizabeth Peters, dau of Reece, d. 1/4/1750.
Samuel Walton d. 1/4/1750.
Esther Warner, dau of Joseph, d. 1/4/1750.
Mary Griffits, dau of Isaac, d. 1/8/1750.
Charles Jenkins, son of Charles, d. 1/18/1750.
Elizabeth Greenleaf, wife of Isaac, d. 1/21/1750.
William Warren, son of Isaac, d. 1/21/1750.
Isaac Roberts, son of Phineas, d. 1/26/1750.
Joseph Gray, Jr, d. 1/28/1750.
Abraham Ferris d. 1/30/1750.

MARRIAGE CERTIFICATES
1672-1750

Richard Warder of Chittester, in the county of Sussex, tobacco pipemaker, took to wife Ann Lee, daughter of John Lee of Guildford, in the county of Surry, at the house of Richard Deane in the Park in Nicholasses Parish Park, in Guildford, this 8th day of the 10th month, 1672.

Francis Little of Horslydown Southwark, in the county of Surry, tailor, mar, in London, this 18th day of the 3rd month, 1676, Mary Woodmansey of the same place.

Richard Gove of Plymouth, joyner, mar this one and 13th day of the 3rd month, 1676, at Broad Street Meeting in Plimouth, Bridget Chilston of Plymouth aforesaid.

Francis Richardson of Ratcliff, in the county of Middlesex, marriner, son of Thomas Richardson of Southshields, in the county of Durham, dec'd, mar this 7th and 20th day of the month called January, 1680, at Devonshire House without Bishopsgate, in London, Rebecca Howard, daughter of John Howard of Upbridge, in the county of Middlesex, shoemaker, dec'd.

David Brentnall and Jane Blancher, both of the city of Philadelphia, mar this 6th day of the 10th month, 1683.

Philip Richards of New York and Mary Potter of same, mar this 20th day of the 6th month, 1684.

Samuel Carpenter of Philadelphia and Hannah Hardiman of the same, mar this 12th day of the 10th month, called December, 1684.

John Parsons of Middleroy, in the county of Somerset, carpenter, and Ann Powell of North Curry, county aforesaid, spinster, mar this 23rd day of the 6th month, commonly called August, 1685.

John Marten of Philadelphia, taylor, and Elizabeth Simms of the same, spinster, mar this 17th day of the 10th month, 1685.

Hugh Durborow, clothier, of Thornbey, and Elizabeth Talor of Tinicom, both of the county of Chester, mar this 11th day of the 1st month, 1686.

John Delavall of New York, merchant, and Hannah Loyd, daughter of Thomas Loyd, of the same place, mar this 31st day of the 3rd month, 1686, at Flushing meeting, Long Island.

Caspar Holt of New York, taylor, and Elizabeth Delaplayne, the daughter of Nicholas Delaplayne of the same place, mar this 12th of the 6th month, 1686.

William Dilwyn of the county of Philadelphia, sadeler, and Sarah Fuller, of the county aforesaid, mar this 2nd day of the 7th month, 1687.

John Kinsey and Sarah Stiven mar, in Philadelphia, this 20th day of the 8th month, 1687.

Joshua Tittery of Philadelphia, glassmaker, and Cecily Wolley of the same place, spinster, mar this 4th day of the 2nd month, called April, 1688.

Samuel Preston of Patuxant, in the province of Maryland, and Rachel Loyd, daughter of Thomas Loyd of Philadelphia, mar this 6th day of the 5th month, 1688.

Henry Badcoke (Badcock) of Philadelphia and Mary Browne of the same place, spinster, mar this 14th day of the 9th month, called November, 1688.

Philip England of Philadelphia and Elizabeth Hatton, widow, of Duck Creek, in New Castle County, mar this 1st day of the 10th month, called December, 1688.

Thomas Wharton, taylor, of Philadelphia, and Rachel Thomas of place aforesaid, spinster, mar this 2nd day of the 11th month, called January, 1688.

William Hudson of Philadelphia, tanner, and Mary Richardson of the same place, spinster, mar this 28th day of the 12th month, called February, 1688.

Edward Shippen of Boston, in New England, merch't, and Rebeckah Richardson late of New York, widow of Francis Richardson, merch't, deceased the 15th day of 5th month, called March, 1688, mar, in Rhode Island, the 4th day of the 7th month, called September, 1689.

Joseph Kirll of Pensilvania and Mary Brett, daughter of John and Mary Brett of Michaels Parish, in the Island of Barbadoes, mar this 9th day of the month called October, 1689, at Bridgetown, Island of Barbadoes.

John Busby of Philadelphia, weaver, and Mary Taylor, spinster, daughter of Christopher Taylor, deceased, mar this 1st day of the 2nd month, called April, 1690.

William Say of Burlington in West Jersey, and Mary Guest, the daughter of Alice Guest, widdow, of Philadelphia, mar this 7th day of the 10th month, called December, 1690.

Nathaniel Edgcomb, late of Burlington, in the province of West Jersey, and Sarah Elis of Darley, province aforesaid, spinster, mar this 29th day of the 11th month, 1690.

Daniel Pegg and Barbara Jones mar this 5th day of the 3rd month, called May, 1691.

Thomas Griffith of Philadelphia, cordwainer, and Judith Delaplane of the same place, spinster, mar this 12th day of the 9th month, called November, 1691.

James Coate of Philadelphia, carpenter, and Mary Watson of the same place, spinster, mar this 8th day of the 12th month, called February, 1691.

Thomas Morris of Philadelphia, glover, and Margarett Wivell of the same place, widdow, mar this 13th day of the 8th month, 1692.

Samuel Cart of the county of Philadelphia, yeoman, and Sarah Goodsonn, daughter of John Goodsonn of Philadelphia, Doctor in Physick, mar this 12th day of the 2nd month, 1693.

Samuel Bulkley and Ann Jones mar this 12th day of the 2nd month, 1693.

William Trotter of Philadelphia, labourer, and Rebecca Theach of the same, spinster, mar this 18th day of the 2nd month, 1693.

John Sanders of Philadelphia, bricklayer, and Elizabeth Wood of the same place, spinster, mar this 11th day of the 6th month, 1693.

Arnold Cassel of Germantown, in the county of Philadelphia, wine dresser, and Susanna Delaplain of Philadelphia, mar this 2nd day of the 9th month, 1693.

Isaac Norris, late of the Island of Jamacia, merchant, and Mary Loyd, daughter of Thomas Loyd of Philadelphia, mar this 7th day of the 1st month, 1694.

George Emlen of Philadelphia, vintner, and Hanah Garet of same, spinster, mar this 5th day of the 4th month, 1694.

William Alloway of Philadelphia, chandler, and Elizabeth Southebee, spinster, daughter of William Southebee of the same place, mar this 9th day of the 8th month, 1694.

William Royall and Mary Redman, spinster, daughter of John Redman, bricklayer of Philadelphia, mar this 8th day of the 6th month, 1695.

Ralph Jackson and Elizabeth Rickets mar this 2nd day of the 8th month, called October, 1695.

Arthur Holton of Philadelphia, baker, and Elizabeth Guest, spinster, daughter of Alice Guest, widdow, mar this 5th day of the 10th month, 1695.

Daniel Radley of Philadelphia, woosted comer, and Mary Boyden, spinster, daughter of James Boyden of Neshaminy Creek in the county of Bucks, mar the 16th day of the 2nd month, 1696.

John Hart of Philadelphia, bricklayer, and Mary Seary, in the township of Oxford and county of Philadelphia, mar the 21st day of the 2nd month, 1696.

George Fox, son of James Fox of Philadelphia, baker, and Susannah Hackney of Burlington, in the province of New West Jersey, daughter of Joseph Hackney of Hemstead, in Hartfordshire, in old England, mar this 20th day of the 3rd month, called May, 1696.

Thomas Shute of the county of Philadelphia and Elizabeth Powell, daughter of William Powell of the county aforesaid, spinster, mar this 29th day of the 10th month, 1696.

John Powell, son of William Powell, cooper, and Ann Harvard, daughter of David Harvard, glover, both of the county of Philadelphia, mar this 12th day of the 11th month, 1696.

David Lloyd of Philadelphia and Grace Growdon, daughter of Joseph
  Growdon of the county of Bucks, mar the 31st day of the 1st month,
  1697.
Daniel Flower of Philadelphia, carpenter, and Sarah Fincher of the same
  place, mar this 6th day of the 3rd month, 1697.
Eve Bellonge, weaver, and Christian Delaplain, spinster, both of
  Philadelphia, mar this 10th day of the sixth month, 1697.
William Kelley of Darby, in Chester County, and Meriana von Buyleart of
  the same place, widow, mar this 9th day of the 9th month, called
  November, 1697.
Charles Sanders of Philadelphia and Sarah Whitepain of the same place,
  widdow, mar this 14th day of the 10th month, 1697.
George Harmer of Philadelphia and Honour Oxley of the same place,
  spinster, mar this 20th day of the 11th month, 1697/8.
Matthew Robinson, late of Philadephia, turner, and Sarah Powell,
  daughter of David Powell of the same place, mar this 18th day of the
  2nd month, called April, 1698.
John Bettle and Abigail Mattern mar this 9th day of the 3rd month,
  called May, 1698.
Richard Gove of Philadelphia, joiner, and Patience Gosden of the said
  town and province, spinster, mar this 8th day of the 5th month, 1698.
Richard Sutton of Philadelphia, chandler and sope boyler, and Mary
  Howell of Cecil County, in the province of Maryland, spinster, mar
  this 12th day of the 7th month, called September, 1698.
Robert Thompson of Philadelphia, smith, and Sara Herne of the same,
  spinster, mar this 3rd day of the 8th month, 1698.
James Parrock of Philadelphia, shipp wright, and Martha Hastings of the
  same place, spinster, mar this 29th day of the 9th month, 1698.
William Say of Philadelphia, merchant, and Mary Paschall of the same
  place, spinster, mar this 4th day of the 2nd month, 1699.
Thomas Rich of Philadelphia, baker, and Sarah Sanders of the same
  place, spinster, mar this 5th day of the 2nd month, 1699.
Matthew Prichard of Philadelphia, cardwinder, and Sarah Henley of the
  same place, mar this 9th day of the 3rd month, 1699.
Samuel Spencer of Philadelphia, mariner, and Esther Jennett of the
  same place, spinster, mar this 15th day of the 4th month, 1699.
Edward Pennington of Philadelphia and Sarah Jennings, daughter of
  Samuell Jennings of Burlington, in the province of West New Jersey,
  mar this 16th day of the 11th month, 1699.
Tobias Dimock, late of Rhoad Island and now residing in Philadelphia,
  and Sarah Harding of the same place, widdow, mar this 29th day of
  the 8th month, called October, 1700.
Anthony Morris of Philadelphia and Elizabeth Wattson of the same
  place, mar this 30th day of the 8th month, 1700.

Thomas Makin of Philadelphia, clerk, and Sarah LaRich of the same place, widdow, mar this 3rd day of the 10th month, 1700.

William Powell, son of William Powell of Philadelphia, cooper, and Elisabeth Kelley of the same place, mar this 31st day of the 10th month, 1700.

John Jones, son of John Jones of Philadelphia, merchant, and Margaret Waterman, daughter of Humphrey Waterman of the same place, deceased, mar this 11th day of the 1st month, 1702.

William White of Philadelphia, cordwainer, and Sarah Bye, daughter of Thomas Bye of the same place, mar this 1st day of the 5th month. 1702.

Christopher Blackburn of Philadelphia, taylor, and Rachel Cumberlidge of the same place, mar this 13th day of the 6th month, 1702.

John Roberts of Philadelphia, cordwainer, and Mary Kilcup of the same place, mar this 10th day of the 7th month, 1702.

Joseph Hembey of the Township of Makefield, in the county of Bucks, husbandman, and Eleanor Jackman of Philadelphia, spinster, mar this 1st day of the 8th month, 1702.

Stephen Jackson of Philadelphia, merchant, and Elizabeth Clemison of the same place, widdow, mar this 15th day of the 8th month, 1702.

Solomon Cresson of Philadelphia, turner, and Anna Watson of the same place, mar this 14th day of the 11th month, 1702.

William Till of Philadelphia, joyner, and Ann Warder, daughter of Richard Warder of the same place, pipemaker, mar this 1st day of the 2nd month, 1703.

John Haywood of Philadelphia, cordwainer, and Mary Emley, daughter of William Emley, mar this 10th day of the 4th month, 1703.

Jesse Kendall of the burrough of Willmington in the county of New Castle on Dellaware, cordwainer, son of John Kendall of the same place, and Mary Marshall of the city of Philadelphia, daughter of William Marshall, late of Willmington aforesaid, deceased, mar this 3rd day of the 5th month, 1703.

Henry Carter of Philadelphia, brickmaker, and Susanna Colley, daughter of John Colley of the same place, hatter, mar this 9th day of the 5th month, 1703.

James Parrock of Philadelphia, shipwright, and Sarah Jennet, daughter of John Jennet, late of the same place, deceased, mar this 15th day of the 10th month, 1703.

John Jones of Philadelphia, merchant, and Elizabeth Fox, daughter of James Fox, late of the same place, merchant, deceased, mar this 9th day of the 1st month, 1703/4.

John Hendricks of Philadelphia, shipwright, son of Albert Hendricks of Chester County, yeoman, and Rebeckah Wells of Philadelphia, widow, mar this 13th day of the 2nd month, 1704.

Anthony Morris, son of Anthony Morris of Philadelphia, merchant, and Phebe Guest, daughter of George Guest, late of the same place, deceased, mar this 10th day of the 3rd month, 1704.

Thomas Elridge, son of Jonathan Elridge of Eversham in the County of Burlington, West New Jersey, yeoman, and Mary James of Philadelphia, mar this 11th day of the 3rd month, 1704.

George Claypoole of Philadelphia, merchant, and Martha Hoskins, daughter of Richard Hoskins of the same place, physician, deceased, mar this 29th day of the 3rd month, 1704.

John Cheetam of Philadelphia, taylor, and Anne Eaton of the same place, mar this 1st day of the 4th month, 1704.

Thomas White of Philadelphia, baker, and Rebeckah Harris of the same place, mar this 8th day of the 4th month, 1704.

Mordecai Moore of the county of Ann Arrundall in the province of Maryland, merchant, and Deborah Loyd, daughter of Thomas Loyd, late Deputy Governor Pennsylvana, deceased, mar this 12th day of the 7th month, 1704

John Piggott (Pickett) of Philadelphia, cordwainer, and Alice Reyniers, daughter of Reynier Tansen of the same place, printer, mar this 2nd day of the 9th month, 1704.

Timothy Hanson, Jun, of Frankfort in the county of Philadelphia, carpenter, and Susannah Freeland, daughter of William Freeland, late of Philadelphia, deceased, mar this 9th day of the 9th, 1704.

Griffith Owen of Philadelphia, practitioner in physick, and Sarah Sanders of the same place, widow, mar this 13th day of the 9th month, 1704.

Richard Robinson of Philadelphia and Sarah Jeofferies of the same place, mar this 7th day of the 10th month, 1704.

Silas Pryor of the county of Chester, yeoman, and Susannah Hall of Philadelphia, mar this 28th day of the 10th month, 1704.

Thomas Roberts of Philadelphia, taylor, and Martha Gove, daughter of Richard Gove of the same place, joyner, mar this 4th day of the 11th month, 1704/5.

Joseph Growdon of Bensalem, county of Bucks, gentleman, and Anne Bulkley of Philadelphia, widow, mar this 10th day of the 11th month, 1704/5.

Nathan Faucet of Philadelphia, bodice maker, son of Walter Faucet of the county of Chester, yeoman, deceased, and Jane Breintnal of Philadelphia, daughter of David Breintnal, haberdasher, mar this 11th day of the 11th month, 1704/5.

David Williams of the Township of Plymouth, county of Philadelphia, yeoman, and Mary Maltsby of Philadelphia, mar this 30th day of the 11th month, 1704/5.

Magnes Plowman of Philadelphia, Lawyer, and Sarah Hutcheson, daughter of Robert Hutcheson, late of the same place, deceased, mar this 14th day of the 12th month, 1704/5.

John Watson of Philadelphia, lawyer, and Abigail Hood of the same place, widow, mar this 4th day of the 2nd month, 1705.

William Burge of Philadelphia, merchant, and Elizabeth Stacy of the same place, mar this 17th day of the 2nd month, 1705.

Thomas Iredell of Philadelphia and Rebeckah Williams of the same place, mar this 9th day of the 3rd month, 1705.

Richard Parker of Philadelphia, cordwainer, and Priscilla Love, relict of Richard Love, late of the same place, deceased, mar this 3rd day of the 5th month, 1705.

William Rakestraw of Philadelphia, yeoman, and Elizabeth Archer, widow, of the same place, mar this 4th day of the 5th month, 1705.

Abraham Scott of Philadelphia, merchant, and Hannah Scott of the same place, widow, mar this 10th day of the 5th month, 1705.

Jedidiah Hussey, of the county of New Castle, in the Territories of Pennsylvania, yeoman, and Esther Cooper, daughter of James Cooper of Philadelphia, shopkeeper, mar this 24th day of the 8th month, 1705.

Thomas Story of Philadelphia, Gent, and Ann Shippen, daughter of Edward Shippen of said city, merchant. mar this 10th day of the 5th month, 1706.

George Gray of Philadelphia and Naomi Berry, late of Maryland, widow, mar this 7th day of the 6th month, 1706.

Thomas Redman, son of John Redman of Philadelphia, bricklayer, and Sarah Harriot, daughter of Samuel Harriot of the said city, marriner, mar this 9th day of the 8th month, 1706.

William Coates of Philadelphia, brickmaker, and Mary Smith, daughter of Thomas Smith, late of the same place, also brickmaker, deceased, mar this 13th day of the 9th month, 1706.

Levin Herberdink, of Philadelphia, weaver, and Mary Loof of the same city, mar this 1st day of the 11th month, 1706/7.

Jacob Minshall, son of Thomas Minshall of the Township of Providence and county of Chester, yeoman, and Sarah Owen, daughter of Griffith Owen of the city of Philadelphia, Practitioner in Physick, mar this 18th day of the 1st month, 1706/7.

James Estaugh of Philadelphia, wheelwright, and Mary Lawson of said city, mar this 19th day of the 1st month, 1706/7.

Adam Lewis of Philadelphia, carpenter, and Hannah Watson of the same place, mar this 10th day of the 4th month, 1707.

Ralph Jackson of Philadelphia, locksmith, and Sarah Dymmock of said city, widow, mar this 3rd/30th? day of the 7th month, 1707.

Thomas Bryan, son of Thomas Bryan of the Township of Northampton, county of Burlington, province of West New Jersey, yeoman, and

Susannah Hearn, daughter of William Hearn of Philadelphia, locksmith, mar this 7th day of the 8th month, 1707.

Clement Plumsted of Philadelphia, merchant, and Elizabeth Palmer of the said city, mar this 15th day of the 8th month, 1707.

Isaac Minshall, son of Thomas Minshall of the Township of Providence, county of Chester, yeoman, and Rebeckah Owen, daughter of Griffith Owen of Philadelphia, Practitioner in Physick, mar this 11th day of the 9th month, 1707.

Caleb Ransted, son of Joseph Ransted, of Philadelphia, cordwainer, and Mary Warder, daughter of Richard Warder of the said city, pipemaker, mar this 12th day of the 9th month, 1707.

William Powell, Jun, of Philadelphia, cooper, and Sarah Armitt of said city, mar this 9th day of the 10th month, 1707.

George Fitzwater of Philadelphia, merchant, and Mary Hardiman, daughter of Abraham Hardiman, late of said city, merchant, deceased, mar this 10th day of the 10th month, 1707.

Robert Bonnel of the city of Philadelphia, wheelwright, and Frances Chanders of the said city, mar this 16th day of the 10th month, 1707.

John Sharp of the township of Evesham in the county of Burlington, province of West New Jersey, yeoman, and Elizabeth Green of the city of Philadelphia, mar this 11th day of the 11th month, 1707/8.

John Widdifield of Philadelphia, joyner, and Mary Lawrence, daughter of William Lawrence of said city, taylor, mar this 29th day of the 11th month, 1707/8.

Thomas Godfrey of the township of Bristoll, county of Philadelphia, maltster, and Lucea Russell of Philadelphia, widow, mar this 18th day of the 1st month, 1707/8.

John Hart, merchant, of Philadelphia, and Hannah McComb, daughter of John McComb of said city, taylor, mar this 2nd day of the 12th month, 1708/9.

John Renshaw of the county of Philadelphia, yeoman, and Elizabeth Newcombe of the city of Philadelphia, mar this 22nd day of the 12th month, 1708/9.

Jonathan Coppock, son of Bartholomew Coppock of the township of Springfield, county of Chester, yeoman, and Jane Owen, daughter of Griffith Owen of Philadelphia, Practioner in Phisick, mar this 3rd day of the 1st month, 1708/9.

Samuel Marriott, son of Isaac Marriott of Burlington in the province of West New Jersey, and Mary Whitpaine, daughter of Jehu: Whitpaine, late of Philadelphia, dec'd, mar this 3rd day of the 1st month, 1708/9.

John Warder, son of Richard Warder of the city of Philadelphia, pipemaker, and Agnes Righton, daughter of William Righton of said city, merchant, mar this 10th day of the 1st month, 1708/9.

Thomas Mitchell of the city of Philadelphia, cooper, and Sarah Densey, daughter of John Densey, late of said city, deceased, mar this 10th day of the 1st month, 1708/9.

John Maule, son of Thomas Maule of Salem in the Colony of Massachusetts, in New England, merchant, and Charity Jones, daughter of Robert Jones, late of the city of Philadelphia, dec'd, mar this 17th day of the 1st month, 1708/9.

William Monington of the city of Philadelphia, merchant, and Susanah Webb, daughter of John Webb of said city, taylor, mar this 13th day of the 8th month, 1709.

Joshua Gilbert, son of John Gilbert of the city of Philadelphia, merchant, and Elizabeth Oldman, daughter of Thomas Oldman of said city, carpenter, mar this 19th day of the 8th month, 1709.

Edward Cadwalader, son of Jones Cadwalader of the Township of Meirion, county of Philadelphia, mason, and Rebeckah Moore, daughter of Anthony Moore, late of city aforesaid, locksmith, mar this 24th day of the 9th month, 1709.

Samuel Lewis, Jun, of the Township of Springfield, county of Chester, yeoman, and Hannah Stretch of the city of Philadelphia, mar this 15th day of the 10th month, 1709.

Gilbert Falconar, son of David Falconar of the city of Edinburgh, Kingdom of Great Britain, mercht, and Hanah Hardiman, daughter of Abraham Hardiman of the city of Philadelphia, merchant deceased, mar this 2nd day of the 12th month, 1709/10.

James Crawford of the county of Newcastle upon Delaware, yeoman, and Sarah Bettle, daughter of John Bettle of the city of Philadelphia, carpenter, mar this 9th day of the 1st month. 1709/10.

Pentecost Teague of the city of Philadelphia, mercht, and Elizabeth Janney of said city, mar this 6th day of the 2nd month, 1710.

Israel Pemberton, senior son of Phineas Pemberton, late of the county of Bucks, deceased, Rachel Read, daughter of Charles Read, late of the city of Philadelphia, merchant, deceased, mar this 12th day of the 2nd month, 1710.

Willoughby Warder, son of Willioughby Warder of the county of Bucks, yeoman, and Sarah Bowyer, daughter of John Bowyer, late of the city of Philadelphia, shipwright, deceased, mar this 13th day of the 2nd month, 1710.

Peter Wishart of the city of Philadelphia, wheelwright, and Ann Battson, daughter of Thomas Battson of the said city, carpenter, mar this 22nd day of the 2nd month, 1710.

Benjamin Chandlee, son of William Chandlee of Kilmore, in the county of Kildare, Kingdom of Ireland, miller, and Sarah Cottey, daughter of Abel Cottey of the city of Philadelphia, watchmaker, mar this 25th day of the 3rd month (May), 1710.

John Durborow, son of Hugh Durborow of the city of Philadelphia, maltster, and Sarah Day, daughter of John Day of the said City, deceased, mar this 12th day of the 8th month, 1710.

Edward Pleadwell of the city of Philadelphia, worsted comber, and Grace Day, daughter of John Day, late of said city, deceased, mar this 12th day of the 8th month, 1710.

John Harper of the city of Philadelphia, taylor, and Jane Faucit of said city, widow, mar this 14th day of the 10th month, 1710.

John Carpenter, son of Samuel Carpenter of the city of Philadelphia, merchant, and Anne Hoskins, daughter of Richard Hoskins, late of said city, practitioner in Physick, deceased, mar this 11th day of the 11th month, 1710/11.

Joseph Paull, son of Joseph Paull of the Township of Bristoll, County of Philadelphia, yeoman, and Elizabeth Roberts, daughter of Peter Roberts of Chester in the Kingdom of Great Britain, farmer, mar this 8th and 20th day of the 1st month, 1711.

John Goodsonn of the Northern Liberties of the city of Philadelphia, Practitioner in Physick, and Cicely Tittery of the said city, widow, mar this 6th day of the 4th month, 1711.

Samuel Coombe of the city of Philadelphia, cooper, and Rebeckah Nicholson of said city, mar this 21st day of the 4th month, 1711.

James Steele of Duck Creek, county of Kent upon Delaware, carpenter, and Martha Bowen of the city of Philadelphia, widow, mar this 3rd day of the 5th month, 1711.

Samuel Taylor of the city of Philadelphia, boulter, and Elizabeth Robinson, daughter of William Robinson, late of the county of Middlesex in the province of East New Jersey, Practitioner in Physick, deceased, mar this 12th day of the 5th month, 1711.

John Scott of the Town and county of Chester, cooper, and Mary Humphries of the city of Philadelphia, mar this 11th day of the 8th month, 1711.

Evan Owen, son of Robert Owen, late of Meirion in the county of Philadelphia, deceased, and Mary Hoskins, daughter of Richard Hoskins, late of the city of Philadelphia, Practitioner in Physick, deceased, mar. this 10th day of the 11th month, 1711/12.

Joshua Holt of the county of Philadelphia, husbandman, and Hanah Michineer, daughter of John and Sarah Michineer of County aforesaid, mar this 19th day of the 4th month, 1712.

Thomas Coxe of the city of Philadelphia, cooper, and Mary Chandler of said city, mar this 17th day of the 5th month, 1712.

Nathaniel Allen, son of Nehemiah Allen of the city of Philadelphia, cooper, and Hannah Webb of the said city, mar this 2nd day of the 2nd month, 1713.

Paul Preston, son of William Preston of Frankfort in the county of Philadelphia, yeoman, and Elizabeth Gilbert of the city of Philadelphia, widow, mar this 22nd day of the 2nd month, 1713.

John Zelly of the city of Philadelphia, bodice maker, and Maragret Howell of the said city, mar this 13th day of the 6th month, 1713.

Emanuel Dungworth, son of Richard Dungworth of the county of Philadelphia, yeoman, and Elizabeth Bringhurst, daughter of John Bringworth, late of the city of London in the kingdom of Great Britain, stationer, deceased, mar this 10th day of the 7th month, 1713.

Thomas Nixson of Woodbury Creek, county of Gloucester, province of West New Jersey, yeoman, and Magdalen Bellish (Bellows) of the city of Philadelphia, widow, mar this 12th day of the 9th month, 1713.

George Coates of the city of Philadelphia, saddler, and Grace Snead, daughter of William Snead, late of said city, taylor, deceased, mar this 12th day of the 9th month, 1713.

Joseph Waite, son of John Waite, late of the city of Philadelphia, coller maker, deceased, and Martha Biles of said city, widow, mar this 11th day of the 12th month, 1713.

Arthur Sawier of the city of Philad., mercht., and Elizabeth Test of Said city, mar this 8th day of the 2nd month, 1714.

Edward Roberts of the city of Philadelphia, merchant, and Mercy Hoskins, daughter of Richard Hoskins, late of said city, Practitioner in Physick, deceased, mar this 14th day of the 2nd month, 1714.

Thomas Chalkley of the city of Philadelphia and Martha Brown of said city, widow, mar this 15th day of the 2nd month, 1714.

Nicholas Hitchcock of the city of Philadelphia, carpenter, and Elizabeth Marsey, of said city, mar this 9th day of the 5th month, 1714.

John Lancaster of the city of Philadelphia, taylor, and Sarah Brientnall, daughter of David Brientnall, of said city, haberdasher, mar this 22nd day of the 5th month, 1714.

William Harvey of the city of Philadelphia, maltster, and Judith Osborn, of said city, widow, mar this 12th day of the 6th month, 1714.

Nathaniel Poole of the city of Philadelphia, shipwright, and Anne Till, of said city, widow, mar this 2nd day of the 7th month, 1714.

Benjamin Brian, son of Thomas Brian of Northampton, county of Burlington in the Western Division of Nova Cesarea or New Jersey, yeoman, and Mary Cliffton, daughter of Henry Clifton of the city of Philadelphia, weaver, mar this 7th day of the 8th month, 1714.

Isaac Warner, son of William Warner, late of the county of Gloucester in West New Jersey, yeoman, deceased, and Mary Salway, daughter of William Salway, late of the city of Philadelphia, merchant, deceased, mar this 25th day of the 9th month, 1714.

James Logan of the city of Philadelphia, merchant, and Sarah Read, daughter of Charles Read, late of said city, mercht, deceased, mar this 9th day of the 10th month, 1714.

Dennis Rockford of the city of Philadelphia, potter, and Elizabeth Hudson, daughter of William Hudson, late of said city, bricklayer, deceased, mar this 10th day of the 12th month, 1714.

Daniel Walton, son of Daniel Walton of Byberry Township, county of Philadelphia, yeoman, and Elizabeth Cliffton, daughter of Henry Cliffton of the city of Philadelphia, weaver, mar this 17th day of the 12th month, 1714.

Samuel Stretch of the city of Philadelphia, watchmaker, and Agnes Warder of said city, widow, mar this 3rd day of the 1st month, 1714/15.

Francis Knowles of the city of Philadelphia, book binder, and Sarah Lee of the same City, spinster, mar this 10th day of the 1st month, 1714/15.

John Owen, son of Griffith Owen of the city of Philadelphia, Practitioner in Physick, and Jane Harriott, daughter of Samuel Harriott of said city, mariner, mar this 16th day of the 1st month, 1714/15.

John Dillwyn, son of William Dillwyn of the city of Philadelphia, saddler, and Mercy Pearce of said city, mar this 24th day of the 1st month, 1714/15.

John Hudson of the city of Philadelphia, turner, and Abigail Skelton of said city, mar this 26th day of the 3rd month, 1715.

Francis Hardin, son of Nathaniel Hardin, late of the city of Philadelphia, deceased, and Elizabeth Jackson, daughter of Ralph Jackson, of said city, locksmith, mar this 9th day of the 4th month, 1715.

Thomas Shoemaker, son of Jacob Shoemaker of the city of Philadelphia, turner, and Mary Powell of said city, mar this 8th day of the 7th month, 1715.

Joseph Redkinap of Town and county of Chester, mercht, and Elizabeth Jerman of the city of Philadelphia, widow, mar this 13th day of the 8th month, 1715.

Daniel England, son of Daniel England of the city of Philadelphia, mariner, and Elizabeth Coleman, daughter of William Coleman of said city, carpenter, mar this 20th day of the 8th month, 1715.

James Wood, son of Henry Wood late of the county of Gloucester in the Western Division of Nova Cesarea or New Jersey, carpenter, deceased, and Mary Peller, daughter of James Peller of the city of Philadelphia, carpenter, mar this 27th day of the 8th month, 1715.

George Claypoole of the city of Philadelphia, merchant, and Deborah Hardiman, daughter of Abraham Hardiman, late of said city, merchant, deceased, mar this 2nd day of the 9th month, 1715.

Joseph Knight, son of Gyles Knight of Liberty Township, county of
  Philadelphia, yeoman, and Abigail Anthill of the city of Philadelphia,
  mar this 1st day of the 10th month, 1715.

William Kelley of the city of Philadelphia, haberdasher, and Joanna Mead
  of said city, mar this 2nd day of the 12th month, 1715.

George Shiers of the city of Philadelphia, shop keeper, and Deborah
  Painter, daughter of George Painter, late of the county of Chester,
  yeoman, mar this 5th day of the 2nd month, 1716.

Joseph Taylor of the city of Philadelphia, smith, and Sarah Fisher,
  daughter of John Fisher of said city, smith, mar this 12th day of the
  2nd month, 1716.

Thomas Peters, son of Thomas Peters of the city of Philadelphia,
  cordwainer, and Mary Empson, daughter of Cornelius Empson, late of
  the county of New Castle upon Delaware river, yeoman, deceased,
  mar this 19th day of the 2nd month, 1716.

Jeremiah Elfreth of the city of Philadelphia, smith, and Sarah Oldman,
  daughter of Thomas Oldman, late of said city, carpenter, deceased.
  mar this 12th day of the 4th month, 1716.

John Lock of the city of Philadelphia, lawyer, and Mary Rudson of said
  city, mar this 5th day of the 5th month, 1716.

Thomas Miller of the city of Philadelphia, victualler, and Hanah
  Emberson of said city, mar this 2nd day of the 6th month, 1716.

Samuel Lewis, son of Israel Lewis of the Island of Barbados, yeoman,
  and Elizabeth Morris, daughter of Anthony Morris of the city of
  Philadelphia, merchant, mar this 13th day of the 10th month, 1716.

William Tidmarsh, of the town and county of Chester, cordwainer, and
  Hannah Emlen of the city of Philadelphia, widow, mar this 20th day
  of the 10th month, 1716.

Robert Owen, son of Robert Owen late of Meirion, county of
  Philadelphia, yeoman, dec'd, and Susannah Hudson, daughter of
  William Hudson of the city of Philadelphia, taner, mar this 10th day
  of the 11th month, 1716/17.

John Breintnall, son of David Brientnall of the city of Philadelphia,
  haberdasher, and Susanah Shoemaker, daughter of Jacob Shoemaker
  of said city, turner, mar this 23rd day of the 3rd month, 1717.

Richard Harrison of the county of Calvert, province of Maryland,
  merchant, and Hannah Norris, daughter of Isaac Norris of the city of
  Philadelphia, merchant, mar this 13th day of the 4th month, 1717.

Henry Hodge of the city of Philadelphia, merchant, and Hanah Scott of
  said city, widow, mar this 12th day of the 7th month, 1717.

Joseph Buckley, son of Joseph Buckley, late of the city of London, in the
  Kingdom of Great Britain, merchant, deceased, and Sarah Masters,
  daughter of Thomas Masters of the city of Philadelphia, merchant,
  mar this 5th day of the 10th month, 1717.

James Whitton of the county of Salem in the Western division of Nove Casarea or New Jersey, yeoman, and Catherine Bedward, daughter of William Bedward late of Meirian, in the county of Philadelphia, mar this 10th day of the 5th month, 1718.

Edward Brooks of the city of Philadelphia, victualler, and Elizabeth Snead, daughter of William Snead, late of said city, deceased, mar this 4th day of the 12th month, 1719.

James Parrock of the city of Philadelphia, shipwright, and Hannah England of said city, widow, mar this 13th day of the 2nd month, 1721.

Thomas Pennington, son of William Pennington of the county of Philadelphia, yeoman, and Martha Steele, daughter of James Steele of the city of Philadelphia, mar this 20th day of the 5th month, 1721.

John Fisher of the city of Philadelphia, cordwainer, and Catherine Brooksby of the said city, mar this 11th day of the 11th month, 1721.

Joseph England of the county of New Castle on Delaware, yeoman, and Elizabeth Brown of the city of Philadelphia, widow, mar this 1st day of the 12th month, 1721.

Solomon Rachford, son of Dennis Rachford late of Philadelphia, yeoman, deceased, and Alice James, daughter of Edward James. late of the city of Philadelphia, bricklayer, deceased, mar this 14th day of the 1st month, 1722.

Samuel Austin, son of John Austin, late of the city of Philadelphia, deceased, and Mary Jarman, daughter of Edward Jarman, late of said city, deceased, mar this 25th day of the 2nd month, 1723.

Hugh Durberow of the city of Philadelphia, boulter, and Hannah Albeson of said city, widow, mar this 11th day of the 5th month, 1723.

Samuel Preston of the city of Philada., mercht. and Margaret Langdale of said city, widow, mar this 9th day of the 5th month, 1724.

Edmond Beakes of the county of Burlington in the Western Division of Nova Casarea or New Jersey, yeoman, and Elizabeth Large, late of the same place but now residing in the county of Philadelphia, widow, mar this 23rd day of the 5th month, 1724.

Arnold Cassel, son of Arnold Cassel, late of the county of Philadelphia, yeoman, deceased, and Lydia Fordham, daughter of Benjamin Fordham of the city of Annapolis in the province of Maryland, merchant, deceased, mar this 28th day of the 5th month, 1724.

George Wilson of the city of Philadelphia, joyner, and Mary Oldham (Oldman) of said city mar this 8th day of the 8th month, 1724.

Edward Owen, son of Griffith Owen, late of the city of Philada., Practitioner in Physick, deceased, and Susannah Kearney, daughter of Philip Kearney, mercht., deceased, mar this 15th day of the 8th month, 1724.

Job Goodson, son of John Goodson of the city of Philadelphia, Practitioner of Physick, and Jane Marryott of the said city, widow, mar this 8th day of the 2nd month, 1725.

Richard Smith of the Western Division of New Jersey, merchant, and Eliza. Powell, daughter of David Powell of the city of Philadelphia, yeoman, mar this 27th day of the 3rd month, 1725.

Nehemiah Allen of the city of Philadelphia, cooper, Rebecah Blackfan of said city, widow, mar this 1st day of the 5th month, 1725.

John Kinsey, son of John Kinsey of the Eastern Division of New Jersey, and Mary Kearney, daughter of Philip Kearney, late of the city of Philadelphia, deceased, mar this 9th day of the 7th month, 1725.

Thomas Masters of the city of Philadelphia, merchant, and Hannah Dickinson of said city, mar this 10th day of the 12th month, 1725.

James Claypoole, son of Nathaniel Claypoole of the city of Philadelphia, deceased, and Mary Hood, daughter of Thomas Hood of the county of Philadelphia, yeoman, mar this 19th day of the 3rd month, 1726.

John Elfreth, son of Henry Elfreth, late of the city of Philadelphia, shipwright, deceased, and Elizabeth Heywood, daughter of John Heywood of said city, cordwainer, deceased, mar this 16th day of 4th month, 1726.

Francis Richardson of the city of Philadelphia, goldsmith, and Latitia Swift, late of Great Britain, mar this 30th day of the 4th month, 1726.

Ralph Hoy of the city of Philadelphia, weaver, and Rebecah Cooper, daughter of James Cooper, of the same City, mar this 15th day of the 7th month, 1726.

Isaac Pillar, son of James Pillar, late of the city of Philadelphia, carpenter, deceased, and Sarah Wood, daughter of G. W. of said city, mar this 4th day of the 9th month, 1726.

John Gilbert of Burlington in New Jersey, cooper, and Mary Pryor, daughter of Thomas Pryor of the city of Philadelphia, boulter, mar this 10th day of the 9th month, 1726.

Samuel Powell, son of William Powell of the city of Philadelphia, cooper, and Mary Raper, daughter of Henry Raper, late of the Island of Barbadoes, deceased, mar this 17th day of the 9th month, 1726.

Thomas Nixson of the city of Philadelphia, yeoman, and Rachel Blackbourne of said city, widdow, mar this 5th day of the 11th month, 1726.

Moses Hughs of the city of Philadelphia, taylor, and Sarah Blythe of said city, widdow, mar this 26th day of the 11th month, 1726.

William Griffiths of Bethell Township, county of Chester, weaver, and Susannah Cassel, daughter of Arnold Cassel, late of the county of Philadelphia, deceased, mar this 14th day of the 1st month, 1726/7.

Jacob Coffin of the city of Philadelphia, wheelwright, and Rachel Rakestraw, daughter of William Rakestraw of said city, yeoman, mar this 20th day of the 2nd month, 1727.

Henry Cliffton of the city of Philadelphia, weaver, and Sarah Dunn of said city, widow, mar this 15th day of the 4th month, 1727.

Jacob Durborow, son of Hugh Durborow of the city of Philadelphia, boulter, and Anne Albertson, daughter of William Albertson, late of the county of Philadelphia, yeoman, mar this 9th day of the 9th month, 1727.

John Paschall, son of Thomas Paschall of the county of Philadelphia, yeoman, and Frances Hodge, daughter of Henry Hodge of the city of Philadelphia, merchant, mar this 25th day of the 2nd month, 1728.

Abraham Carleill of the city of Philadelphia, cooper, and Mary Kay, daughter of John Kay of said city, victualler, mar this 28th day of the 3rd month, 1728.

John Fisher, son of John Fisher, late of the city of Philadelphia, dec'd, and Mary Hodge, daughter of Henry Hodge of the same City, merchant, mar this 30th day of the 3rd month, 1728.

Knight Hodge, son of Henry Hodge of the city of Philadelphia, merchant, and Susanah Bickley, daughter of Abraham Bickley, late of said city, merchant, deceased, mar this 25th day of the 5th month, 1728.

William Rawle, son of Francis Rawle, late of the county of Philadelphia, dec'd, and Margaret Hodge, daughter of Henry Hodge of the city of Philadelphia, merchant, mar this 29th day of the 6th month, 1728.

Thomas Gilpin of the county of Chester, yeoman, and Hannah Knowles of the city of Philadelphia, spinster, mar this 26th day of the 7th month, 1728.

Richard Hill of the city of Philadelphia and Mary Stanbury, daughter of Nathan Stanbury, late of this City, merchant, dec'd, mar this 31st day of the 8th month, 1728.

Joseph Wharton of the city of Philadelphia, cooper, son of Thomas Wharton, late of said city, deceased, and Hannah Carpenter, daughter of John Carpenter, late of city aforesaid, deceased, mar this 5th day of the 1st month, 1729.

John Jervis, son of Martyn Jervis of the city of Philadelphia, mercer, and Rebeccah Walton, daughter of Michael Walton of the said city, innholder, mar this 14th day of the 3rd month, 1730.

Robert Jordan, late of Nansimund in Virginia, and Mary Hill of the City and county of Philadelphia, widow, mar this 3rd day of the 4th month, 1731.

Jeremiah Elfreth of the city of Philadelphia and Letitia Richardson of city aforesaid, widow, mar this 6th day of the 5th month, 1731.

William Sandwith of the city of Philadelphia, mariner, and Sarah Jervis, daughter of Martin Jervis of city aforesaid, mercer, mar this 2nd day of the 7th month, 1731.

John Jones, son of Thomas Jones of Sheltnam, county of Philadelphia, and Rebecca Head, daughter of John Head of the city of Philadelphia, mar this 16th day of the 7th month, 1731.

James Parrock, son of James Parrock of the city of Philadelphia, shipwright, and Priscilla Coats, daughter of Wm. Coats of the Northern Liberties of the city aforesaid, mar this 20th day of the 7th month, 1731.

Obadiah Eldridge of the city of Philadelphia, cordwainer, son of Jonathan Eldridge of Evesham in West New Jersey, and Phebe Guest, daughter of George Guest of Burlington in West New Jersey, mar this 7th day of the 8th month, 1731.

George Wilson of the city of Philadelphia and Mary Rakestraw of the city aforesaid mar the 14th day of the 8th month, 1731.

Samuel Dickinson of Talbot County in the province of Maryland, mercht, and Mary Cadwalader, daughter of John Cadwalader of the city of Philadelphia, mar this 4th day of the 9th month, 1731.

William Warner of the city of Philadelphia, turner, and Mary Welton, daughter of John Welton of Southampton in Bucks County, mar this 25th day of the 9th month, 1731.

Samuel Emlen, son of George Emlen, late of the city of Philadelphia, deceased, and Rachel Hudson, daughter of William Hudson of the city aforesaid, mar this 2nd day of the 10th month, 1731.

Joseph Cloud of Chester County and Hannah Baldwin of the city of Philadelphia, widow, mar this 6th day of the 2nd month, 1732.

William Cooper of Newtown in the province of New Jersey and Mary Rawle, daughter of Francis Rawle of the city of Philadelphia, deceased, mar this 25th day of the 5th month, 1732.

Joseph Stretch, hatter, son of Peter Stretch of the city of Philadelphia, clockmaker, and Lydia Knight, daughter of John Knight of said city, mar this 24th day of the 6th month, 1732.

Stephen Armitt, son of Richard Armitt of the city of Philadelphia and Sarah Whitpain, daughter of John Whitpain of the City aforesaid, mar this 24th day of the 9th month, 1732.

Samuel Powell of the city of Philadelphia, merchant, son of Samuel Powel of the city aforesaid, carpenter, and Mary Morris, daughter of Anthony Morris of said city, brewer, mar this 9th day of the 9th month, 1732.

William Parker of the city of Philadelphia, smith, son of Joseph Parker of Shrewsbury in Monmouth County in the province of New Jersey,, deceased, and Elizabeth Gilbert, daughter of Joshua Gilbert of the city of Philadelphia, deceased mar this 23rd day of the 11th month, 1732.

Nathan Cowman of the city of Philadelphia, mariner, son of Matthew Cowman of the county of Cumberland in Great Britain, and Mary Shute, daughter of Thomas Shute of Milksham in the county of Wilts in Great Britain, mar this 1st day of the 8th month, 1732.

Daniel Stanton of the city of Philadelphia, joyner, son of Daniel Stanton of city aforesaid, mariner, deceased, and Sarah Lloyd, daughter of

John Lloyd of said city, smith, deceased, mar this 5th day of the 2nd month, 1733.

William Plumsted, son of Clement Plumsted of the city of Philadelphia, mercht, and Rebecca Kearney, daughter of Philip Kearney of city aforesaid, mercht, deceased, mar this 19th day of the 2nd month, 1733.

Mordecai Lloyd, son of Thomas Lloyd, late of the city of London in Great Britain, mercht, dec'd, and Hannah Fishbourn, daughter of Wm. Fishbourn of the city of Philadelphia, merchant, mar this 19th day of the 3rd month, 1733.

Henry Clifton of the city of Philadelphia, weaver, and Sarah Maule of the city aforesaid, widow, mar this 15th day of the 9th month, 1733.

Wight Massey of the city of Philadelphia, cooper, son of Samuel Massey of the city aforesaid, deceased, and Elizabeth Jones, daughter of John Jones of said city, merchant, mar this 20th day of the 10th month, 1733.

Isaac Zane of the city of Philadelphia, carpenter, son of Nathaniel Zane, deceased, and Sarah Elfreth, daughter of Henry Elfreth of the city aforesaid, ship-carpenter, deceased, mar this 15th day of the 11th month, 1733.

Edward Warner of the city of Philadelphia, carpenter, and Ann Coleman, daughter of William Coleman of city aforesaid, carpenter, deceased, mar this 29th day of 11th month, 1733.

John Dillwyn of the city of Philadelphia and Susanna Painter, daughter of George Painter of city aforesaid, deceased, mar this 7th day of the 12th month, 1733.

Isaac Garrigues of the city of Philadelphia, cooper, son of Matthew Garrigues of city aforesaid, deceased, and Christian Broadgate, daughter of Thomas Broadgate of said city, taylor, mar this 7th day of 1st month, 1734.

William Moode of the city of Philadelphia, cordwainer, son of Alexander Moode of Newcastle County on Delaware, deceased, and Hannah Cockfield of the city of Philadelphia, daughter of Joshua Cockfield, deceased, mar this 11th day of the 2nd month, 1734.

John Morris of Whitemarsh, county of Philadelphia, son of Anthony Morris of the city of Philadelphia, brewer, and Mary Sutton, daughter of Richard Sutton of the city aforesaid, deceased, mar this 18th day of the 2nd month, 1734.

John Burr of Northampton in the county of Burlington, in the province of New Jersey, and Susanna Owen, widow of Robert and daughter of William Hudson, of the city of Pennsylvania, mar this 2nd day of the 3rd month, 1734.

Benjamin Maddock, son of Mordecai Maddock of Springfield in Chester County and Elizabeth Hart, daughter of John Hart of the city of Philadelphia, bricklayer, mar this 9th day of the 3rd month, 1734.

Nicholas Waln, son of Richard Waln of the Northern Liberties of the city
of Philadelphia and Mary Shoemaker, daughter of George Shoemaker
of the city aforesaid, mar this 23rd day of the 3rd month, 1734.

Abraham Mitchel of the city of Philadelphia, hatter, son of Thomas
Mitchel of the city aforesaid and Sarah Robins, daughter of Samuel
Robins of the said city, deceased, mar this 30th day of the 3rd month,
1734.

Benjamin Trotter of the city of Philadelphia, joyner, and Mary Corker of
the city aforesaid, widow, mar this 4th day of the 4th month, 1734.

Jonathan Wright of Burlington in the province of New Jersey and
Elizabeth Preston of the city of Philadelphia, widow, mar this 11th
day of the 4th month, 1734.

Samuel Coates of the city of Philadelphia and Mary Langdale of
Passyunk of the county of Philadelphia, mar this 13th day of the 4th
month, 1734.

Thomas Peters of the city of Philadelphia, cooper, son of Rice Peters of
the said city, and Hannah Newman of the City aforesaid, mar this
15th day of the 6th month, 1734.

William Atkinson of the city of Philadelphia, shipwright, and Sarah
Pawley of the city aforesaid mar this 24th day of the 7th month, 1734.

Samuel Boone, son of George Boone of Oley, county of Philadelphia and
Elizabeth Cassel of the city of Philadelphia mar this 29th day of the
8th month, 1734.

Hugh Thomas of Blockley in the county of Philadelphia and Sarah
Eastburn of the city of Philadelphia mar this 14th day of the 9th
month, 1734.

Jeremiah Elfreth of the city of Philadelphia and Elizabeth Massey of the
city aforesaid mar this 12th day of the 10th month, 1734.

Anthony Nicholas of the city of Philadelphia, son of Samuel Nicholas,
deceased, and Rebecca Shute, daughter of Thomas Shute of the city
aforesaid, mar this 16th day of the 11th month, 1734.

Hugh Roberts, son of Edward Roberts of the city of Philadelphia, and
Mary Calvert, daughter of George Calvert of the City aforesaid, mar
this 29th day of the 3rd month, 1735.

Roger Brooke of the city of Philadelphia, shipwright, and Sarah Bowyer
of the city aforesaid, mar this 10th day of the 4th month, 1735.

Thomas Bond of the city of Philadelphia, Practitioner in Physick, and
Susanna Roberts, daughter of Edward Roberts of the city aforesaid,
mar this 11th day of the 7th month, 1735.

John Gillingham of the city of Philadelphia, joyner, and Ann Jacob,
daughter of Samuel Jacob, of the said city, mariner, mar this 21st day
of the 8th month, 1735.

David Ferris of the city of Philadelphia and Mary Massey of the city
aforesaid mar this 13th day of the 9th month, 1735.

Joseph Cooper of Newtown, Glocester County, province of New Jersey, and Hannah Dent, daughter of Robert Dent of Wenslydale, County of York, in Great Britain, mar this 1st day of the 3rd month, 1735.

Rees Lloyd of the city of Philadelphia and Sarah Cox of the City aforesaid, daughter of Abraham Cox, deceased, mar this 12th day of the 12th month, 1735.

Christopher Marshall of Middletown, county of Bucks, and Sarah Thompson, daughter of Robert Thompson of the city of Philadelphia, mariner, mar this 4th day of the 1st month, 1735.

Jeremiah Warder of the city of Philadelphia, hatter, and Mary Head, daughter of John Head of said city, mar this 13th day of the 2nd month, 1736.

John Reynell (Reynolds) of the city of Philadelphia, merchant, and Mary Nicholas of the said city, widow, mar this 15th day of the 3rd month, 1736.

Obadiah Eldridge of the city of Philadelphia, cordwainer, son of Jonathan Eldridge of Evesham, province of New Jersey, yeoman, and Mary Oldman of the city aforesaid, widow, daughter of Samuel Garret of Darby, in Chester County, mar this 22nd day of the 2nd month, 1736.

Owen Evans of Gwynedd in the county of Philadelphia and Mary Nicholas of the city of Philadelphia, daughter of Samuel Nicholas, yeoman, deceased, mar this 29th day of the 2nd month, 1736.

Anthony Benezet, son of J. Stephen Benezet of the city of Philadelphia, and Joyce Marriot of said city, mar this 13th day of the 3rd month, 1736.

Samuel Redman of the city of Philadelphia, bricklayer, and Martha Wollaston, daughter of Thomas Wollaston of the said city, cordwainer, mar this 21st day of the 8th month, 1736.

Enoch Flower of the city of Philadelphia and Ann Jones, daughter of John Jones of the said city, merchant, mar this 24th day of the 12th month, 1736.

John Biddle of the city of Philadelphia, son of William Biddle of Mansfield in the province of New Jersey, and Sarah Owen, daughter of Owen Owen of the same City, mar this 3rd day of the 1st, 1736.

Edward Evans of the city of Philadelphia and Rebecca Clark, daughter of William Clark of the Province aforesaid, deceased, mar this 5th day of the 3rd month, 1737.

Samuel Rhoads of the city of Philadelphia, son of John Rhoads, deceased, and Elizabeth Chandler, daughter of Samuel Chandler of the said city, deceased, mar this 12th day of the 3rd month, 1737.

Samuel Sansom of the city of Philadelphia, merchant, son of John Sansom of the city of London, in Great Britain, and Sarah Johnson, daughter of Joshua Johnson of the city of Philadelphia, aforesaid, mar this 19th day of the 3rd month, 1737.

William Bennett of the city of Philadelphia, son of Humphry Bennett of Prescott in the Parish of Culmstock, in Great Britain, deceased, and Mary Davies of the city aforesaid, daughter of Evan Davies of Perkyomy in Beaver Township, mar this 4th day of the 8th month, 1737.

Job Yarnall of the Township of Ridley in the county of Chester, husbandman, son of Philip Yarnall of the Township of Edgemont, county aforesaid, deceased, and Rebekah Lownes of the city of Philadelphia, daughter of James Lownes of said city, mar this 13th day of the 8th month, 1737.

Hugh Durborow of the city of Philadelphia, boulter, and Sarah Freeman of the city aforesaid, widow, mar this 29th day of the 9th month, 1737.

Giles Brimble of the city of Philadelphia, cordwainer, son of John Brimble of Woolley, of Somersetshire, Great Britain, deceased, and Cicely Llewellyn of the city aforesaid, daughter of Morris Llewellyn of Harford Township, said Province, mar this 15th day of the 10th month, 1737.

William Coleman of the city of Philadelphia, merchant, son of William Coleman of the city aforesaid, deceased, and Hannah Fitzwater, daughter of George Fitzwater of the said city, mar this 26th day of the 11th month, 1737.

Joseph Marshall of the city of Philadelphia, bricklayer, son of Ralph Marshall of Mansfield in Nottinghamshire, in Great Britain, and Rachel Marle of the city aforesaid, daughter of Thomas Marle of said city, deceased, mar this 9th day of the 12th month, 1737.

Edward Roberts of the city of Philadelphia and Martha Cox of the city aforesaid mar this 13th day of the 2nd month, 1738.

Reese Meredith of the city of Philadelphia, son of Rees Meredith of Landegley, in Radnorshire, Great Britain, deceased, and Martha Carpenter of the city aforesaid, daughter of Jno. Carpenter of said city, deceased, mar this 23rd day of the 3rd month, 1738.

James Cresson of the city of Philadelphia, son of Solomon Cresson of said city and Sarah Emlen, daughter of George Emlem of City aforesaid City, deceased, mar this 25th day of the 3rd month, 1738.

Ralph Loftus of the city of Philadelphia, mariner, son of Ralph Loftus of Hartmoore, County Durham, Great Britain, yeoman, deceased, and Jane Cart of the said city, daughter of Samuel Cart of Abbington, yeoman, deceased, mar this 8th day of the 4th month, 1738.

Joseph Armitt of the city of Philadelphia, joyner, son of Thomas Armitt, late of the city aforesaid, deceased, and Elizabeth Lisle, daughter of Maurrice Lisle, late of the city aforesaid, deceased, mar this 9th day of the 9th month, 1738.

Isaac Andrews, son of Edward Andrews of West Jersey, and Eliza.
Elfreth, daughter of Jeremiah Elfreth of the city of Philadelphia,
blacksmith, mar this 21st day of the 9th month, 1738.

William Fisher of the city of Philadelphia, son of William Fisher of said
city, deceased, and Sarah Coleman, daughter of William Coleman of
the city aforesaid, deceased, mar this 23rd day of the 11th month,
1738.

George Shires of the city of Philadelphia, son of George Shires of the city
aforesaid, deceased, and Hannah Durborow, daughter of Daniel
Durborow of said city, deceased, mar this 15th day of the 1st month,
1738-9.

Charles Jenkins of the city of Philadelphia, son of Stephen Jenkins of
Abington, county of Philadelphia, and Mary Gray, daughter of Joseph
Gray of the city aforesaid, mar this 26th day of the 2nd month, 1739.

Jacob Townsend of Salem, province of New West Jersey, son of Richard
Townsend of Cape May, Province aforesaid, deceased, and Mary
Harper, daughter of John Harper, late of Philadelphia, deceased, mar
this 29th day of the 3rd month, 1739.

Isaac Norris of the city of Philadelphia, son of Isaac Norris, late of
Farhill in the Northern Liberties of Philadelphia, deceased, and
Sarah Logan, daughter of James Logan of Stenton, county of
Philadelphia, mar this 6th day of the 4th month, 1739.

Joseph Chetham of the city of Philadelphia, son of John Chetham, late of
city aforesaid, deceased, and Elizabeth Roberts, daughter of James
Roberts of the city of London in Great Britain, deceased, mar this
17th day of the 5th month, 1739.

Benjamin Shoemaker of the city of Philadelphia, mercht, and Elizabeth
Morris, daughter of Antony Morris of the City aforesaid, brewer, mar
this 6th day of the 7th month, 1739.

Thomas Robinson of the city of Philadelphia, son of Edward Robinson of
White Marsh, county aforesaid, cooper, deceased, and Mary Brown,
daughter of Nathaniel Brown of the city aforesaid, mariner, deceased,
mar this 9th day of the 8th month, 1739.

Thomas Hallowell of the city of Philadelphia, son of John Hallowell of
Darby in Chester County, yeoman, and Ann Thomson, daughter of
Robert Thomson of city aforesaid, mariner, mar this 6th day of the
10th month, 1739.

Anthony Nicholas of the city of Philadelphia and Mary Cowman mar this
3rd day of the 11th month, 1739.

Wm. Lawrance of Middletown, province of East New Jersey, son of Wm.
Lawrence of the Province aforesaid, deceased, and Martha Head,
daughter of John Head of the city of Philadelphia, mar this 3rd day of
the 2nd month, 1740.

John Jones of Germantown, county of Philadelphia, tanner, son of
Griffith Jones of Oxford, county aforesaid, and Elizabeth Hudson,

daughter of Samuel Hudson, late of the said city, deceased, mar this 8th day of the 3rd month, 1740.

Jeremiah Elfreth of the city of Philadelphia and Mary Wells of the city aforesaid, widow, mar this 17th day of the 4th month, 1740.

Jonathan Evans of the city of Philadelphia, son of Evan Evans of Gwynedd, county aforesaid, and Hannah Walton, daughter of Michael Walton. late of the city of Philadelphia, deceased, mar this 19th day of the 4th month, 1740.

James Davis of the city of Philadelphia, son of Samuel Davis, late of said city, deceased, and Rachel Roberts, daughter of Thomas Roberts, late of the city aforesaid, deceased, mar this 25th day of the 5th month, 1740.

Stephen Jenkins, son of Stephen Jenkins of Abbington, county of Philadelphia, and Hannah Widdifield, daughter of John Widdifield, late of the city of Philadelphia, deceased, mar this 21st day of the 8th month, 1740.

John Ogden of the city of Philadelphia and Hannah Owen daughter of Robert Owen, late of said city, mar this 23rd day of the 8th month, 1740.

James Stephens of the city of Philadelphia and Mary Widdowfield, daughter of John Widdowfeild, late of said city, deceased, mar this 11th day of the 9th month, 1740.

Joseph Sanders of the city of Philadelphia, merchant, and Hannah Reeve, daughter of John Reeve of said city, merchant, mar this 8th day of the 11th month, 1740

Richard Blackham of the city of Philadelphia, blacksmith, and Rebeckah Minshall, spinster, daughter of Rebeckah Minshall of said city, widow, mar this 5th day of the 1st month, 1740.

William Logan, son of James Logan of Stenton, county of Philadelphia, and Hannah Emlen, daughter of George Emlen of the city of Philadelphia, mar this 24th day of the 1st month, called Mar, 1740.

Thomas James, son of Thomas James of the city of Philadelphia, mariner, and Hannah Webb, daughter of Joseph Webb, late of the said city, taylor, deceased, mar this 7th day of the month called May, 1741.

Joseph Dubre, son of Jacob Dubre of the Northern Liberties of the city of Philadelphia, yeoman, deceased, and Hannah Bissell, daughter of William Bissell of the same City, blacksmith, mar this 14th day of the 3rd month, called May, 1741.

Joseph Howell, son of Jacob Howell of Chester, tanner, and Hannah Hudson, daughter of Samuel Hudson, late of the city of Philadelphia, tanner, deceased, mar this 19th day of the 3rd month, called May, 1741.

George Gray, son of Joseph Gray of the city of Philadelphia, innholder, and Mercy Warner, daughter of John Warner of Blockley Township, county of Philadelphia, cordwainer, mar this 21st day of the 3rd month, called May, 1741.

Thomas Tillbury, son of Thomas Tillbury, late of the Parish of Gatlick Hill in London, winecooper, and Anne Warner, daughter of Isaac Warner of Blockley Township, county of Philadelphia, yeoman, mar this 26th day of the 3rd month, called May, 1741.

Robert Worril of the city of Philadelphia, cordwainer, son of Richard Worril, late of the Township of Lower Dublin, deceased, and Elizabeth Waln, daughter of John Waln, late of the Northern Liberties of the said city, mar this 11th day of the 4th month, called June, 1741.

Joseph Richardson of the city of Philadelphia, silversmith, and Hannah Worril, daughter of Richard Worril, late of the Township of Lower Dublin, county of Philadelphia, yeoman, deceased, mar this 13th day of the 6th month, called August, 1741.

Joseph Morris of the city of Philadelphia, hatter, son of Anthony Morris of said city, brewer, and Martha Fitzwater, daughter of George Fitzwater of said city, merchant, mar this 18th day of the 12th month, called February, 1741/2.

Isaac Garrigues of the city of Philadelphia, cooper, and Sarah Powell, daughter of Wm. Powell, late of said city, cooper, dec'd, mar this 4th day of the 12th month, called February, 1741/2.

Jacob Cooper, son of William Cooper of the city of Philadelphia, shopkeeper, and Elizabeth Corker, daughter of William Corker, late of said city, plaisterer, mar this 9th day of the 9th month, called Nov., 1742.

Benjamin Hooton, of the city of Philadelphia, hatter, son of Hooton of the City of Philadelphia, hatter, son of Thomas of Philadelphia, and Hannah Head, daughter of John Head of the said city, mar this 21st day of the month, called December, 1742.

Francis Richardson of the city of Philadelphia, merchant, son of Francis Richardson, late of the said city, goldsmith, deceased, and Mary Fitzwater, daughter of George Fitzwater of the city aforesaid, merchant, mar this 30th day of the 10th month, called December, 1742.

Paul Chaunders of the city of Philadelphia, wool-comber, and Jane Johnson of the city aforesaid, widow, mar this 11th day of the 11th month, 1742-3.

Thomas Kite of the city of Philadelphia, cordwainer, son of Abraham Kite of the Township of Blockly, county of Philadelphia, yeoman, and Mary Bruitnall, daughter of John Brintnall of the city aforesaid, mar this 10th day of the 12th month, 1742-3.

Nehemiah Allen, son of Nathaniel Allen of the city of Philadelphia, cooper, and Rebekah Roberts, daughter of Thomas Roberts of the same place, deceased, mar this 12th day of the 3rd month, 1743.

Samuel Wetherill of the city of Philadelphia, carpenter, son of Thomas Wetherill of Burlington in West New Jersey, and Mary Noble, daughter of Joseph Noble of the city aforesaid, mar this 19th day of the 3rd month, 1743.

Anthony Siddon of the city of Philadelphia, joyner, son of Thomas Siddon of Upper Dublin in the county of Philadelphia, deceased, and Deborah Jones, daughter of John Jones of City aforesaid, cooper, mar this 26th day of the 3rd month, 1743.

Samuel Lippincott of the city of Philadelphia, blacksmith, son of William Lippincott of the Township of Shrewsbury, county of Munmouth in East Jersey and Mary Preston, daughter of Paul Preston of the city aforesaid, deceased, mar this 7th day of the 4th month, 1743.

Thomas Fisher of the city of Philadelphia, cooper, son of William Fisher of the said city, deceased, and Abigail Cooper, daughter of William Cooper of the city aforesaid, shopkeeper, mar this 22nd day of the 7th month, 1743.

Judah Foulke of the city of Philadelphia, shopkeeper, son of Cadwalader of the same place, deceased, and Mary Bringhurst, daughter of John Bringhurst of the city aforesaid, cooper, mar this 16th day of the 12th month, 1743.

John Guest of the city of Philadelphia, cordwainer, son of George Guest of Burlington in West New Jersey, deceased, and Elizabeth Simmons of the city aforesaid, daughter of Stephen Simmons of Salem, in West New Jersey, mar this 23rd day of the 12th month, 1743/4.

Morris Morris of Upper Dublin in the county of Philadelphia, son of Morris Morris of Richland, county of Bucks, and Elizabeth Mifflin, daughter of Jonathan Mifflin of the city of Philadelphia, mar this 22nd day of the 1st month, 1743/4.

John Galloway of the county of Ann-Arundel in the province of Maryland, merchant, and Jane Fishbourn of the city of Philadelphia, widow, mar this 12th day of the 2nd month, 1744.

John Garrigues of the city of Philadelphia, cooper, and Rebekah Oakham of the same place, daughter of Jacob Oakham of Buckingham in the county of Bucks, mar this 19th day of the 2nd month, 1744.

Samuel Gray of the city of Philadelphia, shortcutter, son of Joseph Gray of the city aforesaid and Patience Roberts of the same place, daughter of Robert Roberts, late of the county of Calvert and province of Maryland, deceased, mar this 26th day of the 2nd month, 1744.

Daniel Morris of Upper Dublin in the county of Philadelphia, son of Morris Morris of Richland, county of Bucks, and Tacy Owen, daughter of Owen Owen, late of the said city, deceased, mar this 10th day of the 3rd month, 1744.

John Page of the city of Philadelphia, turner, son of George Page of the same place, and Ann Lownes, daughter of Joseph Lownes of Passiunk, province aforesaid, mar this 24th day of the 3rd month, 1744.

Isaac Lobdell of the city of Philadelphia, carpenter, and Rebekah Cresson, daughter of Solomon Cresson of the same place, mar this 14th day of the 4th month, 1744.

Benjamin Dawson of the city of Philadelphia, hatter, son of John Dawson, late of the same place, deceased, and Eliza Fossell, daughter of Solomon Fossell of city aforesaid, mar this 19th day of the 5th month, 1744.

William Rodman of Burlington in West New Jersey, son of John Rodman of the same place, Practitioner in Physick, and Mary Reeve of the city of Philadelphia, daughter of John Reeve, late of Burlington, aforesaid, deceased, mar this 6th day of the 7th month, 1744.

Thomas Maule of the city of Philadelphia, joyner, son of Thos. Maule of Salem, in New England, deceased, and Susannah Hogg of the city aforesaid, daughter of James Hogg of New Castle, deceased, mar this 18th day of the 10th month, 1744.

Robert Adams of the city of Philadelphia, cooper, son of Robt. Adams of the same place, Ann David of the city aforesaid, daughter of Evan David of Montgomery in the county of Philadelphia, mar this 17th day of the 11th month, 1744/5.

Joseph Saull of Haddonfield, county of Gloucester, West New Jersey and Mary Mariot of the city of Philadelphia, mar this 24th day of the 11th month, 1744/5.

Thomas Marriott of the Burrough of Bristol. county of Bucks, and Mary Foulke of the city of Philadelphia, widow, mar this 31st day of the 11th month, 1744/5.

Herman Casdorp of the city of Philadelphia, shipwright, and Mary Woodley of the same place, widow, mar this 21st day of the 12th month, 1745.

John Elliot of Darby, county of Chester, son of Thomas Elliott of St. George, county of New Castle, and Elizabeth Warner daughter of John Warner of the city of Philadelphia, mar this 18th day of the 2nd month, 1745.

Joseph Hallowell of the city of Philadelphia, cordwainer, son of John Hallowell of the Township of Darby, county of Chester and Eliza. Holcombe, daughter of Jacob Holcombe of Buckingham, county of Bucks mar this 13th day of the 4th month, 1745.

John Robins of the city of Philadelphia, shipwright, and Mary Skelton of the same place mar this 11th day of the 5th month, 1745.

Isaac Griffitts of the city of Philadelphia, merchant, son of Thos. Griffitts of the same place, merchant, and Sarah Fitzwater, daughter of

George Fitzwater of the city aforesaid, merchant, mar this 25th day of the 5th month, 1745.

Mordecai Yarnall of the Township of Willis-town, county of Chester and Mary Roberts of the city of Philadelphia, daughter of Edward Roberts, late of said city, deceased, mar this 8th day of the 6th month, 1745.

Henry Van Aken of the city of Philadelphia, shopkeeper, and Jane Goodson of the City aforesaid, widdow, mar this 22nd day of the 6th month, 1745.

James Lindley of the city of Philadelphia, blacksmith, and Susanna Lowns, daughter of Joseph Lowns of Passiunk, county of Philadelphia mar this 12th day of the 7th month, 1745.

Moses Forster of the city of Philadelphia, chairmaker, son of Reubon and Alice Benson, daughter of John Benson of the City aforesaid, mar this 26th day of the 7th month, 1745.

Joseph Warner of the city of Philadelphia, shipwright, and Rebekah Boyer of the same place, mar this 15th day of the 8th month, 1745.

John Hall of the Township of Springfield, county of Chester, yeoman, and Mary Tomlinson of the city of Philadelphia, widow mar this 17th day of the 8th month, 1745.

Joseph Jones of the city of Philadelphia, joyner, son of Samuel Jones of the same place and Ann Lawrance, daughter of Joshua Lawrance, late of said city, deceased, mar this 24th day of the 8th month, 1745.

John Jones of the city of Philadelphia, merchant, son of John Jones, late of the city aforesaid, deceased, and Sarah Mifflin, daughter of Jonathan Mifflin of the city aforesaid, mar this 28th day of the 8th month, 1745.

Paul Kripner of the city of Philadelphia, shopkeeper, and Eliza. Van Aken of the city aforesaid mar this 7th day of the 9th month, 1745.

Ebenezer Robinson of the city of Philadelphia, bricklayer, and Amey Jones, daughter of John Jones, late of the city aforesaid, deceased, mar this 21st day of the 9th month, 1745.

Samuel Howel of the city of Philadelphia, hatter, son of Thos. Howell of the Township of Chichester and Sarah Stretch of the city aforesaid mar this 12th day of the 10th month, 1745.

Hugh Forbes of the city of Philadelphia, cooper, and Rachel Thompson, daughter of Robert Thompson of said city, mar this 16th day of the 11th month, 1745/6.

Daniel Williams of the city of Philadelphia, baker, son of Edward Williams of Blockley, county of Philadelphia, and Jane Oldman, daughter of Thos. Oldman of said city, deceased, mar this 27th day of the 1st month, 1746.

Samuel Shoemaker of the city of Philadelphia, merchant, son of Benj. Shoemaker of the city aforesaid, merchant, and Hannah Carpenter, daughter of Samuel Carpenter of the city of aforesaid, merchant, mar this 8th day of the 2nd month, 1746.

Samuel Bonnel of the city of Philadelphia, blacksmith, son of Ro___ Bonnel of said city, deceased, and Sarah Thomson, daughter of Adam Thomson of the same place, dec'd, mar this 22nd day of the 2nd month, 1746.

John Head of the city of Philadelphia, hatter, son of John Head of the same place, and Mary Hudson, daughter of Sam'l Hudson, late of the said city, deceased, mar this 15th day of the 2nd month, 1746.

William Attmore of the city of Philadelphia, joyner, son of Thomas Attmore of the Township of Newton, county of Gloucester in West New Jersey, and Mary Stubbs of the city aforesaid, daughter of Thos. Stubbs of the county of Chester, mar this 8th day of the 3rd month, 1746.

Peter Brown of the city of Philadelphia, shipwright, and Sarah Fisher of the same place, widow, mar this 13th day of the 3rd month, 1746.

Eden Haydock of the city of Philadelphia, glaizer, son of Robert Haydock of Long Island and Elizabeth Forster, daughter of Reuben Forster of the said city, mar this 29th day of the 3rd month, 1746.

Samuel Abbott of the city of Philadelphia, house carpenter, son of John Abbott of Crosswicks in West New Jersey, deceased and Eliza. Hastings, daughter of John Hastings of the said city, deceased, mar this 3rd day of the 4th month, 1746.

William Savery of the city of Philadelphia, chairmaker, and Mary Peters of the same place, daughter of Reas Peters of the City aforesaid, mar this 19th day of the 4th month, 1746.

Henry Wood of the township of Waterford, county of Gloucester, province of West New Jersey, yeoman, and Mary Williams, daughter of Isaac Williams of the city of Philadelphia, shopkeeper, mar this 30th day of the 8th month, 1746.

Joseph Fox of the city of Philadelphia, carpenter, and Elizabeth Mickle, daughter of Samuel Mickle of the city aforesaid, merchant, mar this 25th day of the 9th month, 1746.

Joseph Richards of the city of Philadelphia, son of Philip Richards of the said city, deceased, and Mary Allen, of the same place, daughter of Nehemiah Allen, late of the city aforesaid, deceased, mar this 29th day of the 11th month, 1746/7.

Samuel Bryan of the city of Philadelphia, shipwright, son of Thomas Bryan of the Township of Northampton, county of Burlington in West New Jersey, deceased, and Sarah Head, of the city of Philadelphia, daughter of John Head of the city aforesaid, joyner, mar this 17th day of the 12th month, 1746/7.

Thomas Paschall of the city of Philadelphia, hatter, son of Thos. Paschall of Goshen, county of Chester, deceased, and Ann Chandler of the city aforesaid, daughter of Samuel Chandler of the said city, deceased, mar this 19th day of the 12th month, 1746/7.

Abel James of the city of Philadelphia, merchant, son of George James, late of the said city, deceased, and Rebecca Chalkley, daughter of Thomas Chalkley, late of the Northern Liberties in the county of Philadelphia, mar this 9th day of the 2nd month, 1747.

Isaac Jenkenson of the city of Philadelphia, carpenter, son of John Jenkenson, of Philadelphia aforesaid, deceased, and Mary Bould of the same place, daughter of Samuel Bould of the said city, deceased, mar this 16th day of the 2nd month, 1747.

David Cooper of the Township of Dedford, county of Gloucester, West New Jersey, son of John Cooper, late of the same place, deceased, and Sybil Matlack, daughter of Timothy Matlack of the city of Philadelphia, mar this 23rd day of the 2nd month, 1747.

John Miflin of the city of Philadelphia, carpenter, son of John Mifflin of Kent County on Delaware, deceased, and Hannah Taylor of the city aforesaid, daughter of Joseph Taylor of said city, deceased, mar this 7th day of the 3rd month, 1747.

David Edwards of the city of Philadelphia, wheelwright, son of Griffith Edwards, deceased, and Christian Lloyd, daughter of William Lloyd of the city aforesaid, mar this 21st day of the 3rd month, 1747.

Solomon Rochford of the city of Philadelphia, potter, and Rebecca Bolton of the same place, daughter of Everard Bolton of the Township of Cheltenham, county of Philadelphia, deceased, mar this 11th day of the 4th month, 1747.

William Dilworth of the city of Philadelphia, carpenter, son of James Dilworth of the Township of Bristol, county of Philadelphia, and Ann Wood of the city aforesaid, daughter of William Wood, late of Chesterfield, county of Burlington in West New Jersey, deceased, mar this 23rd day of the 4th month, 1747.

Thomas Priestly of the city of Philadelphia, joiner, son of John Priestly of the county of Bucks, Burrough of Bristol, deceased, and Mary Fairman of Kensington in the Northern Liberties of the said city, daughter of Benjamin Fairman, late of Kensington, aforesaid, deceased, mar this 7th day of the 5th month, 1747.

Joseph Lynn of the Northern Liberties of the city of Philadelphia, shipwright, son of Joseph Lynn, late of the same place, deceased, and Sarah Fairman, daughter of Benja. Fairman of the city of Philadelphia, deceased, mar this 27th day of the 8th month, 1747.

Jonathan Lewis of the city of Philadelphia, merchant, son of Evan Lewis, late of the Township of Newton, county of Chester, deceased, and Rachel Brintnall, daughter of John Brintnall, late of the said city, deceased, mar this 26th day of the 9th month, 1747.

Israel Pemberton, Junior, of the city of Philadelphia, merchant, son of
Israel Pemberton, merchant, of the same place, and Mary Jordan,
widow, of the same place, mar this 10th day of the 10th month, 1747.

Isaac Bartram of the city of Philadelphia, cordwainer, son of John
Bartram of Kingsess, county of Philadelphia, and Sarah Elfreeth of
the city aforesaid, daughter of Kaleb Elfreeth, late of said City,
deceased, mar this 17th day of the 10th month, 1747.

Peter Widdifield of the city of Philadelphia, blacksmith, son of John
Widdifield of the same place, deceased, and Rebekah Meredith,
daughter of John Meredith, late of the said city, deceased, mar this
24th day of the 1st month, 1747/8.

John Burroughs, Junior, of Haddonfield, county of Gloucester, province
of West New Jersey, son of John Burroughs of the same place, and
Barbara Fossell, daughter of Solomon Fossell of the city of
Philadelphia, mar this 7th day of the 2nd month, 1748.

Joseph Richardson of the city of Philadelphia, goldsmith, son of Francis
Richardson of the same place, deceased, and Mary Allen, daughter of
Nathaniel Allen of the city aforesaid, mar this 14th day of the 2nd
month, 1748.

Abraham Carlile of the city of Philadelphia, carpenter, son of John
Carlile of Burlington, province of West New Jersey, deceased, and
Ann Brooks, daughter of Edward Brooks of the city aforesaid, mar
this 19th day of the 2nd month, 1748.

Stephen Stapler of the city of Philadelphia, plaisterer, son of John
Stapler of the Township of Middletown, county of Bucks. and Mary
Giffin of the said city, daughter of Thos. Giffin, late of Chester,
deceased, mar this 21st day of the 2nd month, 1748.

Benjamin Hough of the city of Philadelphia, cooper, son of John Hough,
late of the Township of Makefield, county of Bucks, deceased, and
Elizabeth West of the city aforesaid, daughter of Thomas West, late
of Wilmington in New Castle County on Delaware, deceased, mar this
9th day of the 4th month, 1748.

Davis Bassett of the city of Philadelphia, carpenter, son of Elisha Bassett
of Pilesgrove, county of Salem in New Jersey, and Mary Elwell, of the
city aforesaid, widow, mar this 16th day of the 4th month, 1748.

Samuel Burge of the city of Philadelphia, merchant, son of William Burge
of the same place, deceased, and Beulah Shoemaker, daughter of
Benjamin Shoemaker of the same City, mar this 18th day of the 4th
month, 1748.

Francis Harding of the city of Philadelphia, taylor, and Rebekah
Ballenger of the city aforesaid, daughter of Henry Ballenger of
Evesham, Burlington County, in New Jersey, deceased, mar this 7th
day of the 5th month, 1748.

Nathaniel Parr of the city of Philadelphia, baker, son of William Parr,
late of Nottingham in Great Britain, deceased, and Elizabeth Young,

daughter of John Young, late of the said city, deceased, mar this 1st day of the 7th month, 1748.

John Moore of the city of Philadelphia, blacksmith, son of John Moore of the same place, deceased, and Elizabeth Chaunders, daughter of Paul Chaunders of the city aforesaid, mar this 6th day of the 10th month, 1748.

John Smith of the city of Philadelphia, merchant, son of Richard Smith, Junior, of Burlington, province of New Jersey, and Hannah Logan, daughter of James Logan of Steton, county of Philadelphia, mar this 7th day of the 10th month, 1748.

Joseph Baker of the city of Philadelphia, hatter, son of Samuel Baker, late of the Township of Makefield, county of Bucks, deceased, and Esther Head, daughter of John Head of said city, mar this 18th day of the 2nd month, 1749.

Henry Cliffton of the city of Philadelphia, joiner, son of John Cliffton of the said city, and Hannah Reynear of the same place, daughter of Joseph Reynear, late of Chester, deceased, mar this 11th day of the 3rd month, 1749.

John Lynn of the Northern Liberties of the city of Philadelphia, shipwright, son of Joseph Lynn, late of the same place, deceased, and Mary Cooper, daughter of William Cooper of the city aforesaid, mar this 25th day of the 3rd month, 1749.

William Ransted of the city of Philadelphia, cooper, son of Caleb Ransted of West Chester, in Great Britain, and Mary Peters, daughter of Thomas Peters of Philadelphia aforesaid, mar this 15th day of the 4th month, 1749.

William Hinton of the city of Philadelphia and Susanna Bale of the said city, daughter of Thomas Bale, late of Wiltshire in Great Britain, deceased, mar this 30th day of the 9th month, 1749.

James Chattin of the city of Philadelphia, printer, son of Abraham Chattin of the Township of Depford in the county of Gloucester in New Jersey, and Sarah Cox of Passiunk, county of Philadelphia, widow, mar this 5th day of the 2nd month, 1750.

Isaac Greenleafe of the city of Philadelphia, merchant, son of Isaac Greenleafe, late of Ipswich in the county of Suffolk, in Great Britain, deceased, and Elizabeth Calvert, daughter of George Calvert, late of Philadelphia, deceased, mar this 12th day of the 2nd month, 1750.

William Montgomery of the city of Philadelphia, merchant, and Margret Paschall of the same place, widow, mar this 19th day of the 5th month, 1750.

Robert Parrish of the city of Philadelphia, carpenter, son of John Parrish, late of Baltimore County, province of Maryland, deceased, and Mary Wilson, daughter of George Wilson, late of Philadelphia aforesaid, mar this 26th day of the 5th month, 1750.

James Stackhouse of the city of Philadelphia, plaistere, son of Robert
    Stackhouse of the Township of Makefield, county of Bucks, and
    Martha Hastings, daughter of Samuel Hastings of the said City,
    shipwright, mar this 13th day of the 9th month, 1750.
Joseph Saul of the city of Philadelphia, turner, and Sarah Knubley of the
    same place, daughter of John Knubley, late of the county of
    Cumberland in Great Britain, deceased, mar this 11th day of the 8th
    month, 1750.

MISCELLANEOUS MARRIAGES
1682-1750

Seamery Adams and Mary Brett, 8/28/1687
Benjamin Acton and Christian England, 7/4/1686
Joseph Ambler and Sarah Jerman, 9/30/1688
Thomas Andrews and Elizabeth Owen, 8/23/1689
Nathaniel Allen and Hannah Webb, 1/27/1713
Richard Allen and Mary Goforth, 4/27/1718
Nehemiah Allen, Jr, and Hannah Lownes, 7/26/1718
Richard Armitt and Sophia Johnson, 7/26/1701
John Armitt and Mary Emlen, 7/27/1728

Richard Basnett and Elizabeth Frampton, 9/30/1688
John Barnes and Mary Arnott, 7/28/1688
John Baldwin and Catherine Turner, 3/31/1689
Robert Baker and Susanna Packer, 12/24/1709
Thomas Bradford and Priscilla Parker, 8/31/1712
William Blackfan and Eleanor Wood, 1/31/1721
Benjamin Batterson and Mary Thomson, 1/27/1730; 2/1730
Edmund Bennett and Elizabeth Potts, 10/7/1685
William Bethell and Eleanor Claypoole, 11/27/1687
William Beaks and Elizabeth Worriloe, 1/28/1690
John Beasor and Esther Whitehead, 12/21/1694
Matthias Bellows and Maudlin Waight, 11/29/1696
John Bettle and Lydia Bolton, 1/31/1721
Joseph Brientnall and Esther Parker, 10/27/1723
Charles Brigham and Hannah Renager, 7/12/1685
David Brientnall, Jr, and Grace Parker, 12/23/1710
William Bisseland and Hannah Warrington, 6/30/1717
Matthew Birchfield and Alice Goforth, 6/29/1718
John Brock and Elizabeth Rowdon, 6/5/1684
Edward Boulton and Eleanor Jones, 1/30/1694
William Brown and Catherine Williams, 3/26/1699
Thomas Broadgate and Christian Armstrong, 11/6/1710
Thomas Brooks and Martha Hart, 3/27/1748; 4/1748

Benjamin Chambers and Hannah Smith, 3/3/1686
Thomas Canby and Sarah Jervis, 8/27/1693
George Claypoole and Mary Righton, 12/23/1699
George Calvert and Mary Wilson, 11/27/1708
Edward Chadler and Grace Day, 7/29/1710
Samuel Carpenter, Jr, and Hannah Preston, 3/25/1711
William Carter and Mary Sutton, 5/28/1721
Edward Cathrall and Rachel Harron, 11/29/1730; 12/1730
James Claypoole and Rachel Shenton, 5/29/1737; 6/1737
David Clark and Elizabeth Eastbourn, 5/29/1737; 6/1737
Francis Cook and Mary Claypoole, 4/24/1687
Thomas Coate and Beulah Jacobs, 7/25/1695
William Corker and Mary Fisher, 2/29/1709
Joseph Cooper, Jr, and Mary Hudson, 6/28/1713
Abraham Cox and Martha Nicholas, 2/30/1714
Jonathan Cookshall and Martha Kite, 8/28/1715
Thomas Coburn and Elizabeth Cockfield, 3/25/1722
Enoch Coates and Rose Tidmarsh, 2/26/1723
Daniel Cooper and Mary West, 7/27/1739; 8/1739
William Cooper and Mary Rawle, 5/23/1732
John Carver and Isabel Welding, 9/30/1716

John Davies and Dinah Borden, 12/23/1699
Samson Davis and Christian Shute, 5/16/1717
John Densey and Sarah Hollyman, 10/28/1688
Cornelius Denise and Mary Durborow, 5/30/1725
Joseph Drinker and Mary Janney, 6/27/1708
Thomas Duckett and Ruth Wood, 10/31/1686
John Dublonvis and Whankey Taney, 2/29/1687
James Dubery and Elizabeth Waln, 2/24/1719
John Durborow and Rebecca Haywood, 4/24/1720
William Dunn and Sarah Garrett, 11/27/1720
Robert Duncan and Esther Marie, 8/29/1736; 9/1736

John Eastbourn and Margaret Jones, 2/27/1694
Thomas England and Hannah Decow, 4/28/1700
Henry Elfreth and Sarah Gilbert, 12/27/1701
James Estaugh and Hannah Mereday, 10/27/1717
George Emlen and Hannah Garrett, 3/25/1694
Caleb Elfreth and Mary Roberts, 7/24/1725
Joshua Emlen and Mary Hudson, 9/23/1726
Abraham England and Jane Rawle, 3/31/1728
Joshua Emblen and Deborah Powell, 9/29/1728
Joseph England and Sarah Baily, 11/30/1729

William England and Sarah Durborow, 6/28/1741; 7/1741

Thomas French and Elizabeth Stanton, 7/26/1696
Thomas Fitzwater and Elizabeth Palmer, 4/3/1684
William Fisher and Blodget Hodgkins, 11/18/1686
William Fishbourn and Hannah Carpenter, Jr, 10/26/1701
Joshua Fincher and Elizabeth Harwood, 2/24/1702
William Fisher and Tabitha Janney, 2/29/1709
William Fishbourn and Jane Roberts, 6/29/1729; 7/1729
James Fox, Jr, and Ann Wills, 1/31/1699
Abel Fordham and Jane Ireson, 3/29/1724

John Gardner and Elizabeth Walter, 4/3/1684
Joseph Gray and Mary Hastings, 8/25/1717
Andrew Griscom and Sarah Dole, 2/7/1685
Thomas Griffith and Elizabeth Knowles, 12/23/1699
John Gibbons and Sarah Haywood, 7/27/1700
Nathaniel Griffitts and Elizabeth Badcock, 7/30/1715
Samuel Gilpin and Jane Parker, 11/25/1722
Tobias Griscom and Grace Rakestraw, 2/29/1737; 3/1737
Abraham Griffiths and Elizabeth Lynn, 7/24/1742; 8/1742
George Goldsmith and Ellen Harrison, 11/29/1695
George Gottshick and Elizabeth Oliver, 4/25/1697
Aaron Goforth and Mary Pool, 8/25/1717
John Guest and Mary Signey, 6/29/1701
John Guy and Jemima England, 11/30/1701
John Guest and Susanna Truman, 2/29/1736; 4/1737

Thomas Harding and Mary Bullock, 2/5/1686
John Harper and Jane Fawcett, 9/24/1710
Samuel Hanson and Joan Townsend, 11/29/1713
Thomas Harding and Elizabeth Jackson, 3/27/1715
Thomas Hart and Mary Combs, 3/25/1722
John Hastings and Hannah Townsend, 3/29/1724
Robert Heaton and Grace Pearson, 2/26/1700
David Hews and Dorothy Bomstead, 8/30/1719
Richard Hill and Hannah Delavall, 7/27/1700
Samuel Hillary and Jane Waterman, 10/28/1711
William Hinton and Jane Knubly, 6/29/1718
John Holstone and Ann Gibbs, 8/7/1684
Philip Howell and Jane Luffe, 3/3/1686
Thomas Hooton, Jr, and Elizabeth Stanly, 9/26/1686
Arthur Holton and Elizabeth Guest, 9/29/1695
Thomas Howell and Sarah Kilcup, 1/29/1700
Samuel Hood and Mary Hudson, 1/28/1701

Joseph Hood and Sarah Brown, 1/28/1701
Caspar Hoodt and Sarah Coleman, 4/27/1701
Thomas Hodges and Hannah Waller, 12/25/1703
William Hudson and Ann Ways, 6/2/1686
John Hutchins and Mary Davis, 10/30/1692
Samuel Hudson and Mary Holton, 12/24/1715
Richard Hough and Deborah Guinley, 7/27/1717
Daniel Hoodt and Esther Oldman, 2/24/1719
John Hood and Mary Snead, 1/29/1723
Jacob Horner and Mary Corbet, 5/28/1727
William Horne and Elizabeth Davis, 6/26/1737; 7/1737
Benjamin Humphries and Esther Warner, 12/24/1726

Randal Janney and Francis Righton, 8/31/1701
Caleb Jacobs and Mary Widdowfield, 12/28/1723
Ellis Jones and Jane Jones, 11/28/1686

Robert Kent and Margaret Thompson, 6/2/1686
William Kelley and Elizabeth Person, 6/31/1722
Thomas Kitchen and Mary Mace, 10/7/1685
Abraham Kite and Mary Peters, 6/27/1708
John Knight and Hannah Badcock, 10/26/1718
Thomas Knight and Sarah Clifton, 8/30/1719
John Kilbourn and Rachel Strickland, 2/24/1730; 3/1730
John Koster and Elizabeth Hood, 8/25/1717

Joseph Lewis and Susanna Waln, 9/30/1737; 10/1739
John Linton and Joan Watlin, 5/27/1722
Joseph Low and Elizabeth Taylor, 3/29/1713
Joseph Lownes and Sarah Tidmarsh, 3/26/1731
Peter Lloyd and Mary Masters, 12/23/1727
Thomas Lloyd and Susannah Owen, 3/31/1734; 4/1734

Thomas Masters and Elizabeth Herd, 9/2/1685
John McComb and Elizabeth Middleton, 6/21/1688
John Maddock and Elizabeth Kemp, 1/28/1690
John Marle and Elizabeth Elfreth, 6/30/1734; 7/1734
Daniel Medlicott and Martha Tankee (Zankee), 10/2/1684
John Mifflin and Elizabeth Hardy, 2/1/1684
Archibald Michael and Sarah Watts, 12/25/1686
George Mifflin and Esther Cordery, 11/29/1723
Samuel Mickle and Thomazine Marshall, 10/28/1716
Jonathan Mifflin and Sarah Robinson, 2/26/1723
William Miller and Ann Emblen, 3/26/1732; 4/1732
David Morris and Mary Philpin, 3/4/1685

Thomas Morris and Jane Jones, 6/3/1685
Anthony Morris and Agnes Boon, 8/25/1689
John Morton and Mary Way, 5/25/1701
Owen Morris and Mary Jones, 4/30/1704
Richard Moore and Margaret Preston, 3/27/1709
John Morton and Abigail Watson, 12/27/1729; 1/1730
James Morris and Elizabeth Kearney, 12/27/1729; 1/1730
Anthony Morris, Jr and Sarah Powell, 11/29/1730; 12/1730
Samuel Morris and Hannah Cadwallader, 2/29/1737; 3/1737
Luke Morris and Mary Richards, 1/31/1749; 2/1749

John Nailor and Margaret Greenup, 8/30/1713
John Nichols and Jane Roberts, 11/31/1723
Samuel Nichols and Mary Coates, 2/29/1726
Humphrey Norris and Rachel Williams, 6/29/1718

Joseph Oldman and Sarah Massey, 2/29/1726
John Otter and Mary Blinston, 8/29/1686
John Ogden and Hannah Davise, 2/26/1723

John Parker and Mary Doe, 10/27/1700
Thomas Palmer and Sarah Mitchener, 1/30/1705
Richard Parks and Susanna Carlton, 3/29/1713
Joseph Pascal and Elizabeth Coates, 2/28/1721
Alexander Parker and Sarah Thompson, 1/27/1730; 2/1730
Isaac Pearson and Elizabeth Hall, 9/2/1685
Reese Peters and Ann Brooksby, 5/27/1711
Reese Peters and Elizabeth Clark, 1/29/1728; 2/1728
Samuel Pennock and Elizabeth Widdowfield, 5/29/1737; 6/1737
Joshua Pearson and Elizabeth Biddle, 8/29/1742; 9/1742
Nicholas Pile and Ann Webb, 2/25/1713
Edward Pilkington and Mary Webb, 5/30/1714
David Potts and Alice Croasdale, 11/26/1693
Samuel Powell and Abigail Wilcox, 11/31/1700
Michael Poince and Elizabeth Nicholson, 5/26/1728
Samuel Powell and Sarah Roberts, 9/27/1730; 10/1730

Francis Rawle and Martha Turner, 7/27/1689
Caleb Ransted and Rachel Pratt, 1/26/1731; 2/1731
John Realow and Mary Rencho, 10/31/1697
Isaac Ricketts and Elizabeth Palmer, 2/29/1687
Daniel Riggs and Martha Cobron, 10/29/1689
Samuel Richardson and Elizabeth Webb, 5/28/1704
Francis Richardson and Elizabeth Growdon, 1/30/1705
William Rodney and Mary Hollyman, 11/25/1688

John Rhoads and Hannah Wilcox, 8/28/1692
Ebeneezer Robinson and Mary Hugg, 11/30/1718
Isaac Roberts and Hannah Paschal, 3/1741; 4/1741
John Russel and Mary Woodward, 12/5/1683

John Smith and Margaret Penrose, 2/29/1720
John Smith, Jr, and Rebecca Blackbourn, 1/30/1722
Jacob Shoemaker and Elizabeth Roberts, 2/24/1724
Benjamin Shoemaker and Sarah Coates, 3/29/1724
Thomas Shoemaker and Sarah Read, 6/27/1742; 7/1742
William Shute and Elizabeth Steel, 4/30/1721
Jacob Shute and Mary Boyden, 6/27/1725
William Salway and Sarah Pennock, 7/28/1688
James Shaddock and Martha Moon, 8/25/1689
James Stanfield and Mary Hutchinson, 4/27/1690
Nathan Stanbury and Mary Ewer, 1/31/1699
Paul Saunders and Anne Folle, 4/30/1699
Richard Saunders and Sarah Steel, 6/29/1718
John Stacy and Mary Haywood, 5/28/1721
William Saunders and Esther Skinely, 1/30/1722
George Smedley and Sarah Gooden, 4/24/1687
William Snead and Mary Thomas, 10/28/1688
Thomas Skelton and Hannah Salaway, 12/27/1718
Thomas Smith and Priscilla Allen, 11/9/1682
Nathaniel Sikes and Eleanor Pain, 4/7/1686
Christopher Sibthorpe and Mary Fincher, 2/26/1689
Thomas Sisam and Priscilla Smith, 8/27/1693
Randolph Spikeman and Mary Cockin, 8/29/1697
Randolph Spikeman and Grace Smith, 8/25/1700
John Simcock and Mary Waller (Wallen), 2/26/1706
Jacob Simcock and Sarah Waller (Wallen), 5/27/1711
Richard Smith and Anna Marshall, 1/29/1714
Richard Smith and Sarah Wait, 8/30/1719
Daniel Smith and Mary Hoodt. 9/27/1719

Thomas Taylor and Rachel Minshall, 10/27/1700
James Thomas and Ellen Barber, 5/26/1689
Micah Thomas and Givenlin Thomas, 12/28/1689
James Thomas and Ann Warner, 2/26/1695
Joseph Trotter and Dinah Skelton, 1/28/1718
Daniel Thomas and Aletta Piggot, 10/29/1732; 11/1732
Richard Tucker and Jane Batchelor, 2/1/1684
Edward Turner and Catherine Carter, 1/25/1687

Jacob Usher and Ruth Wood, 12/23/1699

Nathaniel Walton and Martha Bowling, 12/1/1685
William Walker and Elizabeth Morgan, 8/25/1689
Thomas Walton and Priscilla Hun, 12/28/1689
Joseph Walker and Margaret Cutler, 1/27/1691
Isaac Warner and Ann Craven, 10/30/1692
Emanuel Walker and Margaret Matthews, 4/30/1699
Solomon Walker and Elizabeth Howell, 10/29/1699
John Walker and Sarah Langston, 9/29/1700
John Warder and Elizabeth Goodson, 3/30/1701
Michael Walton and Elizabeth Moore, 2/29/1709
Isaac Warner and Veronica Cassel, 12/24/1715
John Waller and Jane Mifflin, 6/30/1717
Benjamin Waite and Jane Nickson, 9/29/1717
Richard Warder and Rebecca Pool, 1/29/1723
Joseph Webb and Mary Allen, 1/28/1718
Zachery Whitpain and Sarah Songhurst, 9/26/1686
Joseph Wilcox and Ann Powell, 1/25/1687
James White and Mary Kitchen, 8/28/1698
Benjamin Wright and Barbara Peppiott, 12/23/1699
Richard Witten and Elisabeth Iylife, 12/27/1712
Thomas Wilson and Elizabeth Trafford, 3/29/1713
William Williams and Hannah Carver, 8/31/1729; 9/1729
John Wood and Sarah Sanders, 2/26/1695
William Woodmancy and Dorothy Scott, 9/29/1700
Thomas Worrilow and Susanna Brightwen, 12/27/1701
Joseph Wood and Mary Pound, 6/23/1726
Daniel Worthington and Mary Wood, 4/29/1739; 5/1739
Nathaniel Wycombe and Anne Heskett, 1/28/1701
Thomas Wyner and Mary Warner, 10/28/1722

Nathaniel Zane and Grace Rakestraw, 6/27/1697
Daniel Zachary and Elizabeth Lloyd, 1/29/1700
Jonathan Zeanes and Mary Shenton, 4/28/1728

CERTIFICATES RECEIVED
1686-1750

5/11/1686 - Samuel Toms, on account of marriage - from Newtown in New Jersey.
27/11/1686 - Sarah Watts - from Radnor.
14/1/1686/7 - Edward Turner - to marry Catherine Carter, from Concord Monthly Meeting.
15/4/1687 - George Smedley, on account of marriage - from Darby Monthly Meeting.
19/4/1687 - Francis Cooke, clearness to marry - from Duck Creek.
14/7/1687 - William Bethel, clearness to marry Helena Claypoole - from Amboy - Perth.
5/8/1687 - Seemerrie Adams, to marry Mary Britt - from Falls Monthly Meeting, Bucks County.
26/1/1688 - Joshua Tittery, to marry Cicely Tittery - from Abington Monthly Meeting.
19/6/1688 - John McComb, clearness to marry Elizabeth Middleton.
22/6/1688 - William Salway, to marry Sarah Pinnock - from Abington Monthly Meeting.
24/7/1688 - John Barnes, to marry Mary Arnell - from Abington Monthly Meeting.
18/10/1688 - William Rodeney, in regard to marriage with Sarah Edmondson - from Talbot County, Maryland. William Rodeney, clearness to marry - from William Dixon.
3/12/1689/90 - James Stanfield, to marry Mary Hutchinson - from Chester Monthly Meeting.
3/8/1688 - Thomas Carle, to marry Catherine Brientnall - from Falls Monthly Meeting.
5/8/1690 - William Say, to marry Mary Guest - from Burlington Monthly Meeting.
24/7/1697 - Thomas Turner, on a religious visit - from the quarterly meeting of Coxall in Essex.
17/5/1699 - Mary Doe, late servant to John Field - from Brewers Hall Monthly Meeting, London.
4/11/1699 - Joan Hall - from Moniash Monthly Meeting, Derbyshire, England.
4/2/1700 - Robert Heaton, to marry Grace Pearson - from Middletown Monthly Meeting.
27/3/1700 - Thomas England - from Chester Monthly Meeting.
27/6/1700 - Richard Webb and his wife - from Gloucester quarterly meeting.
25/7/1700 - John Parker - from Chester Monthly Meeting.

28/8/1700 - Thomas Taylor, to marry Rachel Minshall - from Chester Monthly Meeting.

27/10/1700 - Certificate from Hugh Cordry - from Ratclif Monthly Meeting in England. Deborah Cordry, with her husband, Hugh Cordry - from Ratclif Monthly Meeting in England.

5/12/1700 - Samuel Hood, to marry Mary Hudson - from Darby Monthly Meeting. Joseph Hood, to marry Sarah Browne - from Darby Monthly Meeting.

7/8/1701 - Alex'r. Lamplee - from Barbadoes.

9/12/1701 - James Logan - from Bristol Monthly Meeting.

14/2/1702 - James Estaugh - from Felsted Division, Essex.

4/9/1702 - Thomas Janney - from Morley in Cheshire.

8/10/1702 - William Robinson - from Thirsk in Yorkshire.

23/6/1704 - Thos. Coleman - from Horslydown.

6/7/1704 - Abigail Hood, widow - from Darby Monthly Meeting.

16/7/1704 - Richard Gove, to visit Barbadoes - from yearly meeting of Ministers.

11/11/1704 - David Williams, to marry Mary Maltsby - from Haverford.

1/1/1704/5 - Ann Chapman, to visit New England - from Middletown Monthly Meeting.

12/4/1705 - John Widdowfield, respecting clearness to marry - from Thirsk in Yorkshire.

4/6/1705 - Jedediah Hussey, on account of marriage - from Newark.

28/1/1706 - Mary Newcome, a minister - from Leicester quarterly meeting. Naomy Berry - from Choptank.

29/2/1706 - Joseph Brown, removed with wife Lucia - from Salem Monthly Meeting in New Jersey.

9/7/1706 - Edward Scull - from Cork, sent after him.

30/10/1706 - Jacob Minshall, to marry Sarah Owen - from Chester Monthly Meeting.

2/11/1706 - Samuel Lewis, to marry Grissell Kite - from Haverford.

8/11/1706 - John Hart - from Cecil County, Maryland.

26/12/1706 - A letter concerning John Tanner - from Lurgan in Ireland.

27/12/1706 - Elizabeth Palmer - from Bridgetown in Barbadoes.

7/4/1707 - Joseph Grifen - from Newark.

6/6/1707 - Ebenezer Large - from Falls Monthly Meeting.

1/7/1707 - Thomas Brian, Junr, to marry Susanna Kearn - from Burlington Monthly Meeting.

13/7/1707 - Frances Chanders - parents consent to marriage.

24/7/1707 - Abraham Scott - from London.

7/7/1707 - Isaac Minshall, to marry Rebecca Owen - from Chester Monthly Meeting.

13/9/1707 - Certificate from Edward Goodwin and wife - consent to daughters marriage.

8/11/1707 - John Sharp - from the Monthly Meeting at Thos. Shakles, in New Jersey.

23/12/1707/8 - Thomas Godfrey, to marry Lucy Russell - from Abington Monthly Meeting.

23/12/1707/8 - David Brintnall - from Chester Monthly Meeting.

29/1/1708 - John Crocton - from Chester Monthly Meeting.

3/3/1708 - Allen Trustrum, on a religious visit - from Shrewsbury Monthly Meeting in New Jersey.

12/6/1708 - John Maule - from Lynn in Massachusetts.

23/6/1708 - John Camm - from Cork. Caleb Jacob - from Cork.

27/10/1708 - Jonathan Coppock, to marry Jane Owen - from Chester Monthly Meeting.

12/11/1708 - John Hart - from Cecil, Maryland.

18/11/1708/9 - Samuel Marriot, in order for marriage - from Burlington Monthly Meeting.

13/3/1709 - Richard Moore - from West River in Maryland.

4/5/1709 - John Camm - from Cork, explaining former certificate.

1/6/1709 - Esther Parker - from Burlington Monthly Meeting.

6/6/1709 - Martha Griffitts - from Cork, Ireland, to Kingston, Jamaica.

8/6/1709 - Joseph Bond, son of James and Ann Bond - from Brighouse Monthly Meeting in York.

7/7/1709 - John Large, to marry Sarah Corker - from Falls Monthly Meeting.

13/8/1709 - Edw. Cadwalader, to marry Rebecca Moore - from Haverford Monthly Meeting.

31/8/1709 - Samuel Levis, to marry Hannah Stretch - from Chester Monthly Meeting.

2/9/1709 - Willoughby Warder, to marry Sarah Boyer - from the Monthly Meeting at the Falls.

9/9/1709 - Gilbert Falconer - from Cecil, Maryland.

19/10/1709 - James Crawford, on account of marriage - from Duck Creek.

26/10/1709 - Robert Baker, to marry Susannah Packer - from Chester Monthly Meeting.

9/12/1709/10 - Owen Roberts and wife - from Haverford.

24/12/1709 - Robert Baker, fathers consent to marry - from Chester Monthly Meeting.

27/12/1709/10 - Peter Wishart, in order to marry - from Abington Monthly Meeting.

27/4/1710 - Thos. Broadgate, son of John Broadgate - consent to marry.

6/5/1710 - Thos. Broadgate, son of John of Enfield - from Tattenham.

2/6/1710 - John Harper - from Herring Creek.

18/7/1710 - Sarah Massey, wife of Samuel - from Cork. Jacob Mott - from the yearly meeting of Ministers, to Rhode Island.

28/3/1711 - Samuel Taylor - from Abington Monthly Meeting.

3/4/1711 - Mark Carleton - from Mountmellick.

10/4/1711 - Samuel Hillary - from Wexford.

17/4/1711 - Richard Parks and two children - from Liverpool.

18/4/1711 - James Steel, on account of marriage - from Duck Creek.

25/4/1711 - Jacob Simcock, to marry Sarah Wall - from Chester Monthly Meeting.

11/7/1711 - Thos. Nicholson and wife - from Rugely in Staffordshire.
   Peter Osborne and Judith his wife - from Rugely in Staffordshire.

22/8/1711 - John Knight - from Cork.

14/11/1711 - Thomas Bond, formerly of Lancashire - from London.

7/12/1711 - Charles Brockden - from Middletown Monthly Meeting in Bucks County.

7/1/1711/12 - James Morris, unmarried - from Dublin.

10/1/1711/12 - James Watson - from New Castle.

2/2/1712 - Jane Marriot, wife of Isaac - from Gutershedge in Middlesex.

13/2/1712 - William Moore, unmarried - from Waterford. Joshua Baker - from Waterford.

24/2/1712 - James Hurd - from Limington in Somerset.

26/11/1712 - Richard Whitten, to marry Elizabeth Jyliff - from Abington.

31/1/1713 - Rachel Merrick - from Frandley in Cheshire.

13/2/1713 - Nicholas Pile, to marry Ann Webb - from Concord Monthly Meeting.

11/3/1713 - Joseph Low, to marry Eliz. Taylor - from Newton in New Jersey.

13/5/1713 - James Logan - from Devonshire House.

10/6/1713 - Joseph Cooper, to marry Mary Hudson - from the Monthly Meeting at Thos. Shakles.

7/10/1713 - John Naylor, to marry Mary Greenhope - from Radnor Monthly Meeting.

28/10/1713 - Dorothy Bumstide - from London.

2/1/1713/14 - William Clare and family - from Newton in Cheshire.

7/1/1714 - Katherine Martin - from Bull and Mouth.

2/6/1714 - Benj. Bryan - from Burlington Monthly Meeting.

21/12/1714/15 - Wm. Bissell and four children - from Stourbridge.

6/1/1715 - Mary Pace - from Worcester.

18/2/1715 - Ann Chalkley, widow of Robert - from London.

21/2/1715 - John Shiers - from Marsden.

_/7/1715 - Gabriel Newby, to return to N. Carolina - from the yearly mtg. of Ministers.

12/8/1715 - Jonathan Cogshall, to marry Martha Kite - from Haverford.

31/8/1715 - Joseph Knight, to marry Abigail Antill - from Abington Monthly Meeting.

20/12/1715/6 - Thomas Denham - from Bristol.

13/2/1716 - Thomas Skelton - from Carlisle.

20/6/1716 - Deborah Gumley, widow of John - from Duck Creek.

20/7/1716 - Samuel Lewis, son of Israel - from Bridgetown.

16/8/1716 - Thos. Griffitts - from Cork.
17/8/1716 - Thos. Griffitts - from his parents Geo. and Frances Griffitts.
16/9/1716 - Richard Harrison - from West River, Maryland.
25/12/1716 - William Tidmarsh - from Chester Monthly Meeting.
24/1/1716/7 - William Taylor - from Clomnell. Thos. Barger and wife - from Clonmell.
8/2/1717 - Joseph Wood and his family - from Mountmellick.
29/2/1717 - Sophia Siverts - from Abington.
21/3/1717 - Christo. Penrose - from Dublin.
21/4/1717 - John Head - from Mildenhall.
20/6/1717 - Edward Owen, son of Griffith - from Hartshaw.
4/7/1717 - Richard Hough, to marry Deborah Gumley - from Falls Monthly Meeting.
30/7/1717 - George Gray - from Abington Monthly Meeting.
12/10/1717 - Edward Jones, Jr - from Radnor Monthly Meeting.
6/11/1717 - William Hinton - from Nailsworth.
17/12/1717 - Humphrey Norris - from Bristol.
7/1/1717/8 - James Lloyd and wife Ann - from Dudley.
17/1/1718 - Sarah Lee, daughter of Thomas and Martha - from London.
26/3/1718 - James Whitten, to marry Katherine Bedwort - from Salem.
4/5/1718 - John Brown and wife - from Barking.
11/6/1718 - Daniel Flexney, Jr - from Witney.
1/10/1718 - Ann Pyle, widow - from Concord Monthly Meeting.
17/12/1718 - John Wilson - from Hartshaw.
30/1/1719 - Hugh Clifton - from Abington Monthly Meeting.
27/5/1719 - Elizabeth Whartnaby, on a religious visit - from Nantucket.
25/6/1719 - Elizabeth Whartnaby, on religious visit - from Portsmouth, R. I. Hester Kingsley, returning - from Portsmouth, Rhode Island.
1/8/1719 - Elizabeth Whartnaby, on a religious visit - from Flushing.
17/8/1719 - Samuel Overton - from Coventry, England.
9/9/1719 - Thomas Whitehead - from London.
20/9/1719 - Amy Liberty - from Market Street Monthly Meeting, County of Hartford, in England.
2/10/1719 - Jane Ireland, wife of Nicholas Ireland - from Darby Monthly Meeting.
28/10/1719 - Edward Brooks, to marry Eliz. Snead - from Abington Monthly Meeting.
1/1/1719/20 - John Reeves, from Whitley with his wife - from Scarborough.
30/1/1720 - William Adams - from Bridgetown in Barbadoes, clear of marriage.
12/2/1720 - Joseph Elgar and wife - from Folkestone, Kent.
11/5/1720 - Mary Rakestraw - from Newton in New Jersey.
3/6/1720 - Elizabeth Large - from Falls Monthly Meeting.
15/6/1720 - Mary Thompkins and son James - from London.

3/8/1720 - William Dunn, addressed to Bristol in England - from Burlington Monthly Meeting.

2/12/1720 - Mary Ellis - from Chesterfield.

29/3/1721 - Thomas Pennington, to marry a daughter of James Steel - from Abington Monthly Meeting.

12/12/1721/2 - Sarah Griscom - from Newton in New Jersey.

12/1/1721/2 - Hannah Coffin - from Newtown in New Jersey.

14/5/1721 - Elizabeth Teague, on a religious visit - from Newport.

26/6/1721 - Elizabeth Teague, on a religious visit - from Chester Monthly Meeting.

?/7/1721 - Sarah Fisher - from Burlington Monthly Meeting.

20/9/1721 - Joseph England, to marry Elizabeth Brown - from Duck Creek.

3/11/1721 - Esther Tomlinson - from Darby Monthly Meeting.

26/12/1721/2 - Samuel Ogden and wife Hester - from Chester Monthly Meeting.

7/1/1722 - Isaac Marriott and wife Jane - from Hendon in Middlesex. Mary Oldman - from Darby Monthly Meeting.

26/1/1722 - William Saunders, returning - from London. John Smith - from Salem Monthly Meeting.

23/2/1722 - Geo. and Eliz. Deeble, children of Richard, dec'd - from Corke.

4/5/1722 - William Garrett - from Darby.

9/6/1722 - Mary Preston, daughter of Wm. and Jane Bedward - from Merion.

22/6/1722 - Mary Davis, widow of John - from Evesham in Worcester.

18/7/1722 - John Stamper - from Pardshaw Cragg.

28/11/1722/3 - Frances Burd - from Chester Monthly Meeting.

27/3/1723 - Martha McDonald (Mackdaimell) - from Chester Monthly Meeting.

5/4/1723 - Mary Cooper - from Falls Monthly Meeting.

10/4/1723 - Hannah Albertson - from Haddonfield.

4/6/1723 - Susanna Morris, on religious visit - from Perquimans, N. C.

13/6/1723 - Ann Roberts, on religious visit - from Nansemond in Virginia. Susanna Morris, on a religious visit - from Nansemond, Va.

24/6/1723 - Ann Roberts, on religious visit - from Perquimans, N. C.

30/7/1723 - Mary Gray - from Abington Monthly Meeting.

16/10/1723 - Edward Horne and wife Elizabeth - from Horsham quarterly meeting.

3/11/1723/4 - Ann Roberts, on religious visit - from Clifts in Maryland.

9/11/1723/4 - Sarah Worthington, wife of Daniel - from Haverford.

23/11/1723/4 - Mary Miller and son James - from Carlisle. Susanna Morris, on a religious visit - from Clifts, Maryland.

27/2/1724 - Daniel Evans, with wife Emma, a minister - from Abington Monthly Meeting.

4/4/1724 - Edmund Beakes - from Chesterfield Monthly Meeting, in order to marry. Elizabeth Large - from Chesterfield Monthly Meeting.
10/7/1724 - Mary Roberts - from Radnor Monthly Meeting.
28/10/1724 - John Weldon and family - from Bristol.
22/12/1724 - Griffith Owen, returning - from London.
12/23/1724 - Ann Farmer, daughter of John and Mary - from Saffron Walden.
1/1/1724/25 - Hannah Brientnall - from Burlington Monthly Meeting.
26/1/1725 - Ann Tatnall and son Thomas - from Leicester.
20/2/1725 - Bridges Jackson - from Pardshaw Cragg.
7/5/1725 - Sarah Hodgson - from Falls Monthly Meeting.
3/12/1725/6 - Ralph Hoy - from Middletown Monthly Meeting.
25/2/1726 - John Iden, with wife Hannah, a minister - from Chester Monthly Meeting.
25/3/1726 - Mary Finlow, returning to Philadelphia - from Limerick.
28/9/1726 - Catherine Wister - from Abington Monthly Meeting.
2/1/1726/7 - Wm. Callander, Jr - from Barbadoes.
12/1/1726/7 - Robert Woodcock and his wife - from Cooldine.
1/20/1726/7 - Mary Bones - from Bristol Monthly Meeting.
13/2/1727 - Joseph French, Jr - from Barbadoes.
7/4/1727 - Joseph wood, apprentice, returning - from Falls Monthly Meeting.
12/4/1727 - Jacob Hornor, in order to marry - from Haddonfield Monthly Meeting.
?0/6/1727 - Robert Robertson, son of Samuel - from Kelso.
6/1/1727/8 - John Paschall, to marry Frances Hodge - from Darby Monthly Meeting.
22/2/1728 - Abraham England - from Duck Creek.
3/4/1728 - Susanna Bickley, daughter of Abraham, dec'd - from Burlington Monthly Meeting.
24/4/1728 - Michael Poince - from Abington Monthly Meeting. Elizabeth Townsend, returning - from Abington Monthly Meeting.
21/5/1728 - James Hill and wife Margery - from Balandary.
5/7/1728 - Richard Burtos - from Chesterfield Monthly Meeting. William Morris on business - from Heathcots Bay, Barbadoes.
20 /7/1728 - Rebecca Bolton - from Abington Monthly Meeting.
12/10/1728 - John Weldon and family - from Radnor Monthly Meeting.
27/11/1728/9 - Jacob Vernon and wife Elenor - from Chester Monthly Meeting.
28/11/1728/9 - Lowry Siddon, with her small children - from Gwynedd Monthly Meeting.
2/2/1729 - Job Goodsonn - from Horslydown.
28/2/1729 - George Howell and his wife - from Corke.
1/3/1729 - Thos. Baynes and wife - from Middletown Monthly Meeting.

6/3/1729 - Dinah Buzby - from Dublin.

7/3/1729 - John Low - from Lurgan.

15/3/1729 - Thos. Chalkley - from Bridgetown in Barbadoes.

19/3/1729 - Thomas Perry - from Colchester.

1/4/1729 - Sarah Marshall, daughter of Richard and Deborah - from Edenderry.

7/5/1729 - Han. and Esther Woolman, daughters of John, dec'd - from Burlington Monthly Meeting.

19/5/1729 - Elizabeth Whartnaby, on a religious visit - from Lurgan.

28/5/1729 - Geo. Franks and wife - from Abington Monthly Meeting.

29/5/1729 - Ann Cunningham, with nieces Ann, Elizabeth and Mary - from Dublin. Ann Goodbody - from Dublin. Lettice Hatton - from Dublin.

30/5/1729 - Mary Boyes, daughter of Jacob and Lucy T_____ - from Lurgan.

12/6/1729 - Eunice Conolly - from Dublin. Wm. Sitgreaves and his wife - from Bull and Mouth. Elizabeth Whartnaby, returning from visit - from Dublin.

20/6/1729 - Anthony Morris, nephew of Wm. Morris - from Heathcots Bay, Barbadoes.

28/8/1729 - William Williams, to marry Hannah Carver - from Gwynedd Monthly Meeting.

3/10/1729 - Rose Bethell, widow of John - from Darby Monthly Meeting.

19/11/1729 - Anne Dudley - from Bristol Monthly Meeting. Joseph England, on account of marriage - from Duck creek.

21/11/1729 - Sarah Gates, wife of Josiah - from Poole.

8/1/1729/30 - William Sandwith - from Cooledine in Wexford.

16/1/1729/30 - Samuel Emlen, returning - from London.

24/1/1729/30 - William Sandwith - from Dublin.

4/4/1730 - Hannah Hudson - from Dublin.

7/2/1730 - John Hillborn, to marry Rachel Strickland - from Wrightstown Monthly Meeting.

29/2/1730 - John Ogilby - from Barbadoes.

17/6/1730 - John Sparrow - from Devonshire House.

7/8/1730 - Emme Evans, acknowledging visit - from Perquimans, N. C.

27/8/1730 - Emme Evans, acknowledging visit - from Nansemond, Va.

7/9/1730 - Em Evans, acknowledging visit - from near Curles, Va.

9/9/1730 - Mary Jervis, had married out - from Burlington Monthly Meeting. Mary Harvey - from Burlington Monthly Meeting.

28/10/1730 - Alice Paxson, wife of Reuben - from Abington Monthly Meeting.

6/11/1730 - John Dillwyn, returning - from Horselydown.

21/11/1730 - John Kinsey, Junr, and wife - from Woodbridge.

25/11/1730/1 - Ann Evans - from Chester Monthly Meeting. Hannah Baldwin - from Chester Monthly Meeting.

7/12/1730/1 - Robert Jordan - from Isle of Wight.
15/12/1730/1 - Nathaniel Jenkins and wife - from Bristol.
25/12/1730/1 - Isabel Daniel - from Salem Monthly Meeting.
1/1/1730/1 - John Stanes - from Devonshire House.
5/1/1731 - Mary Shute, daughter of Thomas - from Sarum in Wiltshire.
9/1/1730/1 - William Nicholson - from Dublin.
11/1/1730/1 - Armiger and Thos. Trotter - from Chuckertuck, Va.
18/1/1730/1 - Charles Norris, returning - from Bridgetown, Barbadoes.
30/1/1731 - Martha Truman and her two children - from Gwynedd
    Monthly Meeting. Cadwalader Foulke with wife and children - from
    Gwynedd Monthly Meeting.
6/2/1731 - Eliz. Hawkins - from Dublin.
20/3/1731 - Alshee Pickst - from Woodbridge.
27/3/1731 - Samuel Dickinson, unmarried - from Treadhaven.
9/5/1731 - Daniel Stanton, returning - from Newport, R. I.
19/5/1731 - Stephen Payton - from Dudley in Worcester.
26/5/1731 - John Jones, to marry Rebecca Head - from Abington Monthly
    Meeting.
25/7/1731 - William Miller, to marry Ann Emlen - from Newgarden.
11/9/1731 - Meriam Enoch, had married out - from Merion.
27/9/1731 - Robert Jordan, acknowledging visit - from Flushing.
25/11/1731 - Sarah Smith - from Dublin.
4/12/1731 - Benjamin and Sarah Say, she a minister - from Colchester.
14/12/1731 - Lawrence Growdon - from Bristol.
6/1/1731/2 - Joseph Cloud, to marry Hannah Baldwin - from Concord.
10/2/1732 - Martha Clark, wife of Thomas - from Haddonfield Monthly
    Meeting.
12/2/1732 - Edward Walbank and his wife - from Bull and Mouth.
8/3/1732 - Thomas Penn, unmarried - from London.
5/4/1732 - Dorothy Roman, widow - from Concord Monthly Meeting.
9/4/1732 - Samuel Chew and wife Mary - from Cliffs in Maryland.
12/4/1732 - William Cooper, on account of marriage - from Haddonfield
    Monthly Meeting.
30/4/1732 - Samuel Floyd, on business - from Barbadoes.
25/5/1732 - Thomas Gardner and family - from Gwynedd Monthly
    Meeting.
31/5/1732 - John Iden and wife Hannah - from Chester Monthly Meeting.
14/6/1732 - Samuel Sandsom - from London.
26/6/1732 - Richard Waln, acknowledging visit - from Westbury.
29/6/1732 - Sarah Maule - from Gwynedd Monthly Meeting.
26/7/1732 - Richard Waln - from Newport, R. I.
4/8/1732 - John Miller with son and daughter - from Westminster.
11/8/1732 - Robert Jordan - from Nansemond, Va.
1/9/1732 - Sarah Hart - from Darby Monthly Meeting.
2/9/1732 - Mary Emlen, acknowledging her visit - from Flushing.

25/9/1732 - Robert Jordan, acknowledging visit - from Flushing.

27/9/1732 - James Wilson and his wife - from Abington Monthly Meeting.

25/10/1732 - Daniel Thomas, on account of marriage - from Abington Monthly Meeting.

12/12/1732 - Joseph Saunders, nephew of Richard Saunders - from Bull and Mouth.

28/12/1732 - Benj. Tomlinson and wife Mary - from Horselydown.

26/1/1733 - Mary Dubre, wife of Jacob - from Abington Monthly Meeting.

4/4/1733 - William Callander and Katherine his wife - from Burlington Monthly Meeting.

7/4/1733 - Thos. Chalkley - from Dublin.

21/6/1733 - John Richardson - from Pardshaw Hall.

3/7/1733 - Thomas Taylor - from Great Egg Harbor.

6/7/1733 - Mary Nicholas, acknowledging visit - from Pasquotank, N. C.

21/7/1733 - Mary Nicholas, acknowledging visit - from Va. yearly meeting.

24/7/1733 - Giles Brimble - from Bristol. Agnes Eastburn, wife of Robert - from Abington Monthly Meeting.

3/8/1733 - Ann Baldwin, had married out - from Falls Monthly Meeting.

8/8/1733 - Sarah Hopewell, wife of Joseph - from Haddonfield Monthly Meeting.

29/8/1733 - Phebe Dubre, formerly Robinson - from Abington Monthly Meeting.

23/9/1733 - Mary Nichols, acknowledging visit - from West River in Maryland.

31/10/1733 - Sarah Kenderdine and children - from Abington Monthly Meeting.

22/11/1733 - Robert Jordan, acknowledging visit - from London.

7/12/1733/4 - Ann Lambert - from Chesterfield Monthly Meeting.

11/12/1733/4 - Joseph Hopewell - from Haddonfield Monthly Meeting.

_/_/1734 - Pauli_s Kripner - from London.

6/2/1734 - Robert Read and wife Sarah - from Newark.

30/2/1734 - Jonathan Evans, son of Evan Evans - from Gwynedd Monthly Meeting.

4/3/1734 - Elizabeth Widdifield, acknowledging visit - from Flushing.

6/3/1734 - Jonathan Wright - from Burlington Monthly Meeting.

23/3/1734 - Ruth Steer, Jr - from Lisburn.

28/3/1734 - Content Maule, to visit her mother - from Newport, R. I.

30/3/1734 - Margaret Collins, formerly from Ireland - from Gwynedd Monthly Meeting.

24/4/1734 - Sarah Jackson - from Chester Monthly Meeting.

3/5/1734 - John Hank - from Darby Monthly Meeting.

4/5/1734 - Susannah Hastings - from Chesterfield Monthly Meeting.

26/6/1734 - Patrick Ogilby - from Westbury, L. I.

7/7/1734 - Ann Pierce, a minister - from Newark.

30/7/1734 - Thomas Marle and wife - from Abington Monthly Meeting.
21/8/1734 - Sarah Say, respecting her ministry - from Colchester.
30/8/1734 - Margaret Preston, acknowledging visit - from Tredhaven.
25/9/1734 - Ann Hunter - from Abington Monthly Meeting.
2/10/1734 - Rachel Woodcock - from Burlington Monthly Meeting.
12/10/1734 - Benj. Eastburn and his wife - from Radnor Monthly
    Meeting.
7/11/1734 - Jacob Jones and wife Mary - from Wrightstown Monthly
    Meeting.
9/11/1734/5 - Ann Penly - from Cirencester.
14/1/1734 - Daniel Beeby - from Allonby.
26/12/1734/5 - Patrick Ogilby - from Westbury.
31/1/1735 - Benjamin Mason and wife - from Abington Monthly Meeting.
1/2/1735 - Rachel Allen - from Scarborough in York.
10/2/1735 - David Clarke, son of John and Mary - from Painswick.
11/3/1735 - Thomas Bond - from Herring Creek in Maryland.
26/3/1735 - John Jones and wife Mary - from Salem Monthly Meeting.
2/4/1735 - Edward Thompson and his family - from Concord.
6/4/1735 - Samuel Walker, to Charleston, S. C. or elsewhere - from
    Richmond at Chantrey.
28/4/1735 - Alice Harper - from New Garden Monthly Meeting.
25/6/1735 - Alice Lewis - from Chester Monthly Meeting.
30/7/1735 - Daniel Stanton, acknowledging visit - from Newport, R. I.
9/8/1735 - Robert Jordan, acknowledging visit - from Nansemond, Va.
27/8/1735 - James Sperry - from Chester Monthly Meeting.
19/9/1735 - Mary Williams, a widow with children - from Anstle.
25/9/1735 - Daniel Stanton - from Flushing. Mary Davis, unmarred - from
    Gwynedd Monthly Meeting.
26/11/1735 - Israel Pemberton, Junr, returning - from Devonshire
    House.
20/11/1735 - John Freeman with wife and 2 sons - from Lankford.
16/12/1735 - Stephen Payton, of Dudley - from Stourbridge.
23/12/1735 - Thos. Chalkley - from London. Obadiah Eldridge, fathers
    consent - from Evesham in N. J.
28/12/1735/6 - William Morrison - from Abington Monthly Meeting.
8/1/1735/6 - Joseph Saunders, returning - from Bull and Mouth.
31/1/1736 - Ruth Webb, addressed to Chester Monthly Meeting - from
    Lurgan.
6/2/1736 - Thos. Strickland - from Wrightstown Monthly Meeting.
10/2/1736 - Elizabeth Deane, unmarried - from Bellnacree in Antrim.
21/2/1736 - Isaiah McNiece, widower with children - from Coote Will,
    Cavan.
26/2/1736 - Thomas Knight and wife Sarah - from Abington Monthly
    Meeting. Rebecca Ogilby - from Abington Monthly Meeting.

30/2/1736 - John Ambler - from York at Selby. Wm. Callender Jr,
    returning - from Heathcots Bay in Barbadoes.
4/3/1736 - John Glenny - from Henly upon Thames. John Strickland and
    wife Mary - from Wrightstown Monthly Meeting.
17/3/1736 - John Armitt, returning - from Devonshire House. Sarah
    Harry - from Goshen Monthly Meeting.
3/25/1736 - John Paterson - from Dublin.
31/3/1736 - Hester and Rachel Marle, daughters of Thomas Marle - from
    Abington Monthly Meeting.
3/4/1736 - Christo. Marshall - from Middletown Monthly Meeting.
10/4/1736 - Elizabeth Thomas, wife of Richard - from Radnor Monthly
    Meeting.
25/5/1736 - William Bennett, late of Collum Stork in Devon - from
    Spiceland.
26/5/1736 - Daniel Dawson and wife - from Abington Monthly Meeting.
    Thomas Hodgkins and wife Mary - from Salem Monthly Meeting.
8/6/1736 - Rebecca Richardson, widow - from Horselydown.
9/6/1736 - Ralph Loftus, returning - from Bridgetown.
6/8/1736 - Eliz. Clarke - see Richardson.
6/11/1736 - Robert Jordan, acknowledging visit - from Charleston, S. C.
26/11/1736 - Robert Strettill, with his family - from Horselydown.
1/12/1736/7 - Leonard Snowden - from Scarborough in York.
7/12/1736/7 - Lewis Weston - from Bull and Mouth.
28/12/1736/7 - Sampson Davis, his wife and family - from Abington
    Monthly Meeting.
7/1/1736/7 - John Guest - from Burlington Monthly Meeting.
10/1/1736/7 - Rees Roberts - from Radnor Monthly Meeting.
27/1/1737 - Sarah Wilcocks, wife of Issachar - from Mountrath.
29/1/1737 - Robert Jordan, acknowledging visit - from Newport, R. I.
18/2/1737 - Elizabeth Winder, had married out - from Salem.
12/3/1737 - John Bushel - from Bridgetown.
25/4/1737 - Samuel Pennock, to marry and settle - from New Garden.
27/4/1737 - Elizabeth Naylor - from Abington Monthly Meeting.
14/5/1737 - Eleanor Bevan - from Haverford Monthly Meeting.
25/5/1737 - Joseph Marshall, with letter from parents - from Mansfield in
    England.
1/6/1737 - Mary Williams, daughter of John Piggott - from Hopewell, Va.
3/6/1737 - Sarah Pemberton - from Falls Monthly Meeting.
11/6/1737 - Cicely Lewellyn - from Merion.
5/7/1737 - Richard Tomlinson, late apprentice - from Burlington Monthly
    Meeting.
12/7/1737 - Mary Sharp, unmarried - from Haddonfield Monthly
    Meeting.
25/7/1737 - Nathaniel Hopewell, a letter from his mother - from
    Mansfield.

31/8/1737 - Hannah Paschall - from Chester Monthly Meeting.
10/9/1737 - Isacc Lobdell, returning - from Boston. Elizabeth Mifflin, lately married - from Boston.
17/9/1737 - Ann Lewis, daughter of Evan Lewis - from Bradford.
26/10/1737 - Sarah Powell, returning - from Abington Monthly Meeting.
3/1/1737/8 - Martha Walker and daughter Rebecca - from Richmond at Chantr_y.
7/1/1737/8 - Benjamin Callender - from Bridgetown.
28/1/1738 - Mary Sharp, wife of James - from Dublin.
7/2/1738 - Isaac Roberts - from Cliffs, Maryland.
24/2/1738 - Isaac Dawson - from Abington Monthly Meeting.
8/3/1738 - Ruth Adams - from Haddonfield Monthly Meeting.
28/4/1738 - Rachel Elfreth - from Westbury.
13/5/1738 - Rachel Peasley, endorsed by Flushing - from Marmoneck.
18/5/1738 - Rachel Spence - from Warrington in England.
3/6/1738 - Hannah Growden - from Middletown Monthly Meeting.
7/6/1738 - Isaac Andrews, in order to marry - from Burlington Monthly Meeting. Susanna Rumford, formerly Nooks - from Concord.
19/7/1738 - Paul Chaunders, his wife and children - from Hartshaw.
26/7/1738 - Jonathan Rumford - from Gwynedd Monthly Meeting. Catherine Jones, with Mary Woodle - from Gwynedd Monthly Meeting. Mary Woodle, with Catherine Jones - from Gwynedd Monthly Meeting.
6 - 8/8/1738 - Robert Jordan, acknowledging visit - from North Carolina.
12/8/1738 - Robert Jordan, acknowledging visit - from Nansemond, Va.
19/8/1738 - John Luke, son of Jacob - from Bridgetown.
4/9/1738 - Robert Jordan, acknowledging visit - from Isle of Wight County, Va.
16/9/1738 - James Steel - from Duck creek.
11/10/1738 - James Estaugh and wife Hannah - from Haddonfield Monthly Meeting.
25/10/1738 - Sarah Cramer - from Abington Monthly Meeting.
7/12/1738/9 - Phinehas Bond - from Herring Creek, Maryland.
15/1/1738/9 - Mary Stubbs, daughter of Thomas and Mary - from Bradford.
17/3/1739 - Benjamin Callender - from Bridgetown.
28/3/1739 - Samuel Hurford and wife Hannah - from Abington Monthly Meeting.
19/4/1739 - Mary Erwin, going with husband - from Dublin.
2/5/1739 - John Pole and wife Rachel - from Burlington Monthly Meeting.
3/5/1739 - John Hillborn and wife Rachel - from Wrightstown Monthly Meeting.
9/5/1739 - John Howell and wife Katherine - from Haddonfield Monthly Meeting.

30/5/1739 - George James and wife Sarah - from Abington Monthly Meeting.

9/6/1739 - Jane Shally - from Boston.

21/7/1739 - Hannah Jenkinson, on a religious visit - from West river.

28/8/1739 - John Houlton and wife - from Exeter Monthly Meeting.

26/9/1739 - Joseph Levis, to marry Susanna Waln - from Chester Monthly Meeting. Rebecca Minshall, a minister - from Chester Monthly Meeting.

27/9/1739 - Margaret and Ann Davis, sisters - from Gwynedd Monthly Meeting.

17/10/1739 - Mary Waln, a minister - from Goshen Monthly Meeting.

31/10/1739 - Edward Wells and wife - from Abington Monthly Meeting. Rebecca Minshall, Jr - from Chester Monthly Meeting.

28/11/1739/40 - Samuel Jackson - from Abington Monthly Meeting.

25/12/1739/40 - Margaret Williams - from Chester Monthly Meeting.

30/12/1739/40 - Dorothy Griggs - from Abington Monthly Meeting.

12/1/1739/40 - Thomas Rooke - from Dublin.

31/1/1740 - Samuel Bell, his wife and children - from Chester Monthly Meeting.

25/2/1740 - Mary Foulke, acknowledging visit - from Spightstown in Barbadoes.

29/2/1740 - Samuel Norris - from Gwynedd Monthly Meeting.

5/3/1740 - Caleb Burchal and wife, he something of a Minister - from Concord.

8/3/1740 - Evan Evans and wife - from Gwynedd Monthly Meeting.

26/3/1740 - Jacob Durburow and wife - from Chester Monthly Meeting. Isaac Davenport and son Benjamin - from Abington Monthly Meeting.

30/4/1740 - Mary Lewis, wife of John - from Concord.

14/5/1740 - Joseph Deane, son of Alexander Deane - from Antrin.

28/5/1740 - Stephen Jenkins - from Abington Monthly Meeting.

25/6/1740 - John Carver and wife Isabella - from Abington Monthly Meeting.

26/6/1740 - Mary Foulke, acknowledging visit - from Portsmouth, R. I.

4/7/1740 - Mary Foulke, acknowledging visit - from Flushing, L. I.

8/7/1740 - James Stephens, to marry and settle - from Haddonfield Monthly Meeting.

11/7/1740 - John Jones and family - from Radnor Monthly Meeting.

25/8/1740 - Thomas Lightfoot - from New Garden.

3/9/1740 - Thomas Gilpin and wife Hannah - from Concord Monthly Meeting.

5/11/1740 - Richard Blackham, to marry and settle - from Burlington Monthly Meeting.

26/11/1740 - Abel Chamberlain - from Cork.

5/12/1740/1 - Samuel Abbott, an apprentice - from Chesterfield Monthly Meeting.

12/12/1740 - Robert Jordan, acknowledging visit - from Bridgetown.

18/12/1740/1 - Isaac Whitelock - from Leeds.

23/12/1740/1 - Charles Jones and wife Sarah - from Chester Monthly Meeting.

6/1/1741 - James Moore, a widower - from Waterford.

30/1/1741 - Joseph Howell, to marry and settle - from Chester Monthly Meeting.

3/2/1741 - Hugh Canady, a widower with children - from Charlemount. Hugh Kennedy, widower with children - from Charlemont in Ireland.

14/2/1741 - Thomas Tilbury, to marry Ann Warner - from Haverford.

27/2/1741 - _elty Thomas - from Abington Monthly Meeting. Hannah Worrell - from Abington Monthly Meeting.

29/3/1741 - John Robins - from London.

16/4/1741 - Ann Rhoads - from Goshen Monthly Meeting.

18/4/1741 - John Bringhurst, acknowledging visit - from Bridgetown.

30/4/1741 - Robert Jordan, acknowledging visit - from Portsmouth, Rhoad Island. Caleb Raper, acknowledging visit - from Portsmouth, R. I.

1/5/1741 - John Hallowell, Junr, and wife Hannah - from Darby Monthly Meeting.

21/5/1741 - Joseph Stiles, son of Benjamin - from Newbury, Berks.

27/5/1741 - Isaac Shoemaker, to marry H. Roberts - from Abington Monthly Meeting.

6/6/1741 - Anne Emlen - from Chesterfield Monthly Meeting.

20/6/1741 - Hannah Harlan with daughter Hannah - from Bradford.

29/7/1741 - Anne Carver, had married out - from Gwynedd Monthly Meeting.

6/11/1741 - Jacob Lewis and wife Hannah - from Darby Monthly Meeting.

20/11/1741/2 - Joseph Saul - from Pardshaw Hall.

18/1/1741/2 - Samuel Noble, returning - from Bridgetown.

26/2/1742 - Martha James - from Abington Monthly Meeting.

10/3/1742 - Elizabeth Johnson - from Sunderland in Durham.

31/3/1742 - Mary Barton - from Chester Monthly Meeting. John Dawson, wife Dorothy and daughter Deborah - from Abington Monthly Meeting.

28/4/1742 - Jonathan Carmalt and wife - from Abington Monthly Meeting.

29/4/1742 - Samuel Morris - from Gwyedd Monthly Meeting.

17/5/1742 - Hannah Hurford, acknowledging visit - from Dover.

26/5/1742 - Abigail Townsend - from Abington Monthly Meeting. Joseph Garnett - from Dublin.

13/6/1742 - Amos Lewis and his wife - from Merion.

21/6/1742 - Hannah Jenkinson, acknowledging visit - from Dover.

30/6/1742 - Sarah Warner, wife of John - from Chester Monthly Meeting.
Sarah Baker - from Abington Monthly Meeting.

31/6/1742 - Hannah Hurford, acknowledging visit - from Portsmouth, R.
I. Abraham Griffith, to marry Elizabeth Lynn - from Gwynedd
Monthly Meeting.

13/7/1742 - Hannah Jenkinson, acknowledging visit - from Salem, Mass.

27/7/1742 - Abraham Mason and his wife - from Abington Monthly
Meeting. Joel Neave - from London.

4/8/1742 - Samuel Brian - from Burlington Monthly Meeting.

6/8/1742 - Rebeckah Wood - from Darby.

12/8/1742 - Richard Hayes and his wife - from Haverford.

25/8/1742 - Rebeckah James, wife of Edward - from Salem, N. J.

12/9/1742 - Owen Jones and wife Susanna - from Merion.

29/9/1742 - Margaret Mason - from Abington Monthly Meeting.

6/10/1742 - Mary Jackson, late Mary Pyle - from Concord Monthly
Meeting.

11/11/1742/3 - Isaac Taylor and wife Catherine - from Haverford.

31/11/1742/3 - Hannah Carpenter - from Salem, New Jersey.

14/12/1742 - Jesse Bourne, son of Benj. Bourne - from London.

2/1/1742/3 - John Parker - from Darby Monthly Meeting.

12/1/1743 - Sarah Holloway - from Chester Monthly Meeting.

7/2/1743 - John Oxley - from Bridge Town.

25/2/1743 - Anthony Benezet and Joyce his wife - from Abington Monthly
Meeting.

2/3/1743 - John Young and family - from Buckingham Monthly Meeting.

9/3/1743 - Rebeckah Ballinger - from Haddonfield Monthly Meeting.

3/31/1743 - Thomas Robinson, with copy of former certificate - from
Dublin.

27/4/1743 - Thomas Brown, wife and daughter Ann - from Abington
Monthly Meeting.

2/5/1743 - Joshua Gill - from Newark at K___t.

25/5/1743 - Thomas Parry, Jr. and wife - from Abington Monthly
Meeting.

26/5/1743 - Hannah Jenkinson, acknowledging visit - from Newport, R. I.

5/6/1743 - John Boddy - from Richmond in York.

8/6/1743 - Abigail Cooper, daughter of Wm. Cooper - from Haddonfield
Monthly Meeting.

27/6/1743 - Hannah Jenkinson, acknowledging visit - from Westbury, R.
I.

29/6/1743 - John Marl and his wife - from Abington Monthly Meeting.
John Needham, his wife and children - from Chester Monthly
Meeting.

7/9/1743 - Samuel Jones and children Joseph and Esther - from Sadsbury.

11/9/1743 - Lewis Jones and wife Katherine - from Merion. John Galloway - from West River in Maryland.

28/9/1743 - Elizabeth Simmons - from Salem Monthly Meeting.

28/11/1743 - Michael Lightfoot and Mary his wife - from New Garden.

31/11/1743 - Morris Morris, to marry Eliz. Mifflin - from Gwynedd Monthly Meeting.

2/12/1743 - Jane Hicks, endorsed at New York - from Flushing, L. I.

6/12/1743/4 - Thomas Marshall and his wife - from Concord.

27/12/1743/4 - Isaac Shoemaker, lately married - from Abington Monthly Meeting.

7/1/1743/4 - Joseph Hallowell - from Darby Monthly Meeting.

8/1/1743/4 - Mary Truman - from Radnor Monthly Meeting.

26/1/1744 - Daniel Morris, in order for marriage - from Abington Monthly Meeting.

7/2/1744 - Isaac Lobdel - from Newark.

24/2/1744 - John Morris, his wife and children - from Gwynedd Monthly Meeting.

3/3/1744 - James Danford - from Chesterfield Monthly Meeting.

7/3/1744 - John Smith - from Burlington Monthly Meeting.

29/3/1744 - Morris Morris - from Gwynedd Monthly Meeting.

2/5/1744 - Mary Reave (see Rodman) - from Burlington Monthly Meeting. William Rodman, to marry Mary Reve - from Burlington Monthly Meeting.

31/5/1744 - Mary Emlen, acknowledging visit - from Newport, R. I.

13/6/1744 - Rebeckah White - from Haddonfield Monthly Meeting. David Elwell and his wife - from Haddonfield Monthly Meeting.

25/6/1744 - Mary Emlen, acknowledging visit - from Westbury. John Hutton, wife Sarah and children - from New Garden. Katherine Lightfoot - from New Garden.

27/6/1744 - Bartholomew Wyatt and wife Elizabeth - from Salem.

13/7/1744 - Katherine Jones, "our ancient friend" - from Radnor.

20/7/1744 - John Bringhurst, Jr - from Bridge Town.

1/8/1744 - Elizabeth Holcomb - from Burlington Monthly Meeting.

9/9/1744 - Daniel Williams - from Merion.

26/9/1744 - Aaron Watson - from Chester Monthly Meeting.

29/10/1744 - Sarah Knubley - from Beckfoot in Cumberland.

3/11/1744 - John Smith and his wife - from Chesterfield Monthly Meeting.

8/11/1744/5 - Isachar Price - from Haverford. Prudence Colbourne, daughter of Joseph - from Chester Monthly Meeting.

31/111/1744 - Mary Wiley - from Exeter.

2/1/1744/5 - Eden Haydock - from Newark.

6/1/1744/5 - Joseph Parker - from Darby. Sarah Richardson - from Chesterfield Monthly Meeting.

10/1/1745 - George Cozens, with wife Eliner and family - from Haddonfield Monthly Meeting.

3/2/1745 - Daniel Stanton, acknowledging visit - from Newtown, L. I.

8/2/1745 - Elizabeth Delzel - from Haddonfield Monthly Meeting.

29/2/1745 - Thomas Wooley, his wife and children - from Chester Monthly Meeting.

4/3/1745 - Ebenezer Robinson - from Burlington Monthly Meeting.

10/4/1745 - Joseph Saul - from Haddonfield Monthly Meeting.

1/5/1745 - Joseph Govett and wife Esther - from Burlington. Elizabeth Harmon - from Buckingham Monthly Meeting.

6/5/1745 - Alexander Seaton and Rebecca his wife - from Newark.

11/5/1745 - Rebecca Wardell - from Salem, Mass.

15/5/1745 - Mordecai Yarnall, to marry Mary Roberts - from Goshen Monthly Meeting.

29/5/1745 - George Mifflin, returning - from London. Samuel Shoemaker, returning - from London.

6/6/1745 - John Shaw and family - from Maidenhead, Berks.

7/6/1745 - Martha Paschall - from Darby Monthly Meeting. Hannah Talbot, wife of John - from Darby.

26/6/1745 - Henry Dennis, with wife Grace and children - from Salem, N. J. Margaret Newberry - from London.

5/7/1745 - Mary Brown - from Chesterfield Monthly Meeting. Preserve Brown, his wife and son Preserve - from Chesterfield Monthly Meeting.

28/7/1745 - William Lightfoot, with wife Jane - from New Garden.

30/7/1745 - Thomas Pedrick, apprentice to Benj. Kendall - from Chester Monthly Meeting. John Cummings, with Benjamin Kendall and c. - from Chester Monthly Meeting. Peter Howard, apprentice to Benjamin Kendall - from Chester Monthly Meeting. Benjamin Kendall with wife and apprentices - from Chester Monthly Meeting.

4/9/1745 - Mary Lightfoot, wife of Thomas - from Burlington Monthly Meeting.

6/9/1745 - John Bonsall - from Darby. Israel Jones, late apprentice - from Darby.

9/9/1745 - Jane Rakestraw - from Merion.

10/9/1745 - John Heritage, had married out - from Haddonfield.

11/9/1745 - Nixon Chattin - from Haddonfield Monthly Meeting.

12/10/1745 - Martha Petel - from Lynn, Mass. Phebe Taylor - from Radnor Monthly Meeting.

3/11/1745 - Elizabeth Guest - from Burlington Monthly Meeting.

4/11/1745 - Rachel Canby - from Newark.

7/11/1745/6 - Thomas Furnis and wife Rachel - from Wrightstown Monthly Meeting.

26/11/1745 - Daniel Stanton, acknowledging visit - from Newport, R. I.
18/11/1745/6 - Robert Strettell, Jr - from Dublin.
31/1/1746 - Mary Marriott, wife of Joseph - from Salem, N. J.
2/2/1746 - Ann McCormish, wife of Patrick - from Darby.
6/2/1746 - Benjamin Hough - from Falls Monthly Meeting.
8/2/1746 - Elizabeth Webster - from Haverford Monthly Meeting.
9/2/1746 - Joshua and Thos. Crosby - from Jamaica.
22/2/1746 - Joshua Fisher, his wife and daughter - from Duck creek.
12/3/1746 - Timothy Matlack, wife Martha and daughter - from
    Haddonfield Monthly Meeting.
2/4/1746 - Susanna Chandler - from Concord.
4/4/1746 - Elizabeth Elfreth - from the Falls Monthly Meeting.
12/4/1746 - Blandana Palmer - from Radnor Monthly Meeting.
10/5/1746 - Francis Nash - from Leominster.
19/5/1746 - William Griffitts, returning - from Swanzey.
6/6/1746 - Robert Willson and his wife - from Falls Monthly Meeting.
7/6/1746 - Sarah Allen - from Chesterfield Monthly Meeting.
11/6/1746 - Samuel Bryan, returning - from London.
14/6/1746 - William Dickinson - from Pontefract in Yorkshire.
15/6/1746 - Sarah Knubley - letter from her shipmate, Jonathan Willis.
6/7/1746 - Edith Webb - from Kennet Monthly Meeting.
8/7/1746 - Henry Wood - from Haddonfield Monthly Meeting.
4/8/1746 - Anthony Woodcock - from Newark. Stephen Stapler, with
    John and Esther White - from Newark. John White, his wife and
    family - from Newark.
6/8/1746 - Christopher Dingee, with wife and sister Sarah Dingee - from
    Concord Monthly Meeting.
3/9/1746 - Sarah Knight and daughter Rebecca - from Buckingham
    Monthly Meeting.
14/9/1746 - Edward Jones - from Merion.
24/9/1746 - David Edward - from Abington Monthly Meeting. Margaret
    Holland - from Abington Monthly Meeting.
5/11/1746 - Samuel and Mary Lippincott - from Shrewsbury Monthly
    Meeting.
7/11/1746 - Joseph Hough and wife Lydia - from Falls Monthly Meeting.
4/12/1746/7 - John Milnor and his wife - from Falls Monthly Meeting.
16/12/1746 - John Mifflin - from Duck Creek.
24/12/1746/7 - Daniel Morris and wife - from Gwynedd Monthly Meeting.
9/1/1746/7 - David Cooper, in order to marry - from Haddonfield Monthly
    Meeting.
4/2/1747 - Joshua Woolaston, to marry Priscilla Jones - from Newark.
13/2/1747 - Lydia Noble, wife of Samuel - from Haddonfield.
27/2/1747 - Rebecca Birchall - from Abington Monthly Meeting. Isaac
    Gleave - from Chester Monthly Meeting.
4/3/1747 - Hezekiah Williams - from Shrewsbury Monthly Meeting.

6/3/1747 - Mary Gleave - from Darby Monthly Meeting. Rebecca Hunt - from Darby Monthly Meeting.
7/3/1747 - John Haydock, son of Robert - from Flushing.
8/3/1747 - Jonathan Edwards and wife - from Merion.
11/3/1747 - Elizabeth Evans, a minister - from Haddonfield Monthly Meeting.
25/3/1747 - John Henry Apple and wife Mary - from Salem Monthly Meeting.
1/4/1747 - Lydia Canady - from Buckingham Monthly Meeting.
3/4/1747 - Joshua Pearson and wife - from Darby Monthly Meeting. David Palmer - from Falls Monthly Meeting. David Gibson and wife Mary - from Darby.
1/5/1747 - Hannah Heans - from Darby Monthly Meeting.
14/5/1747 - Isaac Bartrane, late apprentice - from Haverford Monthly Meeting.
5/6/1747 - Deborah Hudson - from Falls Monthly Meeting.
2/7/1747 - Sophia Hume, to visit S. C., Penna., and c. - from Devonshire House.
3/7/1747 - John Armitt, acknowledging visit - from Flushing.
7/7/1747 - John Burr - from Burlington Monthly Meeting.
29/7/1747 - Mehetable Redwood, daughter of Abraham - from Newport. Jonas Redwood, son of Abraham - from Newport.
3/8/1747 - Isaiah Bell - from Newark.
10/8/1747 - Francis Nash, respecting clearness - from Leominster.
13/8/1747 - Phinehas Roberts and wife Ann - from Haverford.
26/8/1747 - Mary Giffing - from Chester Monthly Meeting.
4/9/1747 - Samuel Preston Moore and wife Hannah - from Herring Creek.
24/9/1747 - Owen Roberts and wife Jane - from Gwynedd.
26/9/1747 - Samuel Mifflin - from Accomac Co., Va.
1/10/1747 - Mordecai Yarnall, his wife and children - from Goshen Monthly Meeting.
14/10/1747 - Grace Fisher, a minister - from Haddonfield Monthly Meeting.
4/11/1747/8 - James Clothier - from Burlington Monthly Meeting.
7/11/1747/8 - Joanna Brooks - from Chesterfield Monthly Meeting. Mary Brown, Jr. - from Chesterfield Monthly Meeting.
21/11/1747/8 - Patrick Ogilby and wife Rebecca - from Richland Monthly Meeting. Anne Stubbs, daughter of Thos. and Mary - from Bradford.
25/11/1747/8 - Hannah Neale - from Chester Monthly Meeting.
2/12/1747 - Dr. Robert Willan - from Scarborough.
7/1/1747/8 - William Herves - from Concord.
14/1/1747/8 - John Burrough, Jr, in order to marry - from Haddonfield Monthly Meeting.

17/1/1747/8 - William Lightfoot, returning - from Bridgetown.
2/2/1748 - Elizabeth West - from Newark.
26/2/1748 - Joseph Davies and wife Mary - from Gwynedd Monthly Meeting. Thomas Burgess - from Gwynedd Monthly Meeting.
28/2/1748 - Elizabeth Stevens, a minister - from Treadhaven.
29/2/1748 - Charles Moore - from West River. Deborah Hill - from West River.
6/3/1748 - Content Nicholson - from Newark.
7/3/1748 - John Crew, addressed to Haverford - from Dunn Creek, N. C.
13/3/1748 - Thomas Tilbury - from Merion.
24/3/1748 - John Williamson - from Pardshaw.
11/6/1748 - Benjamin Bagnall and wife Ann - from Boston.
14/6/1747 - Ellen Shoemaker - from Merion.
29/6/1748 - Abraham Moss and daughter Rebecca - from Salem. Rebecca Vanakin - from Abington Monthly Meeting.
8/7/1748 - John Moore and wife Rachel - from Radnor. Daniel Stanton, acknowledging visit - from Barbadoes.
3/8/1748 - James Moore and wife Anne - from Burlington Monthly Meeting.
16/8/1748 - Daniel Stanton, acknowledging visit - from Tortola.
25/8/1748 - Musgrave Evans and brother David - from Gwynedd Monthly Meeting.
31/8/1748 - Mary Jones - from Abington Monthly Meeting.
2/9/1748 - John Hallowell, his wife and daughter - from Darby Monthly Meeting.
30/9/1748 - Elizabeth Edmondson, daughter of Elizabeth - from Treadhaven.
7/10/1748 - John Davis - from Horslydown.
4/11/1748 - Martha Stapler - from Falls Monthly Meeting.
19/11/1748 - Joshua Howell, returning - from Bridgetown.
29/11/1749 - Sarah Stevens, daughter of Elizabeth - from Treadhaven.
30/11/1748/9 - Joseph Ogden - from Chester.
6/12/1748/9 - William Lawrence and his wife Martha - from Shrewsbury Monthly Meeting.
8/12/1748 - William Nichols - from Horslydown.
24/12/1748 - Rachel Moore - from West River.
27/12/1748/9 - Thomas Hill and wife - from Abington Monthly Meeting.
5/1/1749 - Mary Glading, daughter of Richard and Ann - from Hertford.
19/1/1749 - James Wagstaffe - from London.
1/3/1749 - Samuel Bettle and wife - from Concord.
3/3/1749 - Ezekiel Jones - from Abington Monthly Meeting.
11/3/1749 - John Luke - from Bridgetown.
17/3/1749 - Grace Fisher, acknowledging visit - from West River.
29/3/1749 - Mary Ogden - from Chester Monthly Meeting.

1/4/1749 - Jeremiah Woolstone - from Middletown Monthly Meeting.
    James Arbuckle and daughter Hannah - from Middletown Monthly
    Meeting.
5/4/1749 - Jane Burgess, wife of Thomas - from Burlington Monthly
    Meeting.
8/4/1749 - Sarah Walter - from Radnor Monthly Meeting.
11/4/1749 - John Bringhurst, son of John of Phila. - from Bridgetown.
12/4/1749 - Reuben Haines - from Haddonfield Monthly Meeting.
17/4/1749 - William Brown, his wife and children - from Nottingham
    Monthly Meeting.
26/4/1749 - Mary Moss, wife of Isaac - from Chester Monthly Meeting.
    David Bacon - from Salem Monthly Meeting.
24/5/1749 - Samuel Burge - from Grace Church Street. James
    Pemberton, returning - from London.
1/6/1749 - Elizabeth Gridley - from Ives, in Co. of Huntingdon.
2/6/1749 - Richard Parker - from Darby.
7/6/1749 - Mary Holcomb and two daughters - from Buckingham Monthly
    Meeting. Hannah Woolston - from Burlington Monthly Meeting.
    Samuel Smith and wife Jane - from Burlington Monthly Meeting.
21/6/1749 - Hannah Ashton, wife of Peter Ashton - from Goshen Monthly
    Meeting.
18/7/1749 - Charles Norris, returning - from Grace Church Street.
22/7/1749 - William Fisher, returning - from Bridgetown.
9/8/1749 - Hannah Bettle, endorsed on parents certificate - from
    Concord.
30/8/1749 - Joseph Parker - from Grace Church Street. William Garrett -
    from Grace Church Street.
4/9/1749 - Susanna Beal - from Newark.
8 - 10/9/1749 - Daniel Stanton, acknowledging visit - from Dublin half
    years meeting.
27/9/1749 - Mary Dennis - from Salem.
1/12/1749/50 - Mary Fishbourn - from Chesterfield Monthly Meeting.
19/12/1749 - John Davis - from Grace Church Street.
12/1/1750/1 - Elizabeth Little - from Dublin.
27/1/1750 - Ann Jones - from Gwynedd Monthly Meeting.
8/2/1750 - John Britten, his wife and children - from Cooldine.
9/2/1750 - Jane Siddons - from Haddonfield Monthly Meeting.
10/2/1750 - Margaret Pascal, had married out - from Haverford. William
    Montgomery - from Kingwood.
21/2/1750 - Nathan Baker - from Nottingham.
24/2/1750 - Margaret Bell - from Gwynedd Monthly Meeting.
26/2/1950 - William Shipley, his wife and child - from Stafford.
14/3/1750 - Mary West - from Haddonfield Monthly Meeting.
19/3/1750 - Hezekiah Williams, returning - from Bridgetown.
28/3/1750 - Thomas Graves - from Salem Monthly Meeting.

5/4/1750 - John Wyly, on business - from Dublin. Joseph Mickle, on business - from Dublin.

6/4/1750 - John Houlton, his wife and children - from Darby Monthly Meeting.

11/5/1750 - John Tagart and wife Mary - from Lurgan.

10/6/1750 - Ann Tilbury - from Merion.

25/6/1750 - Grace Fisher, acknowledging visit - from Westbury.

28/6/1750 - Patience Richardson - from Dublin.

30/6/1750 - John Willson, schoolmaster - from Askwith.

3/7/1750 - John Pole, returning - from Bristol.

4/8/1750 - Adam Harker - from Middletown Monthly Meeting.

9/8/1750 - Catherine LLewelin - from Haverford.

1/9/1750 - Grace Fisher, acknowledging visit - from Newport, R. I.

24/10/1750 - Joseph Ogden, returning - from London.

25/10/1750 - Elizabeth Jones, daughter of Robert - from Gwynedd Monthly Meeting.

31/10/1750 - Mary Wagstaff, with her sister - from Abington Monthly Meeting. Martha Hughs, with Mary Wagstaff - from Abington Monthly Meeting.

8/11/1750/1 - Jane Lewis - from Haverford Monthly Meeting. Margaret Barry - from Haverford.

28/11/1750/1 - William Lightfoot - from Chester Monthly Meeting. 31/11/1750/1 - David Beavirge - from Edinburgh.

5/12/1750 - Thomas Davis, not in full membership - from Dacer.

28/12/1750 - Augustine Mellor - from Barbadoes.

MISCELLANEOUS CERTIFICATES ISSUED
1698-1750

27/11/1698 - Richard Gove - to accompany Thomas Chalkley.

6/3/1704 - Elizabeth Webb -to visit Virginia.

28/5/1704 - Thomas Turner - to visit Barbadoes.

_/_/1706 - Susanna Freeborn - on a religious visit.

_/_/1706 - Richard Townsend - to visit his native land.

29/1/1706 - Abraham Scott - to London. Daniel Gaunt - to Abington Monthly Meeting, to marry.

29/4/1706 - Joseph Brown - to Newtown, in New Jersey.

29/9/1706 - Pentecost Teague - to visit his native land.

30/6/1706 - Martha Chalkley - to visit New England.

29/8/1706 - Susanna Freeborn - to Rhode Island. Patience Anthony - to Friends in Rhode Island.

26/9/1708 - James Steel - to Duck Creek. Israel Pemberton - to Barbadoes on business.

31/10/1708 - Sam'l Wilkinson - to Barbadoes and Ireland.

25/12/1708 - Griffith Owen - to visit Long Island.

29/2/1709 - John Hewlet - to Great Britain.

26/6/1709 - George Gray - to East Jersey and Long Island.

26/7/1709 - Richard Hill - to Bucks County. James Logan.

25/9/1709 - John Richmond - to Great Britain.

24/12/1709/10 - Richard Webb - to Concord Monthly Meeting.

31/1/1710 - Richard Webb - to Concord Monthly Meeting.

30/4/1710 - John Ball - to Abington Monthly Meeting, on account of marriage.

27/8/1710 - John Hart - to Great Britain.

29/10/1710 - Thomas Iredell - to Abington Monthly Meeting. John Picket and wife - to Concord Monthly Meeting. Gilbert Falconer - to Great Britain.

27/2/1711 - Anthony Morris - to visit New England.

25/11/1711 - John Oxley - to New England.

28/1/1712 - Samuel Hudson - to Great Britain.

27/4/1712 - Joseph Bond - to Bristol Monthly Meeting, in Bucks County. James Estaugh and wife Mary - to Duck Creek. George Gray - to Abington Monthly Meeting.

25/5/1712 - Benjamin Fairman - to Chesterfield Monthly Meeting.

26/7/1712 - Richard Brown - to the West Indies.

31/8/1712 - Abraham Shotwell - to Woodbridge to marry.

26/10/1712 - James Hurd - to Limington in Somerset.

27/12/1712 - Jeremiah Allen - to Jamaica.

31/5/1713 - Andrew Godfrey - to Salem Monthly Meeting.

25/10/1713 - David Lloyd and wife - to Chester Monthly Meeting.

26/12/1713 - Richard Parks and wife Susanna - to Concord Monthly Meeting.
30/2/1714 - Stephen Jackson - to visit Great Britain. Edward Mifflin - to Virginia, on account of marriage.
28/3/1714 - Samuel Stretch - to Maryland. James Morris -returning to Bristol.
29/5/1715 - John Oxley - to England on business.
28/2/1721 - Elizabeth Teague - to Long Island and New England.
24/2/1724 - Elizabeth Whartnaby - to visit Long Island and c.
29/2/1726 - Margaret Preston - to visit Long Island and c.
28/5/1727 - Elizabeth Whartnaby - to visit Ireland and c.
26/5/1728 - Margaret Preston - to visit Maryland, Va. and c.
28/6/1730 - Emm Evans - to visit Virginia, Carolina and c.
30/2/1731 - Daniel Stanton - to Rhode Island.
24/7/1731 - Robert Jordan - to visit Nansemond, Virginia.
26/3/1732 - Richard Waln - to visit Long Island and c.
25/6/1732 -Phebe Robinson - to Abington Monthly Meeting.
24/7/1731 - Robert Jordan - to visit Long Island and c.
27/8/1732 - Robert Jordan - to visit Long Island and c.
23/12/1732/3 - Robert Jordan - to London and elsewhere.
29/4/1733 - Mary Nicholas - to visit Md., Va. and c.
26/8/1733 - Isaac Norris, Jr. - to London.
30/6/1734 - Margaret Preston - to visit Maryland and c. Joyce Marriott - to visit Maryland and c.
27/7/1734 - Robert Jordan - to visit New York, L. I. and c.
25/2/1735 - Daniel Stanton - to visit New England.
29/6/1735 - Robert Jordan - to visit Virginia.
26/1/1736 - Robert Jordan - to visit Nansemond, Va.
29/8/1736 - William Hall - to E. Greenwich, R. I. with wife. Robert Jordan - to South Carolina and c.
29/9/1736 - Hannah Jenkinson - to West River, acknowledging visit.
29/2/1737 - Thomas Chalkley - to visit Long Island and c.
16/1/1737/8 - Jeremiah Elfreth - to Westbury, to marry.
25/6/1738 - Robert Jordan -acknowledging visit.
28/10/1739 - Mary Foulke - to visit Barbadoes.
30/4/1738 - Ruth Courtney - to Grange, Ireland. Susanna Hudson - to Grange.
25/3/1739 - Eliphal Harper - to Sandwich, New England.
28/10/1739 - Robert Jordan - to Long Island.
30/3/1740 - Ann Lewis - to Bradford.
28/9/1740 - Robert Jordan - to visit Barbadoes.
29/3/1741 - Robert Jordan - to visit Rhode Island.
26/1/1742 - Hannah Jenkinson - to visit Long Island and c.
25/9/1743 - Edmund Peckover - to London, acknowledging visit.
27/2/1744 - Mary Emlen - to visit Long Island and c.

28/7/1744 - Elizabeth Jordan - to Sunderland, England.

25/11/1744 - Daniel Stanton - to visit Long Island and c.

19 -22/7/1747 -Thomas Gawthrop -acknowledging visit.

25/7/1747 - John Jervis - to Ireland, on business.

27/8/1749 - Jeremiah Martin - to return to Tortola.

30/8/1747 - Thomas Gawthrop - to England, acknowledging visit. Isaac Greenleafe - to return to London.

26/12/1747 - Elizabeth Hudson - to visit England.

27/3/1748 - Cadwalader Evans - to London.

24/4/1748 - Daniel Stanton - to visit Barbadoes, England and c.

29/5/1748 - Samuel Nottingham - to England, acknowledging visit.

28/8/1748 - Sophia Hume, to England, acknowledging visit. James Pemberton - to Grace Church street.

25/9/1748 - Charles Norris - to Grace Church Street.

31/1/1749 - Sarah Warner - to Goshen.

28/2/1749 - Grace Fisher - to visit Maryland and c.

29/7/1749 - Hannah Jenkinson - to return to England.

30/1/1750 -Monthly Meeting. William Brown - to visit Great Britain and c. John Pole - to Bristol, England.

28/10/1750 - Esther White - to visit Southern Provinces.

MEN'S MINUTES
1682-1750

9/11/1682 - Thomas Smith of the county of Philadelphia, Husbandman, and Priscilla Allen, of the same, Spinster, his parents being deceased and her parents consenting, having declared their intentions of marriage before a Monthly Meeting at Shacamaxon, are clear to marry.

6/12/1682 - A letter from John Brnyatt was read.

3/2/1683 - A certificate from Clanbrazill in the county of Armagh in Ireland, for James Atkinson, who now resides at Griffith Jones, concerns his coming into this province contrary to the consent of Friends of the meeting whereunto he belonged, he signified to be very much in debt and care. John Test desires Right against Griffith Jones upon the account of a contract for a plantation, the said Griffith Jones having given Ernest in order to purchase same did unjustly deny to perform the bargain.

5/4/1683 - Thomas Home and Griffith Jones shall speak unto James Atkinson to appear and give satisfaction to Friends touching his arrivall in this province. A difference depending betwixt John Test and Griffith Jones, said Jones stood and requested Friends be appointed to judge of and end said difference.

3/5/1683 - Thomas Holme, Thomas Wynne and Griffith Jones appointed to satisfy, by way of a few lines, the Friends of the meeting at Canbrazill concerning James Atkinson, touching his departure out of England and Ireland into Pennsylvania.

7/6/1683 - Touching the disposal of the Widow Mason's children, it was agreed they should remain at the place of their present being until the next meeting and then be disposed of as Friends see convenient.

4/7/1683 - Agreed and concluded that Richard Mason, son of the Widow Mason shall continue as an apprentice with Thomas Fairman for the term of ten years so he may be educated in the art and mystery of Husbandry; Robert Mason, another son of the Widow Mason, do remain with Christian Closse, where at present he resides, until the next Monthly Meeting, and then to be further disposed of; John Mason, eldest son of the Widow Mason, do remain with his mother, with whom he now resides.

2/8/1783 - John Hart and Thomas Fairman do take care that Widow Mason and her family be duly provided for until further order.

6/9/1683 - Charles Pickering made his appearance, being concerned in paying and passing moneys not current.

4/1/1683/4 - John Gooden and Sarah Kitchen declared their intention to marry.

1/2/1684 - James Claypool and Thomas Lloyd to see to the securing, ordering and disposal of Elizabeth Palmers estate so far as relates to her children by her former husband, according to her said husbands will.

6/3/1684 - Charles Lee and Ann Barrett declare their intention to marry. Nathaniel Ible and Elizabeth Annis declare their intention to marry.

3/4/1684 - Charles Lee and Ann Barret clear to marry. Nathaniel Ible and Elizabeth Annis clear to marry.

1/5/1684 - Thomas Wynn requests a certificate to Friends in England, Wales and elsewhere. There is a difference depending between Walter King and Dennis Rochford touching payment for a hired servant and care. Thomas Wynn, father in law to Elizabeth Rowden, being immediately to depart for England with his wife, moves that the marriage be accomplished sooner than usual.

5/6/1684 - A certificate for James Claypool and his wife, from Friends in London, mentioned his three daughters to be clear from all engagements in relation to marriage.

2/7/1684 - James Atkinson and Hannah Newby declare their intention to marry. There is a difference depending between James Atkinson and Griffith Jones.

7/8/1684 - The difference between James Atkinson and Griffith Jones was composed and ended. James Atkinson clear to marry and a certificate to Friends in Jersey signifying same was drawn up. Thomas Philips requests a certificate of his clearness relating to marriage. Thomas Lloyd proposed his intentions of marriage with Patience Story of New York.

4/9/1684 - Certificate for William Brinton and his wife from Friends, another from his dealers. One for John Boweter and his wife. One for George Pearce from Friends and another from his dealers. One for John Bant and Nicholas Prince from Friends. One for John Taylor from Friends and another from magistrates. One for William Garrett and wife from Friends. One for Robert Cliffe and wife from Friends. One for John Smith and wife from Friends. One for Samuel Lewis from Friends and for Joseph Hembray and Hugh Durborough from Friends.

2/10/1684 - The business of the Widow Walker presented by the womens meeting, desiring Friends to take care of said Widow. Thomas Lloyd clear to marry Patience Story, a certificate signed to signify same to Friends of New York.

6/11/1684 - John Austin and Christian England, widow, declare their intention to marry, Friends being acquainted that John Austin had been concerned with a woman in England by proposal of marriage. John Austin to write for a certificate of clearness from the woman. Lent Widow Warner twenty pounds and put into the hands of Mary Bowman for the said Widows use.

3/12/1684 - Andrew Griscom and Sarah Dole declare their intention to marry, John Bristoll and her brother John Dole giving a certificate of her clearness from all persons in England. William Morgan requests a certificate to England. William Alloway and Elizabeth Prothero declare their intention to marry, her father and mother being present and consenting. Derrick Isaacs, a dutch friend of Germantown, acquainted this meeting of the wants of some of the dutch there.

9/12/1684 - Business concerning the relief of the Widow Warner presented.

2/1/1684/5 - There is a difference between John Day and John Redman.

4/3/1685 - Joshua Tittery, a glassmaker belonging to the Free Society of Traders, complains that they deny him his wages. Ralph Fretwell and John Eckley request certificates to go out of this province. A report concerns Peter Dalbo and his father in law, Peter Rambo. Henry Lee to acquaint the magistrates of the disorderly doings at Passyunck last first day.

1/4/1685 - Barnabas Willcox complains to this meeting that John Fisher has greatly abused him with bad words and names.

3/6/1685 - A letter from Friends in Barbadoes mentions one William Hunt, a minister now in these parts. Thomas Morris and Jane Jones clear to marry, she producing a certificate from Merioneth. George Emlen requests a certificate to marry Ellinor Allen of Bucks County.

12/7/1685 - The difference between Barnabas Wilcox and John Fisher continues. Thomas Rutter requests a certificate of his clearness to marry.

5/8/1685 - Edmond Bennett and Elizabeth Potts declare their intentions to marry, he to bring a certificate from the meeting in Bucks County to which he belongs. Certificate issued to the Falls meeting for Thomas Rutter. Thomas Kitchen and Mary Mace declare their intention to marry, he to bring a certificate from the Monthly Meeting to which he belongs and she, being a widow, to be assisted to settle concerns so that her children be duly provided for and taken care of.

2/9/1685 - Thomas Hollyman complains of Henry Badcock for some uncivil carriage and care. A letter from William Curtis concerning the children of John Lowe, deceased, was read. They are to send up the children to Griffith Jones and he be spoke with in the meantime to receive them.

7/10/1685 - Daniel Peg desires a certificate of his clearness relating to marriage. Bernard Littlejohn desires a certificate of his clearness.

4/11/1685 - A certificate of William Bradford and his wife was read from Devonshire - house meeting. Frances Taylor is deceased. A certificate signed for Bernard Littlejohn. Isaac Ricketts desires advice relating to his case with his employers.

1/12/1685 - Richard Orme desires a certificate of his clearness as he doth intend to take Mary Tedder of Hartford to be his wife. Nathaniel Walton and Martha Bowling clear to marry, he bringing certificates of his clearness from England and from Poquessin.

1/1/1685/6 - David Hammond desires a certificate to England. Richard Orme clear for a certificate. John Curtis desires the meeting to send for John Lowe's children. The meeting desires William Frampton to send the said children up by the first opportunity to be disposed of by the meeting.

5/2/1686 - The children of John Lowe, deceased, presented for concurrence for their putting forth. Archibald Mickle was concluded to having the boy, Griffith Jones the middle girl and the youngest one to be disposed of by the women Friends. Edward Eaton desires a certificate of his clearness, proposing to take a wife from Oxford meeting. Philip Howell and Jane Luffe declare their intention to marry, Friends appointed to enquire into the said Philips clearness and to see the concern of the widow relating to her child settled. Samuel Carpenter, intending to Barbadoes, desires a certificate from this meeting. Friends appointed to speak to John Moon and advise him in regard to marriage.

3/3/1686 - Nathaniel Sikes and Ellinor Pain declare their intention to marry, he producing a certificate from England. Friends to take a view of John Lowe's goods in the hands of John Curtis and settle accounts with him.

7/4/1686 - Whereas William Alloway and Elizabeth Protherough did many months since declare their intention to marry, and have not proceeded, this meeting desires him to come to the next meeting to clear himself of send his reasons for not proceeding in the aforesaid intentions. Evan Oliver hath in his hands goods of some orphans and refuseth to give security for said goods.

5/5/1686 - Thomas Fitzwater hath spoken to Evan Oliver and said Evan told him that he will do what Friends should think fit for him to do for securing the orphans estate.

2/6/1686 - Benjamin Acton and Christian England declare their intention to marry, Benjamin to bring a certificate from the meeting at Salem.

27/6/1686 - Friends appointed to speak to James Harrison that if he has any effects in his hands in order to supply the wants of Richard Merryweather that he will take some care in that respect. John Austin desires a certificate of his clearness.

24/7/1686 - John Otter and Mary Blinston declare their intention to marry, Friends to speak to said Mary that she make over to her child and settle upon her what part of her estate she is willing to bestow. Alexander Beardsley appointed to go to the Widow Frampton and get those books that belong to this meeting which her husband had in his custody.

29/8/1686 - John Otter and Mary Blinston clear to marry, John having
brought a certificate from the Monthly Meeting at Neshaminy.
Friends are desired by this meeting to inquire in behalf of Mary
Blinstons daughter to whom security is to be given that what she
hath to bestow on her daughter may be secured. Zachary Whitpain
and Sarah Songhurst declare their intention to marry, the said
Zachariah having no certificate from his father, Friends are appointed
to write to his father that he signify his mind concerning his sons
proceedings in order to marry.
26/9/1686 - William Fisher and Bridget Hodgkins declare their intention
to marry, he having no certificate of his fathers approbation in the
case, was desired to write for one. Zachery Whitpain and Sarah
Songhurst declare their intention to marry for a second time. Friends
refer him to the last meetings advice, which was to forebear
consummating the same till Friends receive an answer from his
father. Robert Turner and Susannah Welsh declare their intention to
marry, Robert desiring a certificate for this purpose.
31/10/1686 - A certificate for Robert Whitton from Snape meeting in
Yorkshire. One for Michael and Elizabeth Hammond from the Peel
meeting in London. One for Thomas and Mary Peart from Thursk
Monthly Meeting in Yorkshire. Friends appointed to draw up a
certificate for Robert Turner. A certificate from the Monthly Meeting
in Chesterfield in Staffordshire for Henry Lakin who declares his
intention to marry with Ann Lee, widow. Zachariah Whitpain and his
wife have proceeded in order to take each other as man and wife,
contrary to the advice and consent of Friends. The twenty pounds
that Rachel Warner formerly had of Friends, she hath returned.
28/11/1686 - A certificate for John Hayton, who intends to journey
towards New England. Friends appointed to go to Zachariah Whitpain
and his wife returned answer that the said Zachariah did not
understand, neither was convinced wherein he had acted contrary to
truth. Henry Jones and Rachel Walner declare their intention to
marry. A difference between Thomas Smith and Thomas Cross.
Henry Laking and Ann Lee declare their intention to marry. Thomas
Cooper requests a certificate to England.
25/12/1686 - Certificate issued for Samuel Thomas [Tombs]. The
difference between Thomas Smith and Thomas Cross has ended.
Henry Jones and Rachel Walner clear to marry. Joseph Willcox and
Ann Powell declare their intention to marry, both their parents being
present, give consent. Edward Turner and Katherine Carter declare
their intention to marry, Edward to bring a certificate from Concord
meeting, where he hath lately resided.
7/1/1686/7 - James Kite has received of late great damage by fire.
25/1/1686/7 - Joseph Wilcox and Ann Powell clear to marry, he producing
a writing under the hand of one Mary Gardner, that he was never any

ways engaged to. Isaac Ricketts and Elizabeth Palmer declare their intention to marry, her parents being present and giving consent.

9/2/1687 - John Duplonvis and Whanky Zaney clear to marry, he producing a certificate of clearness, and her mother being present and giving consent. Thomas Bowman, signifying his intention to return to England, desires a certificate from this meeting. Francis Richardson and Elizabeth Frampton have some matter of controversy. Thomas Thurston hath made some complaint to this meeting concerning some Friends in Maryland. Joseph Moss requests a certificate in order to marry at the Monthly Meeting held at John Harts.

27/3/1687 - George Smedley and Sarah Gooden declare their intentions to marry. Friends appointed to assist them in securing something for the woman's child. A certificate issued for Joseph Moss.

6/4/1687 - James Kites condition is very low and his loss reported to be about sixty pounds. Friends are cautioned to be careful that they buy neither hoggs, bells, nor any other things of the indians, which may be suspected that they came not honestly by.

24/4/1687 - George Smedley and Sarah Gooden clear to marry, he to give a bond unto Thomas Kitchen for what is due unto Sarah Goodens child by a former husband. John Ithell hath laid some matters of complaint against Robert Turner.

29/5/1687 - A certificate of clearness to marry issued for William Dillwin. Benjamin Whitehead hath put in a complaint against Robert Turner,

6/6/1687 - Thomas Marl laid before this meeting that his wife hath been gone from him this 8 or 9 years and desires their advice relating to his marrying again. A certificate for the satisfaction of Robert Turner to be sent to England and Ireland for the clearing him of those scandalous reports that hath been spread concerning him. Francis Gamble, late of Barbadoes, produced a certificate from the Monthly Meeting whereunto he belonged in the island aforesaid and desires a certificate from us.

3/7/1687 - The matter of Thomas Marl and his wife Eleanor, gone from him about 8 or 9 years, is referred to the Yearly meeting. A communication received from the meeting of Ulster in Ireland concerns Francis and Mary Cornwall.

13/7/1687 - In consideration of the difference depending between Samuel Carpenter and Griffith Jones upon the account of George Thorp, Friends do judge that Griffith Jones shall pay unto Samuel Carpenter in current money of Pennsylvania the full contents of the bond due to George Thorp. Also, there is a difference depending between Samuel Carpenter and Griffith Jones upon the account of a bill of Exchange which came protested from England and due first to Stephen Kent and afterwards to Daniel Wharley of London, whose attorney Samuel Carpenter is. Friends do judge that the said Griffith Jones shall pay unto Samuel Carpenter in the behalf of Daniel Wharley the money due. The said Samuel Carpenter put in another complaint against Griffith Jones on the behalf of John Dowden of London concerning a parcel of hats that Griffith Jones hath received of the aforesaid Dowden and hath not made satisfaction to him. Friends do agree that the said Griffith Jones shall pay unto Samuel Carpenter in the behalf of the aforesaid John Dowden twenty one pounds 2/6. current money of Old England with interest. It is the judgement of this meeting that Griffith Jones ought to give satisfaction to Friends for his conduct in these affairs.

28/8/1687 - Joshua Cart requests a certificate, which was issued, he intending to transport himself to England.

5/10/1687 - John Hayden desires a certificate from this meeting. A certificate to be drawn up for Roger Longworth. Thomas Hootton. Sen, requests assistance in the management of the Christopher Taylors? children and estate.

27/11/1687 - John Day, intending for England, desires a certificate from this meeting.

24/12/1687 - Benjamin Whitehead requests assistance in accomplishing the judgement of Friends in the difference between the said Benjamin and Robert Turner.

5/1/1687/8 - A certificate drawn up and signed on behalf of Roger Longworth. A paper from Burlington concerning Joseph Paul was read. A certificate on behalf of John Hayton was drawn and signed.

30/1/1688 - Joshua Tittery and Cicely Woollery clear to marry, Joshua producing a certificate and a discharge from whom he was concerned in England.

7/2/1688 - James Fox intends to transport himself to England and desires a certificate from hence. John Day likewise requested a certificate upon the same occasion. A conference with John Shelson concerning the letters of John and Martha Moon.

25/3/1688 - Certificates for James Fox and John Day approved. Two papers, one from Francis Cornwall and the other by Thomas Wynn and William Clark concerning the said Cornwall, were read and not well approved. Thomas Bond, being upon his voyage for England, requested a certificate of his clearness.

29/4/1688 - A certificate signed for Thomas Bond. There is some difference in accounts between Henry Waddy and William Southerby.

26/5/1688 - Philip England requests a certificate to Duck Creek meeting of his clearness relating to marriage. James Goodrick requests a certificate to Friends elsewhere, he not knowing if he shall stay in this country until another Monthly Meeting.

31/6/1688 - The certificate requested by Philip England to be deferred as it doth appear that his wife hath not been dead one year. Robert Drew requests a certificate, he being minded to transport himself to England.

28/7/1688 - Friends appointed to end the difference between Ellis Jones and Thomas Fitzwater. Thomas Kiell and Catherine Brientnall declare their intention to marry, he to bring a certificate from the meeting to which he belongs. Rees Preese desires a certificate of his clearness in order to take Elizabeth Williams of Harford to wife. John Wait and Magdalen Morris declare their intention to marry.

26/8/1688 - Friends appointed to inspect into the necessity of Thomas Smith and supply his present occasion and to advise him to place out which of his children he may conveniently spare. Richard Basnett and Elizabeth Frampton declare their intention to marry, he to bring a certificate from Burlington and she to make what reasonable provision she could for her children.

13/9/1688 - Thomas Smith is willing to leave it to Friends to assist him in putting out his youngest children, a boy of about ten years of age and a girl of about four years. Nathaniel Watson is deceased. William Rodney and Mary Hollyman declare their intention to marry, William formerly having lived among Friends in Maryland, he is to bring a certificate from the Monthly Meeting there. John Densey and Sarah Hollyman declare their intention to marry, he producing a letter from his father and mother wherein they do not object against his marriage.

28/10/1688 - Edward Jermins condition is very low.

25/11/1688 - Friends to continue to supply the necessity of Thomas Smith. Friends appointed to end the difference between Benjamin Chambers and Owen Foulks. Friends appointed to inspect into the difference between John Gardner and Philip England. John Jones proposed his intentions to go to Barbadoes and desires a certificate.

22/12/1688 - The differences are ended between Owen Foulk and Benjamin Chambers and John Gardner and Philip England. A certificate issued for John Jones. John Jones brother is lately deceased.

29/1/1689 - Friends appointed to advise the Widow Morgan and to hire some convenient place for her to live, they thinking it not convenient for her to build at present. John Murray and Sarah Budd declare their intention to marry. Thomas Budd, intending a voyage to England, requested a certificate which was accordingly issued.

26/2/1689 - John Murray and Sarah Budd clear to marry.

31/3/1689 - The widow, Catherine Morgan, being in want of some assistance, Friends are willing to lend her four pounds. Andrew Griscomb brings in a complaint against Richard Townsend concerning his servant. Friends are appointed to put an end to said difference and advise that the young man may return to his master Townsend.

13/4/1689 - Samuel Richardson is gone to Jamaico. There is a difference between Isaac Ricketts and his mother Elizabeth Fitzwater. Thomas

Roberts being in necessity and great want of habitation, Friends have consented to lend him five pounds toward his assistance.

26/5/1689 - James Thomas and Ellin Barber declare their intention to marry, requesting they may perfect their intentions sooner than usual he being master of a ship and not at liberty to stay until next meeting. After inquiry, they are clear to marry. Concerning the difference between Isaac Ricketts and his mother in law, Elizabeth Fitzwater, she being willing to let him have his part in the Liberty land, the meeting desires him to forbear for the present. William Bradford desires a certificate, he intending to transport himself to England.

30/6/1689 - A certificate issued for William Bradford. James Pratt desires a certificate to Oxford meeting where he intends to take his wife. The difference between Isaac Ricketts and his mother was again heard.

27/7/1689 - Friends are to endeavour to reconcile the difference between Elizabeth Fitzwater and her son in law. Anthony Morris and Agnes Boom declare their intention to marry, she being a widow, Friends are appointed to make it their endeavour to settle a proportionate part of her estate upon the children. William Walker and Elisabeth Morgan declare their intention to marry, William to procure a certificate from England and also the meeting he hath belonged to since he came into these parts. Friends appointed to see a sufficient part of her estate settled upon the child. Thomas Clifford is in need.

25/8/1689 - William Walker and Elisabeth Morgan clear to marry, the said Elisabeth being a widow and having a child Friends are appointed to see that a proportionate part of what was his fathers should be settled upon him. James Taylor and Elisabeth Chambers declare their intention to marry, James desired to bring a certificate of his fathers assent from the meeting to which he belongs.

29/9/1689 - There is a difference depending between William Rakestraw and John Redmon. Samuel Carpenter requests a certificate in behalf of John Jones concerning his clearness in marriage to be sent to Barbadoes.

26/10/1689 - There is some difference between William Hard, Paul Saunders and James Jacobs. Joseph Wilcox laid complaint against Griffith Jones.

31/11/1689 - The difference between William Rakestraw and John Redmon is ended. The difference between Griffith Jones and Joseph Willcox has not ended. Anthony Morris to write and sign a certificate to satisfy Friends of Chester County that Daniel Riggs and Martha Cobron hath past through the meeting here according to the practice of Friends.

28/12/1689 - John Maddocks and Margaret Kent declare their intention to marry, he to bring a certificate from the Monthly Meeting where he belongs. The difference between Isaac Ricketts and his mother in law continues, they being willing to leave the matter to Friends. William Beaks and Elisabeth Worriloe declare their intention to marry, he to bring a certificate from the meeting where he belongs and the consent of his mother. James Jacob desires a certificate, proposing his intentions of going to England.

28/1/1690 - Anthony Morris to write a certificate to Chester County where they intend to take each other, to satisfy Friends there. The difference between Griffith Jones and Joseph Willcox continues.

26/2/1690 - The difference between Griffith Jones and Joseph Willcox has not ended. William Bradford on behalf of William Wait requests a certificate, he intending to transport himself to England. Mary Otter and her daughter moving again to this meeting desire a certificate to England. Robert Ewer proposing his intentions of going to Rhoad Island not knowing how he may dispose of himself. There is some difference between Arnall Fincher and his mother, and Philip England.

13/3/1690 - Philip England, having bought a house of Arnall Fincher and his mother not being satisfied, the said Philip hath agreed to yield up the same again. Philip Howell requests a certificate of his clearness relating to marriage. There is a difference between William Rakestraw and Francis Rawles. There is also a difference depending between James Fox and James Shaddock.

27/4/1690 - The difference between Mary Fincher and Philip England and the said Mary Fincher and Arnall Fincher has not ended. The difference between William Rakestraw and Francis Rawle has ended. The difference between James Fox and James Shaddock has also ended. There is a difference between John Williamson and Agnes Morris, late Widow Bom.

25/5/1690 - The difference between Arnall Finsher and his mother continues. Friends have received letter from William Steel out of Bristol in Old England, desiring them to take care of his concerns.

29/6/1690 - The difference between Arnall Fincher and his mother has been ended, at present. Friends appointed to take care of William Steels business desire to examine the matter in dispute between John Ithell and John Bristow concerning six barrels of beef that was supposed to belong to said Steel. Griffith Jones appears dissatisfied with the former judgement in his case.

31/8/1690 - John Bristow appeared and solemnly declared that he never received no more beef out of the Bristol Merchant, and for the aforesaid six barrels John Bristow paid the said Ithell forty five pieces of Eight and this meeting being satisfied with Bristows account doth suppose it was a mistake of William Steel.

28/9/1690 - There being a letter sent from John Bristow concerning a note in Robert Turners hand. Agreed that Widow Eckleys bill of charges be allowed and paid by Alexander Beardsley.

26/10/1690 - Friends have had a sense of great inconveniency by the giving of liquors at buryals here in this town, as also the disorderly walking in the street with Corps to the burying ground, neither have been practiced in the chief cities and great towns in England and Ireland. Some Friends also intimate their dislike against the extravagancies of wedding dinners and too much providing for the same.

30/11/1690 - Robert Turner requests Friends assistance in the matter concerning money due him from the estate of Christopher Taylor. John Day, having misconducted to the dishonor of truth, hath sent a letter of condemnation to this meeting. Samuel Carpenter hath laid a complaint against Griffith Jones for refusing to obey the meetings determination in relation to Daniel Wharleys matter.

27/12/1690 - In the matter concerning John Bristow and Steel and Ithell, they all appeared and satisfied Friends that the said Bristow had paid the 45 pieces of Eight and for the barrels of beef it is supposed to be William Steels mistake, this being a final end of that matter. A letter from William Steel desires this meeting to take further care of his plantation and concerns in these parts. It is the meetings desire that he would appoint some particular Friends as Attorneys to act and do his business, which cannot be conveniently done as a meeting. The difference between Samuel Carpenter and Griffith Jones has not ended. Philip Howell bringing a complaint against Richard Hilliard, this meeting do advise the said Philip to persist no further, it having been ended by Friends long ago and the said Philip hath promised to make a title to a certain piece of land sold unto Richard Tucker by the next County Court, which the said Tucker complained for want of. The Widow Tibby is in need.

27/1/1691 - Funds have been raised to buy the Widow Tibby a cow, her former cow being dead.

24/2/1691 - Robert Turner again requesting the assistance of Friends in the matter concerning a debt due him from the estate of Christopher Taylor. There is a matter of difference between William Sneed and John Day.

29/3/1691 - The difference between John Day and William Sneed is ended. William Bethell, signifying his intentions of transporting himself and wife to Jamaico, requests a certificate from this meeting. Friends appointed to end the business of Robert Turner concerning moneys due from Christo. Taylor find that there is due to Robert Turner forty four pounds, 4/8, and that a title be made to Robert Turner of the eighty acres of Liberty Land formerly bought of Chrisr. Taylor. Hugh Maslin hath requested upon his death bed that Friends take what care they could to see his children placed out so they might be brought up among Friends.

26/4/1691 - The children of Hugh Maslin, both girls, will be left to the consideration of the womens meeting. William Fisher, intending to transport himself and family to Old England, requests a certificate from this meeting.

31/5/1691 - A certificate issued for William Fisher. Robert Turner, being dissatisfied with the result of Friends assistance in the matter concerning the estate of Christr. Taylor, is left to his liberty to take what course he can. There is a difference depending between William Pike and Christopher Sibthorp. The said William proposes his intentions of going to Jamaico and desires a certificate, he being to go away in a day or two more. There is a difference depending between John Busbey on the one part and Thomas Hooton and his mother on the other part. William Southerby lays a complaint against James Stanfield on behalf of one in Maryland for withholding a debt to the said person.

28/6/1691 - The difference between John Busbey and Thomas Hooton has ended, except for that concerning the delivery of the goods belonging to Christopher Taylors other children unto Israel. There is a complaint against Thomas Makins. Michael Thomas hath sued Benjamin Chambers at the court without giving him Gospel order.

25/7/1691 - There was no occasion for what was reported concerning Thomas Makin.

30/8/1691 - There is a difference between John Jones and Peter Baynton.

27/9/1691 - Mary Sibthorp hath presented George Palmers letter to his mother and sister from Masqueness.

9/11/1691 - Robert Turner has presented a copy of one paragraph of John Fullers will wherein he gives ten pounds to the poor of Philadelphia. Nathaniel Poole requests a certificate to the Falls, signifying his intentions of taking Elizabeth Lucas, of that meeting, to wife. There is a difference between William Bradford and William Brightwen. There is also a difference between Samuel Richardson and Joseph Willcox.

26/12/1691/2 - A certificate to the Falls issued for Nathaniel Poole. There is a difference between George Keith and John Day. Abel Noble declares his intentions to marry with Mary Garrett and requests a certificate to the Monthly Meeting at Darby.

25/1/1692 - A certificate to Darby meeting issued for Abel Noble. Edward Walters complains against William Gabitas.

29/2/1692 - The difference between Edward Walters and William Gabitas has ended.

26/3/1692 - It is supposed that William Stockdale hath given George Keith occasion to complain against him. John Whitpain requests a certificate in order to marriage. James Delaplaine also requests a certificate to marriage. Seamercy Adams, about to leave this province, requests a certificate of his orderly walking amongst us.

24/4/1692 - Anthony Morris to write a certificate for John Whitpain to be sent to Friends of Rhoad Island concerning his clearness in relation to marriage, and also one for James Delaplaine to be sent to Long Island. Certificate issued for Seamercy Adams. George Palmer lately a prisoner at Masquenes, in Turkey. A paper of condemnation of George Keith and his adherents in the late Separation was read.

29/5/1692 - There is a difference between William Bradford and Thomas Duckett. A certificate from Barbadoes for George Gray was read and one from Maryland for Ralph Jackson. There is a complaint brought William Boulding.

26/6/1692 - The difference between William Bradford and Thomas Duckett has ended, William Bradford having had no cause of difference. Griffith Jones charges Robert Ewer with several miscarriages. Evan Morris's certificate read.

29/7/1692 - Thomas Paschall desires a certificate to Harford Monthly Meeting of his clearness in relation to marriage. William Stockdale signified his mind to leave this province and desires a certificate of his orderly behaviour.

28/8/1692 - William Stockdales inclinations for removal of his family at present is ceased and Friends are appointed to look into his necessity and relieve him out of the public Stock. A certificate issued for Thomas Paschall to Harford Monthly Meeting. Nicholas Ireland and Elizabeth Humphreys declare their intention to marry. John Carver lost most he had by fire that fell out while he and his wife were at their usual meeting. There being a difference between Edward Farmer and John Goodson.

25/9/1692 - Nicholas Ireland and Elizabeth Humphries clear to marry. The difference between John Goodson and Edward Farmer is not yet ended.

30/10/1692 - A paper from the yearly meeting in Maryland condemns George Keiths spirit of separation.

27/11/1692 - The difference between Edward Farmer and John Goodson is ended. William Boulding still persists in the conduct for which he was complained of. Samuel Cart and Sarah Goodson declare their intention to marry. James Jacobs has of late deserted Friends meetings.

31/1/1693 - Samuel Cart, of Cheltnam in this county, and Sarah Goodson, daughter of John and Sarah Goodson of this town, she having a discharge from Edward Farmer who laid some claim to her, are clear to marry. A certificate for Samuel Cart from the Monthly Meeting at Dublin Township, dated 30/11/1692 - 3, in order to marry. William Boulding acknowledges keeping Elizabeth Evan in his house contrary to the advice of Friends.

28/2/1693 - Richard Whitfield brings a letter from the Monthly Meeting at Hartshaw in Lancashire concerning the estate belonging to the children of Humphrey Hodges.

26/3/1693 - William Harwood desires a certificate, intending for England by the first opportunity. George Gray, likewise, intending to go to Barbadoes. Also, William Laycock, he desiring a certificate to depart this province to Old England. Paul Saunders has absented himself from our meetings. Agreed that 20/ of the legacy given by John Fuller be given to Katherine Morgan towards the maintenance of her children.

30/4/1693 - Mary Rochford has been left a widow with 5 small children. John Pritchard, Junior, has complained that Thomas Knight hath wronged him. Richard Dean has given account that Richard Sutton detained money from him that is due by bond.

28/5/1693 - The difference between Richard Dean and Richard Sutton, the widow Rochford being therein concerned, has not ended. Anthony Morris, intending to go towards New England, and being a single person, requests a certificate of clearness in relation to marriage.

25/6/1693 - There is a difference between Robert Turner and Robert Ewer. Likewise, a difference between John Kinsey and Thomas Roberts. Also, a difference between Thomas Miller and William Rakestraw. John Philly brings a matter to this meeting against Samuel Jennings.

29/7/1693 - The difference between John Kinsey and Thomas Roberts is ended. The difference between John Philly and Samuel Jennings is ended, the said Samuel Jennings cleared from his false charges. Arnold Cassel and Susannah Delaplaine declare their intention to marry, Arnold having brought a certificate from Dublin Monthly Meeting. A paper was given forth by John Philly and since printed by George Keith defaming Samuel Jennings.

27/8/1693 - The business between Robert Turner and Robert Ewer has ended. Thomas Sisam and Priscilla Smith clear to marry, she being a widow having children hath first settled part of what she had upon her former husbands children.

24/9/1693 - Robert Turner hath sent to this meeting an abusive paper. A certificate to be prepared for Samuel Jennings who may, before the next Monthly Meeting, be going towards England. The same for William Walker and Thomas Duckett, they having laid their intentions of going to England. John Gardner hath absented himself from our meeting of worship.

29/10/1693 - Friends have received a letter from Robert Turner which bears several gross reflections on the meeting.

26/11/1793/4 - Griffith Owen requests a certificate to go and visit Friends in Maryland and Virginia.

30/1/1694 - A matter of controversy was mentioned between William Rakestraw and Robert Ewer. Friends appointed to write to John Hiton at Meauvice to endeavour to procure his lot in the second street for and on behalf of Friends.

27/2/1694 - The matter between William Rakestraw and Robert Ewer is ended. George Gray desires a certificate to go to Barbadoes.

29/4/1694 - William Laycock and Gwen Hughs declare their intention to marry. Friends are desired to certify to John Nelson in London that Gerrard Roberts is alive and appeared at our Monthly Meeting.

27/5/1694 - A certificate received from Pentecost Teague, of Cornwall in Old England. William Laycock and Gwen Hughs clear to marry.

31/6/1694 - Griffith Owen desires a certificate, intending to remove with his family to old England.

28/7/1694 - It has pleased God to remove by death our friend Thomas Lloyd. Jeremiah Powell, having formerly belonged to this meeting, requests a certificate of clearness in relation to marriage. The Widow Chaunders condition was laid before this meeting.

28/10/1694 - There is a matter of difference between William Rakestraw and Thomas Miller. A paper brought to this meeting by Patience Lloyd against David Lloyd being not thought fit to be publickly read, because she had not given him Gospel order. The Widow Rochford being lately deceased left five children and considerable debt.

25/11/1694 - A difference between Hugh Durbough and William Carter was laid before the meeting.

21/12/1694/5 - John Beasor and Esther Whitehead clear to marry, he bringing a certificate of his clearness from Chichester meeting. A matter in relation to the Widow Ricketts was mentioned concerning her right in a Lot on the Bank in Philadelphia, which is kept from her by her mother.

29/1/1695 - Thomas Hood desires advice in relation to a son and orphan of Dennis Rochford, deceased, the boy being about four years old, the said Thomas to teach him the trade of a weaver. The matter depending between the Widow Ricketts and her mother was continued. Friends being dissatisfied that Thomas Fitzwater and his wife live apart, Thomas is desired to get an house in order to entertain her, that she may have no excuse to stay from him.

26/2/1695 - John Wood and Sarah Saunders again declare their intention to marry, he producing a certificate thought not sufficient. Friends are appointed to acquaint the Friends of Newton meeting, that they may send another more to the satisfaction of Friends. James Thomas and Ann Warner clear to marry, the young man producing a certificate of his clearness and having the consent of all parents. William Pargeter brings a complaint against William Rakestraw. George Whiteheads letter to Thomas Lloyd relating to a complaint sent by Robert Turner to Friends in England about some acclamations made at the marriage of Thomas Lloyd's daughter to Isaac Norris being read, Friends are desired to write an answer for the clearing of truth and our deceased friend Thomas Lloyd from the gross imputation insinuated against him.

31/3/1695 - John Wood bringing a certificate to the satisfaction of Friends from the meeting at Newton concerning his marriage, they are clear to marry.

28/4/1695 - Friends desired to speak to Richard Sutton concerning his forwardness in proceeding at Law and casting Joseph Ranstead into prison. They are likewise desired to speak to the said Richard Sutton that he may not be too forward in getting into the affections of Hannah Day in order to marriage. A matter of difference was brought between William Carter and Evan Griffith. Friends appointed to meet with Patience Lloyd and David Lloyd about settling the estate of Thomas Lloyd, deceased, and paying Robert Story's children's legacies, have settled the matter.

26/5/1695 - There being a complaint brought by Robert Turner and Joseph Willcox against Joshua Hastins.

30/6/1695 - There being a complaint brought by Joseph Phips against Richard Sutton. A complaint also brought by John Parsons against John Saunders. Richard Suttons answer concerning his casting Joseph Ranstead into prison was he looked on him to be no friend, and being desired not to be too hasty in proceeding with the Widow Day to gain her affections in order to marriage, he seemed content to desist his intentions therein. Ralph Jackson and Elizabeth Ricketts declare their intention to marry, care to be taken that her child's legacy be secured him before marriage.

27/7/1695 - Marget Howell brought a complaint against David Powell in detaining from her a parcell of money. William Biles brought a complaint against David Powell. The matter depending between Joseph Phips and Richd Sutton is ended. The matter depending between John Parsons and John Saunders is ended.

25/8/1695 - A matter of difference being brought between George Heathcott, Cornelius Empson and John Richardson.

29/9/1695 - Arthur Cook brought a complaint against James Coats. Friends appointed to inspect the account depending between Thomas Lloyd, deceased, and the children of Christopher Taylor. Robert Turner sent a complaint against the Widow Bennett in relation to her withholding some part of the estate of Barbara Blackdon. Friends are desired to speak to William Rakestraw and Hannah Day that they may not be too forward to engage each other in relation to marriage till matters are clear to the satisfaction of Friends.

27/10/1695 - The matter depending between Robert Turner and Joseph Wilcox against Joshua Hastings is continued. The matter of difference between Cornelius Empson and George Heathcote has not ended.

Friends advise Hannah Day not to entertain William Rakestraw, Richard Sutton nor any other person in order to marriage untill a certain account shall come of her husband John Days death, and do likewise advise William Rakestraw and Richard Sutton, being both present, to desist all farther applications to her in relation to marriage.

31/11/1695/6 - Daniel Radley desires a certificate concerning his clearness in relation to marriage. William Davis requests a certificate in relation to his clearness in relation to marriage. Friends appointed to place out the orphans of Dennis Rochford. Robert Ewer appointed to draw a certificate for Richard Gove, he proposing to go to Maryland and Virginia or elsewhere along with Thomas Musgrave. John Jennett has given his consent for his daughter to take a husband out of the unity of Friends.

28/12/1695/6 - Friends appointed to get the two boys of Dennis Rochford, deceased, bound until they come to the age of twenty one years; also their dare is desired about the other children. John Powell desires a certificate in order to marriage. John Hart, bricklayer, desires a certificate in relation to marriage. John Gardner and his family are in need. A letter was sent to this meeting from Samuel Jennings in relation to the Widow Hamly. A matter of difference between John Sanders and Daniel Standish, they falling out and striking each other. William Biles complains against David Powell for not standing to the award of those Friends appointed to end the difference between them.

27/1/1696 - John Gardner and family are in great necessity for relief. George Fox desires a certificate concerning his clearness in relation to marriage. George Heathcoat refuses to stand to the judgement of Friends appointed to end the difference depending between him and Cornelius Empson and Ca.

24/2/1696 - Certificate issued for George Fox. The matter between George Heathcoat and Cornelius Empson is desired to be continued. Friends to enquire of John Griffith concerning his giving way to his daughter taking an husband that is out of unity. William Rakestraw having desire to go to for Long Island desires a certificate from this meeting.

29/3/1696 - Thomas Lloyd desires a certificate from this meeting.

26/4/1696 - David Powell to perform the award of those Friends appointed to end the difference between him and William Biles. There is a matter of difference between Daniel Smith and Francis Chads. Eve Belonge desires a certificate of his clearness in relation to marriage.

31/5/1696 - A matter of difference brought depending between Samuel Buckley and John Jones.

28/6/1696 - William Gabitas desires a certificate in relation to marriage.
William Rakestraw desires a certificate in relation to marriage. Daniel
Standish, having an intention to go to England, desires a certificate
from this meeting.

25/7/1696 - Certificate issued for William Grabitas in relation to
marriage. Certificate issued for Daniel Standish.

30/8/1696 - Something mentioned concerning Walter Long selling jews -
harps. Friends desired to speak to him, that he take the said jews -
harps again and return their money to them that he sold them to and
that they be sent from whence they came. Also, that the Widow
Culcop deliver the said jews - harps which she bought, to Walter Long
from whom she had them. John Jones requests a certificate of his
clearness in relation to marriage. Robert Ewer desires a certificate in
relation to his clearness marriage. Considering the ill president of
Thomas Fitzwater and his wife living apart from each other, Friends
are desired to speak to them that they may live together and that
Thomas may provide an house or room to entertain her in.

27/9/1696 - Walter Long promises he will sell no more jews - harps and
he would be at part of the loss of those he sold and take them again to
the satisfaction of the meeting. Certificates drawn for John Jones and
Robert Ewer in order for their consummating their intended
marriages. John Hood and John Mifflin have a difference between
them.

25/10/1696 - The difference between John Mifflin and John Hood is
ended. George Goldsmith and Ellen Harrison declare their intention
to marry, he to bring a certificate from West Jersey Friends. Mathias
Bellos and Maudlin Waight declare their intention to marry and he
belonging to Newtown meeting in West Jersey, tis expected that he
bring a certificate from thence along with him.

29/11/1696 - Thomas Fitzwater signified that he would endeavour to get
a room or two furnished in 2 or 3 months time to receive his wife if
she will then come to dwell with him. Robert Owen brings a paper
wherein David Powell is concerned. Ralph Jackson brought a
complaint against his wife's mother for refusing to let her have her
right according to her fathers will. Friends are appointed to speak to
Elizabeth Fitzwater and endeavour her to comply with her former
husbands will. David Lloyd requests a certificate to signify his
clearness in relation to marriage. John Ithell brings a copy of a letter
from Newton meeting to William Steel, informing him of the condition
of his estate in West Jersey and of said Ithells impotency and poverty.
Certificates drawn for James Dickinson and Jacob Fallowfield.

26/12/1696/7 - Certificate issued for David Lloyd. There being a matter of
difference between Ralph Jackson and Josiah Fearn belonging to the
Monthly Meeting of Derby.

26/1/1697 - A certificate issued for Daniel Standish.

27/3/1697 - George Gottschick and Elizabeth Oliver declare their
intention to marry, he belonging to Germantown meeting, tis
expected that he bring a certificate from Friends there. Jacob
Dewberry requests a certificate of clearness in relation to marriage to
the Monthly Meeting at Oxford.

25/4/1697 - A certificate issued for Jacob Dewberry. A letter from George
Palmer wherein he desires his brothers to dispose of some land to
raise money for his relief. Eve Belonge and Christian Delaplaine
declare their intention to marry, he producing a certificate of
clearness from Virginia.

30/5/1697 - Friends and other people to the eastward of Salem in New
England are under a great necessity, by reason of a great calamity
which is upon them. Richard Gove intends to travel to Maryland and
Virginia, a certificate to be drawn. Daniel Smith desires the meeting
would lend him some money, in order that he may carry on some
trade to maintain him and wife.

27/6/1697 - John Jennett hath signified that he is sorry he gave consent
to the marriage of his daughter. Nathaniel Zane and Grace
Rakestraw clear to marry, he bringing a certificate from Friends of
Newton. Friends are desired to put Joseph Oliver an apprentice to
Evan Morris untill he is of the age of 20 or 21 years and that his
master take care to instruct him in the art of leather dressing and the
glovers trade. David Powell complains of being kept from his just
right by reason of Richard Davis's delays. A complaint brought by
John Morgan of being kept out of 19 pounds these four years by
David Powell. William Rakestraw makes complaint of a difference
between himself and Joshua Tittery. Some difference is mentioned
between William Boulding and his wife.

24/7/1697 - Friends desired to treat with William Boulding and
endeavour to agree with him for Mary Price, his servants, time and to
inspect into her estate. Josiah Ellis desires a certificate of his
clearness in relation to marriage. Friends are desired to deal with
Matthais Bellers for misconduct in relation to his marriage. A letter
received from Thomas Rouse and Ann, his wife.

29/8/1697 - The difference between Ralph Jackson and Josiah Fearne
was debated and brought to a result. John Realow and Mary Rencho
declare their intention to marry, the said Realow to bring a certificate
from the Monthly Meeting of Crosswicks or Burlington. Arthur Cook
makes complaint that James Coates hath not performed his bargain
in finishing his house according to their agreement. Charles Sanders
and Sarah Whitpain declare their intention to marry, she to settle
something on her children if she have it. A paper of condemnation
signed by Charles Sanders read and recorded. A certificate issued for
Josiah Ellis. Friends desired to speak to Francis Daniel Pastorius in
order to write for Friends of this meeting.

26/9/1697 - A paper from Derby Monthly Meeting relates to the difference between Ralph Jackson and Josiah Fearn. Francis Daniel Pastorius has answered, concerning writing for this meeting, was that he thought it would not suit him as he does not live in town. James Kight, intending to alter his condition in relation to marriage, desires a certificate of his clearness.

31/10/1697 - A certificate issued for James Kite.

25/12/1697 - Arthur Cook complains that there is a difference between him and Alice Guest.

25/1/1698 - The difference depending between Ralph Jackson and Josiah Fearne is accommodated. The Friends appointed to endeavour to end the difference between Arthur Cook and Alice Guest report that Alice Guest doth not think herself obliged to pay any debts due from her husband when he was in partnership with Joseph Brown because the said Joseph administered on the estate which was in partnership.

29/2/1698 - A certificate signed for Richard Hoskins, who proposed his intentions of traveling to New England. A letter from Horslydown in London concerning the estate of Edward Collier, deceased. John Lineham is deceased.

27/3/1698 - Friends appointed to inquire into the accounts of Christopher Sibthorp relating to the estate of Edward Collier, deceased, are desired to meet as soon as possible and write to the meeting of Horslydown.

24/4/1698 - George Gray hath some thoughts to go to Barbadoes in some short time. There is a difference between Thomas Siam and Daniel Pegg about the division of the land they live on. Richard Sutton desires a certificate concerning his clearness in relation to marriage.

29/5/1698 - A certificate to be drawn for Richard Sutton concerning his clearness in relation to marriage.

26/6/1698 - Friends are desired to assist John Palmer to endeavour to get a bill of 20 pounds sterling to be sent to England to reimburse Theodore Eccleston for the 20 pounds which he hath laid out for the redemption of George Palmer out of captivity. James Pourteras presented a paper of complaint against Daniel Pegg.

30/7/1698 - Renier Jansen, a dutchman, having no certificate from Holland, Friends are desired to make enquiry of his life and conversation while on shipboard and since his arrival here. George Grays certificate was drawn. A bill of 20 pounds was gott for John Palmer to be sent to Theodore Eccleston of London. James White of Burlington and Mary Kitchen of this town declare their intention to marry, he to get a certificate of his clearness. A paper of Pentecoast Teague's was read, relating to the selling of negroes's at the public market place and it is the sense of this meeting that Friends ought not to sell them in that manner, and it is further agreed that Friends write to Friends in Barbadoes to acquaint them that they forbear sending negroes to this place because they are too numerous here. There is a difference in accounts between Thomas Fairman and John Jones. Certificates to be drawn for Elizabeth Web, Mary Rogers and Elizabeth Gamble and likewise, one for Richard Hoskins.

28/8/1698 - There is a difference between Thomas Harris and Elizabeth Culcop about a party wall. Abraham Hardiman desires a certificate of clearness, intending to take Rebeckah Willsford to wife.

29/9/1698 - A certificate of clearness issued for Abraham Hardiman. James Parrock and Martha Hastings clear to marry, she having the consent of her parents.

30/10/1698 - Nathaniel Lamplugh, by Thomas Duckett, complains of Samuel Carpenter, who, by order of and for the use of Samuel Chew of Maryland, did about 3 years ago, agree with him to build a certain vessel. The said Lamplugh provided plank and timber and put off other work in order to perform according to agreement but when he sent up the dimensions they were about one half as big as the vessel was agreed for, so that he could not carry on the same without great damage, the plank being too thick and the timber too large for so small a vessel. Therefore, he expecteth reasonable satisfaction for his damage. Samuel Carpenter acknowledges the above complaint is just and the reason why Nathaniel Lamplugh is not satisfied for his damage is because Samuel Chew has refused to pay the same.

27/11/1798 - Richard Gove hath some thoughts to travel in company with Thomas into Maryland, Virginia and Carolina and desires a certificate. William Carter will be administrator to the estate of the Widow Rochford, do place out her son Dennis an apprentice to Joshua Tittery to serve till he attains the age of 21 years, the said Joshua to teach him the trade of a potter. John Beetle confesses that he, with some others, had taken up some goods on the marsh below Salem. Thomas Fitzwater, with certain Friends, went to his wife in order that the said Thomas and his wife might be reconciled and live together, but could not prevail with her. Eleanor Lewis and her family are in great necessity. John Southeby intends to marry Patience Wardell and desires a certificate of his clearness.

24/12/1698/9 - Jonathan Dickinson intends to go for Jamaico and desires a certificate. John Askew intends to remove from hence in order to go for England and desires a certificate. William Beaks intends removing from hence in order to go for England and desires a certificate. A certificate for David Powell, late of Radnorshire in Wales, now in Bristol Township, was read in this meeting. Nathan Stanbury and Mary Ewer declare their intention to marry, Mary to settle what thought convenient upon her child. John Southeby clear to marry and a certificate drawn accordingly. Thomas Pryor condemns his concealing some goods taken up by him and some others on the marsh nigh Alloway's Creek. John Beetle likewise condemns his concealing the goods taken by him and others nigh Alloway's Creek.

31/1/1699 - Richard Hoskins hath had some drawing of late to visit Old England and some thoughts to go by way of Barbadoes and desires a certificate. Certificates to be drawn for Jonathan Dickinson, John Askew and William Beaks. Matthew Prichard and Sarah Henley declare their intention to marry, Sarah to settle what may be thought convenient upon her children. Thomas Pryor and Lydia Smart declare their intention to marry, the woman to settle what may be convenient upon her child. John Calew owes some money to the estate of John Lineham and refuses the payment thereof.

28/2/1699 - John Jones, by order of Lydia Wade, executrix of the last will of Robert Wade, deceased, hath paid into this meeting five pounds for the use of the school, which sum the said Robert gave yearly forever. Lydia Smart condemns her former taking an husband out of the unity of Friends. Emanuel Walker condemns his former out - goings. William Brown of the county of Chester and Katherine Williams of this town declare their intention to marry, he to bring a certificate of his clearness. Phillip James desires a certificate, intending to transport himself for England.

26/3/1699 - Arthur Cook complains that James Coate hath not as yet finished his house according to the award of several Friends formerly appointed to end same. James Atkinson and Hannah Day declare their intention to marry, he to get a certificate from Newton meeting of his clearness. A paragraph of John Lineham's will was read wherein he hath given 20 pounds for the use of the public school. A paragraph of Robert Ewers will was read wherein he gave 50 pounds to be distributed according to the advice of the Monthly Meeting. A certificate drawn for Philip James.

30/4/1699 - Whereas James Atkinson and Hannah Day proposed their intention to marry and nothing appearing that her late husband John Day is certainly dead, although long absent, it is the advice of this meeting that they cannot proceed to marry among Friends. A certificate for William Mannington from the city of Gloucester in Old England was read. John Ithell has sent a paper signifying his necessity of having some assistance from his brother Steel, upon which Friends are desired to write to William Steel of Bristol desiring him to give full power to sell his plantation and the interest of what it is sold for be for his relief according to what he formerly wrote to Friends was his mind.

28/5/1699 - Isaac Austin, intending to alter his condition, desires a certificate of his clearness. Margaret Beardsley sent to this meeting ten pounds, which was given by her late husband. Several orphan children of John Potts of Wales came here last year, their passage being paid. Friends are to speak to the persons concerned and see for convenient places in order that the children be bound out apprentices.

25/6/1699 - A certificate for Vincent Cordwell from the Monthly Meeting at Monniash, dated 24/1/1699, was read and recorded. Robert Bonny desires a certificate of his clearness. Friends are desired to advise and assist Daniel Smith's widow. Friends also desired to advise and assist Stephen Colemans widow.

29/7/1699 - Robert Bonny clear to marry, Friends desired to write a certificate to the meeting in East Jersey. John Jones intends to transport himself to Barbadoes and desires a certificate concerning his clearness. Richard Gove hath a concern upon him to travel to Old England and desires a certificate of Friends unity with him.

27/8/1699 - John Jones, shoemaker, is clear in relation to marriage, a certificate to be drawn for him. Richard Gove's certificate read and signed. Tertullian Johnson hath some thoughts of going for England and desires a certificate. Thomas Langston, having in his will desired this meeting to assist his wife.

24/9/1699 - Friends are appointed to assist John Scott in putting out the children of Thomas Wilson, late deceased, and also to assist David Brientnall in putting out an orphan of Thomas Langsdale, about three years old. There being a difference between Edward Shippen and Anthony Morris.

29/10/1699 - Friends are desired to acquaint John Scott that he appear here in order to provide for Thomas Wilson's children and to satisfy this meeting concerning the said Thomas Wilson's estate, which he hath carried out of the county. Elizabeth Meales of London has requested Friends care of her son Samuel Meales. Edward Penningtons certificate from London was read. Solomon Warder and Elizabeth Howell, late of the Isle of Wight, declare their intention to marry and producing a certificate from Friends in the said Isle declare they might have accomplished their intentions had not the ship come away before their next meeting. His certificate, and also hers from London, leave them clear to marry. John Jones and Ann Prichard declare their intention to marry. Thomas Bye, John Warder, James Streater, Randal Janney and Thomas Parsons, Senr, produced certificates from their respective meetings. The Friends appointed to deal with disorderly persons having often spoken to William Boulding, it has not had the desired effect. George Claypoole and Mary Righton declare their intention to marry, it thought needful that he condemn his outgoings. The widow Langston complains against Daniel Pegg for not performing or standing to an award according to his bond.

26/11/1699 - Timothy Hudson, Joseph Austill, Abraham Scott, Thomas Story and James Burton having lately arrived from England, produced certificates which were read and recorded. John Scott being present in order to give satisfaction concerning the children and

estate of Thomas Wilson, deceased, Friends are desired to advise and
assist the said John Scott about putting out the said children and to
see that their fathers estate being out of the county be secured for
them. Thomas Griffith and Elizabeth Knowles declare their intention
to marry, the widow Knowles to settle part of her estate upon her
children. William Boulding condemns his evil practices. Daniel Pegg
has gone into Maryland. Friends are desired to look into the condition
of James Thomas, an antient poor friend. John Austin proposed the
taking of an orphan called John Boss, apprentice. Friends are desired
to take care that he be bound till he attain the age of 21 years.

23/12/1699 - Thomas Griffith and Elizabeth Knowles clear to marry, part
of her estate being settled upon her former husbands children.
George Claypoole and Mary Righton clear to marry, he having
condemned his former outgoings. Daniel Zachary and Elizabeth Lloyd
declare their intention to marry, he producing certificates from Old
and New England. Thomas Howell and Elizabeth Kilcup declare their
intention to marry, he producing a certificate from Cecil County
meeting in Maryland. A request from Neshaminee Monthly Meeting
desiring assistance in dividing or disposing of the estate of Thomas
Pearson, deceased, lying in this county. Matthew Prichard desires a
certificate, intending to transport himself, his brother Benjamin and
family into Carolina. Friends are desired to see how what was made
over to his wifes children is or may be secured. A certificate drawn for
Tertullian Johnson.

29/1/1700 - Friends concerned in placing out Thomas Wilsons children
report that Henry, the eldest, is with Samuel Jennings, Thomas with
Phineas Pemberton and John is with Samuel Buckley, who are
desired to see that they are bound and not assigned to any others
without the direction of the meeting and they are desired to put out
the other three children as soon as they can. There are two orphan
children of one Potts to be put out, Thomas Potts, being their uncle.
William Biles, the Elder willing to take Widow Blake's son named
Edward being about 6 years of age. Friends desired to see him bound
with the appropriation of Richard Hallwell, who is Exer'r. to the childs
father, also left by his mother to care for her estate. Friends are
desired to see the estate of Thomas Pearson divided before his
daughter Grace be married, if possible. A certificate issued for
Matthew Prichard, his wife and brother Benjamin. There is a
difference between Patience Lloyd, widow, on the one part, and David
Lloyd and Isaac Morris, Exec'r. of her late husband, Thomas Lloyd, of
the other part

26/2/1700 - Friends concerned with Thomas Wilson's children are desired
to take care that John Scott be obliged to disburse so much of their
fathers estate as may be required for the maintenance of the three
younger children. Friends are desired to continue their care in

putting out I_es Potts children. Friends appointed to put out the Widow Blakes son report it is not yet done. They are desire to get him some other place. Robert Heaton and Grace Pearson clear to marry, he procuring a certificate of his clearness from England and Neshaminee. Friends give them liberty to proceed in the county of Bucks, where his relations live, she having no settled habitation here. Ive Belonge desires a certificate to Friends at Chichester concerning his and his wifes conversation. Friends appointed to look into the condition of James Thomas.

31/3/1700 - Friends are desired to write a certificate for Ive Belonge. John Roberts desires a certificate to England. Abraham Hooper desires a certificate for England. Christopher Sibthorp desires the advice of Friends concerning his son - in - law Joshua Fincher being put to a trade.

28/4/1700 - Jonathan Dickinsons certificate from Jamaico read and approved. Friends are desired to make publick the former condemnation against William Boulding, he continuing in slanderous conversation.

26/5/1700 - Friends formerly desired to take care of Thomas Wilson's children are desired to see those bound who are provided with masters, with the consent of John Scott, viz: to Samuel Bulkless and Michael Bluneton and they would desire John Scott to see those other two children bound to Phineas Pemberton and Samuel Jennings and that the two youngest be provided for till they can be put out. Edward Shippen to consider taking Edward Blake. Friends are desired to endeavour to reconcile William Say and his mother - in - law Alice Guest.

30/6/1700 - Edward Blake, being small, a master cannot be found for him. Richard Hill and Hannah Delavall declare their intention to marry, he bringing a certificate from the two weeks meeting in London, also a postscript of a letter from his father dated 10th month, 1699, signifying his approbation. A certificate from West River in Maryland is also desired. Jonathan Dennis desires a certificate, intending to return home to Barbadoes. John Askew desires a certificate to England. Edward Jerman and Elizabeth Powell declare their intention to marry. Robert Stacey, one of the Executors of Hannah Salter, deceased, being weak in body, desires Friends to come to be informed of Estate of said Hannah. Friends are appointed to see him and do what they can to serve that part of the estate belonging to Friends and to bring the will which is in the desk. Samuel _____, late of Norwich in England, brought no certificate, having been here about 12 months and being in great necessity which Friends relieved, but he is still weak though upon recovery. Thomas Rouse of Kent County, being out of his estate, stands in need of present relief.

27/7/1700 - Samuel Carpenter to deliver to Richard Hayes 40/ toward the clothing of James Wilson in order to have him bound to the said Richard. John Gibbons, Junr, of Chichester and Sarah Haywood clear to marry, he producing a certificate from the Monthly Meeting to which he belongs and also a paper from his parents expressing their satisfaction therein. Tobias Dimmock and Sarah Harding declare their intention to marry and he being a late resident in Rhode Island, producing a certificate of clearness from thence, and she being a widow with two children, Friends are appointed to assist her in making over to said children what may be convenient. A certificate from the Monthly Meeting in Somerset County concerning George Archer being disowned was read and ordered to be set up in some public place. Anthony Morris is desired to continue his care of the Widow Smiths business. Friends to draw a certificate for Jonathan Dennis. Likewise, J. Askew to have a certificate drawn.

25/8/1700 - James Wilsons indenture to Richard Hayes is prepared but not signed. Henry Wilsons indenture to Samuel Jennings and also Thomas Wilsons (another of the said children) being bound to Phineas Pemberton was produced and left in the custody of Ralph Jackson. Tobias Dimock and Sarah Harding clear to marry, her children having what was thought convenient settled upon them. Thomas Davies and Marget Little declare their intention to marry, he producing a certificate from the Monthly Meeting of French Hay in Gloucester in Old England. John Walker and Sarah Langston declare their intention to marry, he producing a certificate from Maryland and Friends to assist the widow in making over to her child by her former husband what may be thought convenient. Friends to acquaint the Govenor that this meeting requests that some friend be appointed Administrator of the Estate of Daniel Smith, deceased. At the widow Moor's request Friends are appointed to ask the Govenor that a course be taken to determine the cause depending between John Goodson and Thomas Fairman in relation to the 300 acres of land they differ about so that the debt due to the said widow may the sooner be discharged. Friends are desired to write to the Monthly Meeting at Frenchhay in the county of Cloucester in Old England to know whether Thomas Davies certificate came from them. John Jones desires a certificate for his son John Jones who proposes to go to Barbadoes shortly.

29/9/1700 - Nicholas Fairlambs certificate from Stockton in the Bishoprick of Durham and Benjamin Davies certificate from French Hay in the county of Gloucester were both read and approved. Thomas Taylor and Rachel Minshaw clear to marry, the young man producing a certificate from Chester Monthly Meeting and being desired to bring something from his mother to satisfy Friends. Samuel Carpenter to dispurse what is wanting for clothing of Edward

Blakes child that is with John Kinsey out of the meetings stock. The matter of the forgery of Thomas Davies certificate, done by himself, being proven, Friends are desired to deal with him in order to have him take the shame upon himself and repent of the abuse he hath put upon Friends both here and in England. Samuel Carpenter desired to dispurse out of the meetings stock 3 pounds toward paying the charges of William Alloways child and to pay the late widow Smith for cleaning the meeting house.

27/10/1700 - A difference between Henry Willis and William Rakestraw.

31/11/1700 - A certificate from Gloucester in Old England on behalf of John Lee and his family was read. Likewise, one from the quarterly meeting of said county of Gloucester on behalf of John Webb and his family was read. Friends appointed to look into the business of Thomas Wilson's estate report that the Wilson's Executor is dead. Christopher Pennock requests a certificate to the six weeks meeting at Cork in Ireland. The difference between William Rakestraw and Henry Willis is not fully ended. Hannah Emersons certificate from Cockersmouth in Cumberland was read, and Mary Lawsons from Parsdey was read. George Sheffington, late of Newfoundland, having been traveling in the service of truth, requests a certificate from this meeting. Some of the dying words of William Fletcher were read at this meeting.

28/12/1700 - A certificate from Mailsworth quarterly meeting on behalf of Richard Webb, his wife and family was read and likewise one from Shrewsbury on behalf of Thomas Peters and another from Farasfield on behalf of Richard Hodson. A certificate issued for Christopher Pennock. Paul Saunders desires a certificate, intending to remove into Chester County with his family. Samuel Hood and Mary Hudson declare their intention to marry, the young man to bring a certificate from Darby Monthly Meeting where he belongs and also something to signify his father consent. A certificate from Pardsay Cragg in Cumberland on behalf of Sarah and Mary Hudson was read and approved. Friends are appointed to assist George Booker in writing to the Monthly Meeting he belongs to in England that he may obtain a certificate to the satisfaction of this Monthly Meeting. Joseph Hood and Sarah Brown declare their intention to marry, he desired to bring a certificate from the Monthly Meeting to which he belongs and also his fathers consent. The Widow Guest and Edward Pennington complain against William Say. John Walker complains against Daniel Pegg who, notwithstanding the Monthly Meeting hath from time to time advised him to perform the award given between Thomas Langston and him, he still refuseth. William Southeby is to inform him that if he doth not do what is just, Friends must disown him and leave the other party to proceed against him in law.

28/1/1701 - A certificate issued for Paul Saunders. Samuel Codd desires a
certificate to Barbadoes. The matter of difference between Henry
Willis and William Rakestraw respecting the children of Robert Lane
is left to the Friends of their choosing and if the children are found to
be indebted to the said Rakestraw, their estate is to be awarded to
make satisfaction, after the best method the persons chosen can
propose, and that Henry Willis take no advantage by the judgement
of court already obtained in the case.

25/2/1701 - A certificate from Bandon Monthly Meeting in Ireland on
behalf of William Abbott and his daughter and another from Bristol
on behalf of Richard Parker were read, also another from Belly -
hagen on behalf of Gaven Stephenson. A certificate issued for Samuel
Codd.

30/3/1701 - The matter between Alice Guest and Wiiliam Say has not
ended by reason of the Widow Hardiman's being concerned by being
much injured by their difference and Samuel Carpenter appearing on
the said widows behalf subjected her part touching the damages to
the determination of Friends. Caspar Hoodt and Sarah Coleman
declare their intention to marry, friend desired to see what
settlement the widow will make upon her children. John Moorton and
Mary May declare their intention to marry, he producing a certificate
from England. Friends appointed to put out Edward Blake's child
report they have agreed with Nathaniel Edgcomb to take him until he
is 21 years of age. Randall Spikeman informs that he has
administered the Estate of Daniel Smith, deceased, and desires that
some persons be appointed to advise with him.

27/4/1701 - A certificate on behalf of John Salkeld from Cumberland,
Ireland and Barbadoes was read. A letter from Bucks Monthly
Meeting signifies that as soon as the plantation of John Scott,
deceased, can be sold they intend to pay the money belonging to
Thomas Wilsons children, which the persons appointed to look after
the said children are desired to mind and look after. Griffith Owen
desires a certificate, intending to travel into New England. A
certificate from Barbadoes on behalf of Thomas Bartlet was read and
also one from Pardsey in Cumberland on behalf of John Fallowfield.
David Vaughn condemns his former outgoings in London and his
marrying a wife here out of the unity of Friends. Casper Hoodt and
Sarah Coleman clear to marry, a settlement upon the widows children
being made. Samuel Greaves desires a certificate to Friends of
Chester County. Abraham Scott, likewise, desires a certificate, being
bound for London. A certificate from Horsleydown meeting for
Margaret Bye and her two daughters was read. Patience Lloyd
appeared desiring an end to the difference between herself and David
Lloyd. Friends are desired to contribute to the necessity of James
Thomas.

25/5/1701 - A certificate issued for Samuel Groves. Likewise, a certificate issued for Abraham Scott who is clear in relation to marriage and debt but as to his orderly walking Friends cannot say much for him. Upon his appearance before this meeting, making acknowledgement of the extraordinary powdering of his perriwig, which is the main thing Friends had against him, it is hoped he will take more care in the future. Richard Armitts certificate not being judged satisfactory, being not from a Monthly Meeting, he is advised to send for another from London as well as the country. John Fallowfield, intending to transport himself to Barbadoes, desires a certificate. Simon Andrews desires a certificate in order to marriage.

29/6/1701 - The widow Knight desires Friends to assist her in settling her business. Abraham Bickley condemns his folly in casting Quoits near Charles Sober's house. The Widow West desires that some Friends assist her in settling her business. George Gray brought in a bill for accommodating Jonathan Dennis in his sickness and funeral expenses. Christopher Sibthorp desires a certificate to Dublin Monthly Meeting. George Guest and John Borrowdall each desire a certificate to Burlington. John Fallowfield, having gone away before his desired certificate was issued, requested it might be sent after him, however, Friends, hearing a report concerning his conversation, are desired to signify the same in writing to the Friends in Barbadoes. A certificate issued for Simon Andrews. John Jones desires a certificate, intending to transport himself to Barbadoes.

26/7/1701 - Thomas Masters condemns his taking a wife out of unity of Friends. A paper from William Waite, who judges himself for being drawn away and joining with George Keith in that wicked spirit of separation, was read and ordered recorded and made publick by sending copies to New York, East and West New Jersey, Maryland and other places where he has traveled. Randal Janney and Frances Righton declare their intention to marry, the young man producing a certificate from the Monthly Meeting he belonged to in England. Certificates issued for Christopher Sibthorp, George Guest and John Borrowdale. Govenor William Penn, intending to go to England, desires a certificate. Esther Cooper intends to accompany Elizabeth Hess to Maryland Yearly Meeting. A certificate issued for John Jones. Abraham Jagger, intending on going for England, desires a certificate. Robert Burrow hath been sick for some time. Tobias Dimnock desires a certificate, intending on removing his family into Bucks County.

31/8/1701 - Friends are appointed to assist the Widow Knight and the Widow West. The difference between Patience and David Lloyd not yet ended, the said widow and the meeting being dissatisfied that it hath lain this long undetermined. A copy of Samuel Siddon's will was read. A certificate for Thomas Batson from Ratcliff meeting near London was read. Enquiry Tobias Dimnock, his wife and Thomas

Smith, his father - in - law, reveals nothing to obstruct his having a certificate except he seems not willing to pay a subscription toward the school, which this meeting thinks he ought to do, and when he has assured Friends he will do it a certificate will be drawn. A certificate to be signed for Walter Newbury. Likewise, a certificate to be signed for Thomas Bartlett who is going home to Barbadoes. Richard Townsend has lately lost a great part of what he had by a great flood. Friends are desired to look into James Thomas's condition and to supply him with what he may be needful.

28/9/1701 - William Fishbourne and Hannah Carpenter declare their intention to marry, he bringing a certificate from Thirdhaven (his place of former residence in Maryland) is further desired to bring something from his fathers hand to signify his consent. James Knight, in behalf of his son John, desires a certificate, said son intending to go for England. Absolom Cuff condemns his marrying contrary to the advice and consent of the Monthly Meeting. A subscription toward the assistance of Richard Townsend who hath received great loss by a late land flood. Friends appointed to inspect the accounts between Patience and David Lloyd report that cannot find any more estate than will pay the debts. The Executors, David Lloyd and Isaac Norris are desired to sell the land to get in what is due the estate and if any overplus be to help the widow. The widow Moor complaining against Philip England for want of her pay for maintaining Jane Ewer, the court having ordered him to pay it, being Executor to her deceased husband. Friends are desired to get Edward Blake another place, he being at present with David Lloyd who does not have conveniences to keep him any longer.

26/10/1701 - Samuel Carpenter is desired to provide necessary cloathing for Edward Blake. Mary Cook requests that Elizabeth Hamlins that was put to her by Friends and hath been with her for several years, might be bound to her according to agreement.

30/11/1701 - Philip England hath paid the Widow Moor according to the meetings advice. Thomas Woorilaw and Susannah Brightwen declare their intention to marry, he producing a certificate from Chester meeting, the place of his late abode. A Friends child named Mary Potts, having been with Isaac Shoemaker for two years, the time agreed is near out and she wants learning. That she may have what learning is sufficient, he desires to have her bound to him for some time. Friends are desired to write to Bucks Monthly Meeting that they endeavour to have the widow Scott to pay the money belonging to Thomas Wilson's children. Richard Woodworth appeared to give satisfaction for often being drunk. A letter from Frenchay in Gloucester declares that Thomas Davies never had a certificate from them.

29/12/1701 - Patience Lloyd, having been advised to end matters
between her and the Executoers of her deceased husband, Thomas
Lloyd, hath not done so. Evan Powell and Mary Jones declare their
intention to marry, he desired to bring a certificate from the Monthly
Meeting where he belongs. Timothy Hurst desire a certificate to
Newtown Monthly Meeting in order for marriage. Friends are desired
to get Thomas Potts child from where it is in order to have it placed
with a friend. Philip Ford, Junior's, certificate from London being
read, he also desires a certificate from this meeting of his clearness to
marriage. Friends are desired to write a certificate for John
Fallowfield to be sent after him to Barbadoes.

27/1/1702 - Friends are continued to take care concerning the child of
Thomas Potts, deceased, to place it with some honest friend, it being
thought that William Ruttidges might be a fit place for her. A
certificate to be signed for Philip Ford. Jonathan Dickinson desires a
certificate, intending to transport himself to Jamaico. Anthony Morris
is desired to send to Robert Dyer or his widow at New Castle for Tods
Actts and Monuments, books belonging to the Estate of Thomas
Wilson, deceased. Anthony Morris is desired to get a copy of John
Fallowfield's certificate sent to Barbadoes and the original to England
to his father. Randal Janney signifies his intention of transporting
himself to Old England and desires a certificate, the same being
desired by Edward Shippen in behalf of his son Edward, going in the
same vessel. John Estaugh's certificate from Old England, Rhoad
Island and Long Island being read, he desires one from us. John
Leaks certificate from New Garden, county of Carloe, in Ireland, was
read. There is a difference between Philip England and William
Davies.

24/2/1702 - The persons with whom the child of Thomas Potts, deceased,
is with are unwilling to part with it. A certificate written for Jonathan
Dickinson and his wife. A certificate written for Randal Janney.
Abraham Bickleys certificate from Burlington was read. George
Booker desires a certificate, intending to go to England. Likewise,
Thomas Parsons desires a certificate for England. Samuel Rickles
certificate from England was read and he desires one from this
meeting, intending to transport himself to England again.

29/3/1702 - Joseph Roads, having been sundry times spoken to for the
rent due to Friends, from his father, and has refused to pay, it is
desired that this matter be laid before Darby meeting. Daniel Smith
is deceased. William White and Sarah Bye declare their intention to
marry, her Guardians consent desired, she is to bring something from
her uncle Joseph White. Friends to write to England on acct. of
George Booker, to satisfy them of his conversation amongst us and
his clearness in relation to marriage. A certificate to be written for
Samuel Reckless. Friends are desired to enquire what is given

Friends by George Tods will and to endeavour to see whether it may be obtained. Martin Seal desires a certificate to the county of Bucks, where he intends to remove.

26/4/1702 - Thomas Thompson, intending to return to England, and his certificate from there and several other places he hath been traveling being read, desires a certificate from this meeting. Joseph Roads appeared to make some excuses against paying the rent of the house his father lived in but Friends see no cause to excuse him from paying, they having been so kind as to abate a great part of the rent. He must pay it or some other course may be taken with him. Christopher Blackbourne and Rachel Cunberlidge declare their intention to marry, the young woman producing a certificate from London and he saying he had one but had lost it. Thomas Coates hath been abusive to Friends in general and not been disowned for it, therefore, Friends are desired to deal with him once more. Thomas Story desires a certificate to visit Friends on Long Island. A certificate issued for Sarah Clements.

31/5/1702 - Friends are desired to endeavour to bring Thomas Coats to a sense of his miscarriage. It hath been reported that Daniel Flower hath behaved himself wickedly in burning books and many other gross things and having formerly made some profession of truth and having married a wife amongst Friends it is desired that Friends should deal with him. Christopher Blackbourne and Rachel Cumberlidge clear to marry, Friends testifying that they saw him have a certificate from North Shields, which certificate is since lost. There is a difference between Joseph Cooper and Thomas Sisom. A certificate issued for Martin Seal. James Streater desires a certificate, intending to remove to Bucks County. Friends are appointed to bind out Edward Blake.

28/6/1702 - A certificate signed for James Streater. Friends are desired to get Edw'd Blake bound to Thomas England. Stephen Jackson and Elizabeth Clemison declare their intention to marry, he having lived formerly in Chester County, produced a certificate dated a year ago, and she to take care to settle something on her child. It being reported of James Logan's going over to the Reed Island men and arms which were used against Daniel Cooper and as is reported is sent for New York and England.

25/7/1702 - Friends appointed to deal with James Logan about the disorder at the Reed Island report they have not done it by reason of his sickness. Nicholas Waln and John Kinsey desire certificates to visit Friends on Long Island.

30/8/1702 - Daniel Pegg, going to law contrary to Friends advice, is further advised to let his action fall and prosecute no further, but endeavour to make satisfaction to and Reconciliation with John Walker. Patrick Ogilby declaring his intention to marry, desires a

certificate to Bucks County. There is a difference between Henry
Willis and William Rakestraw. Samuel Carpenter, in behalf of
Thomas, the son of Thomas Willson, deceased, requests that some
others be appointed with him to put the said Thomas to some trade,
his late master Phineas Pemberton being dead. A letter from Ratcliff
meeting near London desires us to take care of one Edward
Sweetman, a Friends son from thence for his fathers sake, who put
him apprentice to Nathaniel Lamphigh, who goes about this town in a
miserable condition. Friends are desired to inquire into his condition
and see if they can get his leg cured and if Nathaniel Puckle will carry
him home to his mother. A difference between James Atkinson and
Edward Sanway of London laid before this meeting. A certificate from
Concord and Chichester meetings on behalf of James Swaster and his
wife was read.

27/9/1702 - A certificate issued for Patrick Ogilby. Friends so appointed
have put out Thomas Wilson have placed him with William Till.
Friends appointed to look after Edward Swetman report that his leg
seems to be much mended at present and they are desired to get him
a passage with Captain Guy, that if Friends in London or his mother
will not pay for his passage then Friends here will do it. Friends
appointed Executor's by the last will and testament of John Martin,
who intended his debts be paid and charges defrayed, his estate be
disposed of for the use of poor Friends.

25/10/1702 - A certificate from the County of Sussex in Old England
concerning Stephen Staples was read. James Logan hath sent in a
paper to give satisfaction for being too far in the action at Reed
Island. It is thought fit that a copy be sent to Burlington Monthly
Meeting. Friends that were concerned in said matter with James
Logan may shew Edward Shippen, Jun'r, what the said James hath
written concerning the disorder at Reed Island, where the said Edw'd
Shippen was in company, and desire him to do something to satisfy
Friends and clear truth. A matter relating to John Martin's
apprentice, Herriot Rodeford, was referred to this meeting,
concerning his being free.

29/11/1702 - John Jones, Junr, and Margaret Waterman declare their
intention to marry, their father and mother being present, gave
consent. The Widow Goldsmith requests Friends to write to the
meeting of Hartshaw in Lancashire and desire them that Robert
Hadock might return to her what might be in his hands of her yearly
rent that she left him in trust to receive. A complaint was sent to the
meeting by James Jawl against John Walker. There is a difference
between Joshua Hasims and James Atmore.

26/12/1702 - Friends are desired to agree with Nathaniel Puckle for the
passage of Edward Swetman to London to his mother. Samuel
Carpenter is desired to pay the Widow Gamblin for keeping Edward

Swetman this month past. Thomas Chalkley desires a certificate, intending to visit Friends in Maryland, Virginia and Carolina. Likewise, John Kinsey and Richard Gove, intending to travel into New England, desire certificates.

26/1/1703 - Certificates for Thomas Chalkley, John Kinsey and Rich'd Gove were read, approved and signed. Henry Willis, intending to visit Friends on Long Island, Rhoad Island and New England, desires a certificate from this meeting. Friends are desired to bind out John Alloway, an orphan child, to Lewis Thomas, which is thought might be a good place for it, and approved by his grandfather, William Southeby and the other Executor. An orphan child of Dennis Rochfords which was bound out to Thomas Hood of Darby is not well used, therefore, Friends are desired to look into the matter. There is a matter of difference between Edward Shippen and his son - in - law Francis Richardson. John Austin reports that John Potts, who was bound apprentice to him to learn the carpenters trade doth not like it but would rather have some other employ. Jacob Roads and Margaret Warner declare their intention to marry, her parents being present gave their consent and he, having resided in several places and unsettled, Friends are desired to make inquiry.

30/2/1703 - Friends are continued to get a passage for Edward Swetman and Samuel Carpenter is desired to pay for his last months keeping. Friends are desired to get a suitable place for John Potts, who doth not like the Ship carpenter trade. William Robinsons certificate from Thirsk Monthly Meeting in Yorkshire was read. A certificate issued for Henry Willis. Joseph Parkers certificate from the Peel meeting was read, he being a young lad, Friends are desired to advise him and give him good council. William Abbott, intending to remove himself and daughter to Ireland, by way of Barbadoes, desires a certificate.

28/3/1703 - A certificate to be drawn for William Abbott and his daughter. There was an account brought in concerning what was left by Mercy Rodiford and what she owed. In order to have it settled and paid, Friends are desired to dispose of the goods left and pay what she owed and to keep the overplus for the rest of the children.

25/4/1703 - A letter from the Monthly Meeting of Chesterfield in Old England was read requesting this meeting to inquire concerning the estate of John Lyman, deceased, seeming to claim for debt, which they suppose to be due to said Thomas's children, and also to request something of the estate towards the assistance of the children. There is a difference between William Kelly and John Dans. Henry Carter and Susannah Colley, having consent of parents, are clear to marry. A certificate for Elizabeth Green from Dublin Monthly Meeting in Ireland was read. Whereas Sarah Austin is lodged in a house belonging to poor Friends it is thought fit that she procure a certificate from Newton Monthly Meeting or otherwise she provide herself another house to live in before twenty more days be expired.

30/5/1703 - A certificate from the Monthly Meeting of Morley in the county of Chester in behalf of Samuel Heald and his wife Mary was read. Pursuant to the will of Thomas Willson, deceased, Friends have bound out George Willson, his child, to Cadwallader Morgan of Merrion.

27/6/1703 - Mary Maltsbey condemns her going to a marriage which was performed contrary to the order of truth. A certificate for Peter Stretch and Margery his wife from Leek in Staffordshire and one from London on behalf of Robert Finley was read. William Robinson, intending for England and having brought a certificate with him from Thursk Monthly Meeting in Yorkshire, dated the 10th month, 1702, desires likewise to have a certificate back again. Nicholas Fairlamb, intending marriage with a young woman from Chester County, desires a certificate from hence to the Monthly Meeting where she belongs. Thomas Hood, intending to take to wife a young woman who lives at Darby in Chester County, desires a certificate to Darby Monthly Meeting. There being a complaint by Christopher Sibthorp against Thomas Makin for want of money that he oweth him and hath several times disappointed him in his promising to pay it. Likewise, there is a complaint by Ann Budd against Richard Armitt. Also a complaint by Thomas Story against James Logan.

24/7/1703 - A certificate issued for Nicholas Fairlamb. Friends are continued to speak to Thomas Makin and endeavour to make satisfaction to Christo'r Sibthorp for what he is indebted to him. The difference between Ann Budd and Richard Armitt has not ended. The difference between Thomas Story and James Logan is near ended. Henry Clifton, intending to take to wife a friend that lives in West Jersey, belonging to Newton meeting, and therefore desires a certificate to said meeting. James Streater sent a paper desiring a certificate in order to marriage, which this meeting was not very willing to accept, but considering the man's condition and that his dwelling is far remote from hence and his children dead and nobody at home to look after his business, thought it would be too hard upon him to stay longer, Friends are appointed to make inquiry concerning his clearness. John Parsons brought in the will and inventory of Margaret Leeds, deceased, wherein she gives to the poor amongst Friends to be disposed of as this meeting shall see cause. There is a difference between Arnold Cassel and John Palmer.

29/8/1703 - A certificate issued for Henry Clifton. Likewise, a certificate issued for James Streater. A certificate issued for Thomas Hood. Thomas Bradford, intending to marry, desires a certificate to Dublin Monthly Meeting. A certificate from Pardsey Cragg for Thomas Iredal was read and ordered to be recorded.

26/9/1703 - Friends are desired to treat with Friends at Derby about the maintenance of Ann Bunting, as it is believed she doth properly belong to them to maintain. A certificate from the Bull and Mouth meeting in London for Richard Robinson was read and ordered to be recorded. Friends are desired to treat with Newton Friends about Joseph Austells wife and children. Friends are desired to continue their care to end the difference between Christopher Sibthorp and Thomas Makin. Friends are desired to continue their care in bringing in the account of the estate of Thomas Lloyd. A certificate issued for Thomas Bradford to Dublin Monthly Meeting. The widow Knight making application to this meeting for advice in some of her business. Friends appointed to deal with John Macclear concerning his miscarriages report he hath owned most of them and hath given a paper of condemnation against himself. Friends are desired to go to John Beetle and require him to take the shame of his wickedness upon himself, he having confessed himself to Friends that he is guilty thereof.

31/10/1703 - A paper of condemnation concerning John Bettle and his committing adultery was read. Friends seek advice as to how the portions of George Gray's children, being the legacies left by Margaret Beardsley, shall be secured. John Smith, by his mothers letter from Barbadoes, desires a certificate. John Parsons gives in an account of the legacy of Margaret Leeds. Friends are desired to advise Thomas England about putting out Edward Blake apprentice. Thomas Story desires a certificate in order to visit Friends on Long Island, Rhoad Island and parts of New England.

28/11/1703 - A certificate issued for John Smith of Barbadoes. The legacy left by Samuel Seddon is left in the hands of John Kinsey. A certificate issued for Thomas Story. Clement Plumstead desires a certificate in relation to marriage. There being a complaint laid before this meeting by Katherine Carter against her husband.

25/12/1703 - The business concerning bringing in the account of the estate of Thomas Lloyd, deceased, is continued. Thomas Chalkley and Richard Gove desire certificates to visit abroad, said Thomas Chalkley to New England and Richard Gove towards North Carolina. Anthony Morris to write a certificate on behalf of Clement Plumstead to Croswicks Monthly Meeting. Friends are appointed to inspect the accounts of the estate of Thomas Duckett. John Kinsey desires a certificate on account of marriage. A certificate from Devonshire Monthly Meeting on behalf of Mary Bannister and another from York quarterly meeting for Mary Ellerton were read. John Hendricks and Rebeckah Wells declare their intention to marry, she being a widow Friends are desired to things be settled concerning her children.

31/1/1704 - Joseph Jones intends to take a wife in Maryland and desires a certificate from this meeting. A certificate was signed for John

Kinsey. Anthony Morris Junr and Phebe Guest declare their intention to marry, relatives on both sides being present and giving their consent. Thomas Eldridge and Mary James declare their intention to marry, the father of the young man being present gave his consent, and the young man desired to bring a certificate from Newtown Monthly Meeting. Ellen Goldsmith and Friends from Duck Creek on her behalf desire that Friends from this meeting certify to Robert Haydock of Liverpool that said Ellen Goldsmith is living in order that she might leave some effects belonging to her in England which Robert Haydock could not obtain unless it were certified from here that she is alive. John Guy being suddenly to go for Carolina desires this meeting to give him a certificate. Christopher Sibthorp and his wife desire a certificate to Dublin Monthly Meeting.

18/2/1704 - Edward Shippen hath lately received a letter from William Crouch concerning the money due from the estate of Thomas Lloyd to Edward Man. A certificate on behalf of Ellen Goldsmith signed. Clement Plumstead, intending to Virginia and that way a trading, desires a certificate. Thomas Making having sundry times made application that he might be admitted into the public school, which matter hath been under consideration, and John Every being about to leave it, it was agreed that if Thomas Makin thinks fit to accept it upon the same terms as John leaves it, although we think the consideration is small for him, yet other charges being so high already we cannot well augment it. Thomas Eldridge and Mary James clear to marry, he bringing a certificate from Newtown meeting. Thomas Lyford intends for England and desires a certificate from this meeting. Friends appointed to make enquiry concerning Richard Webb report they cannot find things so clear as they desire and that they do not think it advisable to give him a certificate till things are further enquired into.

26/3/1704 - The business relating to the estate of Thomas Lloyd, deceased, is continued untill the next Monthly Meeting. John Every desires a certificate. Hugh Durborow desires a certificate to visit Friends in Maryland. Richard Gove desires that he may have a certificate to visit Friends in Barbadoes when he shall have occasion for it, he being at present going abroad to visit Friends about Carolina for which he had a certificate before when he traveled with Jacob Mott but could not then get a passage over the Bay in Virginia.

30/4/1704 - A certificate for Christopher and Ann Sibthorp was signed and likewise one for Hugh Durborow concerning his traveling. Samuel Richardson and Elizabeth Webb declare their intentions to marry, he bringing a certificate from Dublin Monthly Meeting.

28/5/1704 - David Lloyd and John Jones are continued to get the legacy given by Robert Wade to the school in Philadelphia. Mordecai Moor and Deborah Lloyd declared their intentions to marry, the said

Mordecai living in Maryland he is desired to bring a certificate from the Monthly Meeting he belongs to. Friends are desired to enquire into the difference between James Jacobs and John Mifflin and endeavour to end the same. Certificates on behalf of Thomas Turner from England and Long Island were read and approved and he desiring a certificate from this meeting to visit Friends in Barbadoes which was issued.

25/6/1704 - There being a legacy of ten pounds left by Richard Love. The widow Finley complains as if some belonging to Friends had kept her out of her right, which being examined we cannot find any occasion for said complaint, and likewise complains for want of maintenance but Friends are not well satisfied that she doth properly belong to us to maintain and she seeming to be a healthy woman and able to work, Friends are appointed to make inquiry into her condition. Mordecai Moor and Deborah Lloyd clear to marry, he bringing a certificate of clearness from the Monthly Meeting in Maryland where he belongs. Timothy Hanson and Susannah Freeland declare their intentions to marry, he to bring a certificate from the Monthly Meeting to which he belongs and the young woman something from her mother to signify her consent. Lewis Thomas being removed from this place into Plimuth Township desires a certificate to that meeting.

28/7/1704 - Certificate issued for Lewis Thomas. The man which married the widow Scott is very willing to pay the money belonging to Thomas Willsons children but wants the accounts to see what he is indebted. Friends are appointed to send the account to the Falls Monthly Meeting.

27/8/1704 - Samuel Carpenter intends to be at the next meeting at the Falls and intends to take up the acctts of Thomas Willsons estate. Samuel is desired to get the money or get it secured after the best manner he can and also to bring in an account how much of the estate is in his hands and how much has been paid after the use of the children. Timothy Hanson and Susannah Freeland clear to marry, he producing a certificate from Dublin Monthly Meeting and Friends reporting that Esther James, the young womans mother - in - law, consenting. Griffith Owen and Sarah Sanders declare their intentions to marry, Friends appointed to that her children to have a settlement made upon them. A paper from Sarah Hall declares her trouble and grief for taking a husband out of the unity of Friends. A certificate received from Norwich in Old England for William Petty Senr and his wife. Joseph Growden and Ann Buckley declare their intentions to marry, Joseph desired to bring a copy of his condemnation and a certificate. Silas Pryor and Susannah Hall declare their intentions to marry, he producing a certificate from the Monthly Meeting of New Castle County which was thought to be a little short in point of his conversation.

24/9/1704 - Silas Pryor and Susannah Hall clear to marry, he producing a
satisfactory certificate from the Monthly Meeting in New Castle
County.

29/10/1704 - A certificate received for Christopher Topham from a
Monthly Meeting in Yorkshire. Magnas Plowman and Sarah
Hutchinson declare their intentions to marry. John Furniss
complained against David Powell, that there is a difference between
them.

26/11/1704 - The difference between John Furniss and David Powell is
not ended. A certificate from Horsley - down Monthly Meeting on
behalf of Thomas Coleman was read and recorded. Thomas Griffith is
ordered to pay Henry Willis 2:8:8 - which he hath disbursed for
cloathing of Richard Newcomb and Abraham Buckley is willing to
keep him at his own charge untill his father may arrive here. George
Claypoole desires a certificate to go to Virginia on account of trade.
David Williams and Mary Maltsby clear to marry, he producing a
certificate from Harford Monthly Meeting. Magnus Plowman and
Sarah Hutchinson clear to marry. Pentecoast Teague desired advice
concerning putting out a child of the widow Wests.

23/12/1704 - The difference between David Powell and John Furniss has
not ended. A certificate issued for George Claypoole. James Swaster,
being about to return into Chester County, desires a certificate. John
Watson and Abigail Hood declare their intentions to marry, Friends
desired to see how her children are provided for, she being a widow.
Friends are desired to look into the condition of John Martyn and
Wm. Woodmansey and endeavour to settle them in such places as
they may think convenient.

30/1/1705 - A certificate issued for James Swaster. Thomas Story desires
a certificate to visit Friends in Maryland, Virginia and North Carolina.
George Gray acquainted this meeting that he is selling his business in
order to have liberty to travel abroad. Friends are desired to joyn
with the executors of Margaret Beardsley to see things settled before
George travels. John Knowles desires a certificate to Dublin Monthly
Meeting in relation to marriage. Richard Webb renewed his request
for a certificate to Concord Monthly Meeting. Friends are appointed
to hear and inquire into reports that have been abroad tending to his
defamation and the dishonor of truth. Robert Roberts desires a
certificate in order to marry. Anthony Morris is desired to provide
clothes to make John Martin three shirts.

27/2/1705 - A certificate issued for John Knowles. A certificate issued for
Robert Roberts.

26/3/1705 - Thomas Makin brings a complaint against Richard Roberson.
Friends are desired to make inquiry concerning the said Williams and
see that things be settled relating to the widow Archers child. Philip
England desires a certificate to Duck Creek, intending to remove with

his family. Abraham Scott and Hannah Scott declare their intentions to marry, he producing a certificate from London.

29/4/1705 - A certificate from the two weeks meeting in London, concerning Thomas Lyford, and one from Thursk meeting in Yorkshire on behalf of John Widdowfield were read and ordered to be recorded. Richard Parker and Priscilla Love clear to marry on signing of a covenant for settling things according to Richard Loves will, which the said Richard and Priscilla promise to do before their marriage. Richard Ireson intends to take a wife at Shrewsbury and desires a certificate from this meeting. A certificate issued for Philip England.

27/5/1705 - A paper of condemnation from Elizabeth Harwood concerning her taking a husband out of the order of truth and contrary to the advice of her mother was read. A certificate for William Harrison from Clifts meeting in Maryland was read and recorded.

21/6/1705 - Jedediah Husey and Esther Cooper declare their intentions to marry, he bringing a certificate from Brandywine Monthly Meeting and her father and mother being present, gave their consent. The young man is desired to bring his fathers consent to the next meeting. William Harrison intends to return to Maryland and desires a certificate from this meeting. Friends are desired to inform Rebeckah Curtis that the meeting is not satisfied with the paper she hath sent in, though she hath promised to give what satisfaction Friends shall require we are informed she is gone to be married, contrary to her great pretensions.

28/7/1705 - John Palmer desires a certificate in relation to marriage with Rachel Marshall. Friends are desired to expose to sale what goods John Martin hath left behind him. Thomas Lyford intends to return to England by way of Jamaica and desires a certificate, he having brought one to this meeting from England.

26/8/1705 - A certificate issued for John Palmer. An account brought in of John Martins goods which did just pay his debts and funeral expenses. An epistle dated 8th of 7th month last from Mary Ellerton in Barbadoes was read. Jacob Taylor is about to print some almanacks on his own account.

28/10/1705 - John Parsons hath left a legacy of ten pounds to the publick school. Amy Read hath also left a legacy of five pounds. A paper from Esther James seeming to condemn her outgoings was read. 25/11/1705 - A certificate from Ireland and another from Colebeck meeting in Cumberland, in relation to Mary Wilson, were read. James Cooper desires a certificate, intending to go to Barbadoes. Mary Bannister is about to return to England and desires a certificate. There is a difference between William Snowdon and William Carter.

22/12/1705 - A certificate issued for Mary Bannister. Daniel Gaunt desires a certificate in order to take a wife at Germantown. John Saunders of London desires a certificate in relation to marriage. Abraham Scott intends with his wife for England and desires a certificate. Thomas Janney likewise proposes his going to England and desires a certificate.

29/1/1706 - A certificate issued for Daniel Gaunt who hath produced a certificate of clearness in relation to marriage from Burlington. Friends appointed to inquire after John Saunders report that they do not find him clear from Susannah, the daughter of Susannah Harwood, who declares that they are engaged on account of marriage she will not clear him. A certificate issued for Abraham Scott. John Simcock and Mary Walln declare their intention to marry, their parents present and giving consent and the young man producing a certificate from Springfield Monthly Meeting. Samuel Lewis and Grissel Kite declare their intentions to marry, he to bring a certificate from the Monthly Meeting where he belongs and the young womans parents being presents, gave consent. Friends are desired to labor with Sarah Hinley that she may put forth her children. Thomas Marle, having removed to another Monthly Meeting, desires a certificate of unity with us. Isaac Norris, intending for England with his wife, desires a certificate. Richard Hill complains that Randal Janney is greatly indebted to him and desires that he may be at liberty to sue him. Friends are appointed to advise George Gray and Thomas Potts and the executor of Margaret Beardsley in matters relating to the estate of said Margaret Beardsley for securing the estate of the children. A certificate issued for Thomas Janney.

26/2/1706 - Friends appointed to deal with Randolph Janney in order to his making satisfaction to Richard Hill report they have done so much as they think sufficient and if he doth not make him satisfaction the meeting judges it hard to hinder him from taking such just course. A certificate issued for Thomas Marle. Thomas Story laid before this meeting that Richard Sutton is in his debt for money lent and he is in want of it and he keeps him out of it he desires liberty to recover it by a due course of law. Samuel Lewis and Grissel Kite clear to marry, he producing a certificate of his clearness. David Powell desires a certificate, intending for marriage.

31/3/1706 - Richard Sutton hath put goods (as he saith) into the hands of Caspar Hoodt to make satisfaction to Thomas Story. A certificate issued for David Powell. James Thomas intends suddenly for England and desires a certificate. Joseph Brown produced a certificate from Salem Monthly Meeting and desires a certificate in order to his taking a wife. John Roberts desires a certificate in order to marriage. The widow Russel is in want, by reason that David Powel, lately belonging to Abington Monthly Meeting, keeps her out of money she lent him.

Friends are desired to assist her in getting the said money due from
the said David Powel or Joseph Mather and that they may prosecute
the matter against the said Friends according to the method of
Friends in gospel order.

28/4/1706 - Thomas Story and Ann Shippen clear to marry, with
certificates from London of their unity with him and of his clearness.
Edward Shippen and Esther James declared their intentions to
marry. Friends are appointed to make inquiry concerning Edwards
clearness and see that things be settled on account of said Esthers
child by her former husband. Friends are appointed to see matters
settled in relation to her child. A certificate issued for Joseph Brown.
A certificate issued for John Roberts. John Caddwallader, on behalf of
Gainer Owen, complains that Richard and Sarah Robinson refuses to
pay what is justly due to the said Gainer.

30/6/1706 - Richard Woodworth continues in his evil practice of
drunkenness. Likewise, George Guest continues in his drunkenness
and other disorders. Pentecoast Teague, intends to go to England to
visit his father and mother and desires a certificate. Richard Walln
desires a certificate, intending on marriage with Ann Heath,
belonging to Dublin Monthly Meeting. Martha Chalkley desires a
certificate to visit Friends in New England, her husband being
present gave his consent.

__/7/1706 - A certificate issued for Richard Waln in relation to marriage.
A certificate issued for Pente Teague.

25/8/1706 - Christopher Topham intends shortly for England by way of
Jamaica and requests a certificate.

29/9/1706 - Maurice Lisle, removing to England, desires a certificate, his
departure being near. A certificate signed for Christopher Topham.
Friends are desired to end the difference between Pente Teague and
Thomas White.

27/10/1706 - Friends are desired to speak to William Carter that he bring
an account of his management of the estate of Dennis Rochford,
deceased, to the next Monthly Meeting. George Painter desires a
certificate in order to marriage with Caleb Puseys daughter.

31/11/1706/7 - Jacob Minshell and Sarah Owen declare their intentions
to marry, both their fathers being present and consenting. Friends
appointed to speak with William Carter about the account of the
estate of Dennis Rochfords children report that he would have the
meeting appoint Friends to come and see his book but it is desired
that Friends request him to send a copy of the account to the next
Monthly Meeting. A certificate issued for George Painter. John
Cadwallader continues his complaint on behalf of his kinswoman
against Richard Robinson. John Rhoads requests a certificate for
himself and wife to the meeting where he belongs.

28/12/1706/7 - Jacob Minshell and Sarah Owen clear to marry, both
fathers having consented and the young man having procured a
certificate from Chester Monthly Meeting. James Estaugh and Mary
Lawson clear to marry, he producing a certificate from the Monthly
Meeting in Helstone Dunscon in Essex in Old England. William
Carter brought an account of the estate of Dennis Rochford,
deceased, and George Gray brought an account of Mercy Rochfords
estate. A certificate issued for John Rhoads and his wife. A certificate
in behalf of Paul Wolf from Dublin Monthly Meeting was read.

28/1/1707 - Copies of Edward Shippens paper of condemnation are
desired to be sent to New England, Long Island, Burlington,
Maryland, Barbadoes, Hirtego and one to London. A certificate from
London on behalf of Robert Chamberlain and another from Rhode
Island on behalf of Jeremiah Williams were read and approved.
Richard Gove desires a certificate to visit Friends in Maryland,
Virginia and Carolina. There is a difference between John Evans of
Radnor and David Powell. There is a difference between Stephen
Sands of Nessheminy meeting and Ellis Jones.

25/2/1707 - A certificate was issued for Richard Gove. Friends are
desired to hear and end the difference between George Gray and
Anthony Morris. A certificate from Cork Monthly Meeting in Ireland
on behalf of Edward Scull was received. Joseph Jones is disowned.

27/4/1707 - The time of Pentecoast Teagues departure towards England
draws near and as it hath been a long time since he has had his
certificate he desires that it be renewed. Thomas Makin complains
against Jno. Parker about a debt due to him.

25/5/1707 - A letter from the mens meeting at Lurgan concerns one John
Tanner that left a wife, as they say very unworthily, and takes no
care concerning her nor to pay his own debts, desires that Friends
here deal with him. Thomas Chalkley, having a concern to travel both
in the West Indies and Europe, desires a certificate from this
meeting, having produced a certificate from Maryland of his
clearness.

29/6/1707 - Ralph Jackson and Sarah Dymmock declare their intentions
to marry, Sarah being a widow and having children. Friends spoke
with John Tanner concerning the accounts come out of Ireland about
him but he gives no satisfaction but rather slights their advice and
says he was going to live with Capt. Hinney, intimating that he should
be out of the reach of Friends. Said Friends are desired to draw up
something concerning him to certify that he is a married man and not
one in unity with us. Philip England, having sometime past upon his
removal from hence, desired a certificate which he now renews. John
Piggott, intending to remove with his family into Maryland, desires a
certificate on behalf of himself and his wife. John Walker and his wife

desire a certificate to the Monthly Meeting at Newtown. Pentecoast
Teagues paper of condemnation, written by himself, was read.

26/7/1707 - Richard Roberts sent in a paper of condemnation of his
joining with that evil spirit of separation that appeared in George
Keith. Richard Gove has it in mind to travel to several of the islands
in the West Indies and to Europe as a companion to Thomas Chalkley
and desires a certificate. A certificate issued for Phiilip England.
Thomas Bryant and Susannah Hearne clear to marry, the fathers of
both being present gave their consent. Isaac Minshell and Sarah
Owen declare their intentions to marry, the fathers of both being
present, gave their consent. Caleb Ranstead and Mary Warder
declare their intentions to marry, the parents on both sides being
present gave their consent. Anthony Morris is desired to search the
records and see what procedure is entered against Philip Howel
concerning his disorderly walking and whether he hath been denied.
John and William Holebrook desire a certificate, intending to move
out of the limits of this meeting. Arnold Cassel finds himself under
great straits concerning his worldly affairs.

31/8/1707 - A certificate issued for Richard Gove, he being gone a
considerable time before this meeting. A certificate issued for Philip
England.

28/9/1707 - Griffith Owen hath received a Power of Attorney from
Ellinor Holney to recover a debt due from the estate of John Martin,
deceased. Friends advise him to write to the woman and let her know
that one of the said Martyns executors [Thomas Chalkley] is gone for
England and hath some effects in his hands. Friends from Barbadoes
requests a certificate on behalf of John Smith but he bringing none
with him, nor behaving himself as a friend, Friends are desired to
write to that meeting and acquaint them that he cannot expect a
satisfactory certificate from our meeting. Jacob Howell intends to
remove into the county of Chester and desires a certificate. A
certificate issued for John and William Holebrook. John Widdowfield
and Mary Lawrence declare their intentions to marry, he having
produced a certificate from England. William Woodmanseys daughter
Mary Davis writ to this meeting that she might be considered out of
what her father left. Thomas Makin desires that a certificate may be
sent to him to Long Island. Joseph Janes intending to Jamiaca desires
a certificate.

26/10/1707 - A certificate issued for Jacob Howel.

13/11/1707/8 - Jeremiah Williams, who is removed from this place to New
York, desires a certificate. Thomas Godfrey and Lucia Russel declare
their intentions to marry, the said Thomas producing a certificate
from Dublin Monthly Meeting. John Sharp and Elizabeth Green
declare their intentions to marry, he producing a certificate from
Newtown Monthly Meeting. William Rakestraw informs this meeting

that there is a difference between him and James Logan and that he is a sufferer by him. Thomas Murrey informs this meeting that there is a difference between his father - in - law Edward Shippen and himself.

27/12/1707/8 - Certificates on behalf of William Mason, George Calvert and David Brientnall Junr, were read. Thomas Godfrey and Lucey Russel clear to marry, he producing a certificate from Dublin Monthly Meeting not satisfactory as could be desired yet not sufficient to obstruct them. The matter between Edward Shippen and Thomas Murrey is ended.

25/1/1708 - Henry Willis intends to remove into New Jersey in order to live with his daughter and desires a certificate in order thereto. Paul Woolf intends to return to Germantown to inhabit and desires a certificate. Anthony Morris hath had it in mind to visit Friends on the western shore of Maryland and desires a certificate. John Potts, who was an orphan bound apprentice to John Austin, complains that he hath served out his apprenticeship and his mistress will not discharge him and he desires assistance.

29/2/1708 - A certificate issued for Henry Willis and his wife. Friends of Martha Chalkley move that she might have a certificate sent after her to Maryland. Friends appointed to make enquiry concerning John Potts servitude report they cannot understand that he hath served his time and therefore could not discharge him. Abraham Bickley intends to remove himself, wife and family to New York and desires a certificate in order thereto.

27/3/1708 - Certificates issued for Thomas Cares and John Ward. John Guest intends to remove himself and family to New York and desires a certificate. Richard Parker moved to this meeting on behalf of William White, who formerly lived in this city, for a certificate. Thomas Story hath a concern to visit Friends in the Islands of Barbadoes and Jamaica and other adjacent islands and desires a certificate.

24/4/1708 - A certificate issued for William White. David Brientnall intends to take a voyage to England for the recovery of his health and desires a certificate. Thomas Fairman sends a paper complaining against David Lloyd. A certificate issued for Thomas Story. Likewise Thomas Caress.

30/5/1708 - A certificate for John Croxton read and entered on record. A certificate was issued for David Brientnall after a great deal of advice and council given him and the danger of the voyage and exercise he might meet withal therein, considering his incapacity to help himself. A certificate issued for John Cox.

27/6/1708 - A certificate issued for William White and his wife. Abraham Kite and Mary Peters clear to marry, the relations of both being present and consenting. An epistle from Thomas Chalkley and

Richard Gove was read. John Showell intends to return to Statten Island and desires a certificate. Reese Peters and wife desire a certificate to Dublin Monthly Meeting.

24/7/1708 - Friends appointed to look into the complaint of Thomas Fairman against David Lloyd report they did not find he had just cause to complain but had wronged the said David and they could not persuade him to give satisfaction. A certificate issued for John Shotwell. A certificate on behalf of John _____ from the Peel meeting in London was read and approved. James Steel intends to remove himself and family down to Duck Creek in the county of Kent and requests a certificate. James Estaugh intends to take a voyage to England by way of Jamiaca and to return as soon as his business will permit and desires a certificate in order thereto. John Oxley intends to remove hence to dwell at New York and desires a certificate.

29/8/1708 - Israel Pemberton intends to take a voyage to Barbadoes and desires a certificate. Susannah Freeborn and Patience Anthony are near ready to return home and desire a certificate. A certificate from the Peel meeting in London on behalf of Abraham Scott and wife was read and approved.

26/9/1708 - A certificate from Cork in Ireland concerning John Camm was read, which is not satisfactory. A certificate issued for Rees Peters and his wife. Pentecoast Teague reports that an orphan child of James Wests wants a place to be put out apprentice. There is a matter in controversy between Samuel Carpenter, Nathan Stanbury and John Jones Boulter concerning the estate of the late widow Walkers child. Casper Hoodt reports that his is much injured for want of being cleared of his engagements which he entered into on behalf of Arnold Cassel. It was reported that John Jones Joyner behaves himself very disorderly. Certificates on behalf of Caleb Jacob, Thomas Jacob, Christopher Thomson, William Green and Pentecoast Teague were read and accepted.

21/10/1708 - Certificates on behalf of Edward Pleadwell and Daniel Standish were read. A certificate from Lurgan meeting for Samuel Wilkenson was read, he requesting in turn a certificate from this meeting. John Croxton again moves that he intends to go to Jamaica and desires a certificate.

28/11/1708 - John Hart and Hannah Maccomb clear to marry, he producing a certificate from Cecil in Maryland. Jonathan Coppeck and Jane Owen declare their intentions to marry, relations on both sides being present, consenting, and also a certificate from Providence Monthly Meeting. John Maul and Charity Jones declare their intentions to marry, John bringing a certificate from the meeting at Lyn in New England as well as something under his fathers hand to show his consent. Samuel Marriott and Mary Whitpain declare their intentions to marry, the parents on both sides being present gave their consent and the young man providing a certificate from Burlington Monthly Meeting. John Warder and Agnes Righton declare their intentions to marry, some of the parents on both sides being present and consenting. Griffith Owen desires a certificate to visit Friends in Long Island, Rhode Island, New England and that way. Patrick Henderson finds himself pretty easy and his service chiefly over in these parts, having produced a satisfactory certificate from the province meeting in Ulster in Ireland, desires a certificate from this meeting. A certificate on behalf of John Peel from Bellshagen meeting in Ireland was read and approved. Likewise one from Newcastle County on behalf of Jos. Griffin. Pentecoast Teague reports that he has provided a place for James West with Jacob Usher, carpenter, but the meeting thinks there is no need to give money with him, considering his age and the time he is to be with him.

25/12/1708 - Certificates on behalf of Patrick Henderson and Griffith Owen were approved. Pentecoast Teague is still desired to continue to care to provide a place to put James West. Hugh Durbrow desires to visit Friends on Long Island, Rhode Island and some parts of New England if a suitable companion presents. A certificate on behalf of Christopher Topin from Richmond in Yorkshire was read and approved. There is a difference between John Goodson, Thomas Masters and Arnold Cassel.

27/1/1709 - William Corker and Mary Fisher declare their intentions to marry, the parents being present. Henry Willis, having had a certificate to Newtown meeting, cannot well have another until that be returned. A certificate issued for Hugh Durborow. James Kite complains against Emanuel Walker having given him gospel order and he refuses to comply. There is a matter of complaint by John Martindale against Nicholas Waln.

29/2/1709 - Richard Moore and Margaret Preston declare their intentions to marry, consent of relations already being obtained and the young man desired to bring a certificate from the Monthly Meeting in Maryland where he belongs. The certificate for Hugh Durborow being neglected, Friends are desired to prepare one. There is a difference between Joshua Granger and Christopher Topham. Casper Hoodt intends to go to Europe and desires a certificate. Joseph Coleman intends to return to New England to his parents and desires a certificate. John Howleft proposes to prosecute his voyage to England and desires a few lines by way of certificate.

27/3/1709 - Friends appointed to enquire concerning Casper Hoodt report that they hear nothing against his conversation but his business is not yet settled, neither doth his wife fully give him up. A certificate issued for Joseph Coleman. A certificate for Hugh Durborow was signed. There are several sums of money due from the estate of Thomas Duckett, deceased. It was moved at this meeting that the necessity of the poor people that were robbed by the French at the town of Lewis might be taken into consideration.

25/4/1709 - Robert Whitton lays a complaint against Christopher Topham. Clement Plumstead intends a voyage to Barbadoes upon his lawful business and desires a certificate. A certificate for Casper Hoodt was wrote and signed, he having given them satisfaction. A letter from Flushing Monthly Meeting concerning David Lloyd prosecuting John Rodman was read. It is the advice of this meeting concerning Arnold Cassel that it will not do well for him and his family to settle upon 20 acres of ground. Joshua Hastings is a poor man and in want.

29/5/1709 - George Gray intends for East Jersey, Long Island and that way and desires a certificate. Richard Hill, shoemaker, desires a certificate in relation to marriage.

26/6/1709 - A certificate for George Gray was read and approved. William Monington and Susanna Webb declare their intentions to marry, the young womans parents being present, gave their consent. Joshua Gilbert and Elisabeth Oldman declare their intentions to marry, the parents on both sides being present gave their consent. A certificate issued for Richard Hill, shoemaker. A certificate from Bristol on behalf of James Logan was read, he informing this meeting that his occasions called him to England suddenly and he desires a certificate from this meeting. A certificate from Burlington on behalf of George Parker was read and recorded.

30/7/1709 - A letter from Flushing Monthly Meeting concerning David Lloyd's suing John Rodman was read. John Large and Sarah Corker declare their intentions to marry, the young man producing a certificate from the Falls Monthly Meeting and the young womans parents being present, gave consent. A certificate on behalf of James Logan was read and approved. Elisabeth Webb desires a certificate for herself, husband and children. There is a difference between Thomas Haywood and John Webb.

28/8/1709 - Thomas Brown, being removed from this place, desires a certificate on behalf of himself and wife to Dublin Monthly Meeting, within whose limits he has gone to dwell. The widow Tittery desires the assistance of this meeting concerning a servant boy, whose name is Dennis Rochford, who hath several years to serve and is entered in the potting trade. Edward Cadwallader and Rebeckah Moore declare their intentions to marry. John Large and Sarah Corker clear to marry. Samuel Lewis and Hannah Stretch declare their intentions to marry, he to bring a certificate from the Monthly Meeting where he belongs and his parents either to come or send to satisfy that his proceedings is with their approbation. Samuel Carpenter, Jun'r, by consent of his father, intends a voyage to England and desires a certificate. Edward Pleadwell intends a trading voyage to Jamaica and desires a certificate. Maurice Lisle intends to return and desires a certificate.

25/9/1709 - A certificate issued for Thomas Brown and his wife. A certificate on behalf of John Richmond was read. William Watson moves for a certificate, he being gone to Jamaica in order for England, he having brought two certificates from England and left them in this meeting. A paper of condemnation against himself was brought in by Hugh Lowdon and read, for being overtaken with passion and unseemly behaviour towards his wife.

30/10/1709 - The widow Griffith hath sustained considerable loss by the late fire, which hath put her under some necessities. Gilbert Falkener and Hannah Hardiman declare their intentions to marry, the said Gilbert producing a certificate from Cecil Monthly Meeting in Maryland. There is some difference between James Atkinson and Joshua Hastings.

27/11/1709 - James Morris intends marriage with a young woman at Chester Monthly Meeting and desires a certificate. James Crawford and Sarah Bettle declare their intentions to marry, the young man producing a certificate from Duck Creek Monthly Meeting and the young womans father being present and consenting.

24/12/1709/10 - Certificates on behalf of William Hudson and James Morris were read and approved. Robert Baker and Susannah Packer clear to marry, they having produced certificates and consent of parents. Israel Pemberton and Rachael Read declare their intentions to marry. Peter Wisehart and Ann Batson declare their intentions to marry, the parents of the young woman being present and consenting, and the said Peter to bring a certificate from the Monthly Meeting to which he formerly belonged. Willoughby Warder, Jun'r, and Sarah Bowyer declare their intentions to marry, he producing a certificate from the Falls Monthly Meeting and it is expected that his father should appear or send something under his hand of his concurrence.

31/1/1710 - There is a difference between Robert Yieldhall and George Painter. Israel Pemberton and Rachel Read clear to marry. Peter Wisehart and Ann Batson clear to marry, the young man bringing a certificate from Abington Monthly Meeting. Willoby Warder, Jun'r, and Sarah Bowyer clear to marry, his father being present, giving his consent. It is desired that something may be certified concerning Rebeckah Freeland to send over to Brittain in order to receive a legacy that is there left for her.

28/2/1710 - John Balle, carpenter, who was servant to Peter Stretch, requested a certificate to Dublin Monthly Meeting on account of marriage. A certificate on behalf of Samuel Combs was read and recorded. A certificate on behalf of Rebeckah Freeland cannot yet be perfected untill it doth further appear from the Friends about Duck Creek where she was born.

26/3/1710 - A certificate issued for John Balle. Nathaniel Edgcomb complains against John Mitchener that he is engaged for him in a great deal of money and cannot get satisfaction from him.

30/4/1710 - Nathaniel Edgcomb renews his complaint against John Mitchener concerning money he is bound for, for him, and Margaret Cook for money due to her and Is. Norris also. Solomon Cresson complains against Caleb Raunstead.

28/5/1710 - A certificate on behalf of William Lingard and Mary his wife from Hoesleydown meeting was read and accepted.

25/6/1710 - Edward Pleadwell and Grace Day declare their intentions to marry, with consent of her parents. John Durborow and Sarah Day declare their intentions to marry, parents on both sides being present gave their consent. A letter from the Monthly Meeting of Flushing, in relation to the difference between John Rodman and David Lloyd, was read. There is a difference between John Parker and John Oxley. John Hart intends for Europe and desires a certificate. George Parker having suffered some loss lately by fire, being poor and not able to bear it, desires the assistance of this meeting. Samuel Preston complains against William Fishbourn.

29/7/1710 - Certificates from Milberton, in the county of Somerset, in Great Britain, on behalf of Francis and Thomas Ferris were read and approved. A certificate issued for John Hart. James Kite complains against Emanuel Walker that he keeps him out of his just due.

27/8/1710 - Two certificates on behalf of Thomas Chalkley from the London meeting of Southampton was read and approved. A certificate on behalf of Nathan Shenton of Leicestershire was read and recorded, the said Nathan Shenton deceased soon after his arrival, made no will and leaving behind him five children, the eldest about 16 years and the youngest about ten months old. The meeting requests Richard Hill and Peter Stretch take care of the children and place them out amongst Friends and administer upon what estate he hath left toward the support of his children, it being what he desired upon his death bed. John Harper and Jane Fawcet declare their intention to marry, he producing a certificate from Friends in Maryland but having resided amongst us for some time. Samuel Carpenter, on behalf of Gilbert Faulkener, who has gone for Great Brittain, desires a certificate. Adam Lewis and Mary Watson declare their intention to marry. John Picket and his wife being removed into Chester County desires a certificate from this meeting. Thomas Iredell and his wife likewise, having moved out of the limits of this meeting, desire a certificate. Thomas Willson, joyner, desires the concurrence of this meeting that he might take his brother apprentice that formerly lived with Cad'w. Morgan who is willing to part with

him in consideration that his wife's deceased and he is about to leave
off house - keeping.

24/9/1710 - Friends appointed to take care of Nathan Shentons children
and estate report they have placed out the children they hope to good
places and they are all provided for except the young one which they
have put out to nurse and hope there may be enough left to discharge
the expense of it. Edward Samway is deceased. Adam Lewis and
Mary Watson clear to marry. John Carpenter and Ann Hoskins
declare their intentions to marry, it being with consent of both
parents who were present. A certificate issued for John Picket and
his wife and likewise for Thomas Iredall.

29/10/1710 - Thomas Story complains that he hath money due to him
from John Gilbert and Daniel England who neglect to make him
satisfaction though he hath often demanded it. The executors of John
Barnes brought to this meeting a writing signed by the said John
Barnes wherein is signified some legacies to both this meeting and
Abington meeting. Thomas Broadgate and Christian Armstrong
declare their intentions to marry, he producing a certificate and also
his fathers consent, they having been in the country some time. David
Briendnall, Junr, and Grace Parker declare their intentions to marry,
with consent of parents who were present. A paper from Susannah
Freeborn was read.

26/11/1710 - A certificate on behalf of Joseph Bond and his wife from
Brighouse Monthly Meeting in Yorkshire was read and approved.
Friends appointed to enquire into the conversation of David
Brientnall, Jun'r, report they hear such things concerning him as is
unbecoming the conversation of anyone professing truth. This
meeting is greatly dissatisfied with him and cannot see that he can be
permitted take a wife amongst us until he gives some satisfaction for
his loose conversation. Joseph Paul, Junr, and Elisabeth Roberts
declare their intentions to marry, the young mans parents being
present, declare it was with their consent. There is a legacy given by
the widow Guest for the use of this meeting, it being in the hands of
Anthony Morris, Jun'r, and her son George Guest who was her
executor, having spent what his mother left him, and his wife and
children brought to poverty. Abraham Cox intends going on a voyage
to Barbadoes and desires a certificate, from which Friends hath used
a great deal of pains to dissuade him but the since of the meeting is
that we first have a certificate from the county of Bucks where he
served his apprenticeship, and then if he will not alter his intentions
the meeting may appoint a friend to write a certificate.

23/12/1710 - Anthony Morris intends to visit Friends in New England
and desires a certificate. David Brientnall, Junr, and Grace Parker
clear to marry, the said David having given in a paper to condemn his
loose conversation and evil practices that he hath been guilty of.

Joseph Paul and Elisabeth Roberts clear to marry, the young man producing a certificate from Abington Monthly Meeting. John Maul intends to return to New England and desires a certificate.

30/1/1711 - Friends appointed to write a certificate for Anthony Morris find something alleged of the dissatisfaction of some Friends belonging to Newtown Monthly Meeting, that he was concerned in encouraging the passing of marriage of William Harrison at Newtown meeting, without the consent of his mother. Therefore, Friends are desired to assist the said Anthony that they may endeavour to reconcile William Harrison and his mother. John Oxley has a mind to go to Rhode Island yearly meeting and desires a certificate.

27/2/1711 - All things being over, a certificate for Anthony Morris was approved and signed. Samuel Carpenter, Junr, and Hannah Preston declare their intention to marry, he having produced a certificate from the two weeks meeting in London. A certificate issued for John Oxley. Anthony Morris requests a certificate, being upon his removall for Maryland.

25/3/1711 - A certificate issued for Thomas Chalkley. James Steel and Martha Bowen declare their intention to marry, the said James to being a certificate from Duck Creek Monthly Meeting where he belongs and Friends, having an understanding that Marthas former husband, being supposed to be lost at sea, having not been heard of for about fourteen years, be very careful and diligent therein. Samuel Taylor and Elisabeth Robinson declare their intention to marry, the said Samuel belonging to Abington Monthly Meeting, to produce a certificate from thence. Jonas Langford is dead. Thomas Story produced a copy of a will of Henry Garydon, a friend in Antigua who is also deceased. Edward Shippen complains against Francis Richardson for some difference that is between them.

29/4/1711 - James Steel and Martha Bowen, she having lost her former husband Cornelius Bowen about fourteen years ago in a vessel bound from Boston to the Island of Barbadoes and none of the mariners or passengers in the said vessel was ever heard of, and he producing a certificate from the Monthly Meeting at Duck Creek, are clear to marry. Jacob Simcock and Sarah Walln declare their intention to marry, the said Jacob producing a certificate from the Monthly Meeting of Chester and also his father Jacob Simcock being present, declared his consent. Reese Peters and Ann Brooksley declare their intention to marry, parents on both sides being present, declared their consent. William Hudson desired the advice of his meeting in an affair he is concerned in by Susannah Worrelow. John Watson, having long been sick, is low in the world and wants some help to carry on his affairs. Thomas Story intends to return to England and visit Friends in some parts of that country and desires a certificate.

27/5/1711 - Jacob Simcock and Sarah Walln clear to marry, they
   intending to accomplish the same at Fairhill meeting house. Friends
   are desired to write to the widow of Jonas Langford and request that
   she please review the legacy given us by her husband. The effects of
   Henry Gradon, late of Antiqua, are in the hands of Nathan Stanbury.
   A certificate issued for Thomas Story.
31/6/1711 - A certificate on behalf of William Dunn from Bristol Monthly
   Meeting was read and approved. Thomas Peters, Jun'r, desires this
   meeting will give him a certificate in order to marry. John Prichard
   desires the meeting will help him with a little money toward his
   passage of journey to North Carolina.
28/7/1711 - A certificate from Brighouse Monthly Meeting in the county
   of York in Great Britain on behalf of Henry Thomson and two
   certificates from the Monthly Meeting of Brigflats in the same county
   of York on behalf of Thomas Barnes and Philip Fawcet were read and
   approved. A certificate on behalf of Thomas Peters was read and
   approved. William Kelly reports that there is a difference between
   him and Thos' Shute.
25/8/1711 - Certificates from Ireland on behalf of Samuel Massey and
   Mark Carlton and his wife were read and approved. The widow of
   Mark Carlton applies herself to this meeting in relation to her affairs,
   having lately come from Ireland.
30/9/1711 - Samuel Hillary and Jane Waterman declare their intentions
   to marry, he producing a certificate from Friends in Ireland which
   also mentions consent of parents. Evan Owen and Mary Hoskins
   declare their intentions to marry, he to bring a certificate from
   Hartford Monthly Meeting, with that he had from Barbadoes. A
   paper of condemnation against one Benjamin Mayne from the
   Monthly Meeting of Cork in Ireland was read.
28/10/1711 - John Oxley, having some business in New England, desires
   a certificate.
25/11/1711 - A certificate from Choptank Monthly Meeting on behalf of
   Enion Williams was read and approved. There being a difference
   between John Parker and John Oxley.
29/12/1711 - Ralph Jackson delivered to this meeting the sum of three
   pounds, being a legacy given by James Atkinson, late of Philadelphia,
   deceased certificate from the Monthly Meeting of Leek in
   Staffordshire on behalf of Joseph Taylor was produced and read. A
   certificate from Redstone meeting on behalf of Francis Jones and
   family was produced and read. A certificate from Haverford West on
   behalf of Samuel Jones and his wife and another from Middletown
   Monthly Meeting in Bucks County on behalf of Charles Brockden
   were read and approved. William Hudson desires a certificate on
   behalf of his son Samuel who is gone forward intending for Great
   Britain. Friends are appointed to enquire into William Mastermanns

circumstances and if he wants some support, to supply him with
necessaries.

28/1/1712 - Friends report that they did enquire into William
Mastermans circumstances, who is since dead, and they were very
low. A certificate on behalf of Samuel Hudson was read and approved.
Joseph Satterthwaite and the Widow Albison are in great necessity
by reason of a great loss sustained by fire. A certificate from Cork in
Ireland dated 5/8/1711 on behalf of John Knight (now of this place)
only in respect of his clearness in relation to marriage was read.

25/2/1712 - Samuel Bradshaw, about to remove to Darby in Chester
County, requests a certificate from this meeting. A certificate from
Maryland Monthly Meeting dated 27/1/1712 on behalf of Ennion
Williams was read and recorded. James Estaugh intends to remove
with his family to Duck Creek in New Castle County to live and
desires a certificate accordingly. Griffith Owen requests a certificate
on behalf of Thomas Chalkley, who is gone forwards on his journey to
visit Friends in Maryland and so to North Carolina. Christopher
Blackburn inclines to visit Friends in Maryland, Virginia and North
Carolina in company with Thomas Chalkley and requests a certificate
accordingly. Thomas Griffith, on behalf of John Roberts, cordwainer,
requests a certificate from this meeting.

30/3/1712 - A certificate issued for Samuel Bradshaw. A certificate issued
for James Estaugh. Thomas Cox and Mary Chandler declare their
intentions to marry, the young man having no relations, Pentecoast
Teague, his guardian, being present, consented. Certificates for
Thomas Chalkley read and approved. A certificate for Christopher
Blackburn signed and delivered to him. Friends report that they have
made enquiry concerning John Roberts, cordwainer, and do not find
that Friends can give him a certificate to do him any service. Joseph
Bond is about to remove to Bristol in Bucks County with his family
and having brought a certificate hither from Great Britain, desires a
one from this meeting on behalf of himself and wife. John Knight
intends marriage with a friend of Abington Monthly Meeting and
desires a certificate accordingly. Anthony Morris, on behalf of his son
James, requests a certificate for himself and wife, they being about to
remove to live at Duck Creek in Kent County. George Gray intends to
remove to Germantown and requests a certificate accordingly. A
certificate from London on behalf of Thomas Bond, late of Lancaster,
was read and accepted. Also. a certificate from Chester Monthly
Meeting on behalf of James Lownes and his wife was read and
accepted.

27/4/1712 - A certificate issued for James Morris. Friends produced to
this meeting a certificate on behalf of Samuel Bradshaw which was
read and approved. Certificates for James Estaugh and his wife,
Joseph Bond and his wife, John Knight and George Gray were read

and approved. Benjamin Fairman requests a certificate, intending to marry a friend belonging to Crosswicks Monthly Meeting. Maurice Lisle and Mary Badcock declare their intentions to marry. Issac Morris, as Guardian to Mary Ducket of Hammersmith in Great Britain, complains that there is a legacy due to her from the estate of Thomas Ducket which he can't get payment of. Everard Bolton complains against Samuel Preston and Clement Plumstead, Trustees of John Jones, merch't, deceased, that they refuse to settle acct's with him in relation to the said Jones estate. A certificate on behalf of Aaron Goforth and his family, from the Monthly Meeting of Horslydown, dated 12/7/1711, was read. Isaac Norris, on behalf of George Walker of Virginia, complains against Joshua Granger and Christopher Topham of a debt due from them to the said Walker.

25/5/1712 - Priscilla Parker, widow of Richard Parker, sent in a legacy left by him to this meeting. Certificate in behalf of Benjamin Fairman and James Morris and his wife were read and signed. Abel Preston requests a certificate, he intending to marry a friend of Shrewsbury Monthly Meeting. Friends appointed to make enquiry concerning Maurice Lisle report that they hear a discourse of his courting a young woman in Ireland and having no certificate from Friends there, nor from Great Britain, nor parents consent, this meeting cannot consent to the passing of their marriage. A certificate from Dublin in Ireland, dated 7/1/1711, in behalf of James Morris was read and recorded. Joseph Jacobs requests a certificate, he being about to remove to New England. Edward Shippen complains against Isaac Morris and David Lloyd, that there is a difference between them.

29/6/1712 - A certificate on behalf of Peter Osbourne, his wife and children and likewise for Thomas Nicholas, Mary his wife and children, from Staffordshire in Great Britain, were read and recorded. A certificate on behalf of Peter Osburne, Judith his wife and children and likewise, Thomas Nicholas, Mary his wife and children from Staffordshire in Great Britain were read and recorded. A certificate on behalf of John Farmer from Colchester and other places was read and approved. Caleb Buffam of Salem in New England, having resided hereabouts in this county for some time, and being about now to return, desires a certificate. A certificate issued for John Roberts, he having sent in a paper to condemn himself for his disorderly walking. Richard Hill, on behalf of Richard Brown, his servant, desires a certificate, being about to go to some part of the West Indies. Ebenezer Large, having been dealt with concerning his having been at a marriage of William Rakestraw, Jun'r, contrary to our discipline, and being at a bull bating, hath given a paper of condemnation against himself.

26/7/1712 - A certificate from the Monthly Meeting of Stafford on behalf of John Carpenter, and another on behalf of William Harvey from

Worcester in Great Britain were read and recorded. Charles Brockden desires a certificate to the Monthly Meeting at Middletown in Bucks County, in relation to marriage. Stephen Stapler desires a certificate in order to return to Nottingham. Benjamin Chandley desires a certificate to Nottingham, intending to remove with his family. Friends are desired to what condition a poor friend, John Carpenter, lately come from England, may be in necessity of. Abraham Shotwell desires a certificate in relation to marriage.

31/8/1712 - Edward Shippen is dead. John Hart made application for a certificate, being about to take a voyage on his lawful occasions of merchandizing.

29/9/1712 - John Vaughn, deceased, hath left a legacy to this meeting. A certificate from Lavington in the county of Wilts on behalf of Thomas Canon and his wife, another from the Monthly Meeting of Limington in the county of Somerset for James Hurd, and another from Reading in the county of Berks on behalf of Thomas Speakman were read and recorded. A certificate on behalf of John Hart was read and approved. James Hurd hath intentions to return to Great Britain and as he produced a certificate to this meeting, so he desired he might have the like again. Thomas Speakman, who came from Great Britain, laid before this meeting his necessity of some money to clear the Shipmaster from what he is indebted to him.

26/10/1712 - A certificate from the Monthly Meeting of New Castle in Brittain on behalf of James Watson was read and recorded. David Lloyd desires a certificate for himself and wife to the Monthly Meeting within who's limits they have moved unto.

30/11/1712 - A certificate on behalf of James Hadwin from Westmoreland Monthly Meeting was read and recorded. Richard Whitten and Elisabeth Jylife declare their intentions to marry, the young man bringing with him a certificate from Abington Monthly Meeting. The widow Hallwell sends to this meeting a complaint against David Brientnall. John Jones complains against Thomas Pryor, that he withholds from him money he owed him. Thomas Griffith, on behalf of Jeremiah Allen that is gone to Jamacia, requests a certificate to send after him.

27/12/1712 - Paul Preston and Elisabeth Gilbert declare their intentions to marry, Issac Norris desired to advise and assist the woman, being a widow, that she may settle what she thinks fit upon her children before marriage. Nathaniel Allen and Hannah Web declare their intentions to marry, the young mans father being present and consenting. The widow Hallwell complains against John Harper as she before had done against David Brientnall, they both being bound to her for money that hath long been due to her. A certificate on behalf of Jeremiah Allen was read and approved. Samuel Comb requested a certificate to the falls meeting in the county of Bucks, in

order to marriage. There is a difference between Edward Scull,
Nathan Stanbury and John Jones. John Richard complains of his
poverty and having been lately sick makes his necessity greater, and
requests the assistance of Friends.

27/1/1713 - Certificates from Waterford in Ireland on behalf of William
Moore and Joshua Baker were read and recorded. A certificate issued
for Samuel Combs. Samuel Jones intends to remove to Chester for
the betterment of his trade and desires a certificate.

25/2/1713 - A certificate issued for Samuel Jones. a certificate for Samuel
Combs was read and approved. Richard Parks and Susannah Carlton
declare their intentions to marry, he producing a certificate from a
meeting in Lancashire.

29/3/1713 - Friends appointed concerning the legacy given by Edward
Shippen, deceased, report that nothing is done by reason that his son
Edward has not returned from Boston. A certificate for Ralph
Jackson was read and approved. Thomas Wilson and Elisabeth
Trafford clear to marry, the young man having no parents and the
young womans father being present, gives his consent. Joseph Low
and Elisabeth Taylor clear to marry, the young man bringing a
certificate from the Monthly Meeting at Newtown. Certificates from
Great Brittain on behalf of Elisabeth Whartnaby, Sarah Lee and
Robert Lodge and his wife were read and recorded. Andrew Godfrey
intends to go down to Salem to follow his trade of combing wool and
desires a certificate. William Rakestraw acknowledged that he had
broke the discipline of the church in exposing Thomas Story contrary
thereunto and likewise in relation to his sons marriage contrary to
the order of Friends. There is a difference between Daniel Standish
and Christopher Blackbourn. A letter from one John Jawart, a
German in Maryland, sets forth the injury he and the German
Company hath sustained wherein he blames David Lloyd as chief
instrument.

26/4/1713 - A certificate issued for Andrew Godfrey. John Zelly and
Margaret Howell declare their intentions to marry, the young mans
mother being present and consenting. William Moore and Hannah
Knight declare their intentions to marry. David Lloyd continues his
request for a certificate. The widow Gilbert desires this meeting to
assist in treating with Joseph Gilbert, her late husbands executor, so
that she might be assisted with what of right belongs to her out of her
husbands estate, if anything is there to be had. Certificates from
Horslydown meeting in Southwark, on behalf of Robert and Mary
Hind, and William Clifton and wife, were read and recorded.

21/5/1713 - Certificates from Great Brittain on behalf of John Chambers
and family, John and David Davis, John Owen, and Richard Lewis, his
wife and sons were read and recorded. Likewise, one from Abington
on behalf of Richard Townsend and wife. A certificate on behalf of

Andrew Godfrey was read and approved. Joseph Cooper, Jun'r, and Mary Hudson declare their intentions to marry, the parents on both sides being present, consenting. There os a difference between George Claypool and John Durborow.

28/6/1713 - Emanuel Daugworth and Elisabeth Bringhurst clear to marry, he bringing a certificate of his fathers free consent. Joseph Cooper, Jun'r, and Mary Hudson declare their intentions to marry, he producing a certificate from the Monthly Meeting of Newtown. A certificate on behalf of Hugh Clifton from Willingborow in Northamptonshire was read and recorded. William Pasmore and Ann Smith declare their intentions to marry. Samuel Lad requests a certificate, intending to marry a young woman belonging to Newtown Monthly Meeting in Jersey. William Hudson complains against Thomas Fairman, that he refuses to pay money due upon bond to him and some other Friends.

25/7/1713 - This meeting cannot give way to permit the marriage of William Pasmore for want of a certificate from England. John Nailer and Mary Greenup declare their intentions to marry, the said John producing a certificate from Radnor Monthly Meeting and also, his father being present, gives his consent. A certificate for Samuel Lad read and approved. George Coates and Grace Sneed clear to marry, the young man's mother being present gives her consent. John Oxley intends to visit Friends in Barbadoes and desires a certificate.

30/8/1713 - Thomas Nixon and Magdalen Bellows clear to marry, he producing a certificate from the Monthly Meeting to which he belongs and things being settled on account of her children. George Coates and Grace Sneed clear to marry. A certificate for John Oxley read and approved. Samuel Hanson and Joan Townsend declare their intentions to marry, Samuel to bring a certificate from the Monthly Meeting to which he belongs and also something to signify his mothers consent.

27/9/1713 - Application being made to this meeting on behalf of the widow Ducket in Great Britain concerning a legacy left her by her brother Thomas Ducket, deceased. Nathan Stanbury complains against John Jones, that he will not an account of James Fox's estate. Edward Scull likewise complains against Nathan Stanbury. Thomas Barnes complains against Thomas Broadgate, that he owes him money and he cannot get it of him. Richard Hill complains against Samuel Taylor, that he is indebted to him.

25/10/1713 - A certificate on behalf of David Lloyd and his wife was read and approved. George Mifflin and Esther Cordery declare their intentions to marry, the parents on both sides being present, give consent. Joseph Wait and Martha Biles declare their intentions to marry, the young mans mother being present, gives consent, and Friends to assist the said Martha, being a widow, to settle things in relation to her children. Richard Parks requests a certificate for himself and wife, upon his removal to the county of Chester. A certificate from West River Monthly Meeting in Maryland on behalf of Mordecai Moore and Deborah his wife was read and recorded.

29/11/1713 - Certificates on behalf of Richard Sunby and Mercy Pearce from the two weeks meeting in Lonson were read and recorded. A certificate for Richard Parks and his wife issued. Samuel Hanson and Joan Townsend clear to marry, he producing a certificate from Abington Monthly Meeting. George Mifflin and Esther Cordery clear to marry. There has been a disorderly marriage of William Pasmore and Ann Smith. Samuel Carpenter, being removed to Bristol in the county of Bucks for some time, desires a certificate. Samuel Carpenter, on behalf of Gilbert Faulkener since his removal to New Castle, moves for a certificate. There is a difference between Edwin Williams and Samuel Burden.

26/12/1713 - A certificate on behalf of Robert Eastbourn, his wife and children, from Brighton Monthly Meeting was read and recorded. a certificate to Concord Monthly Meeting on behalf of Richard Parks and his wife was read and approved. Thomas Chalkley and Martha Brown declare their intention to marry, Friends are appointed to endeavour to settle the widows estate, what she is willing to give her children, if anything more than their father left them. Arthur Sawyer and Elisabeth Test declare their intentions to marry. John Durborow complains that two actions of law are entered against him and his brother Edward Pleadwell by Ralph Jackson and Randal Spikeman.

26/1/1714 - A certificate from the two weeks meeting in London on behalf of Joseph Buckley was read, he being upon departing the province and desires a certificate of this meeting. Thomas Chalkley and Martha Brown clear to marry, the said Thomas producing a certificate from several places in his travels. Richard Smith and Anna Marshall clear to marry, he producing a certificate from the Monthly Meeting of Burlington. George Fitzwater and Samuel Peres complains against Nathaniel Pool, that he refuses to do them justice. Arthur Sawyer and Elisabeth Test clear to marry, he being clear from all persons in relation to marriage, his wife being deceased since he came into these parts. John Lancaster and Sarah Brientnall declare their intentions to marry, the young man bringing a satisfactory certificate and the young womans parents being present, give consent. Abraham Cox and Martha Nicholas declare their intentions to marry. There is a difference between William Joans and William Fisher. Stephen Jackson intends for Great Britain and desires a certificate. John Mifflin desires a certificate on behalf of his son, Edward, who intends to take a wife in Virginia.

30/2/1714 - A certificate from Abington meeting on behalf of Samuel Richardson was read and approved. Abraham Cox and Martha

Nicholas clear to marry. James Morris intends to return to Ireland, having sometime since produced a certificate from thence, desires one from hence. A certificate on behalf of Samuel Stretch from the Monthly Meeting of Stafford of Great Britain was read and approved, he having some intention of removing into Maryland to follow his trade there, desires a certificate of this meeting. James Cooper intends for England upon his lawful occasions and desires a certificate. Joseph Richards condemns his marrying by the priest.

28/3/1714 - Christopher Thomson complains that Caleb Ranstead oweth him money and acknowledges the debt but hath not the money to satisfy him. Joshua Granger intends for Europe upon his lawful occasions and desires a certificate. Friends are desired to enquire into the condition of the widow Burden. Nathaniel Griffith, intending to take a voyage to sea, desires a certificate.

25/4/1714 - Nicholas Hitchcock and Elisabeth Massey clear to marry. Nathaniel Pool and Ann Till declare their intentions to marry, Friends appointed to see some settlement made on behalf of Ann Till's child by her former husband. William Harvey and Judith Osbrow declare their intentions to marry, Friends to see if there be anything for her children. Friends are desired to write to Friends at Barbadoes and inclose the certificate on behalf of Sarah Lee and desire them to show it to Joseph Webb therin concerned and use their endeavors to make him sensible of the evil he hath done. Certificates for Nathaniel Griffith and Joshua Granger were read and approved. John Salkeld brought a complaint against the executors of James Kite. Richard Lewis, having gotten a settlement at Germantown, desires a certificate on behalf of himself, wife and son.

30/5/1714 - A certificate from Hartshaw Monthly Meeting in Lancashire on behalf of John Wright, Patience his wife and their children was read and accepted. Another from Newtown in the county of Chester on behalf of William Clare, his wife and family, and likewise a certificate from Nailsworth in Gloucestershire on behalf of Sansom Cary coming over hither with his wife were read and accepted. A certificate issued on behalf of Richard Lewis, his wife and son. Edward Pilkington and Mary Webb clear to marry, they being desirous to accomplish such at Concord. Benjamin Bryan and Mary Clifton declare their intentions to marry, the parents of both being present, give their consent. Lawrence Growden desires a certificate be sent after him, he being gone for England. Thomas Griffith moves for a certificate on behalf of William Dun.

27/6/1714 - Benjamin Bryan and Mary Clifton clear to marry, the young man producing a certificate from Burlington. Dennis Rochford, a young man who was a Friends son and was put out by Friends, being now out of his time and setting up his trade of a potter, is lame and cannot well carry on his trade without some help, is in want of assistance. A certificate for Lawrence Growden to be sent after him to Great Britain. A certificate for William Dun to go to the Falls Monthly Meeting. Likewise, a certificate for Richard Lewis and his family to Abington Monthly Meeting was read and approved.

24/7/1714 - John Hudson and Abigail Stretton declare their intentions to marry, the young mans parents being present, gave their consent. George Claypoole intends to take a voyage to the West Indies upon his lawful occasions and requests a certificate. Complaint being made that Randal Spakeman and Ralph Jackson have entered an action against Edward Pleadwell and John Derborow again upon the same matter.

29/8/1714 - Isaac Warner and Mary Salway clear to marry, the young man producing in writing his mothers consent. James Logan and Sarah Read declare their intentions to marry, the said James producing a certificate from Great Britain. A certificate on behalf of George Claypoole was read and approved. William Green intends to return to Europe and requests a certificate. Paul Saunders is fallen into poverty and having divers small children, requests assistance from Friends. A certificate on behalf of Issac Barton and his wife from the nation of Ireland was read and recorded. Friends appointed to speak with Randal Spakeman report that he will not withdraw the action entered against John Derborow and Edward Pleadwell. Gabriel Thomas complains against Richard Hill.

26/9/1714 - Application was made concerning the estate of Robert Borrow, deceased, and Deborah his widow, in order to assist her with advice. A certificate on behalf of Henry Miller and his wife from Minehead Monthly Meeting was read and approved. Friends are desired to bring in an account of the estate of Susannah Worrilow, deceased. Hugh Lowden complains against Benjamin Farman. Peter Stretch lays before this meeting that his son Daniel is removed into Salem County in New Jersey and desires a certificate.

31/10/1714 - A letter from Concord Monthly Meeting in relation to Eliza'th Webb was read, which seems not to be satisfactory. There is a difference between Andrew Hamilton and Pente. Teague. Daniel Walton, Jun'r, and Elisabeth Clifton declare their intentions to marry, the parents of both being present and gave their consent and the young man producing a certificate from the Monthly Meeting of Abington. Dennis Rochford and Elisabeth Hudson declare their intentions to marry. Thomas Nicholas and his wife, who are gone out of town into the county of Chester, desire a certificate.

28/11/1714 - A certificate on behalf of Francis Erott from Ireland was read and recorded. Dennis Rochford and Elisabeth Hudson clear to marry. James and Mary Barrot desire a certificate to Springfield Monthly Meeting. Francis Knowles and Sarah Lee declare their intentions to marry, the young mans parents being present and consenting. John Owen and Jane Harriott declare their intentions to marry, the parents of both being present and consenting. John Dillwyn and Mercy Pears declare their intentions to marry, the young man's mother being present and consenting. There is a difference between Samuel Massey and Joseph Growden. Richard Townsend lays before this meeting that it is in his mind to visit Friends in Maryland and Virginia and desires a certificate.

25/12/1714 - A certificate issued for James Barrot.

25/1/1715 - A certificate from Abington Monthly Meeting on behalf of Jacob Shoemaker and his wife and children was read and accepted. Isaac Barton and his wife request a certificate to the Monthly Meeting of Chester. A certificate from Minehead Monthly Meeting in Great Britain on behalf of John Davis was read. Robert Lodge, removing into the country, desires a certificate.

29/2/1715 - A letter from Elisabeth Webb gives satisfaction. John Mitchener, who is gone into the country to dwell, desires a certificate.

27/3/1715 - Samuel Taylor, who has gone to live at Duckcreek, desires a certificate. A certificate on behalf of Robert Lodge and his wife, and another on behalf of John Mitchener and his wife, were read and approved.

24/4/1715 - Anthony Morris, on behalf of William Harvey, desires a certificate for himself and his wife, being gone into the country to dwell. There is a difference between John Widdowfield and Sampson Case. Christopher Blackbourne complains that Thomas Makin oweth him money. John Oxley produced a certificate from Bridgtown in Barbadoes and also desires our certificate, he having business of concern in Great Britain. Thomas Shoemaker and Mary Powell declare their intentions to marry, the young man's parents being present and he producing a certificate from Abington, the relations of the young woman also gave consent. A certificate issued for William Harvey and Judith, his wife. A certificate from the two weeks meeting at London on behalf of Joshua Gill was read and approved. John Richmond from Jamacia, being bound for Great Britain, desires a certificate.

26/6/1715 - Thomas Rakestraw, intending to marry again, requests a certificate to Abington Monthly Meeting. A certificate issued for John Richmond. Joseph Rednap and Elizabeth Germain declare their intentions to marry, Joseph advised to bring a certificate to the next meeting and Friends are appointed to assist the said Elizabeth, being a widow, in settling a due proportion for the service of her former husbands children. Daniel England, Junr, and Elizabeth Coleman declare their intentions to marry, the fathers of both to either come or send their consent in writing. Clement Plumstead desires a certificate, his occasions require his going for England. Anthony Morris, likewise, desires a certificate to England. A certificate on behalf of John Lloyd and Sarah his wife, and another on behalf of William Bissell and four children, from Storbridge Monthly Meeting in Worcestershire were read and recorded. Francis Erritt,, having brought a certificate to this meeting and being about to remove to Chester, desires something be written upon the back thereof to certify his behavior since his arrival amongst us.

30/7/1715 - A certificate issued for Thomas Rakestraw. A certificate requested for Cephas Child. Joseph Rednap and Elizabeth Germain clear to marry, he producing a certificate from Providence. George James, having removed to inhabit in the County of Bucks, requests a certificate. Nathaniel Griffiths and Elizabeth Badcock clear to marry, consent of both parents obtained. Friends appointed to enquire into the necessity of John Prichard report that they find it very miserable. Randall Janey, intending to remove himself to Bermuda, desires a certificate therein unto. Caleb Jacobs intends for Barbadoes and desires a certificate.

28/8/1715 - Jonathan Cockshall and Martha Kight clear to marry, Jonathan producing a certificate from Haverford Monthly Meeting. Francis Daniel Pastorus and Peter Shoemaker complain against Susannah Cassel, that she refuseth to pay them a debt due to the estate of Paul Woolf, deceased.

25/9/1715 - Joseph Knight and Abigail Antin clear to marry, Joseph producing a certificate from Abington and his father being here, declared his consent.

30/10/1715 - Upon enquiry into Thomas Miller's clearness, there does not appear such a certainty of his wife's death in England. Therefore, it is the sense of this meeting that Thomas, before he can marry amongst Friends, must procure an undoubted testimony of said wifes death. Friends appointed to enquire into Thomas Peters, Junr's, clearness informs this meeting that Thomas is under some engagements to a woman in Boston. A certificate for David Palmer read and signed.

27/11/1715 - Thomas Chalkley desires a certificate, he intending to Bermuda upon business. Christopher Blackburn desires a certificate, having upon his mind to visit Friends on Long Island and New England.

24/12/1715 - Elizabeth Whartnaby desires a certificate to visit Friends on Long Island, Rhode Island and the adjacent parts. A certificate on behalf of Christopher Blackburn was read and approved. John Hart, desiring to settle at Salem, desires a certificate from this meeting.

30/1/1716 - Joseph Taylor and Sarah Fisher clear to marry, the young womans parents consenting. Jonathan Dickinson requests a certificate on behalf of his son Jonathan touching his clearness to marry. Christopher complains against Robert Bonell, that he was in his debt. Abraham Bickley complains against Thomas Wilson and David Powell, that they are indebted to him.

27/2/1716 - Certificates for Jonathan Dickins and John Hart were read and approved. Francis Richardson desires a certificate in relation to marriage. Hugh Durborow complained against William Coates, that he is justly indebted to him.

25/3/1716 - Friends appointed to enquire into the complaint of the Widow Fairman against Nathan Stanbury report they find him in debt to her for the sum of four pounds, nineteen shillings. A certificate for Francis Richardson was read and approved. Susannah Cassel complains against Thomas Masters, about the settlement or bounds of her lands.

29/4/1716 - Thomas Thomson and Josiah Langdale, having thoughts of returning home via the West Indies, desire a certificate from this meeting. Their certificates from the Monthly Meetings to which they belong, viz; Thomas Thomsons from Hitching in the County of Harford, in Great Britain, dated 28/12/1714, and Josiah Langfords from Skipsea in the eastern part of Yorkshire, dated 28/1/1714, were read at this meeting. A certificate for Joseph Buckley from the two weeks meeting at Devonshire House in London, dated 16/2/1716, was read and recorded. A certificate for Henry Parsons was read and recorded. A certificate from Abington on behalf of George Shoemaker was read and recorded. Caleb Jacobs, who had been to Brabadoes on business, brought a certificate from thence.

27/5/1716 - Walter Newberry, having thoughts of returning home, desires a certificate from this meeting, he having produced a certificate from Salem in New England and Portsmouth on Rhoad Island. Thomas Miller and Hannah Emerson, having declared their intentions to marry and Thomas producing testimony of the certainty of his first wifes death in England, are clear to marry. Jacob Usher and Jane Brientnall declare their intentions to marry.

31/6/1716 - Anthony Morris, who had been visiting Friends in some parts of Europe, has now returned and brings a certificate from the second days morning meeting in London. Christopher Blackbourne, who has been visiting Friends on Long Island, Rhoad Island and some parts of New England, has returned and brought a certificate from the Monthly Meeting in Newport, Rhoad Island. A certificate for John Cooper and his wife Rachel, dated 25/2/1716 from Swanzey, in Wales, was read and recorded. William Hudson makes application for a certificate on behalf of Thomas Eldridge who is removed from hence with his family into Chester County.

28/7/1716 - John Tomlinson and his wife bring a certificate from the Monthly Meeting at the Moat in Ireland. Abraham Bickley makes application for a certificate on behalf of Samuel Hillary who intends for Ireland at the first opportunity. Hugh Lowdon of the city of Philadelphia, being guilty of some violent and dangerous expressions and actions contrary to christianity, is hereby disowned. Thomas

Nixon, by Anthony Morris, applies for a certificate, he being upon urgent business to Great Britain. Caleb Jacobs intends to Barbadoes on business and has some thoughts of going thence to Europe and requests a certificate.

26/8/1716 - The matter of complaint of Thomas Potts against Thomas Shute is fully ended. William Tidmarsh and Hannah Emlen declare their intention to marry, Friends appointed to assist the widow in the settlement of what shall be proper for her children. Anthony Morris makes application on behalf of his son William Morris who is intended to Barbadoes and desires a certificate.

30/9/1716 - William Tidmarsh and Hannah Emlen clear to marry, but the settlement of the widows estate upon the children as she proposed and William agreed was not perfected. John Carver and Isabel Welding clear to marry, he producing a certificate from Abington Monthly Meeting where he belongs. Samuel Righton and Thomasine Marshall declare their intention to marry. Samuel Lewis and Elizabeth Morris clear to marry, Samuel producing a certificate from the Monthly Meeting in Barbadoes and his father consenting in writing.

28/10/1716 - George Emlen desires a certificate to the Monthly Meeting of Abington in relation to marriage.

25/11/1716 - Griffith Owen desires a certificate , intending on visiting Friends on Long Island, Rhoad Island and some parts of New England. He also makes application for a certificate on behalf of his son Edward who is under necessity of going to Great Brittain upon business. Samuel Lewis desires a certificate , he intending to Barbadoes upon business. Friends appointed to look into the condition of John Sapas report that he is in great want. Isaac Norris requests Friends advice on Margaret Beardsley's will.

22/12/1716 - Certificates for Samuel Lewis and Samuel Taylor were read and signed. John Mifflin makes application for a certificate to Duck Creek with respect to marriage.

29/1/1717 - Thomas Griffith and Mary Norris, Junr, clear to marry, the parents on both sides consenting and Thomas producing a certificate from the three weeks meeting in Ireland and another from Jamacia. A certificate for John Mifflin and another for Thomas Barnes was signed.

26/2/1717 - John Wilson desires a certificate, intending by the first opportunity on business for Great Britain.

31/3/1717 - Richard Harrison and Hannah Norris clear to marry, the parents of the young woman giving consent and the young man producing a certificate from West river, in Maryland. William Armstrong and James Graham, intending to return to Great Britain, desire certificates from this meeting. Richard Robinson, also intending a voyage to Great Britain, desires a certificate. Friends are appointed to assist the widow Parker with advice. William Fishbourne, one of Thomas Story's attorneys, complains against Nathan Stanbury, that he doth not pay the money due the grandchildren of Jonas Langford, one of who's husbands comes as representing Thomas Story. Nathan Stanbury acknowledges himself in debt and says he will take all care to discharge it. Henry Child complains against the widow Mary Howard for want of money she oweth.

28/4/1717 - Friends appointed to get in the money lent Paul Saunders report that his widow is very poor and cannot pay it. The same Friends, having dealt with the widow for her disorderly walking, which they fear is too much ground for and the grossness of which they testify against her, declare her to be no member of this community. Daniel Durborow and Sarah Coleman declare their intention to marry. William Smith complains against Stephen Jackson, that there is a difference between them, as the said Stephen is concerned with the estate of Benjamin Chaymbers. Walter Long desires a certificate from this meeting, he intending to remove and settle in Great Britain. Thomas Masters complains against David Powell. Friends are appointed to deal with David and put him upon paying Thos. Masters what he is indebted to him.

26/5/1717 - Richard Moor reports that his complaint against Mary Howard is ended. Daniel Durdorow and Sarah Coleman clear to marry, relatives on both sides being present and consenting. Samson Davis and Christian Shute clear to marry, their relatives concurring. Jane Brientnall makes application for a certificate, she having a concern to visit Friends in Maryland or elsewhere. Jonathan Dickinson makes application for a certificate on behalf of his son Joseph, he intending, with his parents consent, to Great Britain. John Durborow, intending a voyage to Jamaica on trade, applies to this meeting for a certificate.

30/6/1717 - A certificate for Elisabeth Whartnaby was read and signed. John Waln and Jane Mifflin clear to marry, having parents consent. Nathaniel Edgcomb requests a certificate and, likewise, William Hudson, on behalf of his son William, requests one in order to marry. The business between Nathan Satanbury's and Thomas Story's attorneys being discoursed at this meeting, it is their sense that Nathan ought to pay the eldest daughter part of the money that was left by Jonas Langfords will. Richard Hough and Deborah Gumley declare their intention to marry, Deborah being a widow with two children, Friends are desired to assist her in the settlement of what she thinks fit for her children. Richard Woodworth brings a paper condemning himself for his former miscarriage and desires to be accepted amongst Friends again. John Shiers brought a certificate from the meeting of Marsden in Lancaster and desires a few lines from this meeting. Isaac Shoemaker complains against the widow Austin, that she does him wrong.

27/7/1717 - A certificate for William Hudson, Jr, and one for John Shiers were read. There having been some objection last meeting to Joseph Dickinsons certificate, which is cleared, a certificate was read and signed. Jacob Usher and Mary Bacon clear to marry. Richard Hough and Deborah Gumley clear to marry, the said Richard producing a certificate from the Falls Monthly Meeting and the widow making settlement on her children. Friends are appointed to prepare a certificate for Richard Woodworth. The Friends appointed to enquire into the complaint of Isaac Shoemaker against the widow Austin report that the difference cannot at present be settled, there being an orphan concerned it must lye until he come of age. James Wilkenson desires a certificate, intending for Great Brittain.

25/8/1717 - A certificate on behalf of Robert Penrose, his wife Mary and their two daughters Margaret and Ann Penrose of Ballykenny in the county of Wickloff in Ireland was read and accepted. Also, a certificate from Dublin on behalf of Christopher Penrose, the son of the said Rob't. and Mary. was read and accepted. Aaron Goforth and Mary Pool clear to marry, the parents being present, consenting. Joseph Gray and Mary Hastings clear to marry, the said Joseph producing a certificate from Abington Monthly Meeting. A certificate on behalf of Thomas Barger, his wife and family, from the meeting of Clomwell in the Kingdom of Ireland, was read and accepted. Benjamin Wait and Jane Nixon declare their intention to marry, the parents being present, consenting. A certificate on behalf of John Head, his wife and four children, from a Monthly Meeting in Mildenhall in the county of Suffolk in Great Brittain, was read and accepted. A certificate on behalf of James Wilkenson and one for Richard Woodworth were signed. Thomas Chalkley intends a voyage to Barbadoes on business and desires a certificate from this meeting. Joseph Brientnall desires a certificate in order to his intended voyage to Barbadoes on account of trade.

29/9/1717 - Friends appointed to inquire into the complaint of Thomas Miller against Rob't. Bonnell report they have dealt with Bonnell, who makes no objection to Thomas's complaint and promises he will pay him in a little time but forasmuch as the debt has been long owing and is justly due, the same Friends should let Robert Bonnell know that unless he make Thomas Miller satisfaction he will be testified against and Thomas left to his liberty to take his action at law against him. Benjamin Waite and Sarah Nickson clear to marry, the parents consenting. Enion Williams desires a certificate, he intending to visit Friends in Maryland and the adjacent parts.

27/10/1717 - Randal Spikeman and Ann Nicholson clear to marry. James Estaugh and Hannah Mereday clear to marry, the woman producing in writing her fathers consent. Edward Jones, Jun'r, late of Merion township, produced a certificate from Haverford Monthly Meeting which was read and recorded. Friends are appointed to enquire into Levine Harberdick's circumstances.

31/11/1717 - Edward Owen on his return for Europe brought a certificate from the Monthly Meeting of Hartshaw in Lancashire which was read and accepted. Jonathan Dickenson applied to this meeting on behalf of his kinsman Jonathan Gale for a certificate of his clearness and conversation while among us. William Paschall makes application in writing and desires to take Sarah England, daughter of Thomas England, deceased, in marriage among Friends. Inasmuch that he is neither by education nor profession among Friends, is the sense of this meeting that they cannot permit his marriage. Hugh Clifton makes application for a certificate.

28/1/1718 - Arthur Starr, intending to remove to Great Britain, desires a certificate from this meeting. Elizabeth Whartnaby, upon her return from Maryland, brought in two certificates which were read and accepted.

25/2/1718 - William Gromett brought in a certificate from the Monthly Meeting held at Wrangle in Lincolnshire, Great Brittain, which was read and accepted.

30/3/1718 - A certificate on behalf of Benjamin Dickenson from the Monthly Meeting at Staintondale in Yorkshire was read and accepted. Thomas Rakestraw desires a certificate in relation to marriage.

27/4/1718 - James Whilton and Katherine Bedworth clear to marry, the said James producing a certificate from the Monthly Meeting at Salem. A certificate for Thomas Rakestraw was signed. Joseph Wood brought a certificate from Mountmelick for himself, his wife and two daughters, which was read and recorded. Humphry Norris brought a certificate of clearness from marriage from Bristol Monthly Meeting. Richard Martin brought a certificate from Holme Monthly Meeting in Cumberland in England which was read and recorded. Christopher Blackburn applies for a certificate on behalf of William Kendal, he being removed to Chester County. The meeting consents that the widow Borden may continue in Friends house in Walnut Street till further order. David Flower complains against Abraham Bickley, that he refused to pay him a debt due from the Boulding's estate.

25/5/1718 - John Gale desires a certificate, he, with the consent and direction of his father, is intended to Great Brittain. A certificate from the mens meeting in Clonwell in Ireland for William Taylor was read and recorded. Nicholas Hitchcock applies for a certificate. Nicholas Walln applies for a certificate for his son John who is removed into Chester County.

29/6/1718 - A copy of Lydia Nortons certificate was read and application made for a certificate for her from this meeting. William Hinton and

Jane Knubley clear to marry, he having the probationary consent in a letter from his father. A certificate for John Gale was approved and signed. Ebenezer Robinson produced a certificate from the two weeks meeting in London which was read and recorded. Miles Strickland produced a certificate from the mens meeting in Dublin which was read and recorded. Sampson Cary, per Thomas Cannon, applied for a certificate for him and also for James Higgs who came into these parts with him, he being removed to Bristol in Bucks County. William Taylor applies for a certificate to Chester Monthly Meeting with respect to marriage.

26/7/1718 - Nehemiah Allen, Junr. and Hannah Lownes clear to marry, the parents concerned consenting. Enion Williams makes application for a certificate, intending to go to the West Indies upon business of trade and merchandize.

31/8/1718 - John Davison produced a certificate from Swarthmore Monthly Meeting and Issac Hadman produced one from Sedbergh Monthly Meeting in Yorkshire, which were read and accepted. Anthony Morris makes application for a certificate for his son William Morris in Barbadoes, touching on his clearness and conversation. There being one prepared, it is ordered to be approved and signed. Daniel Flexney, son of Daniel Flexney, produced a certificate from Oxfordshire, which was read and well received. Isaac Shoemaker informs his meeting that Jane Austin did not hold to the former order touching the land that lies in dispute between him and her and her children. Friends are appointed to let Jane Austin know that it is the order of this meeting that she desist from cutting the timber or using the land til the orphans come to age, that the same be fully settled. Sampson Davis and his wife desire a certificate to Abington Monthly Meeting.

28/9/1718 - One of the Friends appointed to speak to Jane Austin reports they had spoken to her, and her brother came to acquaint them that she expressed her conformity to the order of the meeting. William Fishbourne, as attorney to Thomas Story, exec'r. of Jonas Langford reports that Matthew? Langford has not made satisfaction according to the advice of this meeting. There is a difference depending between George Painter and Elias Hugg.

26/10/1718 - John Knight and Hannah Badcock clear to marry, the parents concerned consenting. Isaac Norris applied to this meeting for a certificate for James Robinson, he intending to settle in Nottingham. Anthony Morris applied for a certificate for John Cann, who is removed into Chester County. William Hudson applied for a certificate on behalf of Benjamin Holmes. John Owen applied by Anthony Morris for a certificate. Caleb Jacob applied for a certificate, he intending for Bristol in Great Brittain with his wife to settle there. Dennis Rochford has sustained a considerable loss.

30/11/1718 - Ebenezer Robinson and Mary Hugg clear to marry, the
parents of the young woman being present and consenting. A
certificate for Benjamin Holmes was read and signed - also one for
James Robinson, another for John Cann and one for John Owen.
Joseph Martin applied for a certificate to Ireland, he intending to
return thither to settle. Christopher Penrose applied for a certificate
to Middletown touching on his clearness with respect to marriage.
Rebeckah Richardson complains against Clement Plumstead, that he
with - held from her some writings that she, on her going to
Barbadoes, left in his hands to her great damage. Richard Smith
brought a certificate from Newgarden which was read and recorded.
Joseph Martin produced a certificate from the mens meeting held at
Old Castle in the county of Meath in Ireland, and on the back a
certificate from New Garden, his last abode, which were read and
recorded.

27/12/1718 - Edward Blake applied for a certificate, he intending toward
York and Boston. Joseph Noble applied for a certificate to Burlington
touching his clearness with respect to marriage.

27/1/1719 - A certificate for Edward Blake and one for Joseph Noble
were read and signed. Isaac Norris, on behalf of his son Joseph,
applied for a certificate, he with his parents consent, intending for
Great Brittain. Francis Richardson applied for a certificate.

24/2/1719 - Daniel Hoodt and Esther Oldman clear to marry, the parents
concerned consenting. A certificate on behalf of Hugh Clifton from
Abington was read and recorded. A certificate for Francis Richardson
was read and signed. James Dubry and Elizabeth Waln clear to
marry, the parents on both sides being present and consenting.
Abraham Bickley applied for a certificate to Burlington, touching on
his clearness with respect to marriage. William Robins applied for a
certificate, he intending to remove with his family to settle in
Maryland.

30/3/1719 - Evan Thomas and his wife, lately come from Europe, are in
great want.

26/4/1719 - James Lloyd brought a certificate from Dudley Monthly
Meeting for himself and wife, which was read and recorded.

31/5/1719 - Friends appointed to settle the difference between Rebeckah
Richardson and Clement Plumstead brought to the meeting their
agreement in writing. John Wilson brought a certificate from the
Monthly Meeting at Hartshaw in Lancashire, which was read and
recorded. Daniel Flexney, Junr., produced a certificate from the
Monthly Meeting of Witney in the county of Oxon, which was read.
The said Daniel, being bound for Gr't. Brittain again, applied for a
certificate from this meeting.

28/6/1719 - David Brientnall makes application for a certificate on behalf
of John Tomlinson and his wife who are removed into Kennet in
Chester County.

24/7/1719 - Thomas Knight and Sarah Clifton declare their intention to
marry, the parents of each being present, consented. A certificate
from the Monthly Meeting in Dublin in Ireland certifying Thomas
Lindley's clearness in respect to marriage was read and recorded.

30/8/1719 - Thomas Knight and Sarah Clifton clear to marry, the young
man bringing a certificate from Abington Monthly Meeting. Daniel
Smith, Junr. and Mary Hoodt declare their intention to marry, the
parents of each being present, consented. Isaac Hadwin applied for a
certificate, he intending to return to Europe by the first opportunity.
John Oxley brought a certificate from the two weeks meeting in
London which was read and recorded. He intending on a trading
voyage to the West Indies, requests a certificate from this meeting.

27/9/1719 - A certificate for Jane Harper was approved and signed.
Thomas Linley and Hannah Durborow clear to marry. Application
being made for a certificate for Ann Oxley, she being moved to
Burlington. Daniel Smith, Junr. and Mary Hoodt clear to marry, the
young man bring a certificate from Burlington.

25/10/1719 - It doth not appear that Ann Oxley now stands so related to
Friends that a certificate can be granted. Edward Brooks and
Elisabeth Sneed clear to marry, he bringing a certificate from
Abington Monthly Meeting. Jane Brientnall, on behalf of Rachel
Brooksby, applies for a certificate, the said Rachel being removed to
Nottingham. Aaron Goforth desires a certificate, having it upon his
mind to visit Friends in parts of Maryland in company with our friend
Anthony Morris.

26/12/1719 - Thomas Wharton has left a legacy of five pounds to be
distributed among the poor. Randal Spikeman complains against John
Knight.

25/1/1720 - George Shiers applied for a certificate to Middletown or
Neshaminy in Bucks County with respect to his clearness in marriage.
Christopher Blackthorn on behalf of Benjamin Wait for a certificate
to, Newtown Monthly Meeting.

29/2/1720 - John Smith and Marget Penrose clear to marry, the young
man bringing a certificate from Darby Monthly Meeting. A certificate
from Thomas Whitehead from the two weeks meeting in London was
read and recorded. Robert Penrose applied for a certificate, he
intending to remove with his family to Darby. This meeting desires
Friends to write to Abington meeting on behalf of William Mitchenor,
son of John Mitchenor, that he being underage, was removed as one
of the family. Enion Williams produced a certificate from Barbadoes
and another from Friends in Tredhaven in Maryland and both were

read and well received. Richard Hill applied for a certificate on behalf of Lloyd Zachary, he intending to settle in Maryland.

27/3/1720 - A certificate from Barking Monthly Meeting in Great Brittain for John Brown and his wife was read and recorded. Thomas Chalkley brought a certificate from the Monthly Meeting of Horslydown in Southwark, London, which was read.

24/4/1720 - A certificate from Hammersmith in Middlesex in Great Brittain on behalf of Benjamin Ellis was read and recorded. Mary Wing, having a certificate from the Monthly Meeting at Sandwich in New England, she being on her way home desires a certificate from this meeting. A certificate for Mary Guess was approved. John Goodson applied for a certificate on behalf of his grandson Samuel Cart who intends for a voyage for Great Brittain. Samuel Preston, on behalf of William Saunders, applied for a certificate, he intending to Great Brittain. Whereas John Lock of this city hath wickedly and scandalously behaved himself, leaving his wife and children to the charity of others or to greatly suffer, this meeting gives testimony against him for his wicked practices and disown him from any practices with us.

29/5/1720 - Thomas Carleton applied for a certificate, he intending to remove to Kennett Township in Chester County. Thomas Griffith applies for a certificate on behalf of John Knowles, he being removed to Abington meeting.

26/6/1720 - A certificate ...ary Smith, daughter of Casper Hoodt, was read and signed. Thomas Hood complained of a matter of difference between him and James Steel. Thomas Whitehead and Samuel Overton, having brought certificates from Great Brittain and now proposing to return, desires a certificate from this meeting. A certificate for Elisabeth Teague, who intends on a visit with our friend Marget Paine to Maryland and adjacent parts, was read and signed. A certificate from the Monthly Meeting of Market Street in the county of Hartford in Great Brittain and one from the quarterly meeting of Pullenhall in the county of Bedford, and another from the ministering meeting in London, for Marget Paine were read and recorded. Joseph Edgar brought a certificate from the Monthly Meeting in Folkestone in the county of Kent in Great Brittain for himself and his wife which was read and recorded. Benjamin Ellis applied for a certificate to Chesterfield meeting in West Jersey, touching on his clearness in relation to marriage. Hugh Clifton applied for a certificate, he intending to remove to Newtown, in West Jersey.

28/8/1720 - Isaac Lenior and Mary Cordery clear to marry, the young womans parents being present, consenting. William Adams applied for a certificate, he being on a return to Barbadoes. Jane Ireland and Hannah Albison have applied for certificates. Also Mary Coates. This meeting being informed that John Farmer holds meetings in several places, publishes that he stands disowned.

25/9/1720 - William Dunn, having intended for Great Brittain, produced a certificate from Burlington Monthly Meeting directed to Friends in Bristol in Brittain, but the said William Dunn, determining to settle here, his certificate was read and recorded. Enion Williams, having a concern to visit Friends in parts of Maryland and Virginia, desires a certificate from this meeting. Isaac Marriott applied for a certificate, he intending for Great Brittain, and desired that his wife may be included therein, she being in England, he intends to go to her. Jacob Dubree, on behalf of his son James Dubree, applies for a certificate, he intending to move with his wife to Abington.

30/10/1720 - Thomas Chalkley informs this meeting that John Brown has left by will to this meeting a legacy of ten pounds and asks on behalf of the widow asks the meetings acceptance. Friends appointed to let Richard Robinson know of the resentment of this meeting on the report of his speaking slightingly of the King informs the meeting that Richard acknowledges himself sorry for what he had said. Daniel Hodgson applied for a certificate, he intending for Barbadoes on business.

27/11/1720 - Thomas Miller applied for a certificate to Chester Monthly Meeting touching his clearness in regard to marriage. Friends appointed to enquire into Daniel Hodson's clearness report they found it not proper to draw a certificate for him. Friends report they found John Lloyd in want of some assistance and that they let him have 20 pounds, which this meeting approves. William Blackfan and Eleanor Wood declare their intentions of marriage, the young man expected to bring a certificate from the Falls meeting whence he belongs. Samuel Fisher moved for a certificate to the Monthly Meeting of Burlington, touching on his clearness in respect to marriage.

31/1/1721 - William Blackfan and Eleanor Wood clear to marry, the parents and relations concerned consenting. John Bettle and Lydia Bolton clear to marry, the relations and Friends concerned, consenting. Joseph Paschal and Elisabeth Coates declare their intentions of marriage, the young man to produce a certificate from Darby Monthly Meeting. Application being made on behalf of Robert Bonnall and his wife for a certificate for them who are removing into West Jersey.

28/2/1721 - Friends appointed to dispose of the lot belonging to Friends next to Evan Owens report they have let it to Thomas Cannon at the rate of nine pounds a year for three lives, viz: his life, his wifes and his son Williams, and if they all should not have 21 years then nevertheless, he and his heirs shall hold it that time under the restrictions and limitations that he do not follow the Chandlers business of making soap and candles on that lot.

26/3/1721 - Nathaniel Edgcomb hath several times moved for a certificate. Joseph Lownes and Sarah Tidmarsh clear to marry, the parents being present and consenting.

30/4/1721 - Thomas Pennington and Martha Steel clear to marry, Thomas bringing a certificate from Abington Monthly Meeting and also his mothers consent. William Shute and Elisabeth Steel clear to marry, the parents being present and consenting.

28/5/1721 - Thomas Oldman produced a certificate from Chester Monthly Meeting, he intending to remove there, which was ordered to be recorded. William Carter and Mary Sutton clear to marry, Williams wife having not been dead a twelvemonth but it being almost a year, the meeting permits it. Mary Tomkins, for herself and her son John Tomkins, produced a certificate from the two weeks meeting in London which was read and recorded. Esther Clear hath a concern to visit Friends in Great Brittain.

25/6/1721 - Thomas Denham desires a certificate to Friends in Bristol and elsewhere in Great Brittain, he intending on business. Jacob Coffin, Jun'r, applied for a certificate to Friends in Newtown concerning his clearness in respect to marriage. Benjamin Ellis requested a certificate to Friends in London, he intending on business.

29/7/1721 - A certificate for Esther Clear was signed. A certificate for Margaret Paine was moved for by Richard Hill, she intending to return by John Ainnis to Great Brittain. Samuel Preston moved for a certificate for Ennion Williams with request to marriage. Thomas Oldman applied for a certificate to the Monthly Meeting at Darby, in Chester County, touching on his clearness in respect to marriage. A matter of difference between Joseph Richardson and the Executors of Samuel Richardson is brought before this meeting.

27/8/1721 - Our friend Anthony Morris is deceased. This meeting disowns Stephen Jackson. Edward Brooks made application for a certificate to Abington meeting for him and his wife, they intending to remove to Frankford. There is a matter of difference between John Leech, Ebenezer Large and John Jones.

24/9/1721 - Nicholas Waln applied on behalf of his son William Waln for a certificate to Chester Monthly Meeting in respect to marriage. Application was made for a certificate for Samuel Mifflin, who intends a voyage to the West Indies.

29/10/1721 - The difference between Ebenezer Large, John Leech and John Jones is ended. Edward Weston and Hannah Hambly clear to marry. Friends appointed to speak to John Lawson report that he would not support his conduct, but hoped to be careful not to give offense in the future. Nicholas Tucker moved for a certificate to

Byberry, he intending to settle within the limits of that meeting. Joseph Edger applied for a certificate to Oxford meeting.

26/11/1721 - Joseph England and Elizabeth Brown clear to marry, Joseph producing a certificate from Salisbury Monthly Meeting. A certificate for John Ogden, one for Joseph Elgar and one for Nicholas Tucker were approved and signed. A certificate for Mary Boulding to Abington meeting was read and signed. Elizabeth Cockfeld, who married some years ago from among Friends, sent in a paper ... approving the discipline of Friends. Nicholas Waln, on behalf of his son Nicholas Waln, applied for a certificate to Chester meeting touching his clearness with respect to marriage. Richard Martin applied for a certificate to Great Brittain, he intending on business.

23/12/1721 - Joseph Thornton produced a certificate from the Monthly Meeting of Sherington in Bucks in Great Brittain, which was read and recorded. The said Joseph, intending to return to Great Brittain, desires a certificate from this meeting. Isaac Norris, on behalf of his son Isaac, moved for a certificate for him, intending for business to Great Brittain. Thomas Miller complains against George Shoemaker.

30/1/1722 - Friends appointed to enquire into Joseph Thorntons clearness report they have met with some obstruction and they have not prepared a certificate and he declines his proposed voyage for Europe. John Smith, Jun'r, and Rebeckah Blackbourn clear to marry, John Smith producing a certificate from Salem meeting. Samuel Ogden, on himself and Esher his wife, produced a certificate from Chester meeting which was read and recorded. George House and Esther Warner declare their intentions of marriage. Jacob Medcalf and Hannah Hudson, Jun'r, declare their intentions of marriage. Joseph Barger applied for a certificate of his clearness with respect to marriage.

27/2/1722 - George House and Esther Warner clear to marry. Jacob Metcalf and Hannah Hudson clear to marry, Jacob producing a certificate from Newtown Monthly Meeting. Thomas Coborn and Elisabeth Cockfield declare their intentions of marriage.

25/3/1722 - Thomas Cobourn and Elisabeth Cockfield clear to marry, Thomas producing a certificate from Chester Monthly Meeting and the parents on both sides consenting, Friends are appointed to enquire what provision the widow has made for her child. Thomas Hart and Mary Combs clear to marry, his parents consenting. John Maules certificate was read and Thomas Chalkley is appointed to prepare one for him to Salem Monthly Meeting. Samuel Bolton produced a certificate for himself and wife from Abington Monthly Meeting. which was read and recorded. A certificate for Esther Tomlinson was read. Application was made for a certificate on behalf of Richard Moore and his wife who are removed to Maryland.

29/4/1722 - John Tomson applied for a certificate, he being removed to Chester. William Lawrence complains against James Steel, that contrary to discipline, James had sued him. Robert Jordan of Virginia produced his certificate from the Monthly Meeting of Chuckatuck, in Nansemond, in Virginia, which was read and approved. A certificate for John Tomkins and his mother was read and signed. Robert Jordan, who has visited these parts in the ministry, now going hence, requested a certificate. William Garrett produced a certificate from the Monthly Meeting at Darby which was recorded.

31/6/1822 - Friends appointed in the complaint of Wm. Lawrence against James Steel report the business ended. William Clear complains against John Cadwallader. Whereas one John Lawson who came into these parts from Great Brittain ... we testify against him, the said John Lawson ... a person not owned by us. A certificate for George and Elisabeth Deeble from the Monthly Meeting of Cork in Ireland was read and recorded. Joshua Lawrence and Amey Liberty declare their intentions of marriage. Thomas Griffith complains against Caleb Jacob and John Haight. James Cooper applied to this meeting for a certificate of his clearness with respect to marriage, to the Falls meeting in the county of Bucks.

28/7/1722 - Joshua Lawrence and Amy Liberty clear to marry.

26/8/1722 - One of the Friends appointed in the case of Samuel Hudson reported they had endeavored to persuade him to the a conformity to the discipline of Friends but he appeared obstinate .... This meeting therefore testify's against him ... for which this meeting disowns him ... and leaves the complainant to his liberty to take what legal measures be best. A certificate from Flushing Monthly Meeting in behalf of Arnold Castle was read and recorded. John Pritchard applied to this meeting for some assistance, he being very poor and unable to support himself. William Shute complained against Thomas Miller, that he was in his debt and would not pay him.

28/10/1722 - The business of Thomas Griffiths, Caleb Jacob and John Haight, Thomas Griffiths, the complainant reported to be over. Thomas Wynn and Mary Warner clear to marry, Thomas bringing a certificate from Haverford meeting and the parents and relations concerned, consenting. Samuel Gilpin and Jane Parker, daughter of John Parker, dec'd, declare their intentions of marriage. Friends are appointed to deal with Clement Plumstead for his late marriage from among Friends. A certificate for Owen Owen and his wife from Darby Monthly Meeting was read and recorded. Richard Lundy complains against Christopher Topham for that he has, contrary to our discipline, sued him.

25/11/1722 - Samuel Gilpin and Jane Parker clear to marry, Samuel bringing a certificate from Concord Monthly Meeting. John Oxley produced a certificate from the Monthly Meeting in Barbadoes and he

intending to return homeward to Barbadoes in a little time, requested
a certificate from this meeting. John Hood and Mary Sneed, daughter
of Wm. Sneed, dec'd, declare their intentions of marriage. Nicholas
Rogers produced a certificate from Chester Monthly Meeting for
himself and Mary his wife.

22/12/1722 - A certificate for John Oxley to Barbadoes was read and
signed. William Hudson applied for a certificate, he with his wife
intending to Great Brittain upon a visit to his folks and business.
Griffith Owen applied for a certificate to Friends in Great Brittain.

29/1/1723 - A certificate from Goshen for William Cundell and his wife
Elisa, who were removed to this place, was read and recorded. A
certificate for Samuel Gray to Chester meeting was read and signed.
Application being made for a certificate for John Appleton ... and
intending to return home to Great Brittain. William Passmore
appeared at this meeting and acknowledged the breach of discipline
he made many years past in marriage ... which acknowledgement
Friends accept well of William and are glad that he has reconciled
himself to Friends in England.

26/2/1723 - The matter of difference between Joseph Richardson and the
Exec'. of Samuel Richardson is ended. Friends appointed upon the
complaint of John Durborow against the Exec'rs. and Trustees of
James Atkinson ... report that Ralph Jackson, pursuant to a minute
of this meeting in 1714, did not proceed with Randal Spikeman in law
against John Durborow and Edward Pledwell, but that Randal,
notwithstanding the sense and direction of this meeting in 1714,
carried on the action commenced at law against the said Durborow
and Pledwell and justifies his proceeding therin in opposition to the
rule and discipline of Friends, upon which this meeting testifies
against him and disowns him.

31/3/1723 - A paper of Clement Plumstead ... was read ... desiring this
meeting to pass by the offense and breach of discipline which he had
made in his marriage from among Friends, which the meeting was
disposed and doth accept his acknowledgment. Hugh Durborow and
Hannah Allison declare their intentions of marriage, Friends
appointed to enquire into the widows circumstances and what she has
done for her children. Robert Daws, from Barbadoes, produced a
certificate from Bridgetown Monthly Meeting and he proposing to
return in a little time, desired a certificate from this meeting. Joseph
Barger applied for a certificate to Duck Creek Monthly Meeting, he
intending to settle in those parts.

28/4/1723 - Benjamin Kidd, who is upon a visit of love among us,
produced a certificate from the Monthly Meeting of Settle in
Yorkshire, and another from the meeting in York city, both of which
were read. Samuel Dickes brought a certificate from the Monthly
Meeting in Bristol which was read and accepted well. Likewise, John

Stamper brought a certificate from the Monthly Meeting of Pardsay Cragg in Cumberland, in Great Brittain, which was read and well accepted. Joseph Barger, desiring that his wife may be joined with him in the certificate he applied for, the same is deferred until next meeting. A certificate for Josiah Langdale, Margaret his wife and their two children, from Bridlington Monthly Meeting at Skypsea in Great Brittain, and another one from the quarterly meeting held in the City of York, were read and well accepted, and tho' our dear friend Josiah did not live to reach us, yet his widow and children being here, these certificates are ordered to be recorded.

26/5/1723 - A certificate from Westbury Monthly Meeting on Long Island for Robert Dunkan was read.

30/6/1723 - Thomas Masters, on behalf of his son Thomas, applied for a certificate to the Monthly Meeting at Flushing on Long Island in respect to his clearness in marriage. Thomas Graisley, for himself, wife and two children, and his aged father and mother, produced a certificate from the Monthly Meeting of Rudgley in Stafford in Great Brittain , which was read, approved and given up to him again, he intending to the Jerseys for settlement. James Logan made application for a certificate to Friends in Great Brittain, he intending there in the ship Lonson Hope, John Annis, Commander, now near sailing, upon business.

27/7/1723 - A certificate for Thomas Masters, Jun'r, to the Monthly Meeting at Flushing on Long Island, one for James Logan to Great Brittain, one for Joseph Holms, wrote on the backside of that he brought from London, one for Jonathan Biles to Crosswicks, one for John Roberts to Merrion, one for Caleb Ranstead to Abington and one for Philip James to Great Brittain were read and signed. A certificate for Lloyd Zachary from Westhaven in Maryland was read, and he, with the approbation of his uncle Hill, intending on a voyage to London, this meeting certifies on his Maryland certificate their concurrence.

27/10/1723 - Joseph Brientnall and Esther Parker clear to marry, their parents being present and consenting. Isaac Bolton produced a certificate from Abington Monthly Meeting which was read and recorded.

31/11/1723 - John Nichols and Jane Roberts clear to marry, their parents consenting. Esther Clear produced the certificate she took from this meeting when she went on her visit to Great Brittain. Application was made on behalf of George Dible for a certificate to Providence meeting in Chester County, he proposing to settle thereabouts.

28/12/1723 - Caleb Jacobs and Mary Widdowfield clear to marry, Friends appointed to enquire that due care was taken for the widows children. Samuel Ogden applied for a certificate to Chester Monthly

Meeting, he intending to remove with his wife and family into Chetser County.

27/1/1724 - Benjamin Clark applied to this meeting for a certificate to Haddonfield Monthly Meeting touching on his clearness with respect to marriage. Isaac Bolton applied for a certificate to Abington Monthly Meeting with respect to clearness ... of marriage. John Williams complained against James Estaugh, that he was in his debt. Ann Bellows has married contrary to our rules of discipline.

24/2/1724 - Jacob Shoemaker and Elizabeth Roberts clear to marry, their parents consenting. Friends are appointed to deliver Humphrey Norris a copy of the minute against him (of disownment for drunkenness and etc.).

29/3/1724 - Abel Fordham and Jane Ireson clear to marry, the meeting satisfied in the consent of parents. John Salkeld having declared he was intrusted by the young mans father in the case and did consent. Benjamin Shoemaker and Sarah Coates clear to marry, parents on both sides consenting. A certificate from the Monthly Meeting of Bridgetown in Barbadoes on behalf of Roberts Davis, who being here on business for a short time, ... Friends are appointed to prepare a few lines on the back of said certificate. A certificate on behalf of Daniel and Emm Evans from the Monthly Meeting of Abington was read and sent to the Womans meeting.

26/4/1724 - Thomas Oliver produced a certificate from the Monthly Meeting at Dolobran in North Wales, dated 25/12/1723/4 was read and recorded. Joseph Richardson, husbandman, lately arrived in this province, produced a certificate from the Monthly Meeting held at Chantry, in the county of York, in Great Brittain, on behalf of himself, his brother Joshua Richardson and their sisters Ann and Rachel Richardson was read and recorded. Ralph Hay, weaver, produced a certificate from the same Monthly Meeting of Chantry, dated 7/12/1734/4 which was read. Thomas Griffith intends shortly to take a voyage for Ireland and desires a certificate from this meeting. William Passmore desires a certificate, intending to go for England. Samuel Preston and Margaret Langdale clear to marry, a settlement on her children agreed to by the widow. Edmund Beaks and Elizabeth Large clear to marry, Edmund producing a certificate from the Monthly Meeting of Chesterfield in Jersey. Arnold Cassel and Lydia Fordham clear to marry, the young man having only his mother living, has her consent and the guardians of the young woman giving theirs.

31/5/1724 - Daniel Thomas and Margaret Zeely clear to marry, Daniel having produced a certificate from Abington Monthly Meeting. Edward Harn produced a certificate from the quarterly meeting held at Horsham in the county of Sussux, Great Britain, for himself and wife which was read and recorded. Richard Clayton applied to this meeting for a certificate to Concord Monthly Meeting. John Brientnall applied for a certificate to Burlington touching his clearness with respect to marriage.

28/6/1724 - A certificate for Richard Clayton to Concord and one for John Brientnall to Burlington were read and signed. Evan Jones brought a certificate from Great Choptank in Maryland, directed to Merion Monthly Meeting or elsewhere, which was read, and he now being a resident of this city tis lodged with Thomas Griffith. Thomas Griffith has publically read William Fishbournes paper of condemnation.

25/7/1724 - Benjamin Kidd, having visited Friends both southward and eastward, has thoughts of leaving us soon and desires a certificate .... Application was made on behalf of Clement Plumstead for a certificate to London in Great Britain.

27/9/1724 - A certificate from Carlisle in Cumberland in Great Brittain for Mary Miller and her son James Miller was read and recorded. Robert Penrose applied for a certificate for himself, wife and family to Darby Monthly Meeting, he removing thither.

25/10/1724 - Thomas Miller complains against Thomas Pryor, that there is a difference between them.

29/11/1724 - William Kelly is disowned. Myles Strickland brought a certificate from Abington Monthly Meeting for himself, wife and daughter Rachel, which was read and well received. William Hudson, on behalf of his son John, applied for a certificate to Newtown Monthly Meeting in respect to his clearness regarding marriage. William Hudson applied to this meeting for a certificate for his son Samuel, he intending for Great Brittain on business and for his health.

26/12/1724 - The difference between Thomas Miller and Thomas Pryor is ended. Friends appointed to deliver to William Kelly the proceedings against him brought a paper from him ... and his hopes of amendment of life, upon which this meeting, in tenderness to him and his family, suspend the publication of the judgement entered against him. John Warder, on behalf of John Williams, son of Enion Williams, applied for a certificate to Nottingham Monthly Meeting where he is removed. Job Goodson and Jane Marriet declare their intentions to marry, John Goodson, Jobs father, being present, approves.

26/1/1725 - Richard Smith and Elisabeth Powell declare their intentions to marry, the said Richard producing a certificate from Burlington. A certificate for George Deeble to Chester Monthly Meeting was read and signed. Richard Orem produced a certificate from Radnor Monthly Meeting. John Warder applied for a certificate on behalf of one Richard Sunly who many years since removed hence into Bucks County,

30/2/1725 - A paper from Nehemiah Allen the Elder wherin he acknowledges his last marriage from among Friends, was accepted.

28/3/1725 - Griffith Owen brought a certificate from the two weeks meeting in London which was read and recorded. Richard Hill, on behalf of Peter Lloyd, requested a certificate, he intending a voyage to London. This meeting being informed that the relatives of the widow Mary Real decline to support her, Friends are appointed to enquire whether she has right to anything left by her father John Redman or her brother Joseph.

25/5/1725 - A certificate for Joshua Emlen from Chester Monthly Meeting was read and accepted. A certificate from Abington Monthly Meeting on behalf of Joseph Edgar and his wife Mary was read and accepted. Friends appointed to inspect into the widow Mary Reals condition report that nothing can be had from the legacies left by her father and bother.

30/5/1725 - Cornelius Denise and Mary Durborow clear to marry, the parents on both sides being present and consenting. John Kinsey, Jun'r, and Mary Kearney declare their intentions to marry, her mother being present, consenting and John bringing a certificate from Woodbridge Monthly Meeting in East Jersey and some lines from John Kinsey and his wife wherin they give their consent. Jacob Shute and Mary Boydon declare their intentions to marry, Jacobs father Thomas Shute being present and consenting. Application made on behalf of Thomas Wharton for a certificate of clearness in respect to marriage to the Monthly Meeting in London.

27/6/1725 - John Kinsey and Mary Kearney clear to marry. James Brethwaite brought a certificate from Newgarden Monthly Meeting which was accepted. Joseph Hughes brought a certificate from Horsleydown meeting, London. A certificate for Rich'd Sundly was read and signed.

24/7/1725 - Caleb Elfrey and Mary Roberts clear to marry, parents and relatives properly concerned, consenting. Edward Horne sent a paper acknowledging himself sorry for his offense against the church in printing that letter called a letter to Joseph England. Isaac Pillar and Sarah Wood clear to marry, the mother of the young woman being present, consenting. A certificate from the Monthly Meeting at the Falls in the county of Bucks on behalf of Aaron Beeswick was read and received. Friends are desired to show unto William Fishbourn the copy of said paper (copy of disownment) and act therein. Benj'n Burley desires a certificate, he intending to move to New Castle. Likewise, Samuel Jobson desires a certificate. George Claypoole, on behalf of his sister Mary Cook, complains against Evan Roberts, that he does not pay her a just debt.

26/9/1725 - Friends appointed to prepare a certificate for Benj'n Burley report they did not find he brought one to this meeting and therefore they did not prepare one for him. Likewise, they had not prepared one for Samuel Jobson for that he brought none with him from

Europe nor is he intended on a voyage until next summer. A certificate from New Garden Monthly Meeting for Thomas Wollaston, his wife Eleanor and family was read and well received. Also, a certificate for John Benson and Mary, his wife, from Cheshire in Great Brittain was read and received. Mary Widdowfield ... intermarried with one John Moore, not of our society. Francis Richardson and Abigail Golding, having declared their intentions to marry and they not appearing again, Friends are appointed to enquire into the cause.

31/10/1725 - Friends appointed to speak to Francis Richardson report he placeth the blame wholly on the woman, that she refuseth him and thereupon they had discharged each other. A certificate for John Remington and his wife from Chester Monthly Meeting was read and received.

28/11/1725 - Thomas Masters and Hannah Dickinson clear to marry, having the concurrence of guardians and relations. Casper Wistar applied for a certificate to Abington Monthly Meeting touching his clearness in respect to marriage.

25/12/1725 - Application was made on behalf of Robert Hopkins for a certificate to Burlington Monthly Meeting touching on his clearness with respect to marriage. A certificate from Middletown Monthly Meeting in Bucks County for Ralph Hoy was received.

25/1/1726 - James Claypoole and Mary Hood declare their intentions to marry, the parents of the young woman being present, consent, and the young mans not living. Margaret Preston desires a certificate to visit Friends in Long Island, Rhode Island and New England. Samuel Preston proposes to accompany his wife. Elisabeth Teague, who hath been on a visit to Maryland, Virginia and North Carolina with our friend Abigail Bowles, returned their certificates. John Richardson brought a certificate from the Monthly Meeting at Burlington in West Jersey, he intending to settle in this city. Nicholas Cassel applied for a certificate to Burlington Monthly Meeting with respect to his clearness from any engagements.

29/2/1726 - Samuel Nichol and Mary Coates clear to marry, the parents living on each side being present, consent. Joseph Oldman and Sarah Massey clear to marry, the parents living being present, consent. Samuel Jobson, being about to return to London, requests a certificate of his clearness on acct. of marriage. A certificate from the two weeks meeting in London for Lloyd Zachary was read and recorded. A certificate from Chester Monthly Meeting for John Idon and Hannah his wife was read and well received. Aaron Goforth applied for a certificate to Friends in London, he intending to remove to Great Brittain. Martin Jervas applied for a certificate to Ireland, he intending there on trade. John Elfreth and Elisabeth Haywood declare their intentions to marry, the mothers of each being present, consenting, the fathers not living. John Stranger sent a paper condemning his marrying from among Friends.

27/3/1726 - A certificate from Endfield Monthly Meeting in Middlesex concerning Lettice Swift was read and received. A certificate from Radclift Monthly Meeting in London concerning Rebeckah Gray was read and recorded. Thomas Miller sent in a second paper concerning his actions. James Logan brought in a paper concerning his breach of discipline in printing a paper called the Antedote.

24/4/1726 - William Piggott produced a certificate from the Monthly Meeting held in Ratcliff, London. Ralph Jackson, deceased, by his will, gives to the poor two pounds ten shillings. Application was made for a certificate for Joshua Baker, his wife and family, to Concord Monthly Meeting in Chester County.

29/5/1726 - Application was made for a certificate on behalf of Joseph Hewes to Friends in London. Likewise, Thomas Barger applied for a certificate to Concord Monthly Meeting for himself and wife who are removed into Chester County. Application was made on behalf of Benjamin Burleigh for a certificate.

26/6/1726 - Samuel Powell applied for a certificate on behalf of his son Samuel, he being bound on a voyage to London. William Masson applied for a certificate to Center Monthly Meeting touching his clearness in respect to marriage. Richard Hill produced a letter from Dublin Monthly Meeting in Ireland desiring Friends to collect an account of the service our dear deceased friend Thomas Willson had in these American parts.

30/7/1726 - William Davis brought a certificate from Providence Monthly Meeting in Chester County which was read and recorded. Marget Preston, now returned from New England, brought in the certificate she received from that meeting. Application was made on behalf of Abraham Kite and his wife for a certificate, they being removed to Haverford Monthly Meeting. Robert Duncan applied for a certificate to Barbadoes, he being bound thither.

28/8/1726 - John Gilbert and Mary Pryor clear to marry, the young man bringing a certificate from Burlington Monthly Meeting. Samuel Powell and Mary Raper clear to marry, his father being present, consents. Joshua Emlen and Mary Hudson declare their intentions to marry, ... to see that the widows children be secure in what there is left for them.

25/9/1726 - Friends appointed to hear the complaint of Edward Roberts against Thomas Oliver report they hope it ended. Joshua Emlen and Mary Hudson clear to marry, the parents surviving, consenting. Thomas Nickson and Rachel Blackbourne declare their intentions to marry, ... the widow in settlement of her affairs. Moses Hews and Sarah Blith declare their intentions to marry, ... the woman in the settlement of her affairs, especially with respect to her children.

Application was made for a certificate for Joseph Gilpins son, who served apprentice in this town. Also, application was made for a certificate for Francis Richardson, Jun'r, he intending to New England.

30/10/1726 - Moses Hewes and Sarah Blyth clear to marry, his mother and father, by a paper under their hands, signifying their consent. Edward Brooks brought a certificate from Arlington Monthly Meeting for himself and wife who are removed to this city and settled. Reyner Lowden brought a certificate from the Monthly Meeting of Salem which was read and received. John Cassel applied for a certificate to Abington Monthly Meeting touching on his clearness with respect to marriage. Thomas Newland brought a certificate from the Monthly Meeting of M't Troth in Ireland dated 28/6/1726.

27/11/1726 - William Griffith and Susannah Cassell declare their intentions to marry, William producing a certificate from Concord Monthly Meeting and his mother being present, consenting. A certificate for Abigail Bowles, who is intended home for Ireland her first opportunity, was read and signed. A certificate for Peter Lloyd from the two weeks meeting in London was read and received. James Miller applied for a certificate to Carlisle in Great Brittain, the place of his former abode. John Richardson also applied for a certificate to Friends in England, by way of the West Indies. John Iden desires a certificate for himself and wife to Chester Monthly Meeting, he intending to remove thither. Noble Butler requested a certificate to Concord Monthly Meeting in Chester County.

24/12/1726 - Benjamin Humphries and Esther Warner clear to marry, Benjamin having brought a certificate from Merion Monthly Meeting and his mothers consent, his father being absent. Application for a certificate made on behalf of Thomas Lloyd to the two weeks meeting in London. The difference between William Carter and Thomas Shute is ended, William Carter, the complainant is satisfied.

31/1/1727 - Jacob Coffing, Jun'r and Rachel Rackstraw clear to marry, Jacob Coffing not being present, sent his consent and William Rackstraw, the womans father, is present and consents. Emm Evans desires a certificate to visit Maryland, Virginia and North Carolina. John Cross applied for a certificate to the Falls Monthly Meeting touching on his clearness in respect to marriage. Casper Wister applied for a certificate, he intending on a voyage to Great Brittain.

28/2/1727 - Friends appointed to prepare a certificate for Emm Evans report she is disappointed of a companion she expected and declines her visit at present. Casper Wister declines his intended voyage. William Callender, Jun'r, of Barbadoes brought a certificate from the Monthly Meeting of Heathcotte Bay in Barbadoes which was read and accepted. Ebenezer Large requests a certificate of his clearness to marry to the Monthly Meeting of Burlington.

26/3/1727 - William Callender, Jun'r, by John Jones, applied for a certificate to the Monthly Meeting at Heathcotts Bay in Barbadoes. John Oxley, from Barbadoes, on a religious visit to these parts, produced a certificate from a quarterly meeting held at Bridgetown which was read and accepted.

30/4/1727 - Elizabeth Whartnaby applied for a certificate to visit Ireland by way of Barbadoes. A certificate from Falls Monthly Meeting for Joseph Wood was read and accepted. Rachael Richardson, a young woman who came over some years ago from Great Brittain and brought a certificate, hath married from among us and is chargeable with breach of discipline.

28/5/1727 - Jacob Horner and Mary Corbet clear to marry, Jacob bringing a certificate from Haddonfield Monthly Meeting in New Jersey. Martin Gervis brought a certificate from Edenberry in Ireland and also one from the mens meeting in Dublin which were read and well received.

25/6/1727 - Joseph Wood and Mary Pound clear to marry, he having produced under his mothers hand, her consent. John Fallowfield produced a certificate from the two weeks meeting at London in Great Brittain which was read and received. George Claypoole. executer of Mary Cook, brought in a paper signed by her wherin it appears that she hath, in her last will, given to Elizabeth Hill and Elizabeth Teague a legacy of six pounds for the use of Friends. Joshua Johnson, on behalf of his son Isaac Johnson, applied for a certificate to the Monthly Meeting at Burlington touching on his clearness with respect to marriage. Richard Hill complains against Joshua Lawrence, Executor of John Widefield, that he refuseth to pay him a debt due upon bond.

9/7/1727 - Friends appointed to deal with Isaac Pillar report that they have dealt with him and are in hopes that both he and his wife will give Friends satisfaction. Joshua Fielding brought a certificate dated 8/7/1725 from the Bull and Mouth in London and our said friend ... intending to leave us, Friends are appointed to prepare a certificate for him. Thomas Pryor, in behalf of his son Thomas, applied for a certificate touching to Burlington Monthly Meeting touching his clearness in respect to marriage. A certificate for Esther Clare, one for Elizabeth Bumpstead and another for Mary Smith and her daughter were read and signed. Ebenezer Large applied for a certificate to Burlington Monthly Meeting, being removed thither. William Piggott who hath been some time amongst us on a religious visit, intending to return home to London in Great Brittain, moves for a certificate. John Wanton of Rode Island, who is now on a visit to Friends, produced a certificate from the Monthly Meeting held at Newport. Daniel Worthington produced a certificate from a Monthly Meeting held in Leeds in Great Brittain which was read and received.

Daniel Cassell desires a certificate to the Monthly Meeting in Chester County, he intending to settle within the verge of that meeting.

27/8/1727 - Jacob Durborow and Ann Albinson clear to marry, he producing a certificate from Burlington Monthly Meeting and the parents on both sides now living being present, consenting. A certificate from Burlington Monthly Meeting dated 2/8/1727 for Isaac Williams, his wife and children now amongst us was read and received. William Sandwith produced a certificate from the mens meeting in Dublin in Ireland dated 4/5/1727 which was read and received. Richard Ormes applied for a certificate to Harford Monthly Meeting, he being removed within the verge of that meeting.

24/9/1727 - James Lewis applied for a certificate to the Island of Barbadoes.

29/10/1727 - The complaint of Richard Hill against the Executor of John Widdowfield is ended. William Fisher and Mary Pace declare their intentions to marry. Samuel Powell, Jun'r, produced a certificate from the two weeks meeting at the Bull and Mouth meeting house in London dated 10/5/1727 which was read and received. Josiah Gates produced a certificate from the Monthly Meeting at Poole in Great Brittain and the said John? intending to go to Jamacia, has altered his intentions and intends to settle in this city. Jonathan Cagshaw applied on behalf of Thomas Chalkley for a certificate to Barbadoes. James Wilkins applies for a certificate to the Monthly Meeting in London, Great Brittain. Casper Hoodt applied for a certificate on behalf of Regniere Lowdon and his wife to Salem Monthly Meeting, he intending to settle there.

26/11/1727/8 - Friends appointed to enquire into William Fishers clearness respecting marriage report that he declines proceeding any further in respect to marriage with Mary Pace. Samuel Bowns, on a visit from Great Brittain, produced a certificate from the Monthly Meeting of Bridgeport in Dorsetshire dated 18/10/1726 which was read and received. John Casey, who is on a visit from New England, produced a certificate from the Monthly Meeting at Newport in Rhode Island which was read and received. Esther Clare, being returned from her visit from New England, produced a certificate from the Monthly Meeting at Newport on Rhode Island which was read and received.

23/12/1727/8 - Peter Lloyd and Mercy Masters clear to marry, Peters mother being present declared her consent. John Knight, applied in behalf of William Sandwith, for a certificate to the Monthly Meeting at Dublin in Ireland.

29/1/1728 - John Oxley, designing to return home in a short time, applied for a certificate to the Monthly Meeting at Bridgetown in Barbadoes. Richard Hill applied on behalf of John Casey for a certificate to the Monthly Meeting at New Port Rhode Island. John Paschall and

Frances Hodge clear to marry, John producing a certificate from
Derby Monthly Meeting. John Fisher and Mary Hodge declare their
intentions to marry, parents on both sides being present, declared
their assent. Abraham Carlisle, Junr, and Mary Key declare their
intentions to marry, parents on both sides being present were
consenting.

26/2/1728 - Friends report they have been with Sarah Pillar and
delivered to her the testimony which was drawn up against her and
the meeting for the present defers any further publication in regard
to her husband who has shown a disposition to give satisfaction.
James and Mary Cooper sent a paper condemning their behaviour in
differing with each other. Robert Duncan brought a paper
condemning his imprudent behaviour toward Samuel Powell which
was read and received. Mary Bones, a person lately come from
England, is in a weakly position ... Friends are appointed to enquire
into her circumstances and desired to contribute to her assistance.

31/3/1728 - Abraham England and Jane Rawle clear to marry, Abraham
producing a certificate from Duck Creek and the parents on both
sides being present, declared their consent. Knight Hodge and
Susannah Bickley declare their intentions to marry, his father and
her guardian being present, declared their consent. John Fallowfield
applied for a certificate to the Monthly Meeting in London or
elsewhere. William Rabley produced a certificate from the Monthly
Meeting at Plymouth dated 4/5/1727.

28/4/1728 - Robert Eastbourn brought a certificate for himself and wife
from Abington Monthly Meeting. Jonathan Zeanes and Mary Shenton
clear to marry, his mother and her guardian being present,
consenting. Margaret Preston desires to visit meetings in Maryland,
Virginia and North Carolina. A certificate for Edward Robinson and
his wife from Radnor Monthly Meeting, dated 13/4/1728 was read.

26/25/1728 - Michael Poince and Elizabeth Nicholson clear to marry, he
producing a certificate from Abington Monthly Meeting and her
mother being present, consenting. Thomas Gilpin and Hannah
Knowles declare their intentions to marry, he producing a certificate
from Chichester Monthly Meeting in Chester County dated
28/5/1728.

30/6/1728 - Henry Thompson brought a certificate from Abington
Monthly Meeting dated 26/12/1727 and one for his wife dated
27/3/1728, which were read and received. Job Goodson designs
shortly for London and desires a certificate.

27/7/1728 - John Armitt and Mary Emblin clear to marry, their parents
being present and consenting. John Jones, Jun'r, sent in a paper
concerning his breach of discipline in marrying from among Friends.
John Walby produced a certificate dated at Moat in Ireland 10/2/1728
in behalf of himself and wife who removed from thence to settle in

this city. Daniel Worthington applied for a certificate to Abington Monthly Meeting.

25/8/1728 - Richard Hill applied on behalf of Joseph Taylor for a certificate to Raby Monthly Meeting in the county of Durham, he designing to return home in a short time.

29/9/1728 - William Morris produced a certificate from the Monthly Meeting at Heathcoat Bay in Barbadoes dated 5/7/1728, which was read and received. Joshua Emblen and Deborah Powell clear to marry, their parents being present, consenting. Samuel Preston, on behalf of Joseph Norris, applied for a certificate to Friends in Barbadoes, he designing for that place in a short time. Edward Owen, on behalf of Joseph French, applied for a certificate to the Monthly Meeting in Barbadoes.

27/10/1728 - Friends appointed to care for William Sanders wife and children report she is now with her husband, the children likewise. Application made on behalf of Issac Brown for a certificate to Barbadoes. Margaret Preston now returned from her visit to Maryland, Virginia and North Carolina. Thomas Brodgate sent in a paper condemning his disorderly drinking. William and Mary Wood condemn their act before marriage.

31/11/1728 - John Welton produced a certificate for himself and wife dated in Bristol 28/10/1724. Also, one from Radnor Monthly Meeting dated 12/10/1728. Robert Robinson produced a certificate from the Monthly Meeting at Kelso dated 26/6/1727 which was read and received. Friends acquaint this meeting that Sarah Sanders and Lydia Robinson have married from amongst Friends. Likewise, Elizabeth Kelly and Esther Dansey have married from amongst us. Therefore, this meeting finds the necessity of disowning these women from our society. A letter from the quarterly meeting at Oakham to the meeting for sufferings in London, dated 28/4/1728, setting for the disorderly conduct of Edward Mugglestone before he left England was read. Friends are appointed to acquaint said Mugglestone that Friends cannot receive his testimony and to advise him to a speedy return home to his family. William Morris, Luke Morris and Anthony Morris, Jun'r, applied for certificates to Barbadoes.

28/12/1728/9 - Rowland Wilson, designing in a short time to return home, desires a certificate to the Monthly Meeting at Great Strikland in Westmoreland in Great Brittain. Sarah Bartlett, late Sarah Sanders of this city, is disowned for her breach of discipline. Lydia, the daughter of Richard Robinson of the city, having married from amongst us one Oswald Peele, is disowned. Elizabeth Clarkson, late Elizabeth Kelly of this city, hath married from amongst us to one James Clarkson, and is disowned. Esther Dansey, daughter of John Dansey, of this city, has married from amongst us to one Alexander Grant, and is disowned. Thomas Mitchell is disowned. A certificate for

Jacob Vernon and Eleanor, his wife, from a Monthly Meeting at Providence, dated 27/11/1728 - 9, was read. Thomas Shute applied for a certificate for his son Joseph Shute for a certificate to Bridgetown in Barbadoes.

25/2/1729 - Margaret Preston and Mary Nichols desire a certificate to visit Egg Harbour and Long Island. Application made for a certificate for Thomas Biddle to the Monthly Meeting at Concord.

30/3/1729 - The complaint of Mary Lisle against John Heart is ended. Thomas Hall applied for a certificate to Derby, he intending to marry. A certificate for Thomas Barnes and his wife Jennett from Middletown Monthly Meeting in Bucks County was read. Application made for a certificate for Joshua Granger and his wife to Chester Monthly Meeting in Burlington County where they intend to reside.

25/5/1729 - Friends appointed to prepare a certificate for Joshua Granger ... having lived in the Jerseys for a considerable time before he removed hither and it not appearing that he brought a certificate from hence, have not prepared one for him. A certificate for Richard Burton from Chesterfield Monthly Meeting in New Jersey, dated 7th month 1728, was read. A certificate for William Callender, Junr, from a Monthly Meeting at Heathcoat Bay in Barbadoes, dated 21/3/1729, was read.

29/6/1729 - William Fishbourne and Jane Roberts clear to marry, her parents present and consenting. James Levine and Sarah Wright clear to marry, her guardian consenting. A certificate for Sarah Marshall from the Monthly Meeting at Edenderry in Ireland dated 1/4/1729 was read. A certificate for George Franks and Elizabeth his wife from Abington Monthly Meeting, dated 28/5/1729, was read. Isaac Norris brought a letter from Friends in Dublin, dated 22/2/1729, enclosing the Testimony there against William Henderson in order that Friends might not be imposed on by him.

26/7/1729 - Friends appointed in the complaint of Richard Hill against Joshua Lawrence report that Richard Hill's death prevented anything being done, therefore it is discontinued. Sarah Aske, who was Sarah Siddons of this city, widow, has married from amongst us to one Samuel Aske, and she is therefore disowned. A certificate for Rowland Smallman from Waterford Monthly Meeting in Ireland, dated 5/4/1729, was read.

31/8/1729 - William Williams and Hannah Carver clear to marry, he producing a certificate from Gwynedd Monthly Meeting, and they are at liberty to consummate their intentions at North Wales. A certificate for Samuel Emblin to London was signed. Edward Owen is dead. A certificate from Horsleydown Monthly Meeting in Southwark for Job Goodson, dated 2/2/1729, was read. A certificate for Richard Harrison from a Monthly Meeting at the Clifts in Maryland, dated

2/10/1726, was read. Joseph Elger applied for a certificate to Nottingham Monthly Meeting, where he intends to remove with his family. John Cadwallader applied for a certificate to Barbadoes on behalf of his son Thomas Cadwallader.

28/9/1729 - A certificate for Richard Harrison to Hartford Monthly Meeting was signed. Hannah Ashburnham condemns her marrying from amongst Friends.

26/10/1729 - Isaac Pemberton brought in a Testamony against Grace, the wife of David Brientnall, Junr. A certificate for William Sitgrave and wife from Bull and Mouth Monthly Meeting in London, dated 13/6/1729, was read.

30/11/1729 - Joseph England and Sarah Baily clear to marry, there being no ground to believe James Baily alive (with all the Sloops company lost and it being six years since they were heard of). The complaint against Solomon Cresson against Robert Duncan is ended. A certificate for William Callender to Friends in Barbadoes was signed. Joseph Wharton and Hannah Carpenter declare their intentions to marry, his mother and her guardian being present and consenting.

27/12/1729 - Jane Harper condemns her reproachful conduct. Joseph Wharton and Hannah Carpenter clear to marry. James Morris and Elizabeth Kearney clear to marry, his parents being present and consenting and her mother sending a few lines signifying her consent. Jeremiah Elfrith applied for a certificate, on behalf of John Elfrith and his wife, to the Falls Monthly Meeting. Alexander Parker and Sarah Thompson declare their intentions to marry, their parents being present and consenting. Benjamin Betterton and Mary Thompson declare their intentions to marry, her parents present and consenting.

27/1/1730 - Benjamin Betterton and Mary Thompson clear to marry, the young woman's father not being present sent in a paper signifying his consent. John Jervis and Rebeccah Walton declare their intentions to marry.

24/2/1730 - John Hilbourne and Rachel Strickland clear to marry, he producing a certificate from Wrightstown Monthly Meeting. John Jervis and Rebeccah Walton clear to marry, their parents being present and consenting. The following young women have married from among Friends, viz: Sarah Miller to James Cathcart, Sarah Usher to Joseph Fordham and Mary Spencer to Benjamin Leigh.

26/4/1730 - Hannah Shenton and Catherine Borden admitted to one of the Almshouses as tenants. A certificate for Joseph Jackman from the Monthly Meeting at Bridgetown in Barbadoes, dated 28/2/1730, was read and he designing for Long Island, the certificate was returned to him. A certificate for John Lewis from a Monthly Meeting at Heathcoats Bay in Barbadoes, dated 22/2/1730, was read. A certificate for John Dilwin to Friends in London was signed. Application made on behalf of Rowland Smallman for a certificate to the Monthly Meeting at Waterford. Mary Preston has married one Samuel Harison out of unity with Friends.

31/5/1730 - Anthony Morris, Junr, produced a certificate from the Monthly Meeting at Heathcoats Bay in Barbadoes dated 20/6/1729. Adam Lewis stands in need of assistance, Friends are appointed to enquire into his circumstances and to advise him to put out his children.

28/6/1730 - Friends report that Edward Robinson lay in a helpless condition. Reuben Paxton applied for a certificate to the Monthly Meeting at Abington, he intending to marry. Abraham Clibborn produced a certificate from Dublin dated 2/4/1730.

25/7/1730 - Peter Sharp, having been on a religious visit, produced a certificate from Tredhaven Creek in Maryland dated the 27th and 28th of the 3rd month, 1730. John Oxley produced a certificate from a quarterly meeting in Barbadoes and designed to return in a short time, requests a certificate from this meeting. Willian Rably desires a certificate, he intending for Great Brittain. Application made for a certificate for Thomas Gilpin and his wife for a certificate to Concord Monthly Meeting. Application made for a certificate for Thomas Barnes and his wife to Neshaminy or the Falls Monthly Meeting.

30/8/1730 - Testamony against Thomas Broadgate was read and a copy ordered to be delivered to him. Samuel Powell and Sarah Roberts declare their intentions to marry, her parents being present and consenting. A certificate for Cadwallader Evan to Chester Monthly Meeting. A certificate for Abraham Clibbourn to Friends in Dublin.

27/9/1730 - A certificate for John Alment and wife, to Friends at Ballycaine in Ireland. Also one for Mark Eve. Junr. to the same place. Isaac Norris moves on behalf of his son Charles, for a certificate to Barbadoes.

25/10/1730 - A certificate from the two week meeting in London for John Sparrow, dated 17/6/1730.

29/11/1730 - Anthony Morris, Junr, and Sarah Morris clear to marry, their parents present and consenting. Joshua Fielding produced a certificate from the two week meeting in London, dated 28/7/1730.

28/12/1730 - Application for a certificate on behalf of Joseph Shute for a certificate to South Carolina with respect to marriage.

26/1/1731 - Thomas Hatton and wife ... from Ireland ... persists in refusing to produce their certificates, therefor this meeting cannot esteem them to be members. John Kensey and wife produced a certificate from Woodbridge dated 21/11/1730. Henry Frankland ... from Great Britain produced a certificate from York dated 5/4/...? Application on behalf of Aubrey Roberts for a certificate to Goshen Monthly Meeting. Isaac Piller applied for a certificate to Wrightstown.

30/2/1731 - A certificate received from Gwyned Monthly Meeting for Cadwallader Foulke and Mary his wife, dated 30/1/1731. Joseph England and Sarah his wife sent in a paper condemning the unhappy discord that had happened between them. Robert Jordan and Mary Hill declare their intention to marry, he producing a certificate from a Quarterly Meeting in Isle of Wight County, Virginia, dated 7/12/1731. Margaret Preston and Hannah Tidmarsh report that Hannah Lewis and Mary Lewis, daughters of Adam Lewis, had been dealt with. John Dilwin produced a certificate from Horsleydown (London) Monthly Meeting, dated 6/11/1730. Application make in behalf of Daniel Stanton for a certificate to Rhode Island, he designing there on business.

28/3/1731 - Robert Jordan and Mary Hill clear to marry. Friends appointed to acquaint Adam Lewis and his wife with the advice of this meeting respecting the putting out of their children ... report they delivered them a copy of the minute and they promise to comply.

25/4/1731 - Edward Banester produced a certificate from South Kingston in the colony of Rhode Island.

30/5/1731 - Friends appointed to make inquiry concerning Ann, daughter of George Harmer, are continued. Friends appointed to draw testimony against Elizabeth Polgreen, Mary Tongue and Sarah Key are continued. Armiger and Thomas Trotter produced a certificate from the Monthly Meeting at Chuckertuck, Virginia and designing back for Virginia, request a few lines from this meeting. William Sandwith produced two certificates, one from the Monthly Meeting held at Cooledine in Ireland, dated 8/1/1730, and the other from the Mens Meeting in Dublin, dated 24/1/1730. William Sandwith and Sarah Jervis declare their intention to marry, her parents being present, consenting. John Jones and Rebecca Head declare their intentions to marry, he producing a certificate from Abington Monthly Meeting, and her parents being present, consenting. Hannah Bickley was married to John Fordham, a person not of our Society. Paul Johnson, on a religious visit, produced a certificate from the Mens Meeting in Dublin, dated 6/2/1731. Nathaniel Jenkins and wife, come from Great Britain to settle here, produced a certificate from

the Mens Meeting at Bristol .... John Staines produced a certificate from the Two Weeks Meeting in London, dated 1/1/1731. Thomas Clarke applied for a certificate to Haddonfield, intending on marriage.
27/6/1731 - Mary Tongue, late Mary Bickley of this city, hath married from amongst us to one John Tongue. Sarah Williams, late Sarah Keys of this city, hath married from amongst us to one William Williams. William Sandwith and Sarah Jervis clear to marry. Application on behalf of Richard Robinson for a certificate to Burlington Monthly Meeting, he being removed there to live. Bridget Buby sent in a paper condemning her disorderly procedure in marriage. Sarah Owen and Sarah Hudson report they have dealt with Sarah Williams, late Sarah Hadley.
24/7/1731 - Ann Fisher, a daughter of George and Honour Harmer of this city ..., with John Fisher, her present husband ..., we testify against the said Ann Fisher. Obadiah Eldridge and Phebe Guest clear to marry, he producing a paper of consent signed by his father. Samuel Dickinson and Mary Cadwallader declare their intention to marry, he producing a certificate from Tredhaven Monthly Meeting in Maryland and her parents being present, consenting. William Warner and Mary Witton declare their intention to marry, he producing a paper of consent signed by his mother and her father being present, consenting. Application made on behalf of John Day for a certificate to Nottingham Monthly Meeting where he has gone to live.
29/8/1731 - Robert Jordan, being returned from Maryland, delivered unto this meeting the certificate he had with him. Friends appointed to prepare a certificate for Simon Edgle report he did not proceed on his intended journey. Joyce Marriott might be admitted to sit in the Meeting of Ministers and Elders, the meeting consents thereto.
26/9/1731 - Stephen Peyton produced a certificate from the Monthly Meeting at Dudley, in the county of Worcester, dated 19/5/1731. Application made in behalf of Cadwallader Evans and his wife to Chester Monthly Meeting. Edward Bannester applied for a certificate to Haverford Monthly Meeting. Application made in behalf of Thomas Cadwallader for a certificate to Friends in London.
31/10/1731 - Mary Bevan has married a person not in fellowship with us. John Hart, Junr, applied for a certificate to Darby Monthly Meeting respecting his clearness to marry. Application made in behalf of George Franks and his wife for a certificate to North Wales Monthly Meeting. John Jones is desired to provide two cord of wood for Catherine Borden and Mary Davis. Anthony Furnis and his wife sent in a paper acknowledging their outgoing in marriage.
25/12/1731/2 - Friends appointed on the complaint of John Key against Nathaniel Poole report the parties are like to accommodate the matter in controversy. A certificate for Edmund Lewis from this Monthly Meeting on the main in the Government of New York was

read and signed. Joseph Cloud and Hannah Balding declare their
intention to marry, she being a widow and having children, Friends
are appointed to enquire if provision be made for the children. Abel
Preston and wife sent in a paper condemning their disorderly
procedure in marriage and desiring to be reconciled to Friends. Daniel
Evans applied for a certificate to Abibgton Monthly Meeting in
relation to marriage.

31/1/1732 - Joseph Cloud and Hannah Balding clear to marry, he
producing a certificate from Concord Monthly Meeting and his
parents consent in writing, and the Friends appointed to enquire if
provision was made for her children report it was done. Ann
Rakestraw, wife of William Rakestraw, sent in a paper condemning
her disorderly procedure in marriage. Susannah Forrester sent in a
paper condemning her outgoing in marriage.

28/2/1732 - Friends who were appointed to enquire what effects there is
to be found belonging to the estate of Thomas Duckett ... report they
are not certain of any but about 30 pounds in Grace Lloyds hands, for
which ... there was application make in behalf of Benjamin
Tomlinson's wife. Joseph Mather applied for a certificate to
Haddonfield Monthly Meeting. William Miller and Ann Emblen
declare their intention to marry, he producing a certificate from New
Garden Monthly Meeting dated 25/7/1731, and her mother being
present, consenting.

26/3/1732 - Mary Crapp, late Mary Flower of this city, hath lately
married from amongst us to one John Crapp. Application in behalf of
William Lawrence for a certificate to Flushing Monthly Meeting.
Anthony Morris applied on behalf of his son John for a certificate to
Gwynedd Monthly Meeting. Friends from the Womans Meeting
acquaint this meeting that application was made ... for a certificate for
Mary Steele to Duck Creek Monthly Meeting .... They are informed
that she hath received the addresses of a person, with purpose of
marriage, that is not of our society. Therefore, they had not got a
certificate prepared. William Cooper and Mary Rawle clear to marry,
he producing a certificate from Haddonfield Monthly Meeting. A
letter was received from Mary Hilliard, late Mary Steele, respecting
her outgoing in marriage.

28/5/1732 - Joseph Stretch and Lydia Knight clear to marry, his parents
and her grandmother being present, consenting. Benjamin Lay
produced a certificate for himself and his wife from Colchester
Monthly Meeting dated 4/12/1731. William Hudson and Isaac Norris
produced a codicil to William Forrest's will, by which he invests in
them, for the use of this meeting, two lotts and tenements fronting
Chestnut and Fourth Streets in Philadelphia, after his widows death
and she being now dead, this meeting appoints Samuel Powell,
together with the aforesaid Friends, to take care of the premises.

Samuel Powell, cordwainer, and George Coates, sadler, were dealeth with for drinking to excess.

25/6/1732 - Thomas Penn produced a certificate from the Two Weeks Meeting in London, dated 18/3/1732. Edward Wallbank produced a certificate for himself and his wife from Bull and Mouth Monthly Meeting, London, dated 12/2/1732. John Idon produced a certificate for himself and his wife from Chester Monthly Meeting, dated at Providence, 31/5/1732. Jacob Duberry applied on behalf of his sons Jacob and John for certificates to Abington Monthly Meeting. Mungo Bewley, who is on a religious visit from Ireland, produced certificates to this meeting. Samuel Stephens, from Ireland on a religious visit, produced a certificate from Lambs Town Monthly Meeting, dated 28/3/1732. Alice Alderson, from Great Brittain on a religious visit, sent her certificate from the Monthly Meeting of Jedburgh, held at Brigflatts, in Yorkshire. Margaret Coupland, from Great Brittain on a religious visit, sent her certificate from the Monthly Meeting at Kendall. Hannah Dent, from Great Brittain on a religious visit, sent her certificate from the Monthly Meeting at Richmond, in Yorkshire. Samuel Seabrel, from Virginia on a religious visit, produced a certificate from Nansemund Monthly Meeting. Lawrence [Growden] produced a certificate from the Monthly Meeting in the city of Bristol, dated 14/12/1731. Samuel Floyd, from Barbadoes, produced a certificate dated 30/4/1732.

29/7/1732 - William Parker and Elizabeth Gilbert declare their intention to marry, he producing a few lines from his mother signifying her consent, and the young womans mother being present, declares her husband and she were consenting. Thomas Gardner produced a certificate for himself, his wife and his children from Gwynedd Monthly Meeting dated 25/5/1732. A certificate from the Mens Meeting held in Dublin on 9/1/1730, in behalf of William Nicholson, was read ... and the meeting being acquainted that he is gone for Dublin, and application being made for a certificate ..., Friends are appointed to prepare one. Jane Cumen, who was Fordham, sent a paper condemning her outgoing in marriage. ... Womens Meeting acquaints this meeting ... that Mary Cheatham intended to marry one ____ Crook, not of our society ... but since that they understand she is married. Application in behalf of Joseph Davis for a certificate to Gwyned Monthly Meeting.

24/9/1732 - A certificate from Gynedd Monthly Meeting for Ann Gidden. Application made on behalf of Nathaniel Jenkins and his wife for a certificate to New Garden Monthly Meeting.

29/10/1732 - Daniel Thomas and Aletta Piggot clear to marry, he producing a certificate from Abington Monthly Meeting dated the 25th of the present month. Testimony prepared against Ann Kirk, late Oldman, for her outgoing in marriage. Testimony against William

Lingard was read. A certificate for Nathaniel Jenkins and his wife to
New Garden. A certificate dated 27/9/1732 from Abington Monthly
Meeting for James Wilson and his wife was read and they being
removed within the verge of Buckingham Monthly Meeting, request
was made on their behalf for a certificate to that meeting. Nathan
Cowman and Mary Shute declare their intention to marry, he
producing a certificate from the Monthly Meeting at Pardshow Hall in
Cumberland, dated 20/8/1730.

26/11/1732 - Nathan Cowman and Mary Shute clear to marry ..., not met
with any obstruction but from Ann Clifton, of this place, ... but she
hath since, by a paper under her own hand ... acquitted him, and
William Atwood, uncle to the young woman, being present,
acquainted the meeting that her father had committed her to his care
.... Samuel Samson produced a certificate from the Two Week
Meeting in London, dated 14/6/1732.

30/1/1733 - Thomas Parry produced a certificate from the Two Weeks
Meeting at Colchester, dated 19/3/1729, and he, designing for Great
Britain in a short time, requested a certificate from hence.
Application made in behalf of Robert Eastbourne for a certificate to
Abington.

25/3/1733 - Mary Nichols is under a religious concern to visit Maryland,
Virginia and North Carolina, in company with Hannah Dent.

29/4/1733 - Thomas Kemberly, being on a religious visit to these parts,
produced a certificate from Friends in South Carolina, dated 3/4/1733.
William Callender produced a certificate for himself and wife from
Burlington Monthly Meeting, dated 4/4/1733.

27/5/1733 - George Miller, a lad of about 15 years (who's parents were
Friends) came last fall from London in the ship John, which ship was
lost in our Bay, and his father, having lost what effects he had on
board, was soon after drowned in Christeen River, and said lad being
destitute of relations, hath agreed to put himself an apprentice to
Edward Cathrall untill he attains the age of twenty one years. Peter
Stretch, executor of Thomas Cannon, produced an account of one
pound, ten shilling and two pence due to Cannons estate. Samuel
Sanson, intending on returning for London in a short time, requests a
certificate

31/6/1733 - Testimony against Sarah Curry, late Sarah Marriott, for her
outgoing in marriage, was read. Benjamin Tomlinson produced a
certificate for himself and wife from Horsleydown Monthly Meeting
dated 28/12/1732. Isaac Norris requests a certificate in behalf of his
son Charles, who intends in a short time for London. Application
made in behalf of Mary Bowns, that her passage might be paid by
Friends. She being in low circumstances, this meeting agrees.

28/7/1733 - Friends appointed to prepare a certificate for Charles Norris
report he declined the voyage proposed. Application made in behalf of

Richard Renshaw for a certificate to Barbadoes, he going thither on account of trade.

26/8/1733 - A certificate for Isaac Norris, Junr, to London.

30/9/1733 - Testimony against Phebe Plaskett, late Phebe Biles, and Sarah Aldrich, late Sarah England, for going out in marriage. Mary Usher sent a paper condemning her imprudent conduct.

25/11/1733 - John Dilwin and Susanna Painter clear to marry, John Smith and Israel Pemberton being guardian to the young woman. Sarah Ashton, late Sarah Fordham is married to a person not of our society.

22/12/1733/4 - Isaac Garrigues and Christian Broadgate, Junr, clear to marry, her mother sending a paper signifying her consent, and his parents being present, consenting. A certificate for Samuel Hastings to Crosswicks Monthly Meeting. William Moode and Hannah Cockfield declare their intention to marry, William Hudson, the young womans grandfather being present, consents. John Richardson produced a certificate from Pardshaw Hall in Cumberland, dated 21/6/1733. Application in behalf of Lawrence Growden for a certificate to Friends in Bristol, he intending to Great Britain this spring.

29/1/1734 - John Morris and Mary Sutton clear to marry, he producing a certificate from Gwyned Monthly Meeting. Joseph Hopewell, being removed from the Jerseys, produced a certificate from Haddonfield Monthly Meeting dated 11/12/1733/4. Benjamin Lay, removed with his family to settle at Abington, requests a certificate John Burr and Susannah Owen declare their intention to marry, her parents being present and consenting. Benjamin Madox and Elizabeth Heart declare their intention to marry, he producing a certificate from Providence and their parents being present and consenting.

26/2/1734 - John Burr and Susannah Owen clear to marry, he producing a certificate from Burlington Monthly Meeting, and his parents consent in writing in writing. Nicholas Waln and Mary Shoemaker declare their intention to marry a second time, but it appearing they are second cousins (the grandfather of the young man and the grandmother of the young woman having been brother and sister), care was taken ... to discharge them from engaging themselves but that not prevailing, they are clear to marry. Jonathan Wright and Elizabeth Preston declare their intention to marry and she being a widow, Friends are appointed to assist her in the settlement of her affairs ... with respect to her children. Benjamin Trotter and Mary Corker declare their intention to marry, Friends being appointed to see the widows child provided for, and if not, then to assist her in the settlement of her affairs. Robert Read and Sarah his wife, being removed from Chester County in order to settle in this city, produced a certificate from Newark Monthly Meeting held at Center in Chester County, dated 6/2/1734. Elizabeth Widdowfield, intending to

accompany Hannah Dent on a visit to Long Island, requests a
certificate

31/3/1734 - Robert Jordan brought back the certificate he received from
this meeting when he went last for Brittain. Thomas Lloyd and
Susannah Owen clear to marry, his mother being present and hers by
certificate consenting. Certificates for Alice Anderson, Margaret
Coupland and Thomas Chalkley were approved.

28/4/1734. Joseph Sanders produced a certificate from the Two Weeks
meeting in London, dated 12/12/1732. Joseph Callender sent to this
meeting a certificate from Barbadoes dated 2/1734 and Anthony
Morris, on his behalf, applied for a certificate to Barbadoes. Thomas
Kimberly produced a few lines ... dated in South Carolina 27/3/1754
.... Christian Robinson has married one John Brown, one not in
fellowship with us. Thomas Taylor brought a paper condemning his
disorderly conduct ... until Friends are satisfied of his sincerity by his
future conduct.

26/5/1734 - William Atkinson, Junr, and Sarah Pawlin clear to marry, his
father being present, consenting, but she hath neither parents nor
guardian. John Marle and Elizabeth Elfreth declare their intention to
marry, their parents being present, consent. A certificate for
Jonathan Evans from Gwyned Monthly Meeting dated 30/2/1734.
Application made on behalf of Thomas Pryor and his wife to
Burlington Monthly Meeting, they being moved within the verge of
that meeting.

30/6/1734 - John Marle and Elizabeth Elfreth clear to marry, he
producing a certificate from Abington Monthly Meeting. A certificate
for Thomas Kimberly to Friends in South Carolina. A certificate for
John Hanks from Darby Monthly Meeting.

__/7/1734 - Hugh Thomas and Sarah Eastbourn declare their intention to
marry, her parents being present, consenting. Samuel Boon and
Elizabeth Castle declare their intention to marry, the young man
producing a certificate from Gwyned Monthly Meeting.

25/8/1734 - Hugh Thomas and Sarah Eastbourn clear to marry, he
producing a certificate from Hertford Monthly Meeting. Samuel Boon
and Elizabeth Cassel clear to marry, his mother and father having
signified their consent in writing. A certificate from Abington Monthly
Meeting for Thomas Marle and his wife, they having come to reside in
this city. A certificate from the Mens Meeting at Bristol, dated
24/7/1733, on behalf of Giles Brimble who is settled in this city.

29/9/1734 - John Walby reports he read the testimony against Thomas
Broadgate. Jeremiah Elfreth and Elizabeth Massey clear to marry,
her mother being present declared her consent. Anthony Nichols and
Rebecca Shute declare their intention to marry, his mother being
present, declared her consent. Application made in behalf of John
Lewis for a certificate to Chester Monthly Meeting on account of

marriage. Patrick Ogilsby being come to settle in this city, produced a
certificate from Westbury Monthly Meeting on Long Island, dated
28/6/1734. John Salkeld reports he is empowered by a person in
England to receive from Martha Trueman a debt due on bond which
she refuses to pay ....
27/10/1734 - Anthony Nichols and Rebecca Shute clear to marry, the
young womans parents being present were consenting. Margaret
Preston and Joyce Merriott being returned from their visit, produced
a certificate from Tredhaven Monthly Meeting in Maryland. A
certificate for Benjamin Eastbourn and his wife from Heartford
Monthly Meeting, dated 12/10/1734, was accepted.
31/11/1734 - The complaint of John Salkeld against Martha Trueman is
ended.
28/12/1734 - The widow Lingard having requested assistance and advice
respecting a debt due to her from the estate of Jonathan Dickenson,
Junr, the meeting appoints Friends to assist her in this affair. Edward
Tatnall requests a certificate to the Monthly Meeting at New Garden.
28/1/1735 - Friends nominated to end the difference between Sarah
Lancaster and her brother John Brientnall report they have made
some essays but it is not yet ended. Joseph Cooper and Hannah Dent
declare their intention to marry ..., his mother being present declared
her consent and Hannah Dent produced a certificate from the
Monthly Meeting at Richmond in Chentry in Old England, dated
7/4/1734, with her parents consent. Sarah Siddal was married to one
Samuel Haile, a person not of our society. Deborah Hood has been
dealt with for her outgoing in marriage with one John Johnson, not of
our society, as also was Sarah Hood for marrying one Robert
Archpool, also not a Friend.
25/2/1735 - Joseph Cooper and Hannah Dent clear to marry, he
producing a certificate from Haddonfield. Benjamin Mason and his
wife being come to settle within the verge of this meeting produced a
certificate from Abington Monthly Meeting dated 31st of last month.
Roger Brook and Sarah Boyer declare their intention to marry, the
young womans mother being present declared her consent. Isaac
Norris acquainted this meeting that his son, Charles Norris, intended
... a voyage to London and requested a certificate for him.
30/3/1735 - Roger Brook and Sarah Boyer clear to marry, he producing
his mothers consent in writing. A certificate for Hannah Dent to
Wensidel Monthly Meeting in Yorkshire. A certificate for Sarah Lay
from the two weeks meeting at Colchester, dated 21/8/1734 was read.
John Richardson acquainted this meeting that he designed to Brittain
in short time and requests a certificate to Kendall Monthly Meeting in
Westmoreland. Application made in behalf of Joseph Sanders for a
certificate to Friends in London.

27/4/1735 - Testimony prepared against Elizabeth Massey, late Elizabeth
England, Rebecca Scull, late Rebecca Thompson, and Dinah Stamper,
late Dinah Jackson, for their outgoing in marriage. A certificate for
James Estaugh and his wife to Haddonfield Monthly Meeting. A
certificate for Israel Pemberton, Junr, to Friends in London. A
certificate for Joseph Sanders to Friends in London. John Jones
produced a certificate from Salem for himself and wife dated 26th of
3rd month last. Thomas Bond produced a certificate from the week
day Meeting at Herring Creek in Maryland dated 11th day of 3rd
month last. Edward Pledwell sent into this meeting a paper
condemning his disorderly proceeding in marriage.

25/5/1735 - Elisha Gatchell and Simon Edgle, both appearing, acquaint
this meeting that they are in hopes the matter in difference would be
accommodated between themselves. Friends appointed in the affair
respecting Solomon Rotchford report the collection completed, they
having paid the money to him. Friends appointed to prepare
testimony against Ruth Thompson, daughter of James Steele of this
city. Testamony against Deborah Clymer, late Deborah Fitzwater,
and Rebecca Hogg, late Rebecca Fitwater, for their outgoing in
marriage, was read. Testamony against William Masters was read.
Daniel Beeby produced a certificate from Allonby Monthly Meeting at
Louby, dated 14/11/1734.

29/6/1735 - David Farris and Mary Massey declare their intention to
marry, he producing a certificate from his parents showing their
consent, and the young womans mother being present, declared her
consent. A certificate for Robert Reed and his wife, and one for
Abraham Parker, to Concord Monthly Meeting.

26/7/1735 - Testamony against Sarah Price, late Thompson, of this city,
for her disorderly marriage. Joseph Gill, designing to return home in
a short time, requests a certificate to Dublin.

31/8/1735 - A certificate for Patrick Ogilby to Abington Monthly Meeting,
in relation to marriage. James Sperry produced a certificate from
Chester Monthly Meeting dated 27/8/1735. John Armitt, intending
shortly on a voyage to Brittain, requests a certificate to London.

26/10/1735 - A certificate for William Callender to Friends in Barbadoes.
Testamony against Elizabeth Ponce, wife of Michael Ponce, was read.
Ralph Loftus produced a certificate from the Monthly Meeting at
Stockton to Friends in London.

30/11/1735 - A certificate for Samuel Hutton to Friends at Centre
Monthly Meeting in Chester County. Application on behalf of John
Iden and his wife for a certificate to Chester Monthly Meeting.
Elizabeth Dibble, now Gervise, having been dealt with for her breach
of our discipline with respect to marriage.

29/12/1735 - Christopher Marshall and Sarah Thompson clear to marry,
he producing a certificate from Middletown Monthly Meeting in

Bucks County. Owen Evans and Mary Nichols declare their intention to marry, he producing a certificate from Gwyned Monthly Meeting. Application in behalf of Joseph Bethell for a certificate to Derby Monthly Meeting.

26/1/1736 - Obadiah Eldridge and Mary Oldman clear to marry, he producing his fathers consent in writing and Friends appointed to see that provision be made for Mary's children report that their father had provided for them by will. Anthony Benezet and Joyce Merriott declare their intention to marry, their parents being present, declared their consent as did Thomas Merriott, Joyce's Guardian. Hannah Rhodes sent in a paper condemning her outgoing in marriage.

29/3/1736 - Thomas Strickland produced a certificate from a Monthly Meeting in Bucks County.

25/4/1736 - A certificate for John Naylor from Abington Monthly Meeting. William Callender produced a certificate from Friends in Barbadoes dated 2nd day of 3rd month, last. Israel Pemberton, Junr, produced a certificate from the two weeks meeting in London dated 26/11/1735. Thomas Knight produced a certificate for himself and his wife from Abington Monthly Meeting dated the 26th of 2nd month last. Lydia Davis, late Lydia Spencer, dealt with for her breach of our discipline in marrying out of our society.

30/5/1736 - A certificate for Ann Hunter, who is removed to Abington Monthly Meeting. A certificate to Friends at North Wales for Mary Evans, formerly Nicholas. A certificate on behalf of Stephen Peyton from Friends of Worcestershire dated the 12th month last. A certificate from Friends in Bucks County for Christopher Marshall. Christian Brown sent in a paper condemning her outgoing in marriage.

27/6/1736 - A certificate to Friends at the Clifts in Maryland for Samuel Chew, respecting his clearness to marry. A certificate for Patrick Ogleby and wife to Friends at Westbury on Long Island. A certificate for Thomas Redman to Friends at Haddonfield. A certificate on behalf of John Armett from the Two Weeks Meeting in London dated the 17th of the 3rd month last. Thomas Hodgekins produced a certificate from q Monthly Meeting in Salem dated the 26th of the 5th month last, on behalf of himself and his wife. Daniel Dawson produced a certificate from Abington Monthly Meeting dated the 26th of the 5th month last, on behalf of himself and his wife. James Lownes, Junr, sent in a paper condemning his disorderly procedure in marriage. This Meeting acquainted of the death of John Jenkinson and his wife who had left eight children. ... are appointed to get them placed out in suitable places among Friends.

24/7/1736 - A certificate for John Glenny from a Monthly Meeting held at Henly, dated 4/3/1736. A certificate for Isaac McNiece from the Monthly Meeting at Coole Hill in Ireland, dated 21/2/1736. A

certificate for David Clarke from Paynswick in the county of
Gloucester in Great Brittain, dated 10/2/1735. A certificate for Ralph
Loftus from Friends in Barbadoes, dated the 9th month last.

29/8/1736 - A certificate for Mary Hall, who is on a religious visit ... East
Greenwich in the colony of Rhode Island. Also one for her husband
William Hall who accompanied his wife. A certificate for Hannah
Jenkinson from West River in Maryland. She intends to return home
again. Application in behalf of John Hank for a certificate to
Burlington Monthly Meeting respecting marriage. A certificate for
John Patterson from Dublin dated the 25th of 3rd month last.

26/9/1736 - A certificate for James Claypoole to Sissell County, in
Maryland.

31/10/1736 - A testimony against Hannah Gilpin, late Knight, for
outgoing in marriage. A certificate for Samuel C. Walker from the
Monthly Meeting of Richmond, held at Canterbury in Yorkshire,
dated 6/4/1735. A certificate for James Lewis to Friends at
Crosswicks. George Mifflin applied on behalf of his son John Mifflin
for a certificate to Boston Monthly Meeting in relation to marriage. A
certificate for Israel Pemberton, Junr, to the Falls Monthly Meeting
respecting marriage. John Jones reports that he paid William Hudson
and John Bringhurst three pounds on account of John Jenkinson's
son, which they paid to Thomas Vernon towards schooling he is to
give him, the lad being put out to him until he attains the age of 14
years. Richard Renshaw and Ann his wife sent in a paper condemning
their disorderly marriage.

28/11/1736/7 - Friends appointed to see to a certificate for Joshua
Granger, who wished to remove with his family to North Carolina,
report he is not entitled to one. A certificate for John Jones to Salem.
John Hank delivered a paper acknowledging himself to blame in
relation to his proposal of marriage, which he afterward declined, and
desires that Friends would excuse his doing so without tendering the
particular reasons for his not proceeding further and he promises to
be more careful of giving offense in the future. Jacob Jones brought a
certificate from Wrightstown dated 7/11/1734/5. Rebecca Steele sent
in a paper condemning her disorderly marriage.

25/12/1736/7 - A certificate for John Speary to Newmarket Monthly
Meeting. John Biddle and Sarah Owen clear to marry, he producing a
letter signifying his fathers consent and her parents being present,
consenting. John Walby applied for a certificate for himself and wife.

25/1/1737 - A certificate for John Oxley from the Quarterly Meeting at
Barbadoes, and he intending to return home in a short time, requests
a certificate from this meeting. A certificate for William Morrison
from Abington, dated the 28th of last month. Sampson Davis and his
wife, lately settled in this city, sent in a certificate from Abington
Monthly Meeting dated the 28th of last month. Edward Evans and

Rebecca Clark declare their intention to marry, he producing his parents consent in writing and her mother being present, declaring her consent. Sam'l Morris and Hannah Cadwallader declare their intention to marry, their parents being present, consenting. Tobias Griscomb and Grace Rakestraw declare their intention to marry, her mother being present, consenting.

29/2/1737 - Testimony against Moses Hughes prepared. A testimony against Sarah Tuckett prepared. A certificate for John Walby and his wife to Friends in Great Brittain or elsewhere. John Guest and Susanna Truman clear to marry, he producing a certificate from Burlington. Joseph Shoemaker, Junr, sent in a paper condemning his disorderly conduct and breach of discipline in outgoing in marriage.

27/3/1737 - John Jones and John Bringhurst report they have paid to Elizabeth Jackson five pounds, she being in necessity. Considering Nicholas Rogers request, writing certificates, etc, it is thought, considering his deafness he will not be capable of performing to satisfaction. A certificate for David Robinson to Goshen Monthly Meeting. The complaint of Jonathan Cockshaw against Miles Strickland and John Walby is ended. Samuel Pennock and Elizabeth Widdowfield declare their intention to marry, his father and her mother being present, consenting. David Clark and Elizabeth Eastbourne declare their intention to marry, her parents being present, consenting. A certificate for Robert Strettle, his wife, son and two daughters, from the Monthly Meeting at Horsleydown in Southwark, dated 26th of 11th month last. Isaac Morris applied on behalf of his brother Samuel Morris for a Certificate to Gwyned. Application on behalf of William Fishbourne for a certificate to London. Application on behalf of Edward Thompson and his wife for a certificate to Concord Monthly Meeting in Chester County. A certificate for Reese Roberts from the Monthly Meeting at Radnor dated the 10th of 1st month last. John and Rebecca Cresson sent in a paper condemning their outgoing in Marriage. A certificate for John Bushel from Barbadoes dated the 12 of the 3rd month last. Elizabeth and Catherine Ellis sent in a paper setting forth their great trouble in nursing Mary Owen and her daughter in their illness ... they being ill as they set forth 33 weeks .... The Meeting therefore directs John Jones to pay them 4 pounds.

29/5/1737 - Samuel Pennock and Elizabeth Widdowfield clear to marry, he producing a certificate from New Garden Monthly Meeting. No certificate for William Fishbourne, he having altered his intention to go to London. Testimony against Benj. Ray was read. A certificate for Lewis Weston from the Two Weeks Meeting in London, dated the 7th of 12th month last. A certificate for Eleanor Bevan from Harford Monthly Meeting, dated the 14th of last month. Application on behalf of William Warner and his wife for a certificate to Newark Monthly

Meeting. Application on behalf of David Ferris and his wife for a certificate to Newark Monthly Meeting, they being gone to settle at Willingstown in New Castle County.

26/6/1737 - William Horne and Elizabeth Davis clear to marry, his mother being present, consenting and he producing a certificate from Darby Monthly Meeting. A certificate for John Hank to Friends at Burlington respecting his clearness in relation to marriage. Application on behalf of Isaac Lobbden for a certificate to Friends at Boston. It being moved that Sarah Freeman, whose husband formerly presented a certificate from ..., which being deficient was not accepted, ... ought not to appear in public as a minister.

30/7/1737 - Job Yarnall and Rebecca Lownes clear o marry, he producing a certificate from Chester Monthly Meeting. A certificate for Elijah Collins from Friends at Boston, and he designing to return shortly requests a few lines from this meeting. A paragraph of Joshua Tittery's will was read. Application on behalf of Thomas Hodgshin and his wife for a certificate to Salem Monthly Meeting.

28/8/1737 - A certificate for Lewis Weston to Friends in London. Hugh Durborrow and Sarah Freeman, widow, declare their intention to marry, she producing a certificate from Gantford (?Hartford) Monthly Meeting, and Friends appointed to see that care is taken that provision is made for Sarah's two sons. Upon application, a certificate for Lawrence Growden to Friends in Bristol was granted, dated 29/1/1734, but his affairs preventing his return to Brittain he did not make use of it, now being likely to return thither in a very short time, a new certificate is prepared.

30/10/1737 - Joseph Marshall and Rachel Marle declare their intention to marry, he producing a letter from his father and mother, dated at Mansfield 25/5/1737. Joseph Hopewell sent in a paper condemning his disorderly procedure in marriage. Elizabeth Hawkins sent in a paper condemning her conduct.

27/11/1737 - Samuel Powell and John Bringhurst acquainted this meeting that they had bound out John Jenkinson, son of John Jenkinson, deceased, to John Murray of Marlboro, Chester County, until he attains the age of 21 years.

24/12/1737/8 - Testimony against Elizabeth Brockden, alias Elizabeth England, for breach of discipline in marriage. Edward Roberts and Martha Cox declare their intention to marry, Friends appointed to see that provision be made for her children. Application on behalf of Adam Rhodes for a certificate to Goshen Monthly Meeting. A certificate for Jeremiah Elfreth to Westbury Monthly Meeting on Long Island, on account of marriage. Joseph Hitchcock sent in a paper condemning his disorderly procedure in marriage.

31/1/1838 - Edward Roberts and Martha Cox clear to marry, Marthas mother being present, declares her consent. Reese Meredith and

Martha Carpenter declare their intention to marry, he producing a certificate from Leominster, in the county of Hereford, in Great Brittain. Application in behalf of Thomas Cadwallader for a certificate to Chesterfield Monthly Meeting.

28/2/1738 - A testimony of disownment against Ann Lloyd. Ralph Loftus and Jane Cart declare their intention to marry, her mother being present, consenting. William and Sarah Preston sent in a paper condemning their disorderly procedure in marriage. A certificate for Benj. Callender from Bridgetown in Barbadoes.

26/3/1738 - A testimony against John Parrock for his outgoing in marriage. A testimony against Mary Nice, widow. Isaac Browne sent in a paper condemning his disorderly procedure in marriage. A certificate for William Griscomb to Haddonfield. Ruth Courtney and Susannah Hudson, from Ireland, set forward on their visit to the eastward, and after they have performed it, intend to take shipping at Boston to return home. Norton Pryor sent in a paper condemning his unchaste freedom before marriage. Application on behalf of George Wilson for 40/ which was due to him for making a coffin for Daniel Evans.

25/5/1738 - A certificate for Jos. England to Friends at Cecil Monthly Meeting in Maryland. A certificate for John Glaney to North Wales. John and Sarah Langdale sent in a paper condemning their disreputable freedom before marriage. Application on behalf of John Reeves for a certificate to Friends in London. Samuel Powell hath cause of complaint against Isaac Bolton. John Martindale sent in a paper condemning his disorderly procedure in marriage. James Steele hath cause of complaint against Thomas Shute.

25/6/1738 - A certificate for Robert Jordan .... A certificate for Martha Walker and her daughter Rebecca from Richmond Monthly Meeting. A certificate for Leonard Snowden to Grisborough Monthly Meeting in Yorkshire in Great Brittain. William Callender applied in behalf of his brother Joseph for a certificate to Friends in Barbadoes.

29/7/1738 - A certificate for Richard Tomlinson from Burlington Monthly Meeting, dated 5/7/1737. Application in behalf of David Ellwell for a certificate to Haddonfield Monthly Meeting. There having been a charge accrued on the burial of John Staines, the Meeting directs John Jones to pay the money to those it is due. Benjamin Trotter complains against Jacob Shute. Isaac Andrews and Elizabeth Elfreth clear to marry, he producing a certificate from Burlington Monthly Meeting. Joseph Armitt and Elizabeth Lisle clear to marry, he producing a paper signed by his mother in law and her husband, Christopher hunter, signifying their consent. George Howell sent in a paper condemning his disorderly procedure in marriage. Application on behalf of John Hank for a certificate to Burlington, he being removed within the verge of that Meeting.

24/9/1738 - Lydia Cathcart sent in a paper condemning her unbecoming freedom and the manner of her marriage. Application on behalf of Isaiah Mackie for a certificate to Goshen Monthly Meeting.

29/10/1738 - Benjamin Eastburn sent in a paper condemning his unguarded conduct. Testimony against Hannah Boyd, late Bond, for outgoing in marriage, was read. A certificate for James Steele from Little Creek Monthly Meeting. A certificate for James Hill and his wife from a Preparatory Meeting held near Ballenderry in the county of Antrim, dated 21/5/1728, was read. They being lately removed to settle at Williamstown in New Castle County, application was made on their behalf for a certificate to Friends at Newark monthly Meeting.

26/11/1738 - A certificate for Richard Waln to Goshen Monthly Meeting, he intending to marry. A certificate for John Luke from Bridgetown in Barbadoes, dated 19th of 8th month last. A certificate for James Estaugh and his wife from Haddonfield, dated 11/10/1738. Application on behalf of Jacob Durborrow and his wife for a certificate to Chester Monthly Meeting. Cadwallader Foulke complains that Dennis Rochford is indebted to someone in England. Application on behalf of William Welton for a certificate to Newark Monthly Meeting.

23/12/1738 - George Shires and Hannah Durborrow clear to marry, Sarah Hoodt, grandmother of the young woman sent her consent in writing. A certificate for Phineas Bond from a Quarterly Meeting at Herring Creek, in Maryland, dated the 7th instant. Solomon Cresson sent in a paper condemning his imprudent conduct.

30/1/1739 - A certificate for John Roberts from the Monthly Meeting at the Cliffs, in Maryland, dated 7/2/1738.

27/2/1739 - Isaac Morris and Sarah Logan declare their intention to marry, Isaac's mother being present, consenting, and the young womans mother also present, consents and her father sending his in writing. Application on behalf of Anthony Benezet and his wife for a certificate to Newark Monthly Meeting. Application on behalf of Thomas Strickland for a Certificate to Wrightstown. Application made on behalf of Isaac Warren for a certificate to Haddonfield, respecting marriage.

25/3/1739 - Daniel Worthington and Mary Wood declare their intention to marry, Mary being a widow, Friends are appointed to see there be provision made for her children. A certificate for Paul Chanders from Pardshaw, in Lancashire, dated 19/7/1738. A certificate for Eliphal Harper, who landed here on her return from her visit to Great Brittain, to Friends in Sandwich, in New England. Nathaniel Edgecombe has been dealt with for his outgoing in marriage.

29/4/1739 - Daniel Worthington and Mary Wood clear to marry, he producing a certificate from Abington Monthly Meeting and Friends appointed to see provision made for Mary's children report it is done.

7/5/1739 - Adam Rhodes sent in a paper condemning his conduct before marriage. A certificate for Thomas Middleton to Chesterfield Monthly Meeting. A certificate for Anthony Morris to Chesterfield Monthly Meeting at Croswicks.

31/6/1739 - Daniel Cooper and Mary West declare their intention to marry, their parents being present, consenting. A certificate for Isaac Dawson from Abington Monthly Meeting, dated 24/2/1738, but the meeting being apprized he hath married from among Friends, the overseer's are desired to deal with him. William Fishbourne sent in a paper condemning his scandalous practices.

28/7/1739 - A certificate for John Pole and Rachel his wife from Burlington Monthly Meeting.

26/8/1739 - A certificate for Ezeck Fitzrandolph to Woodbury Monthly Meeting. A certificate for Isaac Lobden to Newark Monthly Meeting in New Castle County.

30/9/1739 - Anthony Nichols and Mary Cowman declare their intention to marry. Mary being a widow, Friends are appointed to see that suitable provision be made for her child, and William Atwood, her uncle, being present, declared his consent. Jeremiah Elfreth acquainted this Meeting that there are two poor children in their neighborhood whose parents are dead and the children being young, one is a son of Aaron Goforth, Junr, and the other a son of Robert Abbot, ... to find suitable places for their boarding and that care be taken for their schooling.

28/10/1739 - A certificate for Mary Foulke to Friends in Barbadoes. A certificate for Robert Jordan, to travel with John Hunt on a religious visit, to Friends in Long Island. Joshua Walton complains there is a matter of dispute between him and Hugh Durborrow, which Hugh refuseth to accommodate.

25/11/1739 - A certificate for William Fishbourne, Junr, to Friends in London, respecting his clearness in marriage. The complaint of Joshua Walton against Hugh Durborrow is accommodated to the satisfaction of the parties.

29/12/1739 - A certificate for Benjamin Callender to friends in Barbadoes. A certificate for George Emlen, Junr, to London.

28/1/1740 - Sarah Evans sent in a paper condemning her marriage contrary to the discipline of Friends. A certificate for Daniel Bateman to Friends in Rhode Island. A certificate for Jacob Townsend to Salem.

25/2/1740 - A certificate for Robert Hartshorne to Burlington. Jeremiah Elfreth and Mary Wells declare their intention to marry. Mary being a widow, ... to see that provision be made for her children. Benjamin Mifflin complains against his uncle, George Mifflin, who refuseth to refer. A certificate for William Lawrence to Friends at Shrewsbury.

30/3/1740 - Friends appointed to speak to Sarah Durborrow, late
Freeman, formerly of England, report they had delivered her the
sense of the meeting respecting her ministry and she acquainted
them she was in hopes she would not give friends any trouble in that
respect. Hannah Finney, late Brown, sent in a paper condemning her
outgoing in marriage. A certificate for Abraham Johns to Friends at
the Cliffs in Maryland. John West complains against John Brientnall,
that he is in his debt and refuseth to make satisfaction.

27/4/1740 - Application on behalf of George Howell to Friends at Newark
Monthly Meeting.

25/5/1740 - A testimony against Jacob Jones for his disorderly conduct. A
testimony against Elizabeth Essex for her disorderly proceeding in
marriage. A certificate for John Pearce to Friends at London.

29/6/1740 - A certificate for Joseph Peters to Newark Monthly Meeting.

26/7/1740 - John Ogden and Hannah Owen clear to marry, William
Tidmarsh acquainting this meeting of her grandfathers consent and
her parents sent their consent in writing. James Stephens and Mary
Widdowfield declare their intention to marry, he producing a
certificate from Haddonfield Monthly Meeting and his mother being
present, consenting. Samuel Preston brought a letter from Jacob
Maule, late of this place and now from Salem, in New England,
wherein he condemns his leaving this place in debt and requests that
Friends would receive the same as satisfaction and grant him a few
lines to certify his clearness in relation to marriage.

21/8/1740 - A certificate for Phillip Marriot to Friends at Crosswicks in
the Jerseys. A certificate for George Emlen, Junr, to Friends at
Crosswicks, in relation to marriage.

28/9/1740 - A testimony against Sampson Davis for drinking. Joseph
Sanders and Hannah reeves declare their intention to marry, he
producing a certificate from the Two Weeks Meeting at London,
dated 8/1/1735/6, and her father being present, consenting.

26/10/1740 - A certificate for Lawrence Growden to the Falls Monthly
Meeting, being only in relation to marriage. A certificate for William
Buckley to Friends at Newport in Rhode Island, respecting his
clearness in relation to marry. Sarah Hawkins sent in a paper
condemning her outgoing in marriage.

30/11/1740 - Richard Blackburn and Rebecca Minshall, Junr, declare
their intention to marry, he producing a certificate from Burlington
and his mothers consent in writing. The young womans mother being
present, consents. John Linton has been dealt with for disorderly
procedure in marriage.

27/1/1741 - Joseph Howell and Hannah Hudson declare their intention to
marry, his parents being present, consenting, and as did her
Grandmother and Guardian. Thomas and Joseph Readman complain
against Abraham Bickley, setting forth that he being indebted to

them, refuseth to pay. A certificate for John Jones, his wife, and two
daughters, from Radnor Monthly Meeting dated the 11th day of 7th
month last. A certificate for John Reeve to Burlington. Application
made by William Bull, Govenor of South Carolina, to William Penn,
Esq, our Proprietor, and to George Thomas, Esq, our Governor,
respecting the great distress of many of the inhabitants of that
Colony occasioned by a fire which lately happened in Charlestown,
requesting the charitable contributions of such as are well disposed in
this province.

25/2/1741 - A certificate for Joseph Sanders to Friends in London, he
being on a voyage for Brittain. Thomas Gysom, being very ancient,
desires to go up to his son Thomas in Bucks County and being very
poor, desires some assistance from Friends.

23/3/1741 - A certificate for Joseph Thornton to Friends at Middletown,
in Bucks County. A certificate for Joseph Saul from the Monthly
Meeting at Pardshawhall, in Cumberland, in Great Brittain, dated
20/11/1740/1.

26/4/1741 - Richard Carver sent in a paper condemning his disorderly
procedure in marriage. Samuel Jackson brought in a paper confessing
and condemning his disorderly conduct in accompanying a disorderly
company of people along the streets. Application on behalf of John
Baker for a certificate to friends at Abington, on account of marriage.

31/5/1741 - It appearing by letter from Joseph Shute that he hath been a
considerable sufferer by the fire at Charlestown, S. Carolina, ... this
meeting ... directs the Friends ... to send Joseph Shute one hundred
pounds.

28/6/1741 - A certificate for our ancient Friend Thomas Chalkley to
Friends in the Islands of Tortola and Anguilla. A letter in answer to
one received from John Pickering, Governor of Tortola, was read.
Application on behalf of Joseph James for a certificate to Abington
Monthly Meeting, respecting marriage.

25/7/1741 - Isaac Shoemaker and Hannah Roberts clear to marry. he
producing a certificate from Abington Monthly Meeting and their
parents being present, consenting.

30/8/1741 - Mary Lingard sent in her account for Mary Warner's
accommodation.

27/9/1741 - Joseph Noble applied in behalf of his son Samuel for a
certificate to Barbadoes.

25/10/1741 - A certificate for our ancient Friend Samuel Hopwood on a
religious visit from Great Brittain. Robert Strettle applied on behalf
of his son Amos for a certificate to Friends in London. A certificate for
Benjamin Mason to Abington Monthly Meeting respecting marriage.
Samuel Sansom complains against Robert Strettle, that he hath sued
him contrary to our discipline.

29/11/1741/2 - A certificate for John Warren to Providence Monthly
Meeting in Chester County. Alexander Dean hath a matter of
complaint against John Parrock. Robert Eastburn, Junr, has been
dealt with for his absenting himself from our religious assemblies.

26/12/1741/2 - A testimony against Mary Hudson for outgoing in
marriage. A testimony against William Cannon, clockmaker. Sarah
Durborrow, Tabitha Drinker and Ann Stevenson hath been dealt
with for declining to attend our religious meetings. The widow
Lambert, mother of Ann Stephenson, had some hopes of her
daughter returning to Friends again. William Plumstead dealt with
for his disorderly conduct. Edward Evans dealt with fir declining to
attend our meetings.

26/1/1742 - A certificate for Hannah Jenkinson to Long Island in New
England. Testimony against Martha Williams, late Boyer, Elizabeth
Ashton, late Boyer, Elizabeth Cusak, late Robins, and Mary White,
late Ransted, for outgoing in marriage. A certificate for Joseph
Carlisle to Friends in Burlington. A certificate for Hannah Hurford
and her sister Susannah Morris to visit Friends in New England. A
certificate for John Mifflin, son of John Mifflin, deceased, to Friends
at little Creek.

30/2/1742 - A certificate for Cadwallader Evans from Gwynedd Monthly
Meeting, dated 30th of last month. Benjamin Mifflin brought in a
paper condemning his breach of discipline respecting marriage.
Joseph Wood complains against Elizabeth Griffiths, that she being in
his debt, refuseth to pay.

28/3/1742 - A certificate for Edward James to Friends at Salem, on
account of marriage. A certificate for Samuel Jackson to the Monthly
Meeting at Concord, in Chester County, on account of marriage.

25/4/1742 - Testimony against Ann Shute, late Pendley, having divers
times precautioned against her procedure in marriage, yet not
withstanding, she is since married to her cousin Attwood Shute and
she hath not condemned her disorderly marriage. A certificate for
John Dawson, his wife Dorothy and daughter Deborah, from
Abington Monthly Meeting, dated 31/5/1742.

30/5/1742 - Thomas Shoemaker and Sarah Reed declare their intention
to marry, his father and her mother in law being present, declared
their consent. Rachel Hudson has married to John _ory, a person not
of our society. A certificate for William Thomas from the Island of
Tortola, dated 23/3/1742. A paper from Richard Waln and his wife
condemning their disorderly procedure in marriage. Deborah Butler
sent in a paper condemning her disorderly procedure in marriage.
Nathan Trotter brought in a paper condemning his disorderly
procedure in marriage. Application on behalf of John Harmen for a
certificate to Friends at Abington. Isaac Davenport, having been dealt
with for his disorderly procedure in marriage and not having

condemned it to the satisfaction of Friends, testimony is to be prepared against him. Testimony prepared against Thomas Bond, having been dealt with for his disorderly conduct, especially his taking the oath ....

27/6/1742 - Abraham Griffith and Elizabeth Lynn declare their intention to marry, their parents being present, consenting. Jonathan Cockshaw intends to move to Gwynedd. Jonathan Mifflin complains against David Clark, that there is a difference between them.

24/7/1742 - Joshua Pearson and Elizabeth Biddle declare their intention to marry, their parents being present, consenting. A certificate for Edmund Peckover the from Monthly Meeting at Teckenham in the county of Norfolk, dated the 27th of 4th month last. A certificate for John Haslam from the Monthly Meeting at Wamsworth in the county of York, dated the 4th of last month. A certificate on behalf of Preston Carpenter to Friends at Salem, on account of marriage.

29/8/1742 - Joshua Pearson and Elizabeth Biddle clear to marry, producing a certificate from Darby Monthly Meeting. Samuel and Rebecca Griscom brought in a paper condemning their intimacy before marriage. Tabitha Andrews, late Drinker, and Ann Stephenson have for some time declined attending our meetings, and Hannah Hawkins, late Harper, was married contrary to our discipline, as likewise Esther Scull, daughter of Thomas Mitchell. Application on behalf of John Jones and his wife for a certificate to Abington Monthly Meeting.

31/10/1742 - Andrew Bradford now being deceased. Friends appointed to get the materials belonging to the printing press from him are now desired to continue their endeavors to get them from his Executors. Paul Chandler and Jane Johnson clear to marry, due care being taken of the widows children. Joseph Garrett some months since produced a certificate from Friends in Dublin of which no minute was made, he being uncertain within the verge of what Meeting he should settle, but he being now returned home, application is made on his behalf for a certificate for him to Friends in Dublin. Anthony Morris, one of the Executors of Samuel Hudson's will, complains against Joshua Lawrence, that he refuses to pay a debt due the estate. Honour Harmer being sometime deceased, Joseph Harmer is appointed to dig the graves.

28/11/1742 - Testimony against Frances Strettle, daughter of Robert Strettle, for having joined another Society. A certificate for Moses Thomas to Friends in Burlington, respecting his clearness in marriage. Sarah Kelly, a young woman from Nottingham, in Chester County, came to this city last summer, was taken ill and died, not leaving effects to defray the expenses of her nursing and burial.

15/12/1742 - A testimony against Margaret Williams was read. Thomas Hood applied on behalf of his son, John Hood, for a certificate to Abington Monthly Meeting, respecting marriage.

26/1/1753 - A certificate for Thomas Hood to Abington.

29/2/1743 - Application on behalf of Elias Bland for a certificate to Friends in London.

27/3/1743 - Rebecca Gorsuch, formerly Gray, brought in a paper condemning her conduct ....

25/4/1743 - Stephen Benezet has been lovingly spoke to respecting his declining to attend our Meetings, ... he had joined himself in society with the Moravians. Francis Richardson brought in a paper condemning his conduct before marriage. A certificate for James Truman to Hartford Monthly Meeting, in order for marriage.

29/5/1743 - Friends appointed to consider William Coates will are continued.

26/6/1743 - Testimony against Reese Peters, Junr, for outgoing in marriage.

30/7/1743 - A certificate for John Baldwin to Concord Monthly Meeting. A certificate for John Needham, his wife and three children, John, Ann and Mary, from Chester Monthly Meeting, dated the 9th of last month. Application on behalf of Peter Baker for a certificate to Bristol, in Great Brittain. Application on behalf of Thomas Gilpin and his wife to Concord. Samuel C. Bould and his wife are both dead and have left four children, three of them young and destitute of any substance.

28/8/1743 - John Bringhurst applied on behalf of his son John for a certificate to Friends in Barbadoes. Adam Leis applied to this Meeting for some assistance.

25/9/1743 - A certificate for Edmund Peckover to Takenham in Norfolk, in Great Brittain.

30/10/1743 - A certificate for Silas Carpenter, on a religious visit from Rhode Island Colony. William Trotter brought in a paper signed by himself and his wife. Susanna Williams, late Hodge, and likewise Esther Classe, late Clare, have been dealt with for disorderly procedure in marriage.

27/11/1743 - A certificate for Samuel Lippencott and wife to Shrewsbury. Joseph Oldman complains against William Parker for not paying rent due to Paul Prestons estate. William Davis brought in a paper signed by himself and his wife, condemning their procedure in marriage.

24/12/1743 - A certificate for James Dalzell to Haddonfield Monthly Meeting.

30/1/1744 - A testimony against Samuel Emlen, James Cresson and Enoch Flower. John Galloway and James Fishbourn clear to marry, the father of the children having provided for them by will. A certificate for Mary Emlen to visit Friends to the eastward as far as

New England with our Friend Mary Evans of N. Wales. A certificate
for Richard Waln, to North Wales. Application on behalf of Joshua
Gill for a certificate to North Wales.

27/2/1744 - Isaac Lobdell and Rebecca Cresson declare their intention to
marry, her father being present, declared his consent, and Isaac
producing his mothers consent in writing and likewise a certificate
from Newark Monthly Meeting, held at Centre the 7th inst. A
certificate for Samuel Lippincott and Mary his wife to Shrewsbury
Monthly Meeting. Application on behalf of Thomas Poltney for a
certificate to Laycock Monthly Meeting.

25/3/1744 - Application on behalf of James Moore for a certificate to
Friends at Burlington. Isaac Whitelock hath been dealt with for his
breach in discipline in marrying a person not of our Society.

29/4/1744 - A certificate for Samuel Hopwood to the Monthly Meeting at
Austle in Great Brittain. A certificate for John Haslam to the
Monthly Meeting at Warnsworth, in Yorkshire, in Great Brittain.
Two of the overseer's report they spoke to Richard hayes and he now
attended with his certificate ... ... Harford Monthly Meeting, dated
12/8/1742. A testimony prepared against Joseph Preston. A certificate
for John Low from Lurgan Monthly Meeting in the North of London.
William and Esther Davis sent in a paper condemning their disorderly
procedure in marriage. Application on behalf of Samuel Morris for a
certificate to Gwynedd Monthly Meeting. Application on behalf of
Abraham Whitall to Salem Monthly Meeting. The following have been
dealt with for breach of discipline in marriage: Rachel Tempest, late
Hines; Esther Bankson, late Lynn; Rebecca Hood, late Shute; Mary
Lyon, late Fisher; Elizabeth Durborrow, for her unchaste conduct;
Martha Renshaw, late Shute. Application on behalf of Mary Painter,
widow, that she may have the benefit of one of the rooms at the
Almshouse to live in.

27/5/1744 - A testimony against Isaac Whitlock of the Northern Liberties
of this city, a tanner, for his outgoing in marriage. Thomas Hood,
June, and Rebecca his wife brought in a paper condemning their
disorderly marriage. A certificate for Jane Galloway. Application on
behalf of Thomas Parry and his wife for a certificate to Abington
Monthly Meeting.

31/6/1744 - George James complains against Samuel Predman, that he is
indebted to him. Application on behalf of Thomas Lightfoot to
Burlington Monthly Meeting, on account of marriage. Application on
behalf of William Rakestraw for a certificate to Radnor Monthly
Meeting, on account of marriage.

28/7/1744 - A certificate for Silas Carpenter to the Monthly Meeting at
Greenwich, in the colony of Rhode Island. George Mifflin applied on
behalf of his son George for a certificate to Friends in London. A

certificate for Benjamin Shoemaker for a certificate to Friends in London.

28/8/1744 - Application on behalf of Isaac Thompson to Friends at East Caln.

30/9/1744 - Certificates for Christopher Wilson and Eleazor Shelden. Joseph Stiles has entered himself on board a privateer and has been dealt with for the same.

28/10/1744 - Johanna Smith brought a paper condemning her disorderly procedure in marriage. Moses Thomas hath been dealt with for his disorderly marriage.

25/11/1744 - Thomas Marriott and Mary Foulke clear to marry, he producing a certificate from the Falls Monthly Meeting and provision being made for the young womans son. Samuel Jones brought in a paper signed by his wife and himself to condemn their disorderly marriage. Thomas Stretch and his wife, like wise, brought in a paper condemning their disorderly marriage. A certificate for Daniel Deeby to Newark Monthly Meeting. Application on behalf of Isaac Bolton for a certificate to Abington Monthly Meeting.

22/12/1744 - A certificate for William griffith to Swanzy Monthly Meeting in Great Brittain. Application made last month on behalf of Sarah Lea, hat she may have a room in the Almshouse, Women Friends do now make application on behalf of Mary Warner, for a room for her.

1/29/1745 - Joseph Harmer brought in a paper condemning his conduct as well as his breach of discipline in respect to marriage.

26/2/1745 - A certificate for Issachar Price, his wife and two daughters, Lydia and Letitia, from Haverford Monthly Meeting.

31/3/1745 - A certificate for John Holton and his wife to Derby Monthly Meeting. Ann Eve, formerly Moore, hath been dealt with for going out in marriage.

28/4/1745 - A certificate for Thomas Gardiner to Burlington Monthly Meeting. The complaint of Jonathan Mifflin against Thomas Tilbury report the same is ended. Our Friend, Robert Wade, formerly of Chester County, is deceased. Jonathan Mifflin complains against Thomas Hood. A letter from the Monthly Meeting at Wrightstown respecting Peter Clark ... ... which they allow to be a good reason for refusing his certificate.

26/5/1745 - Joseph and Elizabeth Gardner delivered a paper condemning their disorderly procedure in marriage. A paper from Elizabeth Stinton, late Gardiner condemning her disorderly procedure in marriage. A paper from Rebecca Cruckshank, late Hudson, condemning her disorderly marriage. George Mifflin complains against his brother, Jonathan Mifflin, there being a difference between them. Testimony against William Saunders, who hath for a considerable time declined to attend our meetings.

28/6/1745 - A paper from Mary Hill, lately Hoodt, condemning her disorderly procedure in marriage. A certificate for Griffith Jones, his son Aquila and daughter Priscilla, from Abington Monthly Meeting. A certificate for Ebenezer Robinson from Burlington.

27/7/1745 - A certificate for Joseph Richardson to Friends at Chesterfield, in Burlington County. Application on behalf of Joseph Davis and his wife to Friends at Gwynedd Monthly Meeting. Application on behalf of Joseph Davis and his wife foe a certificate to Gwynedd Monthly Meeting. Adam Lewis requires some further assistance. William Brooks hath been dealt with for going on a privateering voyage, contrary to our known principles. Joseph House has been dealt with for being concerned as owner of a private ship of war fitted out in this city.

25/8/1745 - A certificate for Joseph Marriott to Salem Monthly Meeting. Thomas Brooks brought in a paper condemning his going out privateering. Application on behalf of Samuel Bryan for a certificate to Friends in London.

29/9/1745 - A minute prepared for James Scriven and Stephen Wilcox, here on a visit from New England. A certificate for Nathaniel and Elihu Coleman, here on a religious visit from Nantucket.

27/10/1745 - Friends report the complaint of Samuel Preston Moore against John Langdale is a likely way to be accommodated. William Lightfoot produced a certificate for himself and his wife from New Garden Monthly Meeting, his wife being deceased since the date of said certificate.

31/11/1745 - John Williams brought to this meeting a paper signed by himself and his wife Deborah condemning their disorderly procedure in marriage. Joseph Richardson sent in a paper complaining that he has a debt due from Ralph Loftus, Sarah Cart and John Warder which he apprehends cannot be covered but by a suit of law.

28/12/1745 - Joseph Davis brought in a paper condemning his undue liberty in consenting to his servants going on a voyage with the privateer and receiving part of their profit. A certificate for Joseph Webb to Newark Monthly Meeting, to proceed in marriage. A certificate for Nathaniel Allen, Junr, to Chesterfield Monthly Meeting, on account of marriage. A certificate for Thomas Clifford and Anna, his wife, from Burlington Monthly Meeting.

28/1/1746 - Friends appointed on the affairs respecting Ralph Loftus report that he has paid the debt due to John Richardson. Sarah Cart, one of the Friends bound with him to John Richardson, being deceased since the last meeting. A certificate for Samuel Jordan to the Monthly Meeting at Nansemond in Virginia. A certificate for George Cozins and wife from Haddonfield Monthly Meeting.

25/2/1746 - Peter Brown and Sarah Fisher clear to marry, care being taken that Sarah's children have such provision made for them as her circumstances would admit.

30/3/1746 - Samuel Abbott and Elizabeth Hastings clear to marry, Samuel Hastings, her Uncle present and consenting. A certificate for Joshua Fisher, his wife and two daughters, from Duck Creek Monthly Meeting. A certificate for Timothy Matlock, his wife Martha and daughter Sybil, from Haddonfield Monthly Meeting.

27/4/1746 - Testimony against Joseph Hitchcock for drinking, etc. Application on behalf of George Cozens for a certificate for himself and his family to Haddonfield Monthly Meeting. A certificate for Mary Hall to Friends at Chester Monthly Meeting.

25/5/1746 - It is reported that Hannah, the daughter of Samuel Bolton, was formerly married to John Coombs and is lately married to John Clark, not having a certain account of the decease of her said first husband for which she hath been dealt with. Thomas Shute complains against Thomas Hood, that he refuses to comply with the awards of arbitration appointed to settle the lines of their lands.

29/6/1746 - John Reynell and Israel Pemberton, Junr, signed the deed to Preserve Brown for the 25 feet Bank and Water Lott formerly given to this Meeting by our worthy Friend George Fox. John Wright, hatter, brought into this Meeting a paper signed by himself and his wife, condemning their proceeding in marriage contrary to our discipline. Our Friend Joshua Crosby and his nephew Thomas Crosby, being lately arrived from Jamaica to settle here, acquainted this Meeting of their inclination to be joined to us.

26/7/1746 - A certificate for Joseph Davis and his wife to Gwynedd Monthly Meeting. Joseph Noble applied on behalf of his son Samuel for a certificate to Haddonfield Monthly Meeting, on account of his intended marriage. Hannah Lewis hath been for some time under great indisposition of mind.

31/8/1746 - Samuel Redman, bricklayer, disowned for the irregularity of his conduct. William Cundall complains against Adam Rhodes, that he is in debt to him and neglects to pay.

28/9/1746 - Joseph Richard produced to this meeting a paper acknowledging his breach of our discipline in regard to marriage and desiring to be continued under their notice and care. A certificate for John White, his wife Esther and her son Stephen Staple, from Kennett Monthly Meeting in Chester County. A testimony against Mary, the wife of Ebenezer Doughty, late Mary Allen, for her breach of discipline in marriage. An account of Mary Cribs, for boarding and clothing Samuel Boulds, an orphan child under our care, is desired to be paid. Application on behalf of James Dabzell and his wife for a certificate to Ha____ Monthly Meeting. A certificate for Jonathan Shoemaker to Haverford Monthly Meeting, on account of his

intention to marry. An epistle from John Haslam, dated at
Hansworth Woodhouse, in Yorkshire, was read.

26/10/1746 - A paper from Silas Pryor and Ann his wife, expressing their
concern for their procedure in marriage. A testimony against Thomas
Shoemaker, bricklayer. A certificate for Richard Wood to marry and
settle at Haddonfield. Permission for Rebeckah Bolton to live in one
of the Almshouses is given.

30/11/1746 - Anthony Benezet reports that it appears not to be proper to
grant a certificate for James Debzell at present. Jane Harpers
present circumstances require immediate care in providing a suitable
place. Thomas Gawthorp from Westmoreland, being lately arrived on
a religious visit, produced a certificate from the Monthly Meeting in
Kendall.

27/12/1746 - A paper from William Clark and Beulah his wife,
acknowledging their breach of discipline in marriage. Caspar Wistar
complains against Rob't. and Amos Strettle, that there's a matter of
dispute between them.

27/1/1747 - Papers from Hannah Robinson and Jane Jones, each
condemning their proceeding in marriage. Richard Ireson brought in a
paper signed by him and his wife ... in order to their obtaining a
certificate to Friends at Hopewell in Virginia where they now reside.
Application for a certificate to Sadsbury Monthly Meeting for Thomas
Brown, who served his apprenticeship in this city and now has
removed to settle there. Application for Rebeckah Bellinger to live
rent free in one of the Almshouses is agreed to.

24/2/1747 - Richard Waln disowned for unbecoming behaviour. Joshua
Wollaston and Priscilla Jones declare their intention to marry, their
parents being present and consenting. A testimony against John
Howell, tanner, for not paying his debt. Anthony Woodcock delivered
a paper condemning his breach of discipline in marry out. A certificate
for Joseph Noble Friends in Burlington, in order to marry. Israel
Pemberton, Junr, complains that being appointed by Jane Vanaken,
one of the Trustees in a settlement made by her of her estate before
her last marriage, he hath since her decease applied to her husband,
Henry Vanaken, to deliver up the said settlement to him and the
other Trustees. A certificate for Margaret Holland from Abington
Monthly Meeting.

9/3/1747 - Samuel Lippencott and Mary his wife, received on certificate
from Shrewsbury Monthly Meeting, make application for a certificate
to settle at Haddonfield. James Draper and Rebecca his wife brought
in a paper condemning their breach in discipline in marrying contrary
to the good order of Friends. Priscilla Jones, who at the last Monthly
Meeting proposed her intention of marriage with Joshua Woolaston,
is married to said Joshua Woolaston. A certificate for Isaac Glaves
from Chester Monthly Meeting and one for his wife Mary from Darby

Monthly Meeting, he being lately married to her. A certificate for
Joshua Crosby and his nephew, Thomas Crosby, dated at Kingston, in
Jamaica, 9th of 12th month, last. Cissely Crukshank, late Brimble,
and Rebeckah House, late Fitzwater, are married contrary to our
discipline.

24/4/1747 - Ralph Loftus of this city and Jane his wife are disowned for
debt and unbecoming behaviour. A paper from Ann Bantoft
condemning her misconduct by marrying out. Thomas Nixson
complains against Adam Rhodes, that he is indebted to him which he
neglects to pay.

31/5/1747 - Application on behalf of John Jervis for a certificate to
Friends in England and Ireland, he being about to go thither on
business. Application on behalf of Caleb Ransted, lately gone for
London, for a certificate to England. A certificate for Edward Brooks
to Chesterfield Monthly Meeting, on account of marriage. Application
on behalf of Preston Carpenter, being removed with his wife and
family to settle near Salem.

28/6/1747 - A certificate for Isaac Greenleaf, intending soon to return to
London. Application on behalf of John Elliot and wife for a certificate
to Darby Monthly Meeting. A certificate for Preserve Brown to
Chesterfield Monthly Meeting, on account of marriage. A certificate
for John Fisher for a certificate to Haddonfield Monthly Meeting, on
account of marriage.

25/7/1747 - A certificate for William Lightfoot to Friends in Barbadoes.
Issac Warren, blacksmith, is disowned for drinking. Joseph Wood,
taylor, is disowned for misdemeanor and marrying out. A certificate
for Peter Davis from the Monthly Meeting at South Kingston, in the
colony of Rhode Island.

27/9/1747 - Israel Pemberton, Junr, and Mary Jordan clear to marry,
provision being made for her children. A certificate for Bartholomew
Wyatt, his wife Elizabeth and their son and daughter to the Monthly
Meeting at Salem, in West Jersey. John Bringhurst makes
application, on behalf of his son John, to Friends in Barbadoes, he
being lately gone thither on account of trade.

25/10/1747 - Adam Rhodes, carpenter, disowned for being in debt and
other misdemeanors. A certificate for David Deane from the Monthly
Meeting at Antrin, in Ireland, dated the 25th of 2nd month last. John
Fisher, Junr, delivered a paper acknowledging his blame for marrying
a person not in unity with us. A paper from William Redwood
condemning his conduct. John Clare and Nicholas Cassell hath been
dealt with for their marrying contrary to our discipline.

29/11/1747 - Adam Rhodes requests the publication of the testimony
against him may be deferred some time, which this Meeting consents
to.

26/12/1747 - Testimony against Robert Strettle, William Coleman and John Clare. Application on behalf of Joseph Hough to the Monthly Meeting at the Falls in Bucks County.

25/1/1748 - Amos Strettle, of this city, hath joined with others in fitting out a ship of war for which he has been treated with christian love ... ... the said Amos Strettle is disowned. David Edwards and Christian his wife sent in a paper condemning their unguarded conduct. A certificate for Joseph Hough is deferred as he seems not fully determined about his removal from here. A certificate for Samuel Nottingham from the Monthly Meeting at Wellingborough, in the county of Northhampton, in Great Brittain, dated 22/12/1746. A certificate for Isaac Shoemaker to Abington, he being returned to live in Germantown. A certificate for Henry Vanaken to Abington Monthly Meeting, on account of marriage.

29/2/1748 - Benjamin Hough and Elizabeth West declare their intention to marry, Elizabeth being a widow, proper settlement to be made of her late husbands estate. Isaac Griffitts disowned for contributing to and promoting warlike preparations.

27/3/1748 - A certificate for Isaac Shoemaker and his wife to Abington Monthly Meeting. A certificate for Daniel Morris and Tace his wife to Gwynedd Monthly Meeting. A certificate for William Redwood to the Monthly Meeting in Portsmouth, Rhode Island. A certificate for Cadwallader Evans to Monthly Meeting at Devonshire House and elsewhere. A certificate for Nixon Chattin to the at Haddonfield, in New Jersey. James Wood produced a paper acknowledging his unwatchfulness and marrying contrary to the good rules of society. James Langley produced a paper acknowledging his misconduct in marrying twice out of unity and being desirous to be united to the Meeting where he now lives in Virginia and it appearing that he hath since he left this city resided some years at Nottingham (received a certificate 26/6/1748).

24/4/1748 - A certificate for Joseph noble to friends in Burlington. One for Joshua Howell to Barbadoes and one for Daniel Stanton to Friends in Barbadoes, Great Brittain and elsewhere.

29/5/1748 - Phineas Bond disowned for entering into war preparations. A certificate for Rebecca Minshall to Friends in Derby. William Gray produced a paper acknowledging himself to blame in his breach of discipline in marrying out of unity.

26/6/1748 - Anthony Morris applied on behalf of his son Benjamin for a certificate to Friends in London, he being about to go thither to improve himself in the practice of Physick.

30/7/1748 - Friends appointed to visit Thomas Preston report they found in a disposition to give satisfaction for his misconduct.

28/8/1748 - A certificate for John Hutton, Sarah his wife and his son Thomas, to the Monthly Meeting at New Garden, in Chester County.

A certificate for Benjamin Hough and Elizabeth his wife to the Monthly Meeting at Newark, in New castle County. A certificate for James Pemberton to the Monthly Meeting in Grace Church Street in London. Also for Samuel Burge to the same place. A certificate for Charles Moore to the Monthly Meeting in Edinburgh.

25/9/1748 - A certificate for Thomas Burgess to Burlington Monthly Meeting.

30/10/1748 - John Clifton, Innkeeper. disowned for marrying a woman whose husband was at that time supposed to be living. Sarah Williams, lately Preston, and Ruth Borham, lately Boyer, have been married to persons not of our society. Anthony Benezet laid before this meeting his account of cloathing and boarding Samuel Bould, an orphan child under care of this meeting.

27/11/1748 - This meeting was informed that Thomas Broadgate's paper, wishing to be re - instated into membership, was read and that he is since dead. A certificate for Lewis Jones and his wife to Hartford Monthly Meeting.

24/8/1748 - Testimony against Mercy Denton, lately Roberts, for outgoing in marriage. Testimony against Ann Roth, late Clark, for outgoing in marriage. A paper signed by Doughty Jones and Hannah his wife, condemning their freedom before marriage. A paper signed by Elizabeth Rakestraw, acknowledging her breach of discipline in marrying out of unity. A certificate for Isaac Moss to Chester Monthly Meeting. A certificate for James West to Haddonfield Monthly Meeting, on account of marriage. A paper from Samuel Austin acknowledging his breach of discipline in his marriage. A paper from Preserve Brown, Junr, and Elizabeth Giselin, acknowledging their breach of discipline in marriage. A paper from Spencer Trotter ... ... and marrying contrary to the good order of Friends. A certificate for Jonathan Barrett, he being gone to settle at duck Creek. A certificate for Jonathan Rumford, his wife Susannah and his family, to Wilmington. Testimony against Anthony Nicholas, for drinking. Papers of condemnation against Spencer Trotter, Elizabeth Gervice and Richard Woods read at the First Day morning meeting. William Ransted and Mary Peters, Junr, clear to marry. William producing a letter he received from his father, dated at Chester, in England, expressing his consent. Testimony against Tobias Griscomb for debt and other misdemeanors. Owen Jones produced a certificate from Darby Monthly Meeting on behalf of his brother, Ezekiel Jones, who served his apprenticeship with a person who lived some time there and afterward removed to this city before he was free ... ... that soon after the expiration of the apprenticeship he removed to Barbadoes and intending to settle there, desires a certificate from this Meeting. A paper from Mary Brockden acknowledging that the disregard of our discipline in her marrying had been occasion of much concern to her.

30/4/1749 - A paper from Rebeckah Edgett expressing her disregard for our good order in her marrying out. A certificate for William Brown, Susannah his wife, Sarah their daughter and two younger daughters. A certificate for Jeremiah Martin from Tortola. A certificate for Benjamin Buffington on a religious visit from the Monthly Meeting at Swansy, in New England, and also one for Paul Osborn, who accompanied him. Mary Young, a widow in low circumstances, hath a son who is a cripple. A certificate for Joseph Parker and Edward Pennington to Friends in London. A certificate for Francis Nash to Friends in New York and Flushing Monthly Meeting on Long Island, he being removed to settle there. Application made for John Needham and his wife to live in one of the Almshouses is approved.

28/5/1749 - A testimony against Samuel Head for misdemeanor. Grace Fisher, a minister, returned her certificate from the Yearly Meeting of West River. Obediah Eldridge is lately broke much in debt and both he and his wife refuse to comply with the advice of Friends.

25/6/1749 - John Davis informs the Meeting of his intention of going to London in a short time. Testimony against Joanna Sykes. John Cresson disowned for drinking. A certificate for William Fishbourne to Chesterfield Monthly Meeting, with intention to marry. A certificate for Joseph Ogden to Friends in London, being gone thither on business. A certificate for Samuel Jones and wife to Gwynedd Monthly Meeting.

29/7/1749 - ... Anthony Nicholas desires this Meeting would accept his paper of condemnation. John Iden, Junr, of this city, cordwainer, disowned for debt. A certificate for Hannah Jenkinson to Friends at Pardsley Hall, in Cumberland, she being about to return and settle there.

28/8/1749 - The Friends appointed to make inquiry concerning the cause of Goshen Monthly Meeting objecting to the receiving of Sarah Warner's certificate have now prepared a certificate which mentions her four children; Jacob, Susannah, Jane and Arnold, tho very young. William Parker, blacksmith, disowned. Sarah Barton expressed her concern for marring a person not of our persuasion. Rachel McCulla (McCullough), late Spencer, Mary Neglee (Nagle), late Winter, and Mary Corman, late Cassel, have been dealt with for their breach in discipline in marrying. Israel Pemberton complains due him from the estate of Peter Lloyd.

24/9/1749 - A certificate for James Arbuckle to Abington Monthly Meeting, on acct' of his intention to marry.

29/10/1749 - Jesse Price and Deborah his wife acknowledge their imprudence in marriage. Papers received from Stephen Paschall, John Austin and Thomas Shute, acknowledging their breach of discipline in marriage. A certificate for Isaac Greenleaf from the Two

Weeks Meeting in London. A certificate for Thomas Tillbury to
Haverford Monthly Meeting, on account of marriage.

23/12/1749 - Isaac Greenleaf and Elizabeth Calvert declare their
intention to marry, her mother consenting. Friends appointed to put
Seymour Hood, an orphan, apprentice report they have put him to a
friend on trial. A testimony against Susannah Drinker, late Williams,
for outgoing in marriage. Friends appointed to deal with Francis
Harding, Junr, and George Clare report they have spoke with them.
Sarah Grayson, late Powell, and Mary Morgan, late House, have
married to person not of our society. A certificate for John Pole, soon
to embark for Great Brittain on business, to the Monthly Meeting at
Taunton, in Somersetshire. A certificate for William Lightfoot to
Dublin, he being bound on a voyage thither on business. A certificate
for Nathaniel Brown to Haddonfield Monthly Meeting, on account of
marriage. Benjamin Trotter complains against Nicholas Cassel, that
there is a matter of difference between them.

30/1/1750 - Isaac Greenleaf and Elizabeth Calvert clear to marry.
Charles West and wife Sarah acknowledge their concern for their
breach in discipline in marriage many years since. Benjamin Trotters
complaint against Nicholas Cassel is ended. A paper signed by Mary
Brown, widow, condemning her evil conduct before marriage. A letter
from Benjamin Chew, Junr, signifying that he proposed his intentions
of marriage to Friends at Nottingham Monthly Meeting. Martha
Petell's request to be permitted to live in one of the Alms Houses is
approved. Certificates for John Pemberton, Joseph Gray and James
Logan, Junr, to London, they intending to go on business. A
certificate for Aaron Watson, about to settle at Crosswicks. A
certificate for John Hoskins, to settle at Burlington.

27/2/1750 - ... Priscilla Warren is lately married to one ... Brown, contrary
to our discipline ... and that there is reason to doubt whether husband
Isaac warren be deceased.

25/3/1750 - This Meeting now informed of the decease of our esteemed
friend John Kinsey since the last meeting. William Montgomery and
Margaret Paschall declare their intention to marry, William producing
a certificate from Bethlehem Monthly Meeting in New Jersey, and
Margaret being a widow, ... to see the necessary provision be made
for her children. A paper from Evan Evans and his wife, condemning
their breach of discipline on marriage.

29/4/1750 - A certificate for Thomas Bagnall to the Monthly Meeting of
Lynn. ... Mary Richardson, late Apple, Mary Elton, late Hart, and
Rachel Hatkinson, late Allen, have married to persons not in unity
with us. ... An ... of money expended for the cloathing and etc. of
William Young.

27/5/1750 - Joseph Oldman, of this city, disowned for misconduct. Samuel
Fisher, hatter of this city, joined another Society. John Bringhurst,

continuing on a weak state of body, hath lately embarked in a vessel
for Barbadoes in company with our Friends Thomas Lancaster and
Peter Fearson. A certificate for Isaac Bolton, Sarah his wife, and their
daughters Margaret, Rachel Sarah and Rebeckah, to Abington
Monthly Meeting. Application on behalf of Thomas West to
Haddonfield Monthly Meeting, on account of marriage. James
Wagstaff produced to this Meeting a certificate from the Two Weeks
Meeting in London, dated the 19th of the 1st month last, of his
clearness from marriage engagements there. He having, since his
living in this country, twice married from among Friends now
delivered a paper condemning his conduct therein and afterward
requested a certificate to Abington Monthly Meeting, on account of
his intention to marry there.

31/6/1750 - Friends appointed to put Seymour Hood apprentice report
they bound him to Francis Trumbell to learn the trade of joiner but
that the lad is since run away and gone to sea. This Meeting allows
Anne Wishart five pounds for taking Samuel Farmer apprentice to
learn the trade of tallow chandler. A certificate for James Stackhouse
from Middletown Monthly Meeting. A certificate for John Britton, his
wife, his two sons, Jacob and John and his daughter Susannah from
the Monthly Meeting at Cooledine in the county of Wexford, in
Ireland.

28/7/1750 - A certificate for William Sitgrave to the Monthly Meeting at
Corse Sound, in North Carolina. A certificate for John Davis to
Horsleydown Monthly Meeting. A paper from Rebekah Dussell
acknowledging her breach in discipline in marrying out.

25/8/1750 - A certificate for Jonah Thompson from the Monthly Meeting
at Sherburn, in Dorsetshire, in Great Brittain. A certificate for Aquila
Jones to Goshen Monthly Meeting. A certificate for Amos Jones to
Wilmington Monthly Meeting. A certificate for Lewis Owen to Salem
Monthly Meeting. A certificate for Thomas Williams, on account of
marriage, to Merion. Isaiah Bell and Margaret his wife delivered a
paper condemning their intimacy before marriage.

30/9/1750 - John Hitchcock, carpenter, disowned for his unbecoming
behaviour. Judah Foulke disowned for debt. Edward Cathrall
informed this Meeting that he soon intends to go for Great Brittain
on account of trade. Mary Elton, lately Hart, declines giving Friends
satisfaction for her outgoing in marriage.

28/10/1750 - A certificate for Esther White to Friends in Maryland. A
certificate for John Haydock to Friends in Flushing. A certificate for
David Dean to Wilmington. Lawrence Growden for administering the
oath as magistrate. Thomas Hoodt and wife sent in a paper
condemning their marrying out of unity. Likewise, Simeon Warner
and his wife condemn their marrying out. A paper from Sarah Allen
condemning her misconduct. Samuel Mifflin, son of Jonathan Mifflin,

and Rebekah his wife, daughter of Simon Edgett, deceased, have lately married contrary to our discipline. John Burr complains that Thomas Fisher is indebted to him. Catherine Grandam, a poor widow, and Lucy Griffith, the wife of Thomas Griffith, a man in desperate circumstances with six small children, are in want ... and to recommend the putting out of Lucy's children to some good places.

25/11/1750 - William Gardiner and Jonathan Hood brought in papers condemning their misconduct in marrying out. Application on behalf of the widow of Thomas Wolley, deceased, for some relief.

22/12/1750 - Testimony against Rebecca Wardell, widow, was read. Friends appointed to take care of Hannah Lewis ... got her to a place in the country .... Penelope Redman, a poor widow, is in want of assistance.

INDEX

66; Sarah, 32, 245; Thomas, 62

ASKE, Sarah, 237

ASKEW, J., 174; John, 169, 170, 173

ASPDEN, Dorothy, 79; Mathais, 79

ASTON, Joseph, 25; Sarah, 25

ATKINSON, Christopher, 24; Hannah, 34; James, 32, 34, 149, 150, 170, 181, 197, 201, 225; Joseph, 76; Margret, 24; Margrett, 24; Mary, 69; William, 24, 69, 76, 103, 246

ATMORE, James, 181; William, 79

ATRICH, Sarah, 82

ATTMORE, Mary, 1; Samuel, 1; Thomas, 1, 112; William, 1, 112

ATWOOD, Ann, 76; William, 76, 244, 255

AUSTELL, Joseph, 184

AUSTEN, Edward, 81; Mary, 78; Samuel, 78; Thomas, 81

AUSTILL, Joseph, 171

AUSTIN, Isaac, 170; Jane, 55, 217; John, 55, 98, 150, 152, 172, 182, 193, 269; Samuel, 69, 98, 268; Sarah, 182; Septimus, 69; Widow, 215

AUSTON, John, 150

-B-

BACON, David, 144; Mary, 215

BADCOCK, Elizabeth, 118, 211; Hannah, 119, 217; Henry, 23, 50, 56, 151; Mary, 23, 50, 203; Ruth, 23

BADCOCKE, Henry, 35; Mary, 35

BADCOKE (BADCOCK), Henry, 86

BAGNALL, Ann, 143; Benjamin, 143; Thomas, 270

BAGNELL, Benjamin, 80

BAILOR, _____, 45

BAILY, James, 238; Sarah, 117, 238

BAINBRIDGE, James, 59, 61; John, 59; Rachel, 59, 61

BAKER, John, 69, 257; Joseph, 82, 115; Joshua, 126, 205, 231; Nathan, 144; Peter, 260; Robert, 116, 125, 197; Samuel, 82, 115; Sarah, 138

BALDING, Hannah, 242

BALDWIN, Ann, 132; Hannah, 101, 130, 131; John, 116, 260

BALDWING, Hannah, 242

BALE, Susanna, 115; Thomas, 115

BALEY, James, 39, 41, 43; Mary, 41; Sarah, 41, 43

BALL, John, 146

BALLE, John, 197, 198

BALLENGER, Henry, 114; Rebekah, 114

BALLINGER, Rebeckah, 138

BALSTON, Ann, 1; Thomas, 1

BANESTER, Edward, 240

BANKSON, Esther, 261; Martha, 71; Peter, 71

BANNESTER, Edward, 241

BANNISTER, Mary, 184, 188, 189

BANT, John, 150

BANTOFT, Ann, 266

BANTON, Peter, 19; Pieter, 19; Rebecka, 19; Rebeckah, 19

BARBER, Ellen, 121; Ellin, 157

BARGER, Joseph, 223, 225, 226; Thomas, 127, 215, 231

BARKER, James, 19, 66

BARNES, Jennett, 237; John, 46, 116, 123, 199; Mary, 46; Thomas, 201, 206, 213, 237, 239

BARNEY, John, 32

BARRETT, Ann, 150; Jonathan, 268

BARROT, James, 209, 210; Mary, 209

BARROW, Robert, 22

BARRY, Margaret, 145

BARTLET, Thomas, 176

BARTLETT, Sarah, 236; Thomas, 178

BARTON, Isaac, 209, 210; Mary, 137; Sarah, 269

BARTRAM, Isaac, 114; John, 114

BARTRANE, Isaac, 142

BASNETT, Richard, 116, 156

BASSETT, Abigail, 1; Beulah, 1; Davis, 1, 114; Elisha, 114; Josiah, 1; Mary, 1; Paul, 1; Reuben, 1

BATCHELOR, Jane, 121

BATEMAN, Daniel, 255

Phebe, 245; William, 164, 165, 172
BILLIN, Jane, 37; John, 37
BILTON, Samuel, 38
BIRCHALL, Rebecca, 141
BIRCHFIELD, Alce, 44; Alice, 43; Aron, 44; Mathew, 43, 44, 48; Matthew, 116; Tabitha, 44
BIRMINGHAM, John, 59; Thomas, 59
BISSELAND, William, 116
BISSELL, Hannah, 50, 51, 107; John, 51; Joseph, 51; Mary, 41, 50; Sarah, 42; Thomas, 65; William, 41, 42, 50, 51, 65, 79, 107, 126, 211
BITTLE, Ann, 65; Elizabeth, 59; John, 57, 58, 65, 68, 70, 75; Mary, 57; Robert, 68
BLACKBOURN, Christopher, 205; Rebecca, 121; Rebeckah, 223
BLACKBOURNE, Christopher, 180, 210, 212; Rachel, 99, 231
BLACKBURN, Abigail, 2, 26; Ann, 2, 27; Benjamin, 38; Christopher, 2, 26, 27, 28, 38, 40, 44, 89, 202, 211, 216; Joell, 27; Joseph, 40; Rachel, 2, 27, 28, 38, 40; Rebeckah, 2; Richard, 256
BLACKBURNE, Christopher, 27, 28; John, 28; Rachel, 27, 28
BLACKDON, Barbara, 164
BLACKFAN, Rebecah, 99; William, 116, 221
BLACKHAM, Richard, 107, 136
BLACKLIDGE, Benjamin, 72
BLACKTHORN, Christopher, 219
BLAKE, Edward, 25, 172, 173, 175, 176, 178, 180, 184, 218; Hannah, 25; Widow, 172, 173
BLANCHER, Jane, 85
BLAND, Elias, 260; Susanna, 80
BLANY, Richard, 26
BLINSTON, Mary, 120, 152, 153
BLITH, Sarah, 231, 232
BLUNETON, Michael, 173
BLYTHE, Sarah, 99
BODDY, John, 138

BODY, John, 69
BOICE, John, 76
BOLDING, Mary, 53; William, 53
BOLTON, Everard, 69, 113, 203; Hannah, 264; Isaac, 226, 227, 253, 262, 271; Jane, 77; Lydia, 116, 221; Margaret, 271; Rachel Sarah, 271; Rebecca, 113, 129; Rebeckah, 265, 271; Samuel, 223, 264; Sarah, 271
BOM, Widow, 158
BOMSTED, Dorothy, 118
BOND, Ann, 125; Hannah, 254; James, 125; Joseph, 125, 146, 199, 202; Phineas, 254, 267; Phinehas, 135; Susanna, 59; Thomas, 59, 103, 126, 133, 155, 202, 248, 259
BONELL, Robert, 211
BONES, Mary, 129, 235
BONNALL, Robert, 221
BONNEL, Robert, 92; Ro____, 112; Samuel, 112
BONNELL, James, 83; Robert, 215; Samuel, 83
BONNEY, Frances, 32; James, 32; Robert, 32
BONNY, Frances, 34, 38; Hester, 26; Mary, 34; Robert, 26, 34, 38, 171; Thomas, 26; ____, 38
BONSAL, John, 140
BOOKER, George, 175, 179
BOOM, Agnes, 157
BOON, Agnes, 120; Edward, 51; Samuel, 246
BOONE, George, 103; Samuel, 103
BOOR, Sarah, 83; William, 83
BORDEN, Catherine, 239, 241; Dinah, 117
BORHAM, Ruth, 268
BORROW, Deborah, 209; Robert, 209
BORROWDALE, John, 177
BORROWDALL, John, 177
BOSS, John, 172
BOULD, Mary, 113; Samuel, 113, 268; Samuel C., 260
BOULDING, Ann, 2, 20; Elizabeth, 2, 22, 32; Mary, 223; William, 2, 20, 22, 32, 39, 161, 167, 171, 173

266; Elizabeth, 48, 50;
James, 50; Joanna, 142;
Sarah, 53; Thomas, 116, 263;
William, 48, 74, 263
BROOKSBY, Ann, 120;
Catherine, 98; Rachel, 219
BROOKSLEY, Ann, 200
BROW, Jordan, 73; Thomas, 73
BROWN, ---, 270; Alexander,
2; Ann, 138; Christian, 72,
249; Elizabeth, 2, 74, 98,
128, 223; Ester, 34;
Hannah, 256; Isaac, 67, 80,
236; John, 34, 42, 127,
220, 221, 246; Joice, 67;
Joseph, 28, 67, 124, 146,
168, 189, 190; Lucia, 124;
Lusce, 28; Martha, 95, 207;
Mary, 2, 73, 81, 106, 140,
142, 270; Nathaniel, 106,
270; Peter, 46, 60, 63, 69,
70, 74, 80, 112, 264;
Preserve, 73, 81, 140, 264,
266, 268; Priscilla, 70;
Richard, 146, 203; Sarah,
60, 119, 175, 269; Spicer,
67; Susannah, 269; Thomas,
2, 67, 138, 196, 197, 265;
Tilton, 67; William, 116,
144, 148, 170, 269
BROWNE, Isaac, 253; Mary,
86; Sarah, 124
BRUITNALL, Mary, 108
BRYAN, Benjamin, 126, 208;
Elizabeth, 43; Mary, 43;
Samuel, 112, 141, 263;
Susannah, 43; Thomas, 43,
91, 112
BRYANT, Thomas, 192
BUBY, Bridget, 241
BUCKLEY, Abraham, 187; Ann,
27, 186; Joseph, 27, 46,
47, 97, 207, 212; Phineas,
37; Samuel, 27, 165, 172;
Sarah, 37, 46; Thomas, 82;
William, 256
BUD, James, 42, 45; John,
31, 42, 45; Rebecka, 42, 45
BUDD, Ann, 183; Sarah, 156;
Thomas, 156
BUFFAM, Caleb, 203
BUFFINGTON, Benjamin, 269
BULKLESS, Samuel, 173
BULKLEY, Anne, 23, 90;
Samuel, 23, 27, 87; Thomas,
23
BULL, William, 257
BULLARD, Alexander, 65

BULLOCK, Mary, 118
BUMPSTEAD, Elizabeth, 233
BUMSTIDE, Dorothy, 126
BUNE, Jones, 54
BUNTING, Ann, 184
BURCH, Joshua, 50
BURCHAL, Caleb, 136
BURCHALL, Hannah, 75;
Rebecca, 75
BURCHELL, Caleb, 64
BURD, Frances, 128
BURDEN, Hannah, 42, 51;
John, 52; Katherine, 42,
44, 54; Marmaduke, 44;
Mary, 51, 52; Samuel, 207;
Thomas, 42, 44, 51, 52, 79;
Widow, 208
BURDON, Mary, 56; Thomas, 56
BURGE, Eilliam, 45;
Elizabeth, 45, 71; John,
45; Samuel, 114, 144, 268;
William, 70, 91, 114
BURGER, Joseph, 50
BURGES, Thomas, 82
BURGESS, Jane, 144; Thomas,
143, 144, 268
BURLEIGH, Benjamin, 231
BURLEY, Benjamin, 229
BURNES, Clause, 29; Dyer, 29
BURR, Henry, 84; John, 102,
142, 245, 272; Mary, 84;
William, 52
BURROUGH, John, 142
BURROUGHS, John, 114
BURROW, Robert, 177
BURROWS, Deborah, 41
BURTON, James, 171; Richard,
237
BURTOS, Richard, 129
BUSBEY, John, 160
BUSBY, John, 24, 86; Mary,
24
BUSHEL, John, 134, 251
BUTLER, Deborah, 77, 79,
258; John, 38, 83; Joseph,
77; Noble, 232; Thomas, 79,
83; William, 38
BUZBY, Dinah, 130
BYE, Margaret, 176; Sarah,
89, 179; Thomas, 89, 171

-C-

CADDWALLADER, John, 190
CADWALADER, Edward, 93, 125;
John, 40, 55, 101; Jones,
93; Letitia, 40; Martha,
40; Mary, 101

Susannah, 99, 212;
Veronica, 122
CASSELL, Arnold, 3, 46;
Benjamin, 46; Daniel, 3,
234; Deborah, 65;
Elizabeth, 3; George, 66;
Johannes, 3; Mary, 3;
Nicholas, 3, 59, 65, 66,
266; Peter, 3; Sarah, 3;
Susanna, 3, 46; Susannah,
211, 232; Veronica, 3
CASSLE, Arnold, 48, 51;
Susanna, 48
CASTER, Elizabeth, 40; John,
40; Rachel, 40
CASTLE, Arnold, 224;
Elizabeth, 246; Peter, 25
CATHCART, James, 239; Lydia,
254
CATHRALL, Benjamin, 3;
Edward, 3, 117, 244, 271;
Hannah, 3; Isaac, 3; Mary,
3; Rachel, 3; Sarah, 3
CATHRELL, Edward, 80
CATHRILL, Edward, 66, 67;
Mary, 66, 67; Rachell, 67.
CERRES, Sarah, 21
CHA,KLEY, Thomas, 221
CHADLER, Edward, 117
CHADS, Ann, 78; Francis, 165
CHALKLEY, Abigail, 38; Ann,
126; George, 3, 26, 54;
George (Thomas?), 3;
Martha, 3, 26, 28, 33, 38,
39, 42, 44, 54, 81, 146,
190, 193; Rebecca, 3, 113;
Rebecka, 28; Robert, 3, 28,
126; Thomas, 26, 28, 33,
38, 39, 42, 44, 54, 64, 95,
113, 130, 132, 133, 146,
147, 182, 184, 191, 192,
193, 198, 200, 202, 207,
211, 215, 220, 223, 234,
246, 257
CHAMBERLAIN, Abel, 136;
John, 68; Robert, 191
CHAMBERS, Benjamin, 18, 19,
20, 37, 117, 156, 160;
Elizabeth, 157; Hanna, 20;
Hannah, 18; John, 205;
Sarah, 19; Sarah (Hannah?),
19
CHAMBLISS, Elinor, 84
CHAMPION, John, 51
CHANDERS, Frances, 22, 92,
124; Joseph, 22; Paul, 254;
Thomas, 22; William, 22

CHANDLEE, Benjamin, 93;
William, 93
CHANDLER, Ann, 112;
Catherine, 60; Elizabeth,
65, 104; George, 71; Mary,
94, 202; Paul, 259; Samuel,
104, 113; Susanna, 141
CHANDLEY, Benjamin, 204
CHAPMAN, Ann, 124; William,
80
CHATTIN, Abraham, 115;
James, 115; Nixon, 140, 267
CHAUNDERS, Elizabeth, 115;
Paul, 108, 115, 135; Widow,
163
CHAYMBERS, Benjamin, 214
CHEATHAM, Ann, 32;
Elizabeth, 32; John, 32;
Mary, 243
CHEATOM, An_, 38; John, 38
CHEATUM, John, 37
CHEETAM, John, 90
CHELSEY (SHILLSON), John,
Doctor, 18
CHETHAM, Elizabeth, 80;
James, 65; John, 106;
Joseph, 65, 80, 106
CHEW, Benjamin, 270; Mary,
131; Samuel, 131, 169, 249
CHILD, Cephas, 211; Henry,
214
CHILSTON, Bridget, 85
CHRISTOPHER, Mary, 74
CHUBB, Sarah, 84; Violl, 78,
84
CLARE, Elizabeth, 39, 40;
Ester, 39; Esther, 66, 234,
260; George, 270; Hester,
40, 42; John, 67, 71, 75,
266, 267; Mary, 42;
William, 39, 40, 42, 64,
67, 75, 126, 208
CLARK, Abigail, 67; Ann,
268; Benjamin, 67, 68, 227;
Beulah, 3, 265; David, 117,
251, 259; Elizabeth, 3,
120; Hannah, 264; Jane, 64;
John, 63, 64, 264; Joseph,
3; Martha, 131; Peter, 262;
Rebecca, 104, 251; Rebecka,
32; Samuel, 3; Sarah, 3;
Thomas, 131; William, 3,
32, 75, 84, 104, 155, 265
CLARKE, David, 133, 250;
Elizabeth, 134; John, 133;
Mary, 133; Thomas, 241
CLARKSON, Elizabeth, 236;
James, 236

COLLEY, John, 89; Susanna, 89; Susannah, 182
COLLIER, Edward, 168
COLLINS, Elijah, 252; Margaret, 132; Margrett, 58
COLLY, John, 39; Susannah, 39
COLVERT, George, 46; Mary, 32; Thomas, 32
COMB, Rebecca, 33; Samuel, 33, 204
COMBS, Mary, 118, 223; Samuel, 197, 205
COMER, Margrett, 62
CONDELL, Elizabeth, 68; Lydia, 67; William, 68
CONOLLY, Eunice, 130
COOK, Arthur, 24, 34, 164, 167, 168, 170; Elinor, 34; Francis, 117; Margaret, 198; Margarett, 34; Mary, 47, 178, 229, 233; Samuel, 34
COOKE, Francis, 123
COOKSHALL, Jonathan, 117
COOMBE, Samuel, 94
COOMBS, Hannah, 264; John, 264
COOMS, John, 64; Martha, 64
COOPER, Abigail, 109, 138; Daniel, 117, 180, 255; David, 113, 141; Deborah, 69; Esther, 91, 177, 188; Hester, 42; Jacob, 69, 84, 108; James, 42, 91, 99, 188, 208, 224, 235; John, 113, 212; Joseph, 8, 42, 104, 117, 126, 180, 206, 247; Mary, 115, 128, 235; Rachel, 212; Rebecah, 99; Sarah, 84; Thomas, 153; William, 101, 108, 109, 115, 117, 131, 138, 242
COPPECK, Jonathan, 194
COPPOCK, Bartholomew, 92; Jonathan, 92, 125
CORBET, Mary, 119, 233
CORDERY, Esther, 119, 206, 207; Mary, 220
CORDRY, Deborah, 63, 124; Hugh, 63, 124
CORDWELL, Vincent, 171
CORKER, Elizabeth, 108; Mary, 103, 245; Rebecka, 43; Sarah, 125, 196; William, 43, 46, 53, 108, 117, 195
CORMAN, Mary, 269

CORNE , Jane, 28; John, 28
CORNWALL, Francis, 154, 155; Mary, 154
CORY, Joice, 79; Samuel, 79
COSTER, Samuel, 84
COSTORD, John, 64; Joseph, 64
COTTEY, Abel, 93; Abell, 33; Sarah, 93
COTTY, Abell, 31; Benjamin, 31
COUPER, Charles, 38; Elizabeth, 49; Ester, 29; James, 29, 53; John, 38; Joseph, 49; Mary, 49; Rachel, 38; Rebecka, 50; Samuel, 50, 53, 55; Sarah, 53; , 53
COUPLAND, Margaret, 243, 246
COURTNEY, Ruth, 147, 253
COWMAN, Mary, 106, 255; Matthew, 101; Nathan, 101, 244
COX, Abraham, 55, 57, 104, 117, 199, 207; Ann, 40; Hannah, 77; John, 20, 80, 193; Martha, 49, 57, 105, 252; Samuel, 48, 57; Sarah, 24, 104, 115; Thomas, 40, 48, 49, 202; William, 49
COXE, Thomas, 94
COZENS, Elinor, 140; George, 140, 264
COZINS, George, 263
CRAMER, Sarah, 135
CRAPP, John, 242; Mary, 242
CRAVEN, Ann, 122
CRAWFORD, James, 93, 125, 197
CREAMER, Andrew, 74
CRESSON, Anna, 4, 42, 46, 61; Caleb, 4; Elizabeth, 4; Hannah, 39, 40, 69, 71; Isaac, 4; James, 4, 72, 77, 105, 260; Jane, 4; John, 4, 61, 68, 71, 251, 269; Joshua, 4; Liddie, 4; Mary, 4, 42; Rachel, 4; Rebecca, 4, 251, 261; Rebeccah, 68; Rebekah, 110; Samuell, 39; Sarah, 4, 77; Solomon, 4, 32, 36, 39, 40, 42, 46, 69, 74, 89, 105, 110, 198, 238, 254; William, 40; , 32
CREW, John, 143
CRIBS, Mary, 264
CROASDALE, Alice, 120
CROASDELL, Thomas, 75

DEEBLE, Elizabeth, 128, 224;
George, 128, 224, 228;
Richard, 128
DEEBY, Daniel, 262
DELAPLAIN, Christian, 88;
Susanna, 87
DELAPLAINE, Christian, 167;
James, 160, 161; Susannah,
162
DELAPLANE, Judith, 86
DELAPLAYNE, Elizabeth, 85;
Nicholas, 85
DELAVALL, Hannah, 18, 20,
118, 173; John, 18, 20, 85;
Mary, 18
DELZEL, Elizabeth, 140
DENHAM, Thomas, 48, 126, 222
DENISE, Cornelius, 117, 229
DENNIS, Grace, 82, 140;
Henry, 72, 81, 82, 140;
John, 72; Jonathan, 173,
174, 177; Mary, 144;
Rachel, 81
DENNISS, Benjamin, 34;
Jonathan, 26; Mary, 34;
Thomas, 34
DENSEY, Ann, 28; John, 28,
30, 93, 117, 156; Sarah,
28, 30, 80, 93
DENSY, John, 21; Sarah, 21;
Thomas, 21
DENT, Hannah, 104, 243, 244,
246, 247; Robert, 104
DENTON, Mary, 68; Mercy, 268
DEPLONE, Anthony, 19; John,
18, 19; Whankey, 19
DERBOROW, John, 209
DESHLER, David, 81; Isaac,
81
DEVER, Benjamin, 80
DEWBERRY, Jacob, 167
DIBBLE, Elizabeth, 248
DIBLE, George, 226
DICKENSON, Jonathan, 247
DICKES, Samuel, 225
DICKINS, Jonathan, 212
DICKINSON, Benjamin, 216;
Francis, 48; Hannah, 99,
230; Isaac, 35; James, 166;
John, 4, 50; Jonathan, 4,
22, 35, 41, 44, 50, 169,
170, 173, 179, 211, 214,
216; Joseph, 4, 214, 215;
Mary, 4, 35, 41; Samuel,
101, 131, 241; William,
141; ___, 48
DICKSON, Andrew, 42;
Elizabeth, 42; Margrett, 42

DIDON, John Frederick, 21
DILLWIN, John, 53, 59; Mary,
53; Susanna, 59; William,
154
DILLWORTH, John, 41; Mary,
41
DILLWYN, John, 79, 96, 102,
130, 210; William, 96
DILWIN, Elizabeth, 29; John,
57, 239, 240, 245; Sarah,
26, 29, 50; William, 26,
29, 32, 50
DILWORTH, James, 113;
William, 82, 113
DILWYN, John, 65, 71;
William, 85
DIMMOCK, Tobias, 174, 177
DIMNOCK, Tobias, 177
DIMOCK, Tobias, 88, 174
DINGEE, Christopher, 141;
Sarah, 141
DINGEY, Christopher, 74
DIXON, William, 123
DIXSON, Elizabeth, 31;
Joseph, 42; Mary, 31;
William, 25
DOE, Mary, 120, 123
DOILE, Ambrose, 72
DOLE, John, 151; Sarah, 118,
151
DOUGHTY, Ebenezer, 264;
Edward, 22; Mary, 264
DOWDEN, John, 155
DOWELL, William, 49
DOWTY, Amy, 65
DRAPER, James, 265; Rebecca,
265
DREW, Robert, 155
DRINKER, Henry, 72; Joseph,
66, 81, 117; Susannah, 270;
Tabitha, 258, 259
DUBERRY, Jacob, 243; John,
243
DUBERY, James, 117
DUBLONVIS, John, 117
DUBRE, Jacob, 107, 132;
Joseph, 107; Mary, 132;
Phebe, 132
DUBREE, Hannah, 72; Jacob,
4, 29, 31, 48, 59, 62, 61,
63, 221; James, 4, 221;
Jane, 4, 29, 31, 48; John,
4; Joseph, 4, 29, 55, 62,
66, 72, 79; Mary, 31, 55,
59, 61, 66
DUCKET, Mary, 203; Thomas,
203, 206; Widow, 206

45, 78, 97, 112, 128, 211,
264; Tabitha, 35, 41, 47,
69; Thomas, 6, 70, 72, 78,
109, 272; William, 30, 35,
41, 46, 47, 48, 70, 78, 106,
109, 118, 144, 153, 160,
207, 234
FISHWATER, George, 40; Mary,
40
FITCHWATER, Abraham, 45;
Elizabeth, 42; George, 45,
46, 52; Mary, 45, 46, 52;
Thomas, 24, 46
FITWATER, Rebecca, 248
FITZRANDOLPH, Ezeck, 255;
Hugh, 78
FITZWATER, Deborah, 248;
Elizabeth, 156, 157, 166;
George, 82, 92, 105, 108,
111, 207; Hannah, 105;
Martha, 108; Mary, 108;
Rebeckah, 266; Sarah, 110;
Thomas, 118, 152, 156, 163,
166, 169
FLARNEY, Thomas, 54
FLASCOTT, John, 55; Phebe,
55
FLETCHER, John, 76; William,
25, 175
FLEXNEY, Daniel, 127, 217,
218
FLOWER, Ann, 6, 33;
Benjamin, 6, 28, 33; Caleb,
25; Daniel, 6, 25, 28, 30,
36, 41, 88, 180; Daniell,
32; David, 216; Elizabeth,
28, 60; Enoch, 60, 62, 75,
77, 104, 260; Fincher, 28;
Henry, 6, 28, 33, 48;
Joanna, 48; John, 30, 62,
77; Joseph, 6; Mary, 28,
242; Samuel, 6, 36; Sarah,
6, 25, 28, 30, 32, 36, 41,
66, 75; Thomas, 63
FLOYD, Samuel, 131, 243
FOLK, Cadwallader, 52; Mary,
52
FOLLE, Anne, 121
FORBES, Hugh, 111
FORD, Philip, 179
FORDHAM, Abel, 118, 227;
Benjamin, 98; Jane, 243;
John, 240; Joseph, 239;
Lydia, 98, 227; Sarah, 245
FORDUM, Abell, 52
FORREST, Joan, 53; William,
53, 242
FORRESTER, Susannah, 242

FORRIST, Joan, 19; Mary, 19;
William, 19, 36
FORSTER, Elizabeth, 112;
Moses, 111; Reuben, 53,
112; Reubon, 111; Ruben, 53
FOSSELL, Barbara, 114;
Eliza, 110; Solomon, 110,
114
FOSTER, Reuben, 52; Ruben,
52
FOULK, Cadwalader, 53, 55,
57; Cadwallader, 55, 57;
Mary, 53, 57; Owen, 156;
Thomas, 53
FOULKE, Cadwalader, 109,
131; Cadwallader, 6, 67,
80, 240, 254; Deborah, 70;
Judah, 70, 80, 81, 109,
271; Mary, 6, 81, 110, 136,
147, 240, 255, 262
FOULKS, Owen, 156
FOX, Ann, 26; Dorothy, 20;
Elizabeth, 6, 20, 23, 25,
26; Francis, 6, 26; George,
6, 23, 87, 165, 264; James,
6, 20, 23, 24, 25, 26, 87,
89, 118, 155, 158, 206;
Joseph, 112; Mary, 26;
Richard, 18; Susanna, 6, 23
FRAIM, Robert, 43
FRAMPTON, Elizabeth, 116,
154, 156; Widow, 152;
William, 152
FRAMTON, Thomas, 47
FRANKLAND, Henry, 240
FRANKS, Elizabeth, 237;
George, 130, 237, 241
FREEBORN, Susanna, 146;
Susannah, 194, 199
FREELAND, Rebeckah, 197;
Susannah, 90, 186; William,
90
FREEMAN, John, 133; Sarah,
105, 252, 256
FREMAN, John, 57
FRENCH, Joseph, 129, 236;
Joshua, 58; Thomas, 118
FRETWELL, Ralph, 151
FULLER, John, 160, 162;
Sarah, 85
FURNESS, Daniel, 18; Henry,
18; John, 50; Joseph, 56;
Mary, 56
FURNIS, Anthony, 241; John,
70; Rachel, 140; Thomas,
70, 140
FURNISS, Elizabeth, 34;
John, 187; Thomas, 34

FUSSELL, Solomon, 62, 83;
Susannah, 83

-G-

GABITAS, Abigail, 20;
Jeremiah, 20; William, 20,
160, 166
GALE, John, 216, 217;
Jonathan, 216
GALLOWAY, Jane, 261; John,
109, 139, 260; Susannah, 83
GAMBLE, Elizabeth, 169;
Francis, 154
GAMBLIN, Widow, 181
GARDINER, Elizabeth, 262;
Thomas, 2, 262; William,
272
GARDNER, Elizabeth, 262;
John, 82, 84, 118, 156,
162, 165; Joseph, 69, 77,
262; Martha, 78, 83; Mary,
153; Sarah, 83; Thomas, 69,
84, 131, 243
GARET, Hanah, 87
GARNER, Thomas, 33
GARNETT, Joseph, 137
GARRATT, Ann, 43; James, 57;
William, 43
GARRET, Samuel, 104
GARRETT, Hannah, 117;
Joseph, 259; Mary, 160;
Sarah, 117; William, 128,
144, 150, 224
GARRIGUE, Christian, 63;
Isaac, 63, 76; Mathew, 79;
William, 76
GARRIGUES, Ann, 6; Benjamin,
6; Edward, 6; Isaac, 6,
102, 108, 245; Jacob, 6;
James Ralph, 6; John, 6,
81, 109; Joseph, 81; Mary,
6; Matthew, 102; Rachel, 6;
Rebecca, 6; Samuel, 6;
Susanna, 6; William, 6
GARWOOD, Martha, 76; Mary,
76
GARYDON, Henry, 200
GATCHELL, Elisha, 248
GATES, Cherrish, 67; Josiah,
57, 59, 130, 234; Sarah,
57, 130
GAUNT, Daniel, 29, 146, 189;
Hannah, 29
GAWTHORP, Thomas, 148, 265
GERMAIN, Elizabeth, 210, 211
GERRARD, Robert, 60
GERVICE, Elizabeth, 268
GERVIS, Martin, 233

GERVISE, Elizabeth, 248
GIBBONS, John, 118, 174;
Sarah, 50
GIBBS, Ann, 6, 118;
Benjamin, 6; William, 19
GIBSON, David, 142; Mary,
142
GIDDEN, Ann, 243
GIFFIN, Mary, 114; Thomas,
114
GIFFING, Mary, 142
GILBERT, Elisabeth, 204;
Elizabeth, 95, 101, 243;
John, 26, 33, 93, 99, 199,
231; Joseph, 205; Joshua,
33, 93, 101, 196; Sarah,
117; Widow, 205
GILES, Elizabeth, 24
GILL, Joseph, 248; Joshua,
138, 210, 261; Roger, 24
GILLINGHAM, Ann, 6;
Elizabeth, 6; John, 6, 103;
Mary, 6; Sarah, 6; Susanna,
6
GILPIN, Hannah, 136, 250;
Joseph, 232; Rachel, 82;
Samuel, 118, 224; Thomas,
82, 100, 136, 235, 239, 260
GISELIN, Elizabeth, 268
GLADING, Ann, 143; Mary,
143; Richard, 143
GLANEY, John, 253
GLAVES, Isaac, 265; Mary,
265
GLEAVE, Isaac, 141; Mary,
142
GLENNY, John, 134, 249
GLOVER, Dinah, 67
GODFREY, Andrew, 146, 205,
206; Thomas, 92, 125, 192,
193
GOFORTH, Aaron, 118, 203,
215, 219, 230, 255; Alice,
116; Aron, 43, 44, 47, 54,
55; Elizabeth, 63, 83;
Joseph, 47; Mary, 43, 47,
54, 116; Sarah, 55;
Tabitha, 44
GOLDING, Abigail, 230
GOLDSMITH, Ellen, 185;
George, 24, 118, 166;
Widow, 181
GOODBODY, Ann, 130
GOODEN, John, 149; Sarah,
121, 154
GOODRICK, James, 155
GOODSON, Elizabeth, 122;
Jane, 111; Job, 66, 86,

228, 235, 237; John, 20, 31,
48, 99, 161, 174, 195, 220,
228; Sarah, 20, 31, 161
GOODSONN, Job, 129; John,
87, 94; Sarah, 87
GOODWIN, Edward, 124; John,
56, 79; Sarah, 56; William,
79
GORSUCH, Rebecca, 260
GOSDEN, Patience, 88
GOTTSCHICK, George, 167
GOTTSHICK, George, 118
GOVE, Bridgett, 7, 18;
Elizabeth, 7, 18; Martha,
7, 90; Mary, 7, 27;
Patience, 24; Richard, 7,
18, 24, 27, 85, 88, 90,
124, 146, 165, 167, 169,
171, 182, 184, 185, 191,
192, 194; Sarah, 7
GOVETT, Esther, 82, 140;
Joseph, 78, 140; Lydia, 82
GRACY, George, 24; Mary, 24
GRADON, Henry, 201
GRAHAM, James, 213
GRAINGER, Chalkley, 36;
Elizabeth, 36, 44; Joshua,
36, 44; Miriam, 44
GRAISLEY, Thomas, 226
GRANDAM, Catherine, 272
GRANGER, Joshua, 195, 203,
208, 237, 250
GRANT, Alexander, 236;
Martha, 30
GRAVES, Thomas, 144
GRAY, Charles, 81;
Elizabeth, 76; George, 7,
58, 80, 91, 107, 127, 146,
161, 162, 163, 168, 177,
184, 187, 189, 191, 196,
202; Jeremiah, 36; Joseph,
7, 84, 106, 107, 109, 118,
215, 270; Lydia, 60;
Margrett, 82; Mary, 7, 58,
106, 128; Rebecca, 260;
Rebeckah, 231; Samuel, 60,
76, 109, 225; William, 81,
82, 267
GRAYSON, Sarah, 270
GREAVES, Samuel, 176
GREEN, Elizabeth, 84, 92,
182, 192; John, 29, 54, 68;
Mary, 68; Sarah, 84;
William, 194, 209
GREENHOPE, Mary, 126
GREENLEAF, Elizabeth, 7, 84;
Isaac, 7, 84, 266, 269, 270
GREENLEAFE, Isaac, 115, 148

GREENUP, Margaret, 120;
Mary, 206
GREY, George, 30; Naomy, 30
GRIDLEY, Elizabeth, 144
GRIFEN, Joseph, 124
GRIFFIN, Joseph, 195
GRIFFIT, Mary, 82
GRIFFITH, Abraham, 138, 259;
David, 21; Elizabeth, 39,
47; Evan, 164; Frances, 39;
John, 165; Joseph, 29, 31;
Judith, 22; Lucy, 272;
Mary, 29; Nathaniel, 39,
208; Sarah, 29; Thomas, 22,
47, 86, 118, 172, 187, 202,
204, 208, 213, 220, 224,
227, 228, 272; Widow, 197;
William, 232, 262
GRIFFITHS, Abraham, 118;
Elizabeth, 258; Nathaniel,
211; Thomas, 224; William,
99
GRIFFITS, Elizabeth, 51, 66;
Isaac, 7, 84; Mary, 7, 51,
84; Natha., 51; Nathaniell,
66; Thomas, 7
GRIFFITTS, Ann, 63;
Elizabeth, 40, 44, 46;
Frances, 127; George, 127;
Henry, 40; Isaac, 267;
Issac, 110; Martha, 125;
Mary, 46; Nathaniel, 40,
44, 46, 62, 118;
Nathaniell, 63; Thomas, 74,
110, 127; William, 141
GRIGGS, Dorothy, 136
GRISCOM, Andrew, 118, 151;
Ann, 73; Grace, 7, 83;
Rebecca, 7, 259; Samuel,
74, 81, 259; Samuell, 65;
Sarah, 74, 128; Tobias, 7,
60, 65, 73, 118; William,
60, 81
GRISCOMB, Andrew, 156;
Tobias, 251, 268; William,
253
GRISCUM, Ann, 81; Tobias, 81
GROMETT, William, 216
GROVES, Samuel, 177
GROWDEN, Hannah, 135;
Joseph, 88, 90, 186, 210;
Lawrence, 131, 208, 209,
245, 252, 256, 271
GROWDON, Elizabeth, 120
GUESS, Ann, 74, 75;
Elizabeth, 62; Jean, 77;
John, 62, 63, 75; Jonathan,

HARMOR, George, 53
HARN, Edward, 227
HARNER, Benjamin, 51;
  George, 51; Honour, 51
HARPER, Alice, 133; Eliphal,
  147, 254; Hannah, 259;
  Jane, 7, 80, 219, 238;
  John, 7, 59, 80, 94, 106,
  118, 125, 198, 204; Joseph,
  7; Mary, 7, 106
HARPERS, Jane, 265
HARRIOT, Samuel, 36, 91;
  Sarah, 91; William, 36
HARRIOTT, Jane, 96, 210;
  John, 38; Miriam, 25;
  Samuel, 25, 38, 96
HARRIS, Alice, 33; John, 54;
  Joseph, 46; Rebeckah, 90;
  Sarah, 33; Thomas, 169;
  William, 33
HARRISON, Ellen, 118, 166;
  Hannah, 41; James, 152;
  Mary, 83; Richard, 41, 97,
  127, 213, 237; William,
  188, 200
HARRISS, Alce, 35, 51; Mary,
  51; William, 35; ____, 51
HARRON, Rachel, 117
HARROTT, Samuel, 54
HARRY, Sarah, 63, 134
HART, Elizabeth, 32, 75,
  102; George, 58; Hannah,
  32, 42; Jane, 57; John, 22,
  29, 32, 42, 58, 59, 67, 81,
  87, 92, 102, 124, 125, 146,
  149, 154, 194, 198, 204,
  211, 212, 241; Martha, 116;
  Mary, 22, 29, 42, 270, 271;
  Paul, 22; Rebecca, 81;
  Sarah, 59, 81, 131; Thomas,
  22, 75, 81, 118, 223
HARTLEY, Benjamin, 56, 82;
  John, 54
HARTSHORNE, Robert, 255
HARVARD, Ann, 87; David, 87
HARVEY, Judith, 210; Mary,
  130; William, 95, 203, 208,
  210
HARWOOD, Abigail, 23;
  Elizabeth, 118, 188;
  George, 33; John, 23, 36;
  Mary, 29; Ruth, 29; Samuel,
  22, 29, 33, 44; Samuell,
  44; Sarah, 23; Susanna, 19,
  22, 23, 29, 53; Susannah,
  189; William, 19, 22, 23,
  24, 29, 162

HASELTON, John, 64; William,
  62, 64
HASIMS, Joshua, 181
HASLAM, John, 259, 261, 265
HASTINGS, Elizabeth, 112,
  264; Hannah, 53, 60; John,
  36, 53, 57, 112, 118;
  Joshua, 46, 164, 196, 197;
  Martha, 88, 116, 169; Mary,
  46, 53, 118, 215; Samuel,
  36, 46, 53, 60, 116, 245,
  264; Susannah, 132
HASTINS, Elizabeth, 44, 45;
  Joshua, 45, 164; Mary, 40,
  44; Samuel, 40; Samuell, 44
HATKINSON, Rachel, 270
HATTON, Elizabeth, 63, 86;
  Lettice, 130; Sarah, 52;
  Thomas, 52, 63, 64, 240
HAVARD, John, 23; Mary, 23;
  Sarah, 23
HAWKINS, Elizabeth, 131,
  252; Hannah, 259; Sarah,
  256; Thomas, 73
HAWOOD, Mary, 38; Samuell,
  38
HAY, Ralph, 227
HAYDEN, John, 155
HAYDOCK, Eden, 112, 139;
  John, 142, 271; Robert,
  112, 142, 185; Rv?, 23
HAYES, Richard, 79, 138,
  174, 261; Susannah, 83;
  William, 83
HAYS, Mary, 58
HAYTON, John, 153, 155
HAYWARD, Sarah, 70
HAYWOOD, Elisabeth, 230;
  John, 27, 89; Mary, 27,
  121; Rebecca, 117; Sarah,
  118, 174; Thomas, 196
HAZELTON, Miriam, 76;
  Richard, 76
HEAD, Esther, 115; Hannah,
  108; John, 41, 52, 75, 100,
  104, 106, 108, 112, 115,
  127, 215; Judith, 41;
  Martha, 106; Mary, 15, 104;
  Rachell, 52; Rebecca, 100,
  131, 240; Rebecka, 41;
  Samuel, 75, 269; Sarah, 112
HEALD, Bancroft, 27; Mary,
  183; Samuel, 27, 183
HEANS, Hannah, 142
HEARN, Sarah, 48; Susannah,
  92; William, 48, 92
HEARNE, Sarah, 20; Susannah,
  192; William, 20

INGRAM, Ann, 52, 69; John,
52, 69, 75; Rachel, 52;
Sarah, 77
IREDAL, Thomas, 183
IREDALL, Thomas, 199
IREDEL, Thomas, 198
IREDELL, Thomas, 91, 146
IRELAND, Jane, 127, 220;
Nicholas, 127, 161
IRESON, Benjamin, 27;
Dorcas, 39, 49, 51, 80;
Jane, 118, 227; John, 27,
39, 50; Joseph, 51;
Richard, 188, 265; Sarah,
78; William, 39, 49, 51,
78, 80; ____, 50
ISSACS, Derrick, 151
ITHELL, John, 154, 158, 166,
170
IYLIFE, Elizabeth, 122

-J-
JACKMAN, Eleanor, 89;
Joseph, 239; Mary, 72;
Stephen, 89; Thomas, 72
JACKSON, Benjamin, 50;
Bridges, 129; Charles, 26;
Dinah, 248; Elizabeth, 26,
27, 32, 33, 50, 72, 96,
118, 251; John, 32, 76;
Mary, 60, 71, 138; Palph,
225; Ralph, 26, 27, 46, 56,
87, 91, 96, 161, 164, 166,
167, 168, 174, 191, 201,
205, 207, 209, 231; Samuel,
76, 136, 257, 258; Sarah,
56, 132; Stephen, 32, 33,
50, 60, 147, 180, 207, 214,
222
JACOB, Ann, 103; Caleb, 43,
194, 217, 224; Elizabeth,
43; Joshua, 30; Samuel,
103; Thomas, 194
JACOBS, Beulah, 117; Caleb,
45, 119, 211, 212, 213,
226; James, 157, 158, 161,
186; Joseph, 203
JACQUES, Elizabeth, 21;
Thomas, 21
JAGGER, Abraham, 177
JAMES, Aaron, 81; Abel, 113;
Alice, 98; Ann, 37; Edward,
37, 69, 98, 138, 258;
Esther, 8, 186, 188, 190;
George, 73, 113, 136, 211,
261; Hannah, 70; John, 36,
41, 81; Joseph, 69, 71,
257; Martha, 69, 137; Mary,

90, 185; Philip, 45, 170,
226; Phillip, 8, 170;
Rebeckah, 138; Sarah, 36,
41, 80, 136; Thomas, 36,
41, 69, 70, 107
JAMMEY, Frances, 35;
Randall, 35
JANES, Joseph, 192
JANEY, Randall, 211;
Tabitha, 118
JANNEY, Elizabeth, 93;
Frances, 8, 27; Mary, 117;
Randal, 119, 171, 177, 179,
189; Randall, 8, 37;
Randol, 27; Randolph, 189;
Thomas, 124, 189; William,
8, 27
JANSEN, Renier, 168
JARMAN, Edward, 98; Mary, 98
JAWART, John, 205
JAWL, James, 181
JELSON, Jane, 74
JENINGS, Ann, 19, 21; Henry,
28, 31; Joyse, 21;
Margrett, 31; Samuel, 19,
21; William, 19
JENKENSON, Isaac, 113; John,
113
JENKINS, Abigail, 75;
Charels, 106; Charles, 75,
84; Hannah, 67; John, 57,
67; Mary, 57; Nathaniel,
131, 240, 243, 244;
Stephen, 67, 106, 107, 136
JENKINSON, Hannah, 136, 138,
147, 148, 250, 258, 269;
John, 249, 250, 252
JENNET, John, 89; Sarah, 89
JENNETT, Bridgett, 33;
Esther, 88; John, 23, 33,
165, 167
JENNINGS, John, 8; John,
Doctor, 18; Samuel, 162,
165, 172, 173, 174;
Samuell, 88; Sarah, 88
JEOFFERIES, Sarah, 90
JERMAN, Edward, 8, 32, 36,
173; Elizabeth, 8, 32, 96;
Mary, 8; Sarah, 116
JERMINS, Edward, 156
JERVAS, Martin, 230
JERVIS, Charles, 9;
Elizabeth, 9; Hannah, 62;
John, 9, 62, 63, 72, 82,
100, 148, 238, 266; Martin,
9, 65, 100; Martyn, 100;
Mary, 9, 59, 67, 130;
Rebecca, 9; Richard, 59;

23; William, 9, 23, 88, 97, 119

KELLY, Elizabeth, 21, 46, 236; Joan, 61; Mary, 22; Miriam, 36; Mirianna, 22; Sarah, 19, 46, 66, 259; William, 21, 22, 36, 46, 182, 201, 228

KELTON, Hannah, 61

KEMBERLY, Thomas, 244

KEMP, Elizabeth, 119

KENDAL, William, 216

KENDALL, Benjamin, 140; Jesse, 89; John, 89

KENDERDINE, Sarah, 132

KENNEDY, Hugh, 137

KENSEY, John, 240

KENT, Margaret, 157; Robert, 10, 18, 119; Stephen, 154

KEY, April, 51; John, 42, 48, 51, 59, 67, 241; Mary, 235; Rebecka, 42; Sarah, 42, 59, 240

KEYS, Sarah, 241

KIDD, Benjamin, 225, 228

KIELL, Thomas, 156

KIGHT, Hannah, 37; James, 26, 34, 37, 168; John, 26; Martha, 211

KILBOURN, John, 119

KILCUP, Elizabeth, 172; Mary, 89; Sarah, 118

KILE, Michell, 42

KIMBERLY, Thomas, 246

KINESLY, Charles, 72

KING, Benjamin, 18; Hannah, 78; Joseph, 78; Thomas, 57; Walter, 150

KINGSLEY, Hester, 127

KINSEY, David, 71; Elizabeth, 65; James, 22; John, 18, 22, 26, 52, 65, 68, 71, 79, 82, 85, 99, 130, 162, 175, 180, 182, 184, 185, 229, 270; Mary, 52, 68; Sarah, 22, 26

KIRK, Ann, 243; James, 59; Mary, 59

KIRLL, John, 43; Joseph, 27, 43, 86; Mary, 27

KITCHEN, Mary, 122, 168; Sarah, 149; Thomas, 119, 151, 154

KITE, Abraham, 108, 119, 193, 231; Grissel, 189; Grissell, 124; James, 153, 195, 198, 208; Martha, 117, 126; Thomas, 108

KITES, James, 154

KNIGHT, Gyles, 97; Hannah, 42, 43, 45, 74, 205, 250; Henry, 42, 45; James, 178; John, 34, 38, 42, 43, 45, 50, 74, 80, 101, 119, 126, 178, 202, 217, 219, 234; Joseph, 97, 126, 211; Lydia, 101, 242; Rebecca, 141; Sarah, 34, 38, 133, 141; Thomas, 34, 43, 119, 133, 162, 219, 249; Widow, 177, 184

KNOWLES, Ann, 31, 37, 40; Elizabeth, 118, 172; Elizabeth (now Griffith), 27; Frances, 40; Francis, 10, 43, 46, 61, 65, 96, 209; Hannah, 46, 100, 235; John, 27, 31, 37, 40, 187, 220; Martha, 40; Mary, 40; Sarah, 10, 27, 40, 43, 46, 65; Thomas, 56;   , 37

KNUBLEY, Jane, 217; John, 116; Sarah, 116, 139, 141

KNUBLY, Jane, 118

KOILE, Elizabeth, 41; Michael, 41

KOSTER, John, 71, 119

KRIPNER, Paul, 111; Pauli_s, 132

-L-

LACY, Mary, 57; Thomas, 57

LAD, Samuel, 206

LAKIN, Henry, 153

LAKING, Henry, 153

LAMBERT, Ann, 79, 132; Hannah, 41; John, 41; Samuel, 23; Widow, 258

LAMPHIGH, Nathaniel, 181

LAMPLEE, Alex'r., 124

LAMPLUGH, Nathaniel, 169

LANCASTER, David, 10, 37; Jane, 10, 54; John, 10, 37, 47, 54, 56, 95, 207; Jonathan, 10, 37; Joseph, 8, 47; Sarah, 8, 37, 47, 54, 247; Thomas, 10, 271

LANDALE, Jane, 74; John, 74

LANE, Robert, 176

LANGDALE, John, 253, 263; Josiah, 4, 212, 226; Margaret, 98, 226, 227; Mary, 4, 103; Sarah, 253

LANGDALL, John, 64, 75; Margrett, 75; William, 64

Christian, 55; Elizabeth,
58; James, 58; Jane, 23;
John, 73; Phebe, 41, 45;
Thomas, 23; ____, 45
MORTON, Abigail, 83; John,
50, 120
MOSS, Abraham, 80, 143;
Isaac, 144, 268; Joseph,
154; Mary, 144; Rebecca,
143
MOTT, Asher, 84; Deborah,
83; Jacob, 125, 185; Mary,
8
MUCKANS, Hannah, 57
MUGGLESTON, Edward, 49
MUGGLESTONE, Edward, 236
MUMFORD, Ann, 41; Mary, 41,
43; Thomas, 41, 43
MURRAY, Humphrey, 37; John,
156, 252
MURREY, Ann, 20; Humphrey,
20; Thomas, 193
MUSGRAVE, Thomas, 165

-N-

NAGLE, Mary, 269
NAILER, Elizabeth, 71, 73;
John, 70, 206; Joseph, 71;
Sarah, 73
NAILOR, John, 120
NASH, Francis, 141, 142,
269; Joseph, 63; Mary, 63
NAYLOR, Elizabeth, 134;
John, 126, 249
NEALE, Hannah, 142
NEAVE, Joel, 138; Joell, 67
NEEDHAM, Ann, 260; John,
138, 260, 269; Mary, 68,
260
NEGLEE, Mary, 269
NELSON, John, 163
NEWBERRY, Margaret, 140;
Walter, 212
NEWBOLD, Godfrey, 32; Sarah,
32
NEWBURY, Walter, 178
NEWBY, Gabriel, 126; Hannah,
150
NEWCOMB, Richard, 187
NEWCOMBE, Elizabeth, 92
NEWCOME, Mary, 124
NEWLAND, Thomas, 232
NEWMAN, Hannah, 103; Paul,
24
NEWTON, Barbadoes, 20;
Basill, 20; William, 20
NICE, Mary, 253
NICHOL, Samuel, 230

NICHOLAS, Anthony, 103, 106,
268, 269; Martha, 117;
Mary, 104, 132, 147, 203,
249; Samuel, 103, 104;
Thomas, 203, 209
NICHOLS, Anthony, 63, 83,
246, 247, 255; Antony, 56;
Edward, 61; John, 120, 226;
Joshua, 37; Margrett, 63;
Martha, 207, 208; Mary, 61,
83, 132, 237, 244, 249;
Rebecka, 56; Samuel, 30,
55, 120; William, 143
NICHOLSON, Ann, 215;
Content, 143; Elizabeth,
120, 235; Isaac, 66;
Joshua, 66; Rebeckah, 94;
Thomas, 126; William, 131,
243
NICHOS, John, 48; Samuel, 48
NICKSON, Jane, 122; Sarah,
215; Thomas, 231
NICOLS, Margrett, 67
NIXON, Jane, 215; Thomas,
206, 213
NIXSON, Maudlin, 46; Thomas,
46, 81, 95, 99, 266
NOBLE, Abel, 27; Able, 160;
Anthony, 72; Elizabeth, 49;
Joseph, 12, 49, 52, 54, 80,
109, 218, 257, 264, 265,
267; Lydia, 141; Martha,
12; Mary, 12, 27, 49, 52,
54, 109; Richard, 52;
Samuel, 12, 80, 137, 141,
257, 264
NOOKS, Susanna, 135
NORBURY, Nathan, 79
NORRIS, Charles, 12, 131,
144, 148, 239, 244, 247;
Deborah, 12; Elizabeth, 12;
Hannah, 12, 97, 213;
Humphrey, 45, 120, 127,
227; Humphry, 216; Is.,
198; Isaac, 12, 24, 32, 33,
52, 65, 67, 69, 87, 97,
106, 147, 164, 178, 189,
203, 204, 213, 217, 218,
223, 237, 239, 242, 244,
245, 247; John, 12, 52;
Joseph, 12, 218, 236;
Margaret, 12; Mary, 12, 24,
32, 33, 52, 78, 213;
Prudence, 12, 32; Rachel,
12, 33, 45; Samuel, 12, 71,
136; Sarah, 12, 24, 65, 67,
69; Thomas, 12

REDNAP, Elizabeth, 38;
   Joseph, 38, 210, 211; ____,
   38
REDWOOD, Abraham, 142;
   Jonas, 142; Mehetable, 142;
   William, 266, 267
REECE, Thomas, 62
REED, Anne, 28; Charles, 28;
   John, 67; Robert, 58, 248;
   Sarah, 258
REEVE, Hannah, 107; John,
   13, 107, 110, 257; Mary,
   13, 110; Sarah, 13
REEVES, Hannah, 256; John,
   45, 57, 127, 253; Sarah,
   45, 57
REMINGTON, John, 230
RENAGER, Hannah, 116
RENCHO, Mary, 120, 167
RENSHAW, Ann, 83, 84, 250;
   Elizabeth, 38; John, 38,
   47, 74, 92; Martha, 261;
   Mary, 59; Rebeccah, 66;
   Richard, 66, 74, 83, 84,
   245, 250; Thomas, 38, 47
REVE, Mary, 139
REYNEAR, Hannah, 13, 115;
   Isaac, 13; Joseph, 13, 115;
   Mary, 13; Rachel, 13;
   Stephen, 13
REYNELL, John, 264
REYNELL (RENOLDS), John, 104
REYNIERS, Alice, 90
REYNOLDS, Beulah, 65; John,
   60, 65, 69, 71; Mary, 60,
   69; Samuel, 71
RHOADES, Catherine, 82;
   Samuel, 82
RHOADS, Ann, 137; Elizabeth,
   13; Hannah, 13; John, 104,
   121, 190, 191; Mary, 13;
   Samuel, 13, 104
RHODES, Adam, 65, 73, 77,
   252, 255, 264, 266; Evan,
   73; Hannah, 249; Jacob, 64;
   Margrett, 64; Mary, 65;
   Samuel, 77
RIALL, John, 13; Joseph, 13;
   Mary, 13; Susan, 13;
   William, 13
RICH, Tho:, 24; Thomas, 88
RICHARD, John, 205; Joseph,
   264
RICHARDS, Ann, 26; David,
   13; Elizabeth, 22; John,
   26; Joseph, 77, 112, 208;
   Margaret, 13; Mary, 20, 22,
   24, 120; Philip, 20, 22,

85, 112; Phillip, 23, 24;
   Sarah, 13
RICHARDSON, Ann, 47, 227;
   Benjamin, 36; Deborah, 13;
   Edward, 24; Elinor, 27;
   Elizabeth, 13, 30, 34, 35,
   36, 47; Francis, 13, 30,
   34, 35, 36, 49, 51, 78, 85,
   86, 99, 108, 114, 120, 154,
   182, 200, 212, 218, 230,
   232, 260; George, 13;
   Grace, 13, 68; Hannah, 13,
   74; Jane, 56; John, 13, 30,
   34, 51, 164, 230, 232, 245,
   247, 263; Joseph, 13, 68,
   73, 74, 108, 114, 222, 225,
   227, 263; Joshua, 227;
   Joshuah, 49; Letitia, 51,
   100; Mary, 13, 86, 270;
   Nathaniel, 13; Patience,
   145; Rachel, 227, 233;
   Rebecca, 13, 134; Rebecka,
   34; Rebeckah, 86, 218;
   Samuel, 8, 27, 35, 40, 47,
   120, 156, 160, 185, 207,
   222, 225; Sarah, 73, 78,
   140; Thomas, 13, 85
RICHFORD, Denniss, 42;
   Elizabeth, 42
RICHMOND, John, 146, 197,
   210
RICHMONG, John, 64
RICHRDSON, John, 132
RICKETS, Elizabeth, 87
RICKETTS, Elizabeth, 13,
   164; Isaac, 13, 34, 120,
   154, 156, 157; Isac, 20;
   John, 13, 34; Widow, 163
RICKLES, Samuel, 179
RIGGS, Daniel, 120, 157
RIGHTON, Agnes, 92, 195;
   Frances, 119, 177; Mary,
   117, 171, 172; Samuel, 213;
   Sarah, 74; William, 92
RILEY, Moses, 53
RING, Elizabeth, 39; Hannah,
   39; Samuel, 39
RIPTON, Charles, 38; Josias,
   38
RITTER, Nathaniel, 67
ROADS, Jacob, 182; John, 54;
   Joseph, 179, 180
ROAS, Aquilla, 44
ROBBINS, Lettins, 45;
   Rebecka, 45; Samuel, 53;
   Thomas, 53; William, 45
ROBERTS, Ann, 42, 128, 142;
   Aquilla, 51; Aubrey, 240;

Catherine, 19; Charles, 66;
Daniel, 56; Edward, 42, 45,
51, 63, 95, 103, 105, 111,
231, 252; Elizabeth, 13, 94,
106, 121, 199, 200, 227;
Evan, 229; Gerald, 163; H.,
137; Hannah, 41, 51, 68,
257; Hugh, 68, 74, 76, 84,
103; Isaac, 73, 84, 121,
135; Israel, 19; James, 106;
Jane, 42, 76, 118, 120, 142,
226, 237; John, 13, 26, 47,
51, 56, 57, 61, 89, 173,
189, 190, 202, 203, 226,
254; Margaret, 13; Martha,
14, 34, 41, 42, 54, 72;
Mary, 13, 42, 45, 51, 56,
69, 84, 111, 117, 129, 140,
229; Mercy, 268; Owen, 46,
125, 142; Patience, 109;
Peter, 34, 94; Phineas, 84;
Phinehas, 142; Priscilla,
73; Rachel, 72, 107;
Rebecka, 42; Rebeckah, 109;
Rees, 134; Reese, 251;
Richard, 192; Robert, 109,
187; Samuel, 57; Sarah, 14,
47, 120, 239; Susanna, 74,
103; Thomas, 14, 19, 27, 34,
41, 42, 53, 54, 69, 90, 107,
109, 157, 162
ROBERTSON, Andrew, 72;
Richard, 187; Robert, 129;
Samuel, 129; Thomas, 72
ROBINS, Elizabeth, 258;
Henry, 18; Jaspar, 36;
John, 110, 137; Mary, 63;
Rebecka, 36; Samuel, 83,
103; Sarah, 103; William,
36, 61, 218
ROBINSON, Christian, 246;
David, 14, 251; Doctor, 20;
Ebenezer, 44, 111, 121,
140, 217, 218, 263;
Ebnezer, 42; Edward, 51,
106, 235, 239; Elizabeth,
34, 62, 77, 94, 200;
Hannah, 60, 76, 83, 265;
James, 66, 217, 218; Jane,
51; Lydia, 14, 236;
Margaret, 14; Margrett, 32,
42, 62; Mary, 42, 44;
Mathew, 28, 32, 42, 67;
Matthew, 34, 36, 88; Peter,
78; Phebe, 132, 147;
Richard, 49, 70, 90, 184,
190, 213, 221, 236, 241;
Robert, 236; Sarah, 11, 14,

28, 32, 34, 36, 42, 44, 49,
74, 119, 190; Thomas, 62,
76, 77, 80, 106, 138;
William, 94, 124, 182, 183
ROCHFORD, Alice, 69; Dennis,
51, 150, 163, 165, 169,
182, 190, 191, 196, 208,
209, 217, 254; Denniss, 27;
Elizabeth, 51; Mary, 27,
162; Mercy, 191; Solomon,
69, 113; Widow, 162, 163,
169
ROCKFORD, Dennis, 96
RODEFORD, Herriot, 181
RODENEY, William, 123
RODIFORD, Mercy, 182
RODMAN, John, 110, 196, 198;
William, 110, 139
RODNEY, William, 120, 123,
156
ROGERS, Mary, 169, 225;
Nicholas, 52, 61, 225, 251;
Rachell, 52
ROLAND, Ishmael, 44;
Margrett, 44
ROMAN, Mary, 56; Philip, 56
ROMMAN, Phillip, 55
ROOKE, Thomas, 136
ROTCHFORD, Dennis, 20, 21;
Mary, 21; Solomon, 248
ROTH, Ann, 268
ROUSE, Ann, 167; Thomas,
167, 173
ROW, Christopher, 20; Mary,
20; Robert, 20
ROWAN, Dorothy, 131
ROWDEN, Elizabeth, 150
ROWDON, Elizabeth, 116
ROWLAND, Sarah, 6
ROWN, Margrett, 83
ROYALL, William, 87
RUDMAN, Joseph, 31; Sarah,
31; Thomas, 31
RUDSON, Mary, 97
RUGGLE, Nathaniel, 28
RUMFORD, Jonathan, 135, 268;
Susanna, 135; Susannah, 268
RUSSEL, John, 121; Lucey,
193; Lucia, 192; Widow, 189
RUSSELL, Lucea, 92; Lucy,
125
RUTTER, Thomas, 151
RUTTIDGES, William, 179
RYALL, Israell, 75; Jeremy,
42; Mary, 28, 32, 50;
Thomas, 28, 32; William,
28, 32, 37

-S-

SADDIN, Henry, 55
SALAWAY, Hannah, 121
SALEWAY, William, 21
SALKELD, John, 176, 208, 227, 247
SALTER, Hannah, 173
SALWAY, Mary, 95, 209; William, 95, 121, 123
SAMSON, Samuel, 244
SAMWAY, Edward, 199
SANDERS, Charles, 14, 24, 88, 167; Edy, 22; Elizabeth, 23, 28, 29, 48; Hester, 46; James, 41; John, 23, 24, 26, 29, 46, 87, 165; Joseph, 107, 246, 247, 248, 256, 257; Paul, 22, 38; Richard, 41, 48, 55; Sarah, 14, 29, 41, 55, 88, 90, 122, 186, 236; William, 14, 46, 55, 236
SANDS, Stephen, 191
SANDSOM, Samuel, 131
SANDWITH, Elizabeth, 14; Mary, 14; Samuel, 75; Sarah, 14; William, 14, 75, 100, 130, 234, 240, 241
SANSOM, Elizabeth, 14, 71; Hannah, 14; John, 14, 65, 104; Joseph, 14; Mary, 14, 59; Samuel, 14, 59, 65, 71, 78, 104, 257; Sarah, 14, 78
SANSON, Hannah, 83; Samuel, 83, 244
SANWAY, Edward, 181
SAPAS, John, 213
SATTERTHWAITE, Joseph, 202
SATTERWITH, James, 47
SAUL, Joseph, 72, 80, 83, 116, 137, 140, 257; Mary, 72, 80; Rebecca, 83
SAULL, Anthony, 82; John, 110; Joseph, 82
SAUNDERS, Ann, 84; Esther, 79; John, 164, 189; Joseph, 68, 75, 132, 133; Paul, 121, 157, 162, 175, 176, 209, 214; Peter, 70; Richard, 68, 71, 121, 132; Sarah, 163; Thomas, 70; Timothy, 68; William, 121, 128, 220, 262
SAVERY, Sarah, 78; William, 78, 112
SAWIER, Arthur, 95
SAWYER, Arthur, 207
SAXBIE, John, 18

SAY, Benjamin, 131; Elizabeth, 26; Mary, 22; Sarah, 131, 133; William, 22, 86, 88, 123, 173, 175, 176; ____, 22
SCHREOGLE, Katherine, 81
SCIAMN, Ann, 66; Hannah, 66; John, 66
SCOFIELD, Ann, 39; Henry, 39; Richard, 52
SCOTT, Abraham, 31, 91, 124, 146, 171, 176, 177, 188, 189, 194; Dorothy, 122; Hanah, 97; Hannah, 31, 91, 188; John, 94, 171, 172, 173, 176; Thomas, 31; Widow, 178, 186
SCRIVEN, James, 263
SCULL, Abigail, 81; Edward, 39, 124, 191, 205, 206; Elizabeth, 62, 77; Esther, 81, 259; James, 39, 62, 63; Jasper, 77, 78, 81; Nicholas, 39; Rebecca, 248; Sarah, 39, 78
SEABREL, Samuel, 243
SEAL, Martin, 180
SEARY, Mary, 87
SEATON, Alexander, 140; Rebecca, 140
SEDDON, Samuel, 184
SEWERS, Esther, 68; Francis, 68
SHADDOCK, James, 121, 158
SHALLY, Jane, 136
SHANKLES, Thomas, 125
SHARCROSS, John, 53
SHARP, James, 64, 77, 135; John, 92, 125, 192; Margrett, 72; Mary, 134, 135; Miriam, 64; Peter, 239
SHARPLESS, Benjamin, 14; Edith, 14; Hannah, 14
SHAW, Hezediah, 78; John, 73, 140; Thomas, 73
SHEFFINGTON, George, 175
SHELDEN, Eleazdor, 262
SHELLEY, Abraham, 70; John, 70
SHELLY, Abraham, 66, 69, 75; Elizabeth, 69, 75; William, 66
SHELSON, John, 155
SHELSON (SHILLSON), John, Doctor, 14
SHELTON, Hannah, 78

SMITH, Ann, 76, 206, 207;
Christian, 76; Daniel, 23,
121, 165, 167, 171, 174,
176, 179, 219; Grace, 121;
Hannah, 117; Hugh, 81;
Jane, 144; Joanna, 79;
Johanna, 262; John, 46,
115, 121, 128, 139, 150,
184, 192, 219, 223, 245;
Joseph, 32; Margrett, 46;
Mary, 31, 33, 233;
Priscilla, 121, 162;
Richard, 43, 99, 115, 121,
207, 218, 228; Samuel, 144;
Sarah, 23, 34, 43, 46, 131;
Thomas, 19, 23, 81, 91,
121, 149, 153, 156, 178;
Widow, 174, 175; William,
21, 33, 34, 214; ___ary,
220
SNEAD, Elizabeth, 98, 127;
Grace, 95; Mary, 28, 31,
66, 119; Richard, 28, 31;
William, 28, 31, 95, 98,
121
SNEED, Elisabeth, 219;
Grace, 206; Mary, 225;
William, 159, 225
SNOW, Pater, 82; Peter, 75;
Thomas, 75
SNOWDEN, Ann, 18; Leonard,
134, 253
SNOWDON, William, 188
SOBB, Christopher, 29;
Rachell, 29; Rebecka, 29
SOBER, Charles, 177
SOMNER, Thomas, 69
SONGHURST, John, 56; Sarah,
122, 153
SOPER, John, 30
SOPORS, John, 41
SOUTHBE, Joan, 29; William,
29, 44
SOUTHBY, John, 25, 169;
William, 18, 25
SOUTHEBEE, Elizabeth, 87
SOUTHEBY, William, 175, 182
SOUTHERBY, William, 155, 160
SPAKEMAN, Randal, 209
SPARROW, John, 130, 239
SPEAKMAN, Thomas, 204
SPEARY, John, 250
SPENCE, John, 48, 55;
Rachel, 48; Rachell, 53;
Samuel, 53
SPENCER, Abraham, 51; Ester,
35; Esther, 83; Hester, 30,
31; John, 51; Lydia, 249;

Mary, 30, 239; Rachel, 269;
Rachell, 51; Richard, 31;
Samuel, 30, 31, 35, 88
SPERRY, James, 133, 248
SPIKEMAN, Ann, 45; Grace,
38; Mary, 23; Randal, 207,
215, 219, 225; Randall,
176; Randolph, 23, 38, 45,
46, 121
SPURRIER, Sarah, 56;
Theophilius, 56
STACEY, Alce, 32; Robert,
173; William, 32
STACKHOUSE, James, 116, 271;
Robert, 116
STACY, Alce, 30; Elizabeth,
91; John, 30, 37, 38, 48,
54, 121; Mary, 54; Robert,
25, 38; Thomas, 30
STAINES, John, 241, 253
STAMPER, Dinah, 248; John,
226
STAMPLER, John, 128
STANBERRY, Mary, 37; Nathan,
37
STANBURY, Mary, 27, 33, 100;
Nathan, 27, 33, 43, 100,
121, 169, 194, 201, 205,
206, 212, 214
STANDISH, Daniel, 165, 166,
194, 205; Daniell, 61
STANES, John, 131
STANFIELD, James, 121, 123,
160
STANLEY, William, 18
STANLY, Elizabeth, 118
STANTON, Abigail, 14;
Daniel, 14, 60, 69, 77, 78,
101, 131, 133, 140, 141,
143, 144, 147, 148, 240,
267; Daniell, 62;
Elizabeth, 118; John, 60,
69; Josiah, 78; Samuel, 72;
Sarah, 14, 77
STAPLER, Elizabeth, 32, 34;
Hannah, 34; John, 15, 114;
Margaret, 15; Martha, 143;
Mary, 15; Stephen, 34;
Stephen, 15, 32, 49, 64,
114, 141, 204; Susanna, 50;
Thomas, 15; William, 48,
50; ___, 48
STAPLES, Stephen, 181
STARR, Arthur, 35, 216;
Katherine, 35
STEEL, Elisabeth, 222;
Elizabeth, 121; Hannah, 83;
James, 15, 33, 126, 128,

77; Solomon, 122; Susana,
19; Susanna, 15, 20;
Susannah, 20; Thomas, 74;
Widow, 150; William, 15, 19,
20, 22, 122, 157, 162
WALL, Richard, 18; Sarah,
126
WALLBANK, Edward, 243
WALLER, Hannah, 119; John,
122; Mary, 121; Sarah, 121
WALLICE, Easter, 19;
Elizabeth, 19; Esther, 19;
Robert, 19
WALLN, John, 216; Mary, 189;
Nicholas, 216; Richard,
190; Sarah, 200, 201
WALN, Ann, 15, 45;
Elizabeth, 15, 108, 117,
218; Ellin, 29; Jane, 15,
29, 40, 75; John, 40, 108,
214; Joseph, 15; Mary, 15,
136; Nicholas, 15, 29, 43,
103, 180, 195, 222, 223,
245; Richard, 15, 45, 103,
131, 147, 190, 254, 258,
261, 265; Robert, 15, 80;
Susanna, 15, 119, 136;
William, 15, 222
WALNE, Ann, 30; Nicholas,
30; Richard, 30
WALNER, Rachel, 153
WALTER, Elizabeth, 118;
Sarah, 144
WALTERS, Edward, 160
WALTON, Daniel, 96, 209;
Elizabeth, 40; Hannah, 107;
Joshua, 255; Mary, 40;
Michael, 40, 100, 107, 122;
Michall, 54; Nathaniel,
122, 152; Rebeccah, 100,
238; Samuel, 84; Thomas,
122; William, 64
WANTON, John, 233
WARD, John, 193; Rebecka,
24; William, 34
WARDELL, Charles, 70; Mary,
23; Patience, 169; Rebecca,
140, 272; William, 70, 74
WARDER, Agnes, 35, 96; Ann,
31, 32, 89; Elizabeth, 31,
51; Jeremiah, 15, 16, 62,
69, 73, 104; John, 16, 33,
35, 62, 92, 171, 195, 228,
263; Joseph, 16; Lydia, 16;
Mary, 16, 73, 92, 192;
Rebecca, 16; Rebecka, 49,
51; Richard, 31, 32, 33,
42, 49, 51, 69, 85, 89, 92,

122; Sarah, 16, 35;
Solomon, 171; Susanna, 16;
Willoby, 197; Willoughby,
93, 125, 197
WARNER, Ann, 16, 28, 37, 44,
46, 54, 67, 121, 137, 163;
Anne, 108; Arnold, 16, 269;
Deborah, 84; Edmund, 21;
Edward, 62, 67, 84, 102;
Elizabeth, 16, 79, 110;
Ester, 38; Esther, 62, 84,
119, 223, 232; George, 19;
Hannah, 16, 37, 67; Isaac,
16, 37, 47, 66, 79, 95,
108, 122, 209; Isaiah, 38,
69; Issac, 62; Jacob, 269;
James, 44; Jane, 16, 269;
John, 37, 38, 66, 79, 107,
110, 138; Joseph, 84, 111;
Lydia, 16; Margaret, 16,
182; Mary, 19, 37, 58, 82,
122, 224, 257, 262; Mercy,
107; Rachel, 21, 153;
Sarah, 138, 148, 269;
Simeon, 271; Susanna, 16,
46; Susannah, 269; Swan,
38, 62; Veronica, 16;
Widow, 150, 151; William,
44, 46, 58, 95, 101, 241,
251
WARREN, Isaac, 64, 84, 254,
270; Issac, 266; John, 258;
Mary, 64; Priscilla, 270;
William, 84
WARRINGTON, Hannah, 116
WATERMAN, Humphrey, 89;
Jane, 118, 201; Margaret,
89, 181
WATERS, Edward, 160
WATLIN, Joan, 119
WATSON, Aaron, 139, 270;
Abigail, 41, 120; Abigaill,
28; Anna, 89; Eveny, 37;
Hannah, 91; James, 126,
204; John, 25, 28, 41, 45,
46, 49, 91, 187, 200; Jude,
46; Mary, 80, 86, 198;
Nathaniel, 18, 156;
Rebecka, 49; William, 197
WATTS, Sarah, 119, 123
WATTSON, Elizabeth, 88;
Joseph, 47
WAY, Mary, 120
WAYS, Ann, 119
WEB, Elizabeth, 169; hannah,
204
WEBB, Ann, 120, 126; Edith,
141; Elizabeth, 35, 120,

Heritage Books by Anna Miller Watring:

Accomack County, Virginia, Marriage References and Family Relationships, 1620–1800

Bucks County, Pennsylvania, Church Records of the 17th and 18th Centuries,
Volume 2: Quaker Records: Falls and Middletown Monthly Meetings
Anna Miller Watring and F. Edward Wright

Bucks County, Pennsylvania, Church Records of the 17th and 18th Centuries,
Volume 3: Quaker Records: Wrightstown, Richland, Buckingham,
Makefield And Solebury Monthly Meetings

Civil War Burials in Baltimore's Loudon Park Cemetery

Early Church Records of Monmouth County, New Jersey

Early Quaker Records of Philadelphia, Pennsylvania,
Volume 1: 1682–1750

Early Quaker Records of Philadelphia, Pennsylvania,
Volume 2, 1751–1800

King George County, Virginia, Marriage References
and Family Relationships, 1721–1800
Anne M. Watring and F. Edward Wright

Loudon Park Caretaker Records, A–B, 1853–1986
Anna M. Watring, E. Charles Miller, and R. Scott Johnson

New Jersey Bible Records:
Volume 1, Atlantic, Burlington, Cape May
and Gloucester Counties

New Jersey Bible Records:
Volume 2, Salem and Cumberland Counties